Environmental Regulation

2002 Supplement

2002 Supplement

Environmental Regulation

Law, Science, and Policy

Third Edition

Robert V. Percival
Professor of Law, Robert Stanton Scholar, and Director,
Environmental Law Program
University of Maryland School of Law

Alan S. Miller
Global Environmental Facility
The World Bank

Christopher H. Schroeder
Professor of Law and Public Policy Studies Director,
Program in Public Law
Duke University School of Law

James P. Leape
Executive Vice President
World Wildlife Fund

ASPEN LAW & BUSINESS
A Division of Aspen Publishers, Inc.
New York   Gaithersburg

Printed in the United States of America.

1 2 3 4 5 6 7 8 9 0

ISBN 0-7355-2866-7 (supplement)

Library of Congress Cataloging-in-Publication Data

Environmental regulation : law, science, and policy / Robert V. Percival
. . .[et al.] — 3rd ed.
    p. cm.
    Includes index
    ISBN 0-7355-1233-7 (casebook)
    ISBN 0-7355-2866-7 (supplement)
        1. Environmental law — United States. 2. Environmental law —
    United States — Cases. I.
    Percival, Robert V.
    KF3775.E548 2000
    346.73'046—dc21   99-059664

About Aspen Law & Business Legal Education Division

With a dedication to preserving and strengthening the long-standing tradition of publishing excellence in legal education, Aspen Law & Business continues to provide the highest quality teaching and learning resources for today's law school community. Careful development, meticulous editing, and an unmatched responsiveness to the evolving needs of today's discerning educators combine in the creation of our outstanding casebooks, coursebooks, textbooks, and study aids.

ASPEN LAW & BUSINESS
A Division of Aspen Publishers, Inc.
A Wolters Kluwer Company
www.aspenpublishers.com

Contents

Contents

Contents

Contents

Contents

Contents

Authors' Note

The materials contained in this 2002 Supplement include information on significant developments in environmental law that have occurred since publication of the third edition of *Environmental Regulation: Law, Science, and Policy* in 2000. These include three new Supreme Court decisions (the *American Trucking* case in Chapter 5, the *Solid Waste Agency of Northern Cook Country* case in Chapter 6, and *Palazzolo v. Rhode Island* in Chapter 7), important developments in environmental justice litigation (the *South Camden Citizens in Action* case in Chapter 1 and the impact of the Supreme Court's *Sandoval* decision on it), and renewed debate over opening ANWR to oil drilling (Chapter 1). They also include the use of the Congressional Review Act to veto OSHA's ergonomics standard (Chapter 2), RCRA/CERCLA updates (Chapter 3), a case study of the Bush administration's review of new limits on arsenic in drinking water (Chapter 4) and an analysis of new takings litigation that the Supreme Court has agreed to decide in 2002 (Chapter 7). The supplement includes a new NEPA problem exercise and updates on NEPA and the Endangered Species Act (Chapter 8), revisions to EPA's policy on Incentives for Self-Policing (Chapter 9), the *Bragg* decision on mountaintop mining and the Eleventh Amendment (Chapter 9), and an update on efforts to implement the Kyoto Protocol despite the Bush administration's rejection of it (Chapter 10).

None of these developments requires professors to make significant changes in the organization of the Environmental Law course or in the material in the existing casebook. But professors who wish to keep students informed of the latest developments in the field will want to assign some of the new decisions and the new Notes and Questions that follow them.

The events of September 11, 2001, have stunned everyone and produced a dramatic change in the political climate in Washington. While it is too early to tell how this will affect environmental law, we have included a new note in Chapter 4 of this supplement on EPA's counterterrorism responsibilities and efforts to restrict terrorists' access to information about hazardous chemicals. These efforts include the Chemical Safety Information, Site Security and Fuels Regulatory

Relief Act adopted in 1999.

We plan to continue to post updates to the casebook on our website located at: http://www.law.umaryland.edu/courses/environment (note that the URL listed for this site on page 1 of the Teacher's Manual inadvertently omitted the ".edu").

Professor Percival would like to express his appreciation to Kerri Roman, Marcia Tannian, and Patricia Teck for their research assistance, and his enormous gratitude to Laura Mrozek, Administrator of Maryland's Environmental Law Program, for her continuing help and assistance. Professor Schroeder would like to express his appreciation to Elizabeth Hendrix, Duke Law School class of 2003, for her research assistance.

October 2001

Table of Cases

Principal Cases are in italics

Table of Cases

Table of Cases

Environmental Regulation

2002 Supplement

- 1 -

Environmental Values and Policies: An Introduction

Environmental Justice Concerns (pp. 21-28)

As mentioned in the text, on May 1, 1997, the Nuclear Regulatory Commission's Atomic Safety and Licensing Board ruled that environmental justice concerns must be addressed in environmental impact statements (EIS) prepared in connection with the application by Louisiana Energy Services (LES) for a permit to construct a uranium enrichment facility near Homer, Louisiana. In re Louisiana Energy Services, Docket No. 70-3070-ML. LES subsequently petitioned the full Nuclear Regulatory Commission (NRC) for a review of the Board's decision.

On April 3, 1998, the NRC affirmed the Board's findings that the final EIS for the proposed uranium enrichment facility did not adequately consider "disparate impacts." Stating that "'disparate impact' analysis is our principal tool for advancing environmental justice under NEPA," the NRC agreed that its staff should provide a supplemental EIS with a more thorough analysis of the impacts of road closures and changes in local property values, and whether any actions could be taken to mitigate these impacts. However, the NRC reversed the Board's requirement for further NRC staff investigation of racial discrimination, stating that the Board had made "no finding one way or the other on whether intentional racism had tainted the decisional process." The NRC said that while the National Environmental Policy Act (NEPA) requires agencies to consider not only environmental impacts, but also social and economic impacts ancillary to them, "nothing in NEPA or in the cases interpreting it indicates that the statute is a tool for addressing problems of racial discrimination." The NRC concluded that the Board's proposed racial discrimination inquiry went "well beyond what NEPA has traditionally been interpreted to require," and "stretches NEPA to its breaking point."

1

Following the NRC's ruling, LES abandoned its plans for the Claiborne Enrichment Center and asked the NRC to withdraw its application. LES noted that revision of the EIS would delay the project indefinitely. On April 30, 1998, the Commission granted the motion to withdraw the application, as well as terminate the proceedings.

Title VI and Section 1983 Litigation of Environmental Justice Concerns (pp. 25-26)

Section 601 of Title VI of the Civil Rights Act of 1964 guarantees nondiscrimination in the administration of federal programs, and Section 602, 42 U.S.C. § 2000d-1, authorizes federal agencies who administer such programs to issue regulations implementing that guarantee (pp. 25-26). Environmental justice plaintiffs have been bringing administrative complaints under those regulations. They also have been suing state agencies alleged to be violating Section 602 and those regulations in the course of implementing federal programs that have been delegated to those agencies. On April 19, 2001, a district court in New Jersey issued a significant ruling in such a case, finding sufficient merit in plaintiffs' environmental justice claims to support both declaratory relief and a preliminary injunction against the permitting of a cement processing factory.   South Camden Citizens in Action v. New Jersey Dept. of Envt'l. Protection, 145 F.Supp. 2d 446 (D.N.J. 2001) (SCCIA I).

As the main text notes, however, whether or not Title VI confers such a private right of action has been an open question. On April 24, 2001, the Supreme Court decided this question in a case involving Section 602 implementing regulations issued by the Department of Justice. Alexander v. Sandoval, 121 S. Ct. 1511 (2001). The Supreme Court answered it in the negative. On the afternoon of that same day, the parties in the South Camden Citizens litigation and the district court judge in *SCCIA I* met by telephone to begin assessing the impact of *Sandoval* on the preliminary relief that had been granted.

After an expedited briefing schedule, the court held that *Sandoval* had indeed overruled its earlier decision that Title VI supported the plaintiffs' lawsuit. Simultaneously with the court's review of the Title

Chapter 1. Environmental Values and Policies

VI question, the court had asked the parties to brief whether or not the identical claims of the plaintiffs could be litigated pursuant to 42 U.S.C. § 1983. Section 1983 establishes liability against any "person who, under color of [state law] . . .[deprives any citizen of the United States] of any rights, privileges, or immunities secured by the Constitution and laws [of the United States.]" Relying on Supreme Court and court of appeals precedent, the court found that a Section 1983 claim can be based on rights established by statutes and by regulations implementing statutory rights, as well as on the Constitution. It then analyzed the requisites articulated by those courts for a 1983 claim not based on the Constitution. First, to establish that a federal right is being asserted, plaintiffs must show (a) that Congress intended the provision in question to benefit the plaintiff, (b) that the purported right is not too "vague and amorphous" to be judicially enforceable, and (c) that it unambiguously imposes a binding obligation on the States. Second, defendants can still defeat a 1983 claim if they can show that Congress "specifically foreclosed a remedy under 1983" by providing a "comprehensive enforcement mechanis[m] for protection" of the right. Blessing v. Freestone, 520 U.S. 329, 340-341 (1997). The court found that plaintiffs' environmental justice claims met these standards, and that none of its earlier relief was barred by the Eleventh Amendment. Accordingly, the court ordered that its earlier relief would remain in effect. South Camden Citizens in Action v. New Jersey Dept. of Envt'l. Protection, 145 F.Supp. 2d 505 (D.N.J. 2001) (*SCCIA II*).

The following excerpt from *SCCIA I* focuses on the substantive grounds for finding that the decision by the NJDEP to issue an air permit to the cement processing facility violated Title VI and the EPA regulations by imposing an impermissible disparate impact on the surrounding community. By virtue of *SCCIA II*, the analysis of the NJDEP's obligations under Title VI remains completely germane to plaintiffs' Section 1983 action, unaffected by *Sandoval*'s foreclosing private suits directly under Title VI. The district court presented its findings and conclusions in numbered paragraphs, and for ease in consulting the full opinion, we retain those numbers in the excerpt.

South Camden Citizens in Action v. New Jersey Department of Environmental Protection
145 F. Supp. 2d 446 (D.N.J. 2001)

Orlofsky, District Judge.

I. INTRODUCTION
. . .

To understand the nature of the issues presented, I shall set forth a brief summary of the operative facts. Plaintiff, South Camden Citizens In Action ("SCCIA"), is an unincorporated community organization, whose members are residents of a neighborhood in Camden, New Jersey, known as "Waterfront South." The individual Plaintiffs are residents of Waterfront South and members of SCCIA. Defendant, the New Jersey Department of Environmental Protection ("NJDEP"), a New Jersey state agency, is responsible for enforcing the environmental laws and regulations of the State of New Jersey, as well as federal law, where applicable. The NJDEP receives federal funding and is thus obliged to conform its operations to the restrictions imposed by Title VI and the regulations which have been promulgated to implement Title VI.... Defendant Intervenor, St. Lawrence Cement Co., L.L.C. ("SLC"), manufactures and distributes cement products. SLC has built and proposes to operate a facility in Waterfront South to grind and process granulated blast furnace slag ("GBFS"). SLC sells the ground GBFS as an additive to portland cement.

SLC's proposed facility will emit certain pollutants into the air. These pollutants will include particulate matter (dust), mercury, lead, manganese, nitrogen oxides, carbon monoxide, sulphur oxides and volatile organic compounds. The GBFS will arrive by barge at a Camden port facility. Trucks will then deliver the GBFS to SLC's proposed facility in Waterfront South, a distance of approximately three miles. The GBFS will then be processed and transported back to the port by truck. Annually, there will be approximately 35,000 inbound delivery

4

Chapter 1. Environmental Values and Policies

trucks arriving at SLC's proposed facility and approximately 42,000 outbound truck deliveries departing from the facility. Inbound truck deliveries will occur on about eighty days per year with approximately 500 truck deliveries per day. Outbound truck departures from the SLC facility will occur on approximately 225 days per year, with about 200 trucks departing per day. The contemplated truck routes pass through the Waterfront South Community.

The population of Waterfront South is 2,132, forty-one percent of whom are children. Ninety-one percent of the residents of Waterfront South are persons of color. Specifically, sixty-three percent are African-American, twenty-eight percent are Hispanic, and nine percent are non-Hispanic white. The residents of Waterfront South suffer from a disproportionately high rate of asthma and other respiratory ailments.

The Waterfront South neighborhood is already a popular location for the siting of industrial facilities. It contains the Camden County Municipal Utilities Authority, a sewage treatment plant, the Camden County Resource Recovery facility, a trash-to-steam plant, the Camden Cogen Power Plant, a co-generation plant, and two United States Environmental Protection Agency ("EPA") designated Superfund sites. Four sites within one-half mile of SLC's proposed facility are currently being investigated by the EPA for the possible release of hazardous substances. The NJDEP has also identified fifteen known contaminated sites in the Waterfront South neighborhood.

As described in greater detail in this Court's Findings of Fact and Conclusions of Law set forth below, the NJDEP granted the necessary air permits to SLC to allow its proposed facility to begin operations. In doing so, the NJDEP considered only whether the facility's emissions would exceed technical emissions standards for specific pollutants, especially dust. Indeed, much of what this case is about is what the NJDEP failed to consider. It did not consider the level of ozone generated by the truck traffic to and from the SLC facility, notwithstanding the fact that the Waterfront South community is not currently in compliance with the National Ambient Air Quality Standard ("NAAQS") established by the EPA for ozone levels, nor did it consider the presence of many other pollutants in Waterfront South. It did not consider the pre-existing poor health of the residents of Waterfront South, nor did it consider the cumulative environmental burden already borne by

5

this impoverished community. Finally, and perhaps most importantly, the NJDEP failed to consider the racial and ethnic composition of the population of Waterfront South.

At this stage of these proceedings, this Court must resolve the following complex questions: (1) Whether the criteria and methods used by the NJDEP to evaluate air permit applications, namely, its exclusive reliance on EPA emissions maximums, especially the NAAQS for particulate matter ("PM-10"), without consideration of the totality of the health and environmental circumstances of the community in which the proposed facility will be located, violates the regulations promulgated by EPA to implement Title VI of the Civil Rights Act of 1964, which prohibits discrimination based on race and national origin; and (2) Whether the NJDEP's decision to issue the necessary air permits to SLC to operate its proposed facility in the Waterfront South Community constitutes disparate impact discrimination based on race and national origin in violation of EPA regulations promulgated to implement section 602 of the Civil Rights Act of 1964, 42 U.S.C. § 2000d-1.

For the reasons which follow in this Court's Findings of Fact and Conclusions of Law made pursuant to Fed.R.Civ.P. 52(a), I conclude that: (1) The NJDEP's failure to consider any evidence beyond SLC's compliance with technical emissions standards, and specifically its failure to consider the totality of the circumstances surrounding the operation of SLC's proposed facility, violates the EPA's regulations promulgated to implement Title VI of the Civil Rights Act of 1964; and (2) Plaintiffs have established a prima facie case of disparate impact discrimination based on race and national origin in violation of the EPA's regulations promulgated pursuant to section 602 of the Civil Rights Act of 1964.

Accordingly, I shall grant Plaintiffs' application for a preliminary injunction, vacate the NJDEP's issuance of SLC's air permits, and remand this case to the NJDEP and Commissioner Shinn to make appropriate findings consistent with this Opinion. The NJDEP's findings shall be filed with the Court within thirty days of the date of this Opinion. SLC shall be enjoined from operating its proposed facility pending further order of this Court. This Court shall retain jurisdiction.

Chapter 1. Environmental Values and Policies

III. FINDINGS OF FACT AND CONCLUSIONS OF LAW

. . .

I. Waterfront South

47. Waterfront South is a neighborhood located in the City of Camden, New Jersey. Waterfront South corresponds to United States Census Tract 6018. The population of Waterfront South consists of 2,132 people, approximately 41% of whom are children.

48. The most recent census figures available, from the 1990 census, reveal that 91% of the residents of Waterfront South are persons of color. Specifically, 63% are African-American, 28.3% are Hispanic, and 9% are non- Hispanic White.

49. In 1990, the median household income of residents of Waterfront South was $15,082, and the per capita income was $4,709. Over 50% of the residents of Waterfront South live at or below the federal poverty level.

50. Waterfront South is located in the City of Camden, which is part of Camden County, New Jersey. According to 1990 census figures, the residents of Camden County are 75.1% non-Hispanic white, 16.2% African-American, and 7.2% Hispanic.

51. In 1990, the median household income of residents of Camden County was $40,027, and the per capita income was $15,773.

52. Camden County is one of twenty-one counties in the State of New Jersey. The residents of the State of New Jersey are 79.4% non-Hispanic white and 20.6% non-white.

53. Many pollutant-producing municipal and industrial facilities are located in or near Waterfront South.

56. There are two Superfund sites located in Waterfront South. The first is the Welsbach/General Gas Mantle site, and consists of two abandoned factories and neighboring residential lots on Arlington Street. The site is contaminated with thorium and was discovered to be radioactive in 1981. The second is the Martin Aaron Drum Company site, which is located on Broadway.

Chapter 1. Environmental Values and Policies

57. There are four sites within one-half mile of the proposed SLC facility that the EPA has identified and has already or is currently investigating for the release or threatened release of hazardous subsection of Atlantic and Delaware Avenues; (2) Camden Gas Works, at the intersection of 2d and Spruce Streets; (3) the Front Street Warehouse, at 1229 Front Street; and (4) the Camden Coke Plant, on Front Street between Walnut and Kaighn Streets.

58. The NJDEP has identified fifteen known contaminated sites in the Waterfront South neighborhood. These sites include, *inter alia:* (1) Camden Iron & Metal, located at the intersection of Front and Atlantic Streets; (2) Conrail, located on Chelten Ave.; (3) Lectronic Research Laboratories, at 1423 Ferry St.; (4) Consolidated Chemx Corp., located at 4th and Jefferson Streets; (5) Camden Lime, located at the intersection of South Front and Atlantic Ave.; (6) Atlantic Industrial Tank, at 212 Mechanic Street. Fourteen of these sites are currently active in the NJDEP's site remediation program. Montag Decl., Exh. C at 25-26 (Hearing Officer's Report). The NJDEP is aware of the concentration of contaminated sites in this area and has dedicated a staff member to work directly with the City of Camden to facilitate clean-up and redevelopment.

59. It is uncontested that, in addition to those sites listed above, all of which are subject to some federal or state regulation, there are numerous other industrial facilities in the area. These include: (1) four scrap yards on or near Ferry Avenue; (2) Jen Cyn Industries: (3) Lambertsky Poultry; and (4) four automotive shops.

60. The City of Camden recently commissioned a study of Waterfront South, and, after analyzing the study results, designated Waterfront South as "an area in need of redevelopment," pursuant to N.J.S.A. § 40A:12A-3. The study found that:

> Properties in [unsanitary, dilapidated or obsolete] condition are not only harmful to themselves, but also constitute a clear and present danger to the surrounding community.... The dense arrangement of buildings, the close proximity of residential and industrial uses, and unregulated truck traffic makes the spillover effects of noxious manufacturing or related industrial activity . . . detrimental to

surrounding property users and residents throughout Waterfront South. . . .

J. The Health of the Community and the Effects of the SLC Facility on Health

(1) Current Health of the Community

Plaintiffs offered evidence showing that the current health of Waterfront South residents is already poor. The court found that the proposed facility would worsen the residents' health in several different ways. For one, the particulate matter (PM) generated by the facility would exacerbate asthma, bronchitis, impaired lung function and other respiratory problems. Some of this conclusion was based on studies showing the particular dangers of very small particulates of 2.5 microns in diameter and smaller. Under the PM standards in effect at the time of the permit decision, such small-diameter PM was not separately regulated, although PM of 10 microns or less was. In response to plaintiff's expert testimony, the "NJDEP has not submitted any expert testimony regarding the specific implications of the proposed SLC facility's particulate emissions on the health of the residents of the surrounding community. To support its contention that the proposed SLC facility will not adversely affect the health of the residents of the surrounding community, the NJDEP relies exclusively on the fact that the emissions from the proposed facility will be within the 1987 EPA NAAQS for PM-10. . . . The NJDEP responds to Plaintiffs' concerns regarding the SLC facility's potential PM-2.5 emissions by emphasizing that there is currently no NAAQ standard for PM-2.5. Essentially, the NJDEP argues that unless and until the EPA issues a NAAQ standard for PM-2.5, the NJDEP cannot be held responsible for failing to consider whatever adverse health consequences might result from PM-2.5 exposure. The NJDEP maintains this position despite the fact that the NJDEP has noted that "ozone and particulates are New Jersey's two most pervasive air quality problems and more measures need to be taken to ensure that those health standards are attained in future years."

Other adverse effects would result from emissions of nitrogen oxides and hydrocarbons, which in the presence of sunlight combine to form ozone (smog). " In response to the Plaintiffs' concerns about the effects of the SLC diesel truck traffic on ozone levels, the NJDEP argues only that the Plaintiffs have not adequately demonstrated that the SLC facility's truck emissions will 'significantly' contribute to ambient ozone. . . . Given the large volume of truck traffic which will be traveling to and from the SLC facility, NJDEP's failure to give any consideration whatsoever to the potential increase in ozone levels in an area which is in non-attainment with the existing Ozone NAAQS, I find NJDEP's argument to be disingenuous. In these circumstances, it is clear that ozone levels will only get worse, not better."

The only criterion used by the NJDEP in evaluating SLC's air permit applications in this case was whether, based on emission projections and modeling data, the facility meets the NAAQS established by EPA in 1987. . . . If a proposed facility does not exceed the NAAQS, it will generally be permitted. [It was undisputed that NJDEP modeling showed the the facility complied with the applicable NAAQS requirements.]

N. The Governing Legal Standard for Preliminary Injunctive Relief

[Plaintiffs had presented several claims for relief, including claims based on intentional discrimination. They vigorously pursued only the Section 602 claim, and that is the sole theory that the court addressed.]

122. Plaintiffs also allege that the NJDEP's decision to permit the SLC facility constitutes disparate impact discrimination in violation of the EPA regulations enacted pursuant to section 602 of the Civil Rights Act of 1964, codified at 42 U.S.C. § 2000d-1. Section 602 provides that:

> Each federal agency which is empowered to extend Federal financial assistance to any program or activity, by way of grant, loan, or contract other than a contract of insurance or guaranty, is authorized and directed to effectuate the provisions of section 2000d of this title with respect to such program or activity by issuing rules, regulations, or orders of general applicability which shall be consistent with achievement of the objectives of the statute authorizing the financial assistance in connection with which the action is taken.

42 U.S.C. § 2000d-1. . . .

Chapter 1. Environmental Values and Policies

O. Likelihood of Success on the Merits

127. To prevail on a motion seeking preliminary injunctive relief, the moving party must first show a "reasonable probability of eventual success in the litigation.". . . . To satisfy this standard, "[i]t is not necessary that the moving party's right to a final decision after trial be wholly without doubt; rather, the burden is on the party seeking relief to make a prima facie case showing a reasonable probability that it will prevail on the merits." . . .

129. In order to evaluate the likelihood that Plaintiffs will succeed on the merits of their claim . . . . I shall first consider Plaintiffs' request for a declaratory judgment that the NJDEP violated section 602 of Title VI, and the EPA's implementing regulations to that section, codified at 40 C.F.R. § 7.1 *et seq.,* by failing to consider the potential adverse, disparate impact of its permitting decision with respect to the proposed SLC facility. Second, applying Title VI disparate impact analysis, I must evaluate the likelihood that Plaintiffs will succeed on the merits of their Title VI claim by deciding whether they have carried their burden of establishing a prima facie case of disparate impact discrimination in violation of Title VI.

Q. Declaratory Judgment on the Requirements of Title VI Implementing Regulations

137. This case presents the novel question of whether a recipient of EPA funding has an obligation under Title VI to consider racially discriminatory disparate impacts when determining whether to issue a permit, in addition to compliance with applicable environmental standards. For the reasons set forth below, I conclude that on the facts of this case, the NJDEP had such an obligation and failed to discharge it.

[The court found several sources of law and administrative guidance to support the existence of this obligation. These included EPA's Section 602 implementing regulations, which, inter alia prohibit the use of "criteria of methods" for administering the permit program "which have the effect of subjecting individuals to discrimination" and which prohibit facility site selection "that has the purpose or effect of . . . . subjecting them to discrimination." The court also cited President

11

Chapter 1. Environmental Values and Policies

Clinton's environmental justice Executive Order, No. 12,898. Finally, it relied on EPA's Revised Guidance for Investigating Title VI Administrative Complaints and its "Draft Title VI Guidance for EPA Assistance Recipients Administering Environmental Permit Programs," relying on them "only to the extent necessary to understand the EPA's developing interpretation of a recipient's duties under Title VI," because they were only in draft form. The Court specifically referred to a portion of the Draft Revised Investigative Guidance, which states:]

> Compliance with environmental laws does not constitute *per se* compliance with Title VI. Frequently, discrimination results from policies and practices that are neutral on their face, but have the effect of discriminating . . . [T]here may be instances in which environmental laws do not regulate certain concentrations of sources, or take into account impacts on some subpopulations which may be disproportionately present in an affected population. For example, there may be evidence of adverse impacts on some subpopulations (e.g., asthmatics) and that subpopulation may be disproportionately composed of persons of a particular race, color, or national origin. Title VI is concerned with how the effects of the programs and activities of a recipient are distributed based on race, color, or national origin. *A recipient's Title VI obligation exists in addition to the Federal or state environmental laws governing its environmental permitting program.*

65 Fed.Reg. 39650, 39680 (emphasis added).

The NJDEP, without acknowledging the preceding language, quotes the section of the Draft Revised Investigation Guidance which immediately follows the language above, where the Guidance describes the role of the NAAQS in assessing Title VI compliance:

> If an investigation includes an allegation raising air quality concerns regarding a pollutant regulated pursuant to a primary NAAQS, and where the area in question is attaining that standard, the air quality in the surrounding community will generally be considered presumptively protective and emissions of that pollutant should not be viewed as "adverse" within the meaning of Title VI. However, if the investigation produces evidence that significant adverse impacts may occur, this presumption of no adverse impact may be overcome.

Chapter 1. Environmental Values and Policies

65 Fed.Reg. 39650, 39680.

When considered as a whole, it is clear from this section of the Draft Revised Investigation Guidance that the EPA, when investigating Title VI complaints, will consider a recipient's compliance with NAAQ standards as evidence of its compliance with Title VI, but, significantly, such compliance is not conclusive or determinative evidence. The Court's reading of this section of the Guidance is corroborated by the EPA's footnote to this section, in which it reiterates that:

> [E]ven if an area is in compliance with the NAAQS for a criteria pollutant, there still may
> be Title VI concerns related to other criteria pollutants, to toxic hot spots associated with hazardous air pollutants under section 112 of the Clean Air Act, or to pollutants from other media.

65 Fed.Reg. 39650, 39681 n. 130.

153. The fourth source that undercuts Defendants' theory is the only decision the EPA OCR [Office of Civil Rights] has issued to date on a Title VI complaint. This decision resulted from a challenge to proposed construction of a steel plant in Flint, Michigan. *See* U.S. EPA OCR Investigative Report for Title VI Administrative Complaint File No. 5R-98-R5 (*"Select Steel Investigative Report"* or *"Select Steel"*). [This is the complaint at page 26.] The *Select Steel* Complaint was filed with the EPA on August 17, 1998, by Father Phil Schmitter and Sister Joanne Chiaverini, alleging that the Michigan Department of Environmental Quality ("MDEQ") violated Title VI by permitting the construction of a steel plant in a community which was primarily African-American and already disproportionately burdened with significant pollution- producing facilities. *Id.* at 3. Specifically, the complaint alleged that MDEQ violated Title VI when it issued a "Prevention of Significant Deterioration" ("PSD") permit to the Select Steel Corporation. The Complainants alleged that the proposed steel plant would have a disparate impact on the surrounding, minority community by exposing the community to VOCS, lead, manganese, mercury, and dioxin. The population in the community of the proposed site was 55.2% minority, in comparison with the statewide average of 17.6%. *Id.* at 13-14.

Chapter 1. Environmental Values and Policies

154. In evaluating the *Select Steel* Complaint, the EPA OCR followed a five-step analysis it published in the 1998 Draft Investigative Guidelines, which were a precursor to the 2000 Revised Draft Investigation Guidelines. Specifically, the EPA OCR considered the following data: (1) the proposed facility's emissions, including NAAQ-regulated emissions and non-NAAQ-regulated emissions; (2) the existing level of air toxics in the area, based on data from the EPA's Toxic Release Inventory (TRI); and (3) health data, including children's lead blood-levels from the community where the proposed facility was to be located. Only after evaluating this data did the EPA OCR conclude that the operation of the proposed facility would not adversely affect the health of the residents of the surrounding community. The EPA then concluded that "[i]f there is no adverse affect from the permitted facility, there can be no finding of discriminatory effect which would violate Title VI and EPA's implementing regulations." *Id.* . . .

161. I shall grant Plaintiffs' request for a declaratory judgment that the NJDEP and Commissioner Shinn have violated Title VI of the Civil Rights Act by failing to consider the potential adverse, disparate impact of the SLC facility's operation on individuals based on their race, color, or national origin, as part of its decision to permit SLC's proposed facility.

R. Title VI Disparate Impact Analysis

162. In addition to declaratory relief, Plaintiffs also seek preliminary injunctive relief. Specifically, Plaintiffs ask this Court to rescind the permits which the NJDEP granted to SLC, and enjoin the NJDEP from issuing the SLC permits without first implementing a protocol for reviewing permit applications to ensure compliance with Title VI. Plaintiffs contend they are entitled to injunctive relief because they have established a likelihood of success on the question of whether the operation of the proposed SLC facility will have an adverse, disparate impact on the Waterfront South Community based on the race, color, or national origin of the residents of that community. . . .

166. According to the Third Circuit . . . in case involving alleged disparate impact discrimination in violation of Title VI, the plaintiffs bear the initial burden of establishing a *prima facie* case that a facially neutral practice has resulted in a racial disparity. . . . The plaintiff must

demonstrate, by a preponderance of the evidence, that the disputed practice detrimentally affects persons of a particular race to a greater extent than other races. . . . "It is not enough for the plaintiff merely to prove circumstances raising an inference of discriminatory impact at issue; [the plaintiff] must prove the discriminatory impact at issue. . . . In other words, Plaintiffs must prove that a facially neutral practice disparately and adversely impacts them, and that the disparate impact is causally linked to the contested practice. . . .

167. If the plaintiff meets this burden, then the burden shifts to the defendant to come forward with a "substantial legitimate justification," or a "legitimate, nondiscriminatory reason," for the contested practice.

168. Finally, if the defendant is able to meet its rebuttal burden, the burden shifts back to the plaintiff to "establish either that the defendant overlooked an equally effective alternative with less discriminatory effects or that the proffered justification is no more than a pretext for racial discrimination." *Powell,* 198 F.3d at 394.

169. This Court has been able to identify only one reported federal court decision which: (1) addressed the application of the burden-shifting analysis to a Title VI, section 602 claim alleging disparate impact discrimination; (2) in the context of plaintiff's request for a preliminary injunction; (3) regarding an alleged violation of the EPA's Title VI implementing regulations, codified at 40 C.F.R. § 7.1 *et seq.* In *New York City Environmental Justice Alliance ("NYCEJA") v. Giuliani,* 214 F.3d 65 (2d Cir.2000), the Second Circuit considered a complaint brought by environmental organizations against New York City, alleging that the city's proposed destruction of city-owned lots containing community gardens would violate Title VI's prohibition on discrimination by recipients of federal funds. *NYCEJA,* 214 F.3d at 67. Specifically, the plaintiffs alleged that the destruction of the gardens would have a disproportionate, adverse impact on the mostly minority residents of the communities in which the gardens were located, in violation of 40 C.F.R. § 7.35. *Id.*

170. The Second Circuit held that the plaintiffs had failed to establish a prima facie case of disparate impact discrimination for two reasons. First, the Court found that plaintiffs failed to show a causal link between the elimination of the gardens and the alleged adverse effect

on Plaintiffs, namely, loss of outdoor recreational space. *NYCEJA*, 214 F.3d at 69-70. Second, the Court held that Plaintiffs' proposed indicator, or measure, of disparity, namely, "loss of open space," was not an "appropriate measure" of disparate impact. *Id.* According to the Court, an "appropriate measure" would be one that is adequate to allow the court to "ascribe significance to any alleged disparate impact" of the defendant's action. *Id.*

171. I note, however, that the facts upon which the Second Circuit's decision was based in *NYCEJA* are very different from the facts presented by Plaintiffs in the present action.

172. I conclude, therefore, that the application of the burden-shifting analysis to the claim raised by Plaintiffs in this case, which alleges disparate impact on the basis of a permitting decision, in violation of the EPA's Title VI implementing regulations, presents this Court with an issue of first impression. I note that the application of a Title VI analysis to environmental permitting decisions has been the subject of extensive debate among legal scholars. *See, e.g.,* Sheila Foster, *Piercing the Veil of Economic Arguments Against Title VI Enforcement*, 10 Fordham Envt'l L.J. 331 (1999); Michael D. Mattheisen, *Applying the Disparate Impact Rule of Law to Environmental Permitting Under Title VI of the Civil Rights Act of 1964*, 24 Wm. & Mary Envt'l L. & Pol'y Rev. 1 (2000); Julia B. Latham Worsham, *Disparate Impact Lawsuits Under Title VI, Section 602: Can a Legal Tool Build Environmental Justice?* 27 B.C. Envt'l Aff. L.Rev. 631 (2000); Bradford C. Mank, *Environmental Justice and Title VI: Making Recipient Agencies Justify Their Siting Decisions*, 73 Tul. L.Rev. 787 (1999).

S. Plaintiffs' Prima Facie Case

. . .

(1) Adverse Impact

176. Plaintiffs contend that the operation of the proposed facility will adversely impact them in several ways. After reviewing the record, I have determined that the primary adverse impacts of which Plaintiffs complain are impacts to the health of the residents who live in the Waterfront South neighborhood where the proposed SLC facility is located. While Plaintiffs also complain of adverse effects to their quality of life, caused by the noise, vibrations and dirt associated with the

truck traffic which will traverse the neighborhood if the facility becomes operational, I have concluded that the record in this case is insufficient to support such a claim. Accordingly, I shall deny Plaintiffs' request for a preliminary injunction to the extent that it is based on the alleged adverse impact of the operation of the SLC facility on Plaintiffs' quality of life.

177. The operation of the proposed facility will impact the health of the residents of the Waterfront South community in two specific ways. First, particulate matter emitted from the proposed SLC facility will affect respiratory function in the members of the surrounding community, a disproportionate number of whom already suffer from asthma and other respiratory conditions which will be aggravated by the inhalation of particulate matter. Second, the ozone generated by the annual migration of 77,000 trucks making deliveries to and from the SLC facility will impact residents' health because it aggravates respiratory function and causes cancer. The Court has also found that the Waterfront South community in general, and African-American members of the community in particular, already suffer disproportionately high rates of cardiovascular disease and respiratory disease such as asthma.

178. The question that remains, however, is whether these impacts are sufficiently "adverse" to support a conclusion that Plaintiffs have carried this portion of their burden in making out a prima facie case of disparate impact discrimination under Title VI. . . .

180. Both the NJDEP and SLC respond to Plaintiffs' argument by contending that the SLC facility's emissions are *per se* not adverse. With respect to the PM-10 emissions, the NJDEP insists that because the PM-10 emissions will be in compliance with the governing NAAQS, set in 1987, they cannot be considered "adverse.". . .

182. Defendants rely on four sources to support their claim that emissions which are in compliance with the NAAQS are *per se* not "adverse": (1) the language of the Clean Air Act, codified at 42 U.S.C. § 7409; (2) the EPA OCR's decision in *Select Steel;* (3) the EPA Draft Guidances; and (4) the recent Supreme Court decision in *Whitman v. American Trucking Assoc., Inc.* [excerpted in this Supplement in Chapter 5].

183. The Clean Air Act provides, in relevant part, as follows:

Chapter 1. Environmental Values and Policies

(b) Protection of public health and welfare

(1) National primary ambient air quality standards, prescribed under subsection (a) of this section shall be ambient air quality standards the attainment and maintenance of which in the judgment of the Administrator, based on such criteria and allowing an adequate margin of safety, are requisite to protect the public health. Such primary standards may be revised in the same manner as promulgated.

42 U.S.C. § 7409.

184. Based on this language, Defendants argue that by setting the NAAQS, the EPA has already, after extensive research and study, determined at what level an ambient airborne pollutant becomes "adverse" to public health. In the response issued by the NJDEP to the concerns raised at the public hearing on the SLC facility, Dr. Atay, the NJDEP Hearing Officer, explained the NJDEP's reliance on the NAAQS to determine "adversity":

The primary NAAQS were established to protect public health with an adequate margin of safety. Principally based on human health studies, they are set to protect the most sensitive individuals. Those with respiratory or heart conditions, children and the elderly would be among the groups considered sensitive individuals. Therefore, based on the dispersion modeling analysis of the proposed facility, no adverse health impacts are expected due to PM-10 emissions.

185. To support the NJDEP's application of the NAAQS as the sole indicator necessary to evaluate whether a health impact is "adverse" for the purposes of a Title VI disparate impact analysis, Defendants cite the language of the EPA's OCR's *Select Steel Investigative Report* at length. Specifically, the NJDEP relies on the EPA Investigator's statement that:

[T]he EPA believes that where, as here, air quality concerns are raised regarding a pollutant regulated pursuant to an ambient, health-based standard, and where the area is in compliance with, and will continue after the operation of the challenged facility to comply with, that standard, the air quality in the surrounding community is presumptively protective and emissions of that pollutant should not be viewed as "adverse" within the meaning of Title VI.

Select Steel at 28.

186. After a careful review of the *Select Steel Investigative Report*, however, the Court concludes that the NJDEP's reliance on *Select Steel* is based on a selective reading of that decision and is misplaced. First, the *Select Steel* decision states clearly that a recipient's obligations under Title VI include consideration, with respect to the permitting of pollutant-producing facilities, of factors *independent* of compliance with environmental statutes, such as the NAAQS. *Select Steel* at 28. Second, immediately prior to the language cited by the NJDEP, the Select Steel Investigative Report states:

> Importantly, to be actionable under Title VI, an impact must be both 'adverse' and 'disparate.' The determination of whether the distinction of effects from regulated sources to racial or ethnic communities is 'adverse' within the meaning of Title VI will necessarily turn on the facts and circumstances of each case and the nature of environmental regulation designed to afford protection.

Select Steel Investigative Report at 28.

When considered in context, it is clear that the language cited by Defendants from *Select Steel* reflects the OCR's decision regarding the principal facts of that case. The decision in *Select Steel* does not stand for the blanket proposition that compliance with the NAAQS is always enough to assure that the impacts of a facility are not sufficiently "adverse" as to trigger Title VI, but only for the proposition that such a showing creates a presumption of non-adversity.

187. Furthermore, the methodology used by the EPA OCR to evaluate the "adversity" of the impact in *Select Steel* supports this Court's conclusion that evidence of compliance with the NAAQS is not the end point of an investigation into "adverse impact" under Title VI. The EPA OCR conducted a comprehensive analysis of not only the proposed facility's emissions in *Select Steel*, but also of the health conditions in the complainants' community, and the emissions of other NAAQS- and non-NAAQS regulated facilities in the area. *See Select*

Steel, 13-25.

[With respect to the Revised Draft Guidance, the court found that it endorsed a method of adverse impact analysis consistent with the Select Steel approach. "Specifically, the Draft Revised Investigation Guidance advises that EPA OCR will begin investigation of Title VI complaints by determining the 'universe of sources' affecting the complainant community, including not only those pollutants identified with the permitted activities, but also other sources of environmental stressors."]

194. This understanding of the approach recommended by the Guidances is corroborated by the Preamble to the Guidances, in which the EPA states:

EPA has remained mindful that no single analysis or definition of adverse disparate impact is possible due to the differing nature of impacts (e.g., cancer risk, acute health effects, odors) and the various environmental media (e.g., air, water) that may be involved. EPA did not set an across-the-board definition of adverse impact . . . EPA will use environmental laws, regulations, policy and science as touchstones for determining thresholds for what is adverse.

65 Fed.Reg. 39650, 39654.

196. Thus, the Court concludes, from a review of *Select Steel,* the Draft Recipient Guidance and the Draft Revised Investigation Guidance, that the NJDEP has misconstrued the meaning of EPA's interpretation of its Title VI regulations regarding reliance on the NAAQS as the sole and determinative measure of adversity of impact.

197. The Court also concludes that the methodology the EPA described in the Guidances and used in *Select Steel,* which mandates consideration of the totality of circumstances and cumulative environmental burdens, is inconsistent with the NJDEP's contention that it need not consider SLC's truck traffic when assessing impact because mobile sources of pollution are regulated under a different program than stationary sources. Such an artificial and arbitrary distinction is clearly inapplicable to an assessment of adverse impact under Title VI. The NJDEP has cited no law to support its contention that it is not "autho-

rized" to consider motor vehicle emissions when making a Title VI regarding a permit application. The mere fact that stationary and mobile sources of emissions are regulated differently under the CAA does not, in the view of this Court, prohibit the NJDEP from considering the cumulative effects of the operation of the SLC facility on ambient air quality in the surrounding community pursuant to a Title VI investigation.

198. The Court further concludes that Plaintiffs have demonstrated that the permitting and operation of the SLC facility, when considered in the context of the current health conditions and existing environmental burdens in the Waterfront South community, is likely to adversely affect their health to a degree that meets the standard of "adversity" under Title VI. The NJDEP has not disputed the fact that residents of this community already suffer a significantly disproportionate rate of cancer and asthma. Nor has it disputed, or even considered, the health consequences associated with the cumulative environmental burden this community already experiences as a result of the presence of a sewage treatment facility, power plant, trash-to-steam incinerator, two Superfund sites, fourteen sites the NJDEP has designated as contaminated, and approximately fifteen industrial facilities. Additionally, the area is in "severe noncompliance" with the ozone NAAQS. And, finally, the SLC facility will emit a level of PM-2.5 which exceeds the level that the EPA's research indicates is safe for the general population, to say nothing of its effects on a population which already suffers from significant respiratory ailments. 62 Fed.Reg. 38652. The United States Court of Appeals for the District of Columbia considered the analysis used by the EPA to make this determination, and found that the EPA's decision was based on the demonstration of a statistically significant relationship, proven through regression analysis, between PM-2.5 and negative health effects. *American Trucking Assoc., Inc. v. U.S.E.P.A,* 175 F.3d 1027, 1053-54 (D.C.Cir.1999), *rev'd in part and aff'd. in part, Whitman v. American Trucking Assoc.,* 121 S.Ct. 903 (2001). Based upon my review of the evidence in the record and my application of the analysis recommended and practiced by the EPA to determine adversity, I conclude that Plaintiffs are likely to succeed on the merits of their Title VI claim to the extent that their success depends on their ability to make a prima facie showing of adverse impact.

Chapter 1. Environmental Values and Policies

(2) Disparate Impact

199. Following the test articulated by the Third Circuit...disparity is the second part of the three-part test Plaintiffs must satisfy to establish a prima facie case of disparate impact discrimination in violation of Title VI. Disparity in Title VI cases may be proved through the use of "appropriate statistical measures." . . .

200. To support their claim that pollutant-producing facilities in New Jersey are disproportionately located in communities of color, Plaintiffs rely primarily on the expert report of Dr. Michel Gelobter.

201. Dr. Gelobter analyzed the correlation between race and the distribution of facilities that emit air pollution in New Jersey. Dr. Gelobter performed two different analyses. First, he gathered data on the number of air pollution emitting facilities from the "Airometeric Information Retrieval System, Air Facilities Subsystem" ("AIRS/AFS") database, which is one of thirteen publically available databases which comprise the EPA's "Envirofacts" database. Dr. Gelobter then gathered data on the racial composition of New Jersey ZIP Code areas using the 1990 U.S. Census results. Comparing these data, Dr. Gelobter found that ZIP Code 08104, which includes the Waterfront South Area, has 21 AIRS/AFS facilities, compared to a statewide average of 7.8 AIRS/AFS facilities per ZIP code. Dr. Gelobter further found that ZIP codes with higher than the state-wide average of 20.6% non-white residents had an average of 13.7 AIRS/AFS facilities per ZIP code, or 105% more AIRS/AFS facilities, than those with a below-average number of non-white residents, which had an average of 6.7 AIRS/AFS facilities per ZIP Code. ZIP Code 08104, which corresponds with Waterfront South, has 230% of the statewide average of AIRs/AFS facilities.

202. Second, Dr. Gelobter collected data on the average number of EPA-regulated facilities per ZIP Code in New Jersey, which is 37.8 facilities per ZIP Code. Dr. Gelobter then compared the actual number of such facilities in each ZIP Code with the percentage of that ZIP Code's residents who were above or below the state average of non-white residents. Dr. Gelobter concluded that ZIP Code 08104, which includes the Waterfront South area, contains 70 EPA-regulated facilities, which is 185% of the state-wide average of 36.5 EPA-regulated facilities per ZIP Code.

Chapter 1. Environmental Values and Policies

203. Finally, Dr. Gelobter performed a regression analysis of the relationship between EPA-regulated facilities and the percentage of non-whites in a ZIP Code area. Dr. Gelobter found that for every 10% increase in the percentage of non- white residents in a given ZIP Code, the ZIP Code would experience a 16% increase over the average number of EPA-regulated facilities. According to Dr. Gelobter's Certification, based on his statistical analysis, "the odds that there is no relationship between the percentage of non-white residents and the number of facilities in a ZIP Code area are less than 3 in 10 million.". . .

206. I note that both the databases utilized by Dr. Gelobter, and the methods of statistical analyses he employed, have been identified in the EPA Guidances as appropriate for assessing disparity of impact in permitting decisions pursuant to Title VI. *See* Draft Recipient Guidance, 65 Fed.Reg. 39650, 39661. The Draft Investigation Guidance states that the EPA OCR, in assessing disparate impact, will first characterize the populations to be compared, and then conduct comparisons. 65 Fed.Reg. 39650, 39681-39682. [FN11] Furthermore, the measures Dr. Gelobter selected to use in conducting his analysis, such as the number of EPA-regulated facilities per ZIP code, are culled from databases maintained and specifically recognized by the EPA as appropriate sources of data for conducting disparate impact analysis, such as the EnviroFacts, CERLCIS, AIRS, and AIRS/AQS databases. 65 Fed.Reg. 39650, 39659-60. . . .

209. Based on my review of Dr. Gelobter's testimony, and my consideration of the testimony of Dr. Coursey, I conclude that Plaintiffs have established a prima facie case of disparate impact. Specifically, I conclude that Dr. Gelobter used an appropriate measure to calculate disparity, in that he relied on databases and methodology recommended by the EPA for the purpose of measuring disparate impact.

(3) Causation

210. Applying the Third Circuit's disparate impact analysis for Title VI cases, the final element of a plaintiff's *prima facie* case is the demonstration that the alleged adverse disparate impact is causally linked to defendant's facially neutral policy. [T]he Second Circuit [has] ar-

ticulated the importance of this element in the specific context of an allegation of discrimination in violation of the EPA implementing regulations to Title VI: "[t]he plaintiffs understood, of course, that they were required to do more than demonstrate to the district court that [the alleged discriminatory action] was a bad idea. In order to establish a prima facie case of adverse disparate impact, [plaintiffs] had to allege a causal connection between a facially neutral policy and a disproportionate and adverse impact on minorities."

211. In this case, Plaintiffs rely primarily on the Certification of Dr. Gelobter to demonstrate a causal link between the disparity of distribution of industrial, pollutant-producing facilities in New Jersey and the NJDEP's facially neutral permitting policy, which is based exclusively on compliance with the NAAQS. Specifically, Dr. Gelobter undertook a regression analysis of the relationship between EPA-regulated facilities and the percentage of non-whites in a ZIP Code area. The results of the regression analysis indicate that the odds that there is no relationship between the percentage of non-white residents and number of facilities in a ZIP Code area are approximately three in 10 million. . . .

213. SLC contends that based on Dr. Gelobter's analysis, Plaintiffs make an "unsubstantiated leap" to the conclusion that the NJDEP's permitting process is causally linked to the admitted disparity in the distribution of industrial facilities in the State of New Jersey. According to SLC, this Court must reject Dr. Gelobter's data on causation because he failed to consider all of the factors that could account for the siting of industrial facilities in particular areas, such as access to transportation, existing infrastructure, and available labor force. Thus, SLC asserts that "even assuming the statistical evidence that Plaintiffs have produced is accurate, those statistics are not the result of some defect in NJDEP's permitting process, but are rather the result of hundreds, if not thousands, of individual siting decisions made by private entities searching on the basis of sound business principles for the most appropriate locations for their industrial facilities."

214. I reject SLC's argument for several reasons. First, this Court has already concluded that there is in fact a severe "defect" in the NJDEP's permitting process, namely, that the NJDEP relies exclusively on compliance with environmental regulations such as the NAAQS,

without considering its obligations under Title VI, in issuing permits such as those it issued for the proposed SLC facility.

215. Second, a review of the applicable regulations promulgated by the EPA clearly indicates that the EPA has determined that there is a causal connection between recipients' permitting practices and the distribution of polluting facilities, and enacted the implementing regulations to Title VI to ensure that recipients consider the potential disparate impact of their permitting decisions. *See* 40 C.F.R. § 7.1 *et seq.* In other words, the EPA has acknowledged that because recipients are responsible for permitting, they are also responsible for considering the distribution of the facilities which they permit with respect to the classes protected by the Civil Rights Act of 1964. The regulations therefore support the conclusion that a recipient's permitting decisions are causally linked to the distribution of facilities as a matter of law.

216. Third, SLC ignores the fact that without receiving a permit from the NJDEP, none of the hundreds or thousands of business to which it refers may legally operate in the State of New Jersey. As I just explained, the EPA implicitly rejected SLC's contention that there is no causal connection between the distribution of facilities and the permitting process when it issued the implementing regulations to Title VI. I conclude that SLC's contention that the NJDEP's permitting practices are absolutely irrelevant to the siting of industrial facilities in New Jersey is illogical, and contradicted by the applicable Title VI regulations.

217. Fourth and finally, after reviewing the expert testimony submitted by both Plaintiffs and SLC on the issue of causation, and the facts of this case, I have concluded that the Plaintiffs have carried their prima facie burden of demonstrating that the NJDEP's permitting practices are causally linked to the adverse, disparate impact about which Plaintiffs complain. . . . Plaintiffs in this case have submitted statistical evidence, utilizing measures recommended by the EPA, which causally links the NJDEP's permitting practice to the disparate distribution of facilities in New Jersey.

218. In sum, because I have concluded that Plaintiffs have adequately demonstrated that the NJDEP's permitting practices result in an adverse, disparate impact on the basis of race, color, or national

origin, I conclude that Plaintiffs have made a prima facie case of disparate impact discrimination under Title VI.

T. DEFENDANTS' REBUTTAL BURDEN

219. Under *Powell* [v. Ridge, 189 F.3d 387 (3d Cir. 1999), cert. denied, 528 U.S. 1046 (1999)] after the plaintiff establishes a *prima facie* case of disparate impact discrimination, the defendant has the opportunity to rebut the resulting inference of discrimination by showing that it had a "substantial legitimate justification" or a "legitimate nondiscriminatory reason" for its practice. . . .

221. SLC . . . has offered several justifications for the NJDEP's decision. These include: (1) the fact that the proposed SLC facility was in compliance with the NAAQS and all applicable environmental regulations; (2) the fact that SLC and the NJDEP "consulted with the community"; and (3) the fact that the City of Camden "needs the economic and social benefits that come with a renewed industrial presence attuned to its environmental responsibilities." SLC did not cite any case law or other statutory or administrative source to support its contention that these justifications meet the standard [required to meet the rebuttal burden.]

223. In the absence of guiding legal precedent on the question of what constitutes a "substantial legitimate justification" or a "legitimate nondiscriminatory reason" in the context of this case, I shall look to EPA regulations and practice.

224. According to the Draft Revised Investigation Guidance, once the EPA OCR makes a finding that a proposed facility will have an adverse, disparate impact on the complainants, "[t]he recipient will have the opportunity to 'justify' the decision to issue the permit notwithstanding the adverse disparate impact, based on a substantial, legitimate justification." 65 Fed.Reg. 39650, 39683. The Guidance cautions that "determining what constitutes an acceptable justification will necessarily be based on the facts of the case," but states that "generally, the recipient would attempt to show that the challenged activity is reasonably necessary to meet a goal that is legitimate, important, and integral to the recipient's institutional mission." *Id.* The Guidance identifies the following types of justifications as examples which the EPA

might consider substantial and legitimate: (1) a demonstration that the permitting action will provide a public health or environmental benefit to the affected population; (2) a demonstration that the permitting action will have economic benefit, if the benefit is "delivered directly to the affected population." *Id.* In assessing the validity of an economic justification, OCR will consider both the recipient's perspective, and the affected community's perspective, on whether the permitted facility will in fact provide direct economic benefits to the community. 65 Fed.Reg. 39650, 39683.

225. I conclude that the record in the present case is insufficient for me to determine whether the NJDEP can provide a "substantial, legitimate justification," in the context of Title VI analysis, for its permitting decision. SLC did not cite any applicable legal, statutory, or regulatory source to support its conclusion that the NJDEP provided sufficient justification for its decision to permit the SLC facility. Neither the NJDEP nor SLC has addressed the NJDEP's potential justifications with reference to the guidelines suggested by the EPA, which, as I have stated, are the only source this Court can find that specifically addresses a Title VI rebuttal analysis in permitting decisions.

226. Accordingly, because Defendants have failed to carry their rebuttal burden, Plaintiffs have established a likelihood of success on the merits.

U. IRREPARABLE HARM

[The court concluded that the adverse health effects predicted by plaintiffs' experts assoicated with PM constituted irreparable harm to the Waterfront South community. In addition, "the totality of the circumstances, including but not limited to the additional ozone generated by the diesel truck traffic associated with the proposed facility and the additional environmental burdens which the SLC facility will impose on an already environmentally burdened community" also constituted irreparable harm.]

V. IRREPARABLE HARM TO OTHER PARTIES, AND THE PUBLIC INTEREST

[The court concluded that SLC's economic losses associated with injoining the issuance of its permit was legally insufficient to constitute irreparable harm to it.]

243. Finally, SLC argues that a preliminary injunction is against the public interest because it would "thwart the public interest in a revitalized Camden." What is clear from the record, however, is that the already poor health of the community in which the facility is located is likely to be adversely affected by the operation of the facility, and that the NJDEP did not consider either the health status or the cumulative environmental burdens in this community prior to issuing the permits. Based on these facts, the Court concludes that the public interest clearly weighs in favor of granting Plaintiffs' request to enjoin the operation of the facility until the NJDEP has conducted an adverse disparate impact analysis in accordance with its obligations under Title VI.

244. Finally, this Court concludes that requiring the NJDEP to comply with the EPA's Title VI implementing regulations is inherently in the public interest, insofar as it ensures the protection of civil rights within the context of environmental permitting decisions. *See, e.g., Government of Virgin Islands, Dept. of Conservation and Cultural Affairs v. Virgin Islands Paving, Inc.,* 714 F.2d 283, 286 (3d Cir.1983) (explaining that "one of the most significant factors to be considered is the public interest which underlies [the environmental act]").

245. Thus, having considered the arguments set forth by Plaintiffs, the NJDEP, and SLC concerning the factors of harm to non-moving parties and public interest, I conclude that both factors weigh in favor of a grant of preliminary injunctive relief to Plaintiffs.

IV. CONCLUSION

For the reasons set forth above, Plaintiffs' application for a preliminary injunction is granted. The air permits issued by NJDEP to SLC are vacated. This case is remanded to NJDEP and Commissioner Shinn to make appropriate findings consistent with this Opinion, which shall be filed with this Court within thirty days. SLC shall be enjoined from operating its proposed facility until further order of this Court. This Court shall retain jurisdiction. The Court shall enter an appropriate form of order.

Chapter 1. Environmental Values and Policies

NOTES AND QUESTIONS

1. **EPA's Revised Draft Guidance**. The principal case refers repeatedly to proposed revisions that EPA has issued to modify its earlier guidance regarding compliance with Title VI, which is discussed at page 26. On June 27, 2000, EPA published two new draft guidance documents on how it will respond to environmental justice complaints filed under Title VI of the Civil Rights Act of 1964: "Draft Title VI Guidance For EPA Assistance Recipients Administering Environmental Permitting Programs" and "Draft Revised Guidance for Investigating Title VI Administrative Complaints Challenging Permits." 65 Fed. Reg. 39,650 (2000). Although the purpose of this revised guidance was to clarify how the agency interprets its obligations under Title VI, there has been considerable criticism that the new guidance is still too vague and leaves too many crucial issues unresolved. See Bradford C. Mank, The Draft Title VI Recipient and Revised Investigation Guidances: Too Much Discretion for EPA and a More Difficult Standard for Complainants? 30 Env. L. Rep. 11144 (2000); The Draft Civil Rights Guidance: The Controversy Continues, 17 Envt'l Forum 46 (Sept/Oct. 2000). As of this writing, it is not known how the revised guidance will fare in the Bush Administration.

2. **Section 1983**. The continuing relevance of SCCIA I's disparate impact and duty to consider analysis depends upon whether or not SCCIA II's ruling that such Title VI claims can be litigated as Section 1983 actions is sustained. The controversies over the 1983 question are no less severe than those that the court notes surround how Title VI should be interpreted and applied in permitting decisions. For a review of the issues involved in the 1983 question, see Bradford Mank, "Using Section 1983 to Enforce Title VI's Section 602 Regulations," 49 U. Kans. L. Rev. 321 (2001).

Problem Exercise: Should the Makah Be Permitted to Hunt Whales? (pp. 28-30)

Further whale hunting by the Makah has been halted by the success in the Ninth Circuit of the lawsuit referred to in the last paragraph of the Problem Exercise, page 30. Metcalf v. Daley, 214 F.3d 1135 (9th

Cir., 2000). The opinion is excerpted in Chapter 8 of this Teacher's Update. Portions of the opinion not reproduced there also supply additional factual detail on the Makah's traditions of whale hunting, their treaty rights, and the details of the IWC proceedings. In *Metcalf* the Ninth Circuit ruled that the federal government had violated NEPA by agreeing to support the Makah's whaling proposal before performing an environmental assessment (EA). Even though an EA subsequently had been prepared, the court required that it be redone prior to resumption of the whaling.

On July 13, 2001, the National Marine Fisheries Services released a new EA that endorsed resumption of the whaling. The new EA, which is 89 pages in length, finds that there is no biological reason for restricting the Makah hunt to the period from November through June when whales are migrating. It also recommends expanding the area where the hunt may occur. According to the EA, the population of gray whales is estimated to be around 26,000, the largest it has been since the mid-nineteenth century. The federal government now intends to develop a new cooperative agreement with the Makah that will allow the tribe to strike up to five whales per year until 2002 when the quota expires.

Problem Exercise: Should the Arctic National Wildlife Refuge Be Opened to Oil Exploration and Development? (pp. 62-69)

Oil exploration in the ANWR played a prominent role in the 2000 presidential campaign. Candidate George Bush favored opening the region for exploratory drilling, while candidate Al Gore pledged to preserve the region. President Bush's nominee for Secretary of the Interior, Gale Norton, worked in Interior during the Reagan Administration, and was a part of the working group there that tried to persuade Congress to open the region to exploration. Douglas Jehl, "Interior Choice Sends a Signal on Land Policy," New York Times, Dec. 30, 2000.

After the election, President Clinton was urged by some to issue an executive order declaring the 19 million acre a national monument. This would effectively bar exploration unless and until the status was rescinded by legislation. Among those urging this step was former

Chapter 1. Environmental Values and Policies

President Jimmy Carter. Writing in the New York Times, he wrote that in all the travels that he and Mrs. Carter took to beautiful locations,

> nothing matches the spectacle of wildlife we found on the coastal plain of America's Arctic National Wildlife Refuge in Alaska. To the north lay the Arctic Ocean; to the south, rolling foothills rose toward the glaciated peaks of the Brooks Range. At our feet was a mat of low tundra plant life, bursting with new growth, perched atop the permafrost. As we watched, 80,000 caribou surged across the vast expanse [at home] in an uncorrupted wilderness home, and the wolves, ptarmigan, grizzlies, polar bears, musk oxen and millions of migratory birds. [It] was a profoundly humbling experience. We were reminded of our human dependence on the natural world.

> [When I] signed legislation expanding the protected area to 18 million acres [sic] I listened to scientists who emphasized that the coastal plain is the ecological heart and soul of this, our greatest wildlife sanctuary. [The] law I signed 20 years ago did not permanently protect this Arctic wilderness. It did, however, block any oil company drilling until Congress votes otherwise. That is where the issue stands today.

> President-elect George Bush has. . .unquestioning faith that drilling would have little impact. The simple fact is, drilling is inherently incompatible with wilderness. The roar alone — of road-building, trucks, drilling and generators — would pollute the wild music of the Arctic and be as out of place there as it would be in the heart of Yellowstone or the Grand Canyon.

> Some 95 percent of Alaska's oil-rich North Slope lands are already available for exploration or development. Our nation must choose what to do with the last 5 percent. Oil drilling or wilderness. We cannot have it both ways.

> I am for the wilderness. [As] Teddy Roosevelt [said when] he used the Antiquities Act to protect the Grand Canyon: "Leave it as it is. The ages have been at work on it, and man can only mar it. What you can do is keep it for your children, your children's children and for all who come after you."

Chapter 1. Environmental Values and Policies

Jimmy Carter, "Make This Natural Treasure a National Monument," N.Y. Times, Dec. 29, 2000.

Spurred by rising prices of gasoline, which some had predicted would exceed three dollars per gallon in parts of the country in the summer of 2001, as well as the electricity shortages in California, President Bush took steps soon after his inauguration to act on commitments made during the presidential campaign to reorient American energy policies. He asked Vice President Cheney to chair a National Energy Policy Development Group to assess and make recommendations concerning our national energy policy. On May 17, 2001, the Group issued its National Energy Plan, with a series of recommendations covering energy conservation and development and use of renewable energy sources, energy production, the energy supply and distribution infrastructure, and environmental protection. After noting that at current rates United States oil consumption will increase by about one-third, to 26 million barrels per day, while domestic production will decline slightly to about 7 million barrel per day, the report recommended that a portion of the ANWR be opened to drilling. Here is what the report had to say:

> The Alaska National Interest Lands Conservation Act expanded ANWR from 9 million acres to 19 million acres, and designated 8 million acres as wilderness. Congress specifically left open the question of management of a 1.5 million acre Arctic Coastal Plain area of ANWR because of the likelihood that it contains significant oil and gas resources. Section 1002 of the Act directed the Department of the Interior to conduct geological and biological studies of the Arctic Coastal Plain, "the 1002 Area," and to provide to Congress the results of those studies with recommendations on future management of the area. ... In May 1998, the USGS issued revised estimates of oil and gas resources in the 1002 Area. The 1998 USGS assessment shows an overall increase in estimated oil resources when compared to all previous government estimates. The estimate reaffirms the 1002 Area's potential as the single most promising prospect in the United States. The total quantity of recoverable oil within the entire assessment area is estimated to be between 5.7 and 16 billion barrels (95 percent and 5 percent probability range) with a mean value of 10.4 billion barrels. The mean estimate of 10.4 billion barrels is just below the amount produced

to date from North America's largest field, Prudhoe Bay, since production began 23 years ago. Peak production from ANWR could to be between 1 and 1.3 million barrels a day and account for more than 20 percent of all U.S. oil production. ANWR production could equal 46 years of current oil imports from Iraq. Technological improvements over the past 40 years have dramatically reduced industry's footprint on the tundra, minimized waste produced, and protected the land for resident and migratory wildlife. These advances include the use of ice roads and drilling pads, low impact exploration approaches such as winter-only exploration activities, and extended reach and through-tubing rotary drilling. These technologies have significantly reduced the size of production-related facilities on the North Slope. Estimates indicate that no more than 2,000 acres will be disturbed if the 1002 Area of ANWR is developed. For purposes of comparison, ANWR is about the size of the state of South Carolina, whereas the developed area is estimated to be less than one fifth the size of Washington D.C.'s Dulles International Airport.

National Energy Plan (2001). See http://www.energy.gov/HQPress/releases01/maypr/energy_policy.htm in order to view a copy of the entire energy plan.

How do these facts and arguments influence your views on ANWR?

Most environmental groups and most Americans continue to oppose opening the ANWR. The mean estimate of 10.4 billion barrels of reserves equals a little less than 10 months domestic use, according to the Group's projections. At just over 1% of the world production, it would have little impact on the world price of crude. Public Citizen argues that a 6% increase in auto and light truck fuel efficiency standards would, within three years, produce consumption reductions equal to the total amount of oil in the refuge.

Public Citizen also noted the environmental values at risk in the ANWR. "It is a significant denning ground for polar bears and an important migratory and nesting ground for over 130 species of birds. The coastal plain served as the central, "high-density calving area" for the Porcupine caribou herd 82% of the time between 1983 and 1999. Sarah James, of the Gwich'ins, has said that "there is only one place for the caribou to calve and that's where the oil is." The Gwich'ins continue to be dependent upon the caribou as a key food source. The Wilderness Society named the Refuge one of the 15 Most Endangered Wild Lands in 2000. It is described by the Fish & Wildlife Service as "America's finest example of an intact, naturally functioning community of arctic/subarctic ecosystems." Public Citizen, Oppose Drilling in the National Arctic Wildlife Refuge (May 14, 2001), available at http://www.citizen.org/cmep/alerts/arcticwildliferefuge.htm. That website also contains links to other information sources on the ANWR.

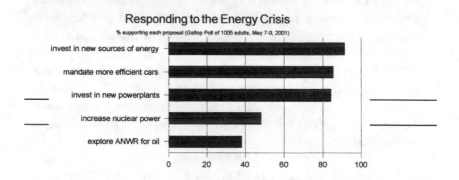

The claim that ANWR drilling will produce a very "small footprint" as the result of new technology has been questioned, because the footprint of the drilling rigs themselves is but a part of the total development needed for oil exploration and production. Pamela Miller, head of Arctic Connection, an environmental consulting firm in Anchorage, says that the first exploratory wells are "only the first step. In the refuge, they imply that development would be confined to a limited area. But actually they would transform a wilderness ecosystem into an industrial zone." At the already developed Arctic fields, more than 10,000 acres of North Slope tundra has been altered by facilities, roads and pipelines. The entire developed area for the existing fields equals 800 square miles.

The most basic environmental argument against many elements of the National Energy Plan, including its recommendation on the ANWR, is that the Plan emphasizes increasing production and improving supply and distribution systems, whereas it would be stressing energy conservation and the use of renewables. As Public Citizen expressed the point: "Oil is a wasteful, inefficient, and polluting energy source, from well to exhaust. To disregard the environmental consequences and promote drilling in the Arctic Refuge is to prop up harmful, outdated technologies and reckless consumption habits without addressing the more fundamental questions of energy security and sustainability. A more forward-looking national energy security act should be developed that actively promotes and funds cutting-edge renewable and sustainable energy sources. A comprehensive plan would include conservation measures and research, development, and implementation of green energy production. We -- and our environment -- can afford nothing less."

The odds that ANWR will be opened to exploratory drilling soon shifted markedly with the dramatic announcement in May by Senator Jim Jeffords of Vermont that he was leaving the Republican party to become an Independent. This changed a Senate that was formerly 50-50 Republicans and Democrats to one that was 50-49-1, resulting in a reorganization of the Senate under a Democratic majority. Hence Jeff Bingaman (D-NM), an announced opponent of ANWR drilling, replaced Frank Murkowski (R-AL), an announced supporter of drilling, as chair of the pivotal Energy Committee in the Senate. This makes it less likely that the Senate Energy Committee will report a bill permitting drilling on the 1002 lands.

Just before it began its summer recess, the U.S. House of Representatives voted on August 1, 2001, to allow drilling in ANWR. The ANWR drilling provision was included in H.R. 4, a package of energy legislation approved by the House. While environmentalists had thought that they had the votes to defeat any proposal to open ANWR to drilling, an effort to strip the provision from the bill was defeated by a vote of 223-206. Proponents of drilling gained votes by including a provision limiting the surface area of ANWR that could be drilled to no more than 2,000 acres. They also gained support from the Teamsters Union, which had been successfully courted by the Bush administration with the prospect of more jobs from ANWR. H.R. 4, the House-passed energy bill, provides $27 billion in tax breaks to promote development of coal, oil, natural gas, and nuclear power and $6 billion to promote conservation. A proposal to increase the required average fuel economy of sport utility vehicles from 20.5 miles per gallon to 27.5 mpg failed by a vote of 269-160.

Chapter 1. Environmental Values and Policies

The fate of ANWR now rests with the U.S. Senate. The Teamsters Union has been trying to convince Democratic Senators to support opening ANWR by arguing that it will generate 735,000 more jobs in the U.S. economy. Others argue that this estimate is a gross exagerration of the employment effects of drilling in ANWR because it is founded on a 1990 study by the American Petroleum Institute that projects that opening ANWR will cause oil prices to decline by $3.60 a barrel, which most believe is highly unlikely. President Bush, who had issued an executive order to ban the use of project labor agreements by federal contractors (Executive Order 13202, 66 Fed. Reg. 11225 (2001), reportedly has cut a deal with the union in which he agreed to support use of such an agreement in ANWR in return for the union's support for drilling.

Proponents of opening ANWR to drilling are hopeful that the legislation will not be killed in a straight party-line vote in the Senate Energy Committee, which now is composed of 12 Democratic senators and 11 Republicans. Key swing votes in the commitee are Democratic Senators Mary Landrieu of Louisiana and Daniel Akaka of Hawaii, who reportedly are leaning in favor of opening ANWR to drilling, and Republican Gordon Smith of Oregon, who reportedly will oppose it.

Following the terrorist attacks on the United States on September 11, 2001, there was concern that efforts to support national defense would be used to provide cover for a host of anti-environmental measures. It was widely rumored that Republican Senator Frank Murkowski of Alaska, with the support of Vice President Richard Cheney, would attach legislation opening ANWR and other protected public lands to oil drilling to the defense authorization bill that was sailing through the Senate. After this brought a sharp outcry from the Senate's Democratic leadership, Senator Murkowski disavowed the idea on the Senate floor. However, Republican Senator James Inhofe of Oklahoma then announced that he had introduced two separate amendments to the defense authorization bill that would do so. Senator Inhofe argued that opening ANWR to oil drilling was vital to military readiness and national security. As one columnist described this effort, "Those who were trying to expedite the drilling in the Arctic wildlife reserve argued that true patriotism dictated wholesale adoption of the pro-industry, pro-drilling House bill, even if it added unstainable weight to the defense authorizaton measure." Mary McGrory, Endangered Point of View, Wash. Post, Oct. 4, 2001, at A3. However, Senators from both parties argued vehemently that this was not the time to decide an issue on which the Congress is so closely divided. Senator Inhofe's tactic drew such widespread condemnation that that on October 2nd, the Senate voted unanimously to cut off debate on the defense bill, rejecting Inhofe's efforts. While both Inhofe and Murkowski have vowed to find alternative means to force Senate passage of legislation opening ANWR to oil drilling, some Democratic senators have vowed to filibuster, if necessary, to block any effort to open ANWR.

- 2 -
Environmental Law:
A Structural Overview

Environmental Statutes: A Historical
Perspective (pp. 101-13)

While there have been no significant amendments to the federal environmental statutes since publication of the casebook, the Bush administration's assumption of power has produced substantial changes in regulatory policy. Upon assuming office, the Bush administration temporarily blocked several regulations that had been adopted in the waning days of the Clinton administration. These included EPA's decision to lower maximum contaminant levels of arsenic in drinking water to 10 ppb under the Safe Drinking Water Act, as discussed in Chapter 4 of this Teacher's Update, and a regulation barring the construction of new roads and logging in millions of acres of national forests. With the Bush administration's support, Congress for the first time used the provisions of the Congressional Review Act, 5 U.S.C. §801-808 (mentioned on p. 173 of the casebook and explained on pages 98-99 of the Teacher's Manual), to veto the Occupational Safety and Health Administration's ergonomics regulations. These and other changes, which are discussed below, are likely to make presidential and congressional oversight of rulemaking a subject of great controversy in the years to come.

Federal Preemption of State Law (pp. 121-122)

Federal preemption issues continued to reach the U.S. Supreme Court with considerable frequency. In 2000 the Supreme Court decided two important preemption cases shortly after the casebook went to press. In United States v. Locke, 529 U.S. 89 (2000), the Court unanimously held that the federal Ports and Waterways Safety Act preempts Washington state regulations that imposed training, English proficiency, navigation watch, and casualty reporting requirements on oil tanker crews operating in state waters. In two other cases, the Court held that aspects of state tort law were preempted by federal safety regulations. Geier v. American Honda Motor Co., 529 U.S. 861 (2000), and Norfolk Southern Railway Co. v. Shanklin, 529 U.S. 344 (2000). In its most recent Term, the Supreme Court also dealt with preemption issues in Lorillard Tobacco Co. v. Reilly, 121 S.Ct. 2404 (2001), where it held that the Federal Cigarette Labeling and Advertising Act (FCLAA) preempted Massachusetts regulations restricting outdoor and point-of-sale advertising of cigarettes. Noting that the FCLAA expressly preempts state regulation of advertising and promotion of cigarettes "based on smoking and health," the Court rejected the notion that the Act preempts only regulation of the content of cigarette advertising and not regulation of its location. However, the Court noted that the FCLAA does not restrict a state's ability to enact generally applicable zoning resrictions that may apply to advertising for reasons of traffic safety or aesthetics.

Constitutional Limits on Federal Regulatory Authority under the Commerce Clause (pp. 129-131)

The Supreme Court's revival of limits on Congress's commerce power in *U.S. v. Lopez* (pp. 129-131) continued to affect environmental law. As discussed in Chapter 6 of this Teacher's Update, in *Solid Waste Agency of Northern Cook County v. U.S. Army Corps of Engineers (SWANCC)* the Court considered whether Congress has the constitutional authority to regulate isolated wetlands used by migratory birds. Relying on *Lopez*, the petitioner in *SWANCC* argued that Congress could not require it to obtain a federal permit under § 404(a) of the Clean Water Act before it filled an abandoned sand and gravel pit to create a landfill. Deciding *SWANCC* by the same 5-4 lineup that prevailed in *Lopez*, the Supreme Court ducked the constitutional issue by interpreting §404(a) narrowly. The Court found that Congress had not clearly indicated its intent to apply §404(a) to isolated wetlands visited by migratory birds. To avoid what it described as "significant constitutional and federalism questions," the Court held that §404(a)'s jurisdictional predicate — "waters of the United States" – did not include isolated wetlands where migratory birds are present. *SWANCC* thus narrows the reach of the federal Clean Water Act, while leaving important questions unanswered concerning the ultimate effect of *Lopez* on federal authority to protect the environment. It remains unclear how the "substantially affects" test is to be applied and whether Congress has lesser constitutional authority to protect the environment from destruction by noncommercial activities than by commercial ones.

The Supreme Court appears reluctant to address these questions, for it declined to review another decision narrowly rejecting similar constitutional challenges to the Endangered Species Act. The Court denied review in *Gibbs v. Babbitt*, 214 F. 3d 483 (4th Cir. 2000), a decision reproduced in Chapter 8 of this Supplement at pp. 243-262. In *Gibbs*, a divided panel of the Fourth Circuit held that the Congress had the authority to protect an experimental population of endangered red wolves on private land in North Carolina. Construing the taking of red wolves to protect farms as economic activity, the Fourth Circuit majority said that individual takings may be aggregated to assess their effect on interstate commerce. The majority noted that many tourists and scientists cross state lines to visit the wolves and that efforts to preserve them create the possibility of a renewed market in wolf pelts. It also observed that the regulation did not interfere with a traditional state function because Congress has historically played an important role in protecting endangered wildlife. A dissenting judge argued that Congress could not regulate a handful of animals in one small region of one state when the activity had no economic character.

Another challenge to Congress's regulatory authority under the commerce clause was rejected in *Allied Local & Regional Manufacturers Caucus v. U.S. Environmental Protection Agency*, 215 F. 3d 61 (D.C. Cir. 2000). The petitioners challenged EPA's Clean Air Act regulations limiting the content of volatile organic compounds in architectural coatings on the grounds that they exceeded the limits of federal authority under the Commerce Clause. The Court upheld the regulations, finding that the Commerce Clause is broad enough to permit regulation of activities causing air or water pollution that may have effects in more than one state.

Dolphin-Safe Tuna Labeling (pp. 135-137)

As noted in the text, p. 137, Congress in 1990 enacted the Dolphin Protection Consumer Information Act, Pub. L 101-627, which provided that tuna sold in the United States could not display "dolphin safe" label if the tuna was harvested using purse seine nets intentionally deployed on or to encircle dolphins. The subsequent history of efforts to promote dolphin safe tuna harvesting practices is discussed in Chapter 10 of this Supplement.

Green Marketing Claims and the *Western Fuels Association* Defamation Suit (p. 137)

In April 2000, the Western Fuels Association filed a defamation suit against environmentalists who claimed that coal-fired power plants contributed to global warming. On March 31, 2001, the lawsuit, *Western Fuels Association, Inc. v. Turning Point Project,* Case No. 00-CV-074-D, was dismissed for improper venue. The suit claimed that statements on a website and in a New York Times advertisement warning of the dangers of global warming, which had been sponsored by several environmental groups, constituted commercial defamation in violation of § 43 of the Lanham Act. The Lanham Act forbids "false or misleading description or fact" designed to create confusion as to a products "characteristics, qualities, or origin." Plaintiffs argued that the ad threatened the Wyoming coal industry by calling for an end to coal-fired electricity. Defendants were several non-profit organizations, including Friends of the Earth, Rainforest Action Network, Earth Island Institute, and others. Defendants denounced the lawsuit as a classic SLAPP (strategic lawsuit against public participation) suit.

Chief Judge William Downes concluded that the lawsuit was improperly brought in Wyoming since the defendants were located in Washington, D.C. and San Francisco. While the plaintiff argued that the defendants' use of an internet website to run a similar ad made venue proper anywhere, the court found that "an Internet advertisement alone" is not "sufficient to subject the advertiser to jurisdiction in the plaintiff's home state, without "something more" to show defendants purposefully directed activity in a "substantial way to the forum state." Judge Downes also disagreed with the plaintiff's "characterization that the subject of this action is coal," finding no specific connection between coal in Wyoming and the defendants' challenged statements.

In response to the court's decision, the Western Fuels Association has decided to abandon the lawsuit. Commenting on the proceedings, the Environmental Forum observed that "the Western Fuels Association has been a party itself to many ads on the opposite side, including one that famously said that a little extra carbon dioxide in the atmosphere was actually probably good for the planet. At last check, Mother Earth has not filed suit, even though evidence of njury is accumulating rapidly." News That's Reused, 18 Envt'l Forum, July/Aug. 2001, p. 21. Further information about the case may be found online at http://www.turnpoint.org,http://www.westernfuels.org and also at http://www.cmht.com/casewatch/cases/cwglobalslapp.htm, where a copy of the opinion may be obtained.

Oil Spill Liability and Regulation (pp. 139-145)

The impact of the Oil Pollution Act (OPA) on the prevention of oil spills continues to receive considerable attention. There has been a sharp decline in the amount of oil spilled in U.S. waters. A study by the National Research Council (NRC) of the National Academy of Sciences concluded that this decline

> "was the result of a number of actions that are in process or emerging, notably: an increased awareness among vessel owners and operators of the financial consequences of oil spills and a resulting increase in attention to policies and procedures aimed at eliminating vessel accidents; actions by port states to ensure the safety of vessels using their ports; increased efforts by ship classification societies to ensure that vessels under their classification meet or exceed existing requirements; improved audit and inspection programs by charterers and terminals; and the increased liability, financial responsibility, and other provisions of OPA 90.

National Research Council, Double-Hull Tanker Legislation: An Assessment of the Oil Pollution Act of 1990 (1998).

The international community has followed the lead of the United States, bv adopting MARPOL regulations requiring oil tankers to be double-hulled (or to use some approved alternative) by no later than 2023. As double-hull requirements are gradually being phased in, the percentage of tankers in the world fleet with double hulls has increased from 4 percent in 1990 to 10 percent in 1994, and 30 percent in 2001. More than 50 percent of very large crude oil carriers (VLCCs) (carriers of 200,000 tons or more) now have double hulls. At the same time, there has been a decline in the percentage of oil shipped in tankers owned by oil companies, a trend attributed by the NRC study to "a decision by some major oil companies to leave the tanker business, in large part to avoid high-liability exposure as well as for other economic reasons."

Greenpeace International was sharply critical of the decision by Exxon Mobil in January 2001 to charter two single-hulled tankers for five years each despite the availability of double-hulled alternatives. A London tanker broker expressed surprise at Exxon Mobil's decision. "I find it strange that such a profitable company can't afford a double-hulled tanker," given their record profits. The broker noted that double hull tankers cost only a few thousand dollars more per day to charter. Pete Harrison, Galapagos Oil Spill Renews Tanker Safety Debate, Reuters News Wire, Jan. 26, 2001.

Several studies have confirmed the conclusion that properly designed double-hulls are the most effective means for preventing oil spills. The NRC study concluded that "complete conversion of the maritime oil transportation fleet to double hulls will significantly improve protection of the marine environment." The committee estimated that the cost of this conversion worldwide will total approximately $30 billion over a twenty-year period. This represents an additional cost of approximately 10 cents per barrel of oil transported. The capital costs of double-hull tankers are estimated to be 9 to 17 percent higher than single-hulls' and their operating and maintenance costs are expected to be 5 to 13 percent greater.

Reinventing Regulation (pp. 176-177)

EPA now has more than 50 signed agreements for projects in its Project XL program. Several states also are pursuing programs similar to Project XL that provide greater regulatory flexibility to companies with superior environmental performance records. In November 2000 the National Academy of Public Administration published another report on efforts to improve environmental regulation. The report, entitled "Environment.Gov: Transforming Environmental Protection for the 21st Century," encourages EPA and the states to continue to expand their use of new approaches to make regulation more flexible and efficient.

Chapter 2. Structural Overview

An assessment of national environmental policy during the Clinton Administration by the American Enterprise Institute-Brookings Joint Center for Regulatory Studies identifies some major themes. First, during the 1990s national environmental standards were made more stringent (particularly the national ambient air quality standards for particulates and ozone) and environmental quality improved. Second, while Congress became more interested in promoting economic efficiency in regulation, the Clinton Administration remained skeptical of cost-benefit analysis and EPA placed much less emphasis on economic analysis. The Clinton Administration placed much more emphasis on expanding the role of information disclosure than previous administrations and interest in tradeable permit system continued to increase. Sheila M. Cavanagh, Robert W. Hahn, and Robert N. Stavins, National Environmental Policy During the Clinton Years (July 2001).

Presidential Oversight of Rulemaking in the Bush Administration (pp. 177-182)

Regulatory review issues again are likely to become more contentious under the Bush administration, which views regulation with far more skepticism than the Clinton administration did. On the day the Bush Administration took office, White House Chief of Staff Andrew Card issued the following memorandum to the heads and acting heads of all executive department agencies. This memorandum provides some indication that the Bush Administration has aggressive plans for regulatory review. It directs agency heads not to send any proposed or final regulations to the Federal Register without the approval of a Bush appointee and to withdraw all regulations that had been sent to the Federal Register which had not yet been published except for rules dealing with emergency situtations.

January 20, 2001

MEMORANDUM FOR THE HEADS AND ACTING HEADS OF EXECUTIVE DEPARTMENTS AND AGENCIES

FROM: Andrew H. Card, Jr.,
Assistant to the President and Chief of Staff.

SUBJECT: Regulatory Review Plan

The President has asked me to communicate to each of you his plan for managing the Federal regulatory process at the outset of his Administration. In order to ensure that the President's appointees have the opportunity to review any new or pending regulations, I ask on behalf of the President that you immediately take the following steps:

1. Subject to any exceptions the Director or Acting Director of the Office of Management and Budget (the "OMB Director") allows for emergency or other urgent situations relating to health and safety, send no proposed or final regulation to the Office of the Federal Register (the "OFR") unless and until a department or agency head appointed by the President after noon on January 20, 2001, reviews and approves the regulatory action. The department or agency head may delegate this power of review and approval to any other person so appointed by the President, consistent with applicable law.

2. With respect to regulations that have been sent to the OFR but not published in the Federal Register, withdraw them from OFR for review and approval as described in paragraph 1, subject to exception as described in paragraph 1. This withdrawal must be conducted consistent with the OFR procedures.

3. With respect to regulations that have been published in the OFR but have not taken effect, temporarily postpone the effective date of the regulations for 60 days, subject to exception as described in paragraph 1.

4. Exclude from the requested actions in paragraphs 1-3 any regulations promulgated pursuant to statutory or judicial deadlines and identify such exclusions to the OMB Director as soon as possible.

5. Notify the OMB Director promptly of any regulations that, in your view, impact critical health and safety functions of the agency

and therefore should be also excluded from the directives in paragraphs 1-3. The Director will review any such notifications and determine whether exception is appropriate under the circumstances.

6. Continue in all instances to comply with Executive Order 12866, pending our review of that order, as well as any other applicable Executive Orders concerning regulatory management.

As used in this memorandum, "regulation" has the meaning set out in section 3(e) of Executive Order 12866. That is, this plan covers "any substantive action by an agency (normally published in the Federal Register) that promulgates or is expected to lead to the promulgation of a final rule or regulation, including notices of inquiry, advance notices of proposed rulemaking, and notices of proposed rulemaking."

This regulatory review will be implemented by the Director or Acting Director of the OMB. Communications regarding exceptions to the review, or questions regarding the review generally, should be addressed to that individual.

Finally, in the interest of sound regulatory practice and the avoidance of costly, burdensome, or unnecessary regulation, independent agencies are encouraged to participate voluntarily in this review.

NOTES AND QUESTIONS

1. Can the Bush Administration legally require agency heads to withdraw regulations that already had been sent to the Federal Register? Would it be legal for a new administration to go further than suggested in the Card memorandum and suspend the effectiveness of regulations that already have been promulgated without first providing public notice and an opportunity to comment?

2. While many last-minute regulations ultimately were allowed to take effect, several high-profile Clinton regulatory initiatives, such as stricter limits on arsenic contamination in drinking water, have been blocked. The fact that regulatory review will again become a battleground for environmental interests is apparent in the battle over the confirmation of Harvard professor John Graham as administrator of OMB's Office of Information and Regulatory Affairs (OIRA). On

Chapter 2. Structural Overview

July 19, 2001, the Senate confirmed Graham's appointment by a vote of 61-37 despite intense opposition by environmental and consumer groups. See, e.g., Dick Durbin, Graham Flunks the Cost-Benefit Test, Wash. Post, July 16, 2001, p. A 15.

3. In an effort to demonstrate that he plans to be even-handed in conducting regulatory review, Graham has announced that OIRA will issue "prompt" letters to agencies to direct their attention to issues that deserve greater regulatory attention. See John D. Graham, Memorandum for the President's Management Council, Presidential Review of Agency Rulemaking by OIRA, Sept. 20, 2001, p. 5 (describing the meaning of "prompt" letters). In September 2001, OIRA sent prompt letters to OSHA and to the Department of Health and Human Services. The letter to OSHA encouraged the agency to require companies to use automated external defibrillators to prevent deaths from heart attacks. The letter to HHS encouraged it to require food labeling that would disclose trans-fatty acid content. Ellen Nakashima, OMB Asks Agencies for Action, Wash. Post, Sept. 21, 2001, p. A30. Are "prompt letters" a good vehicle for ensuring that regulatory review is not biased against regulation?

4. In a recent article, Professor Elena Kagan argues that there has been a significant transformation in the relationship between the President and the administrative state, which she calls "presidential administration." Elena Kagan, Presidential Administration, 114 Harv. L. Rev. 2245 (2001). Kagan argues that President Clinton, building on the regulatory review programs established in the Reagan and Bush administration, acted to assert personal ownership over the executive agencies' regulatory activity. By issuing directives to agencies to influence their regulatory priorities and by visibly taking credit for regulatory initiatives that supported his political agenda, President Clinton demonstrated that enhanced presidential control over executive agencies can serve pro-regulatory objectives. According to Professor Kagan, the President has, at least for now, achieved primacy in directing and influencing the outcome of the regulatory process. Does the Card memo suggest that President Bush plans to continue this pattern, though perhaps in a deregulatory direction? Does the President have the constitutional authority to dictate regulatory decisions entrusted by statute to agency heads?

Chapter 2. Structural Overview

Congressional Oversight of Rulemaking: the Congressional Review Act and the Repeal of OSHA's Ergonomics Standard (pp. 177-182)

As noted in the text (p. 173), when Congress enacted the Small Business Regulatory Enforcement Fairness Act in 1996, it included a provision requiring agencies to send all regulations to Congress for review 60 days before taking effect and creating a special fast-track procedure to enable Congress to enact joint resolutions disapproving regulations. This legislation is known as the Congressional Review Act, 5 U.S.C. §§ 801 to 808. It provides that if Congress enacts a joint resolution disapproving a regulation, the regulation shall not take effect or continue in effect. If a regulation is disapproved by Congress, the Act prohibits the agency that issued it from issuing any new rule that is "substantially the same as" the disapproved rule unless specifically authorized by subsequent legislation. 5 U.S.C. § 801(b)(2). In Immigration and Naturalization Service v. Chadha, 462 U.S. 919 (1983) the Supreme Court held that a legislative veto of regulations is unconstitutional because it bypassed the President's role in approving or disapproving of legislation. The Congressional Review Act avoids this constitutional problem by providing that joint resolutions of disapproval must be signed by the President or enacted over his veto.

While several joint resolutions to disapprove rules have been introduced into Congress, it was not until March 2001 that Congress enacted a resolution disapproving a regulation. The regulation repealed by Congress was the Occupational Health and Safety Administration's ergonomics standard to protect workers from repetitive stress injuries. The regulation, which had been under development by OSHA for a decade, finally had been issued in the closing days of the Clinton administration. OSHA expected that the rule would prevent 500,000 worker injuries per year from carpal tunnel syndrome, back strains, and other ailments. OSHA acknowledged that the rule would be expensive for businesses, estimating that it ultimately could cost $4.5 billion to implement, but it projected that it would save $9 billion per year by reducing worker injuries.

On March 1, Congressional Republicans introduced a resolution of disapproval, which was approved by the Senate on March 6, 2001, by a vote of 56-44. On March 7, the U.S. House of Representatives adopted the joint resolution by a vote of 223-206. Using the fast track procedures of the Congressional Review Act, the joint resolution was adopted without any hearings or committee action, with no opportunity for amendments, and with floor debate limited to 10 hours. President Bush endorsed the disapproval effort and signed the joint resolution repealing the rule.

Many of those who voted to repeal the rule stated that they were not opposed to having an ergonomics standard, but that they objected to the particular standard that had been adopted by OSHA. Labor Secretary Elaine Chao announced that the department would consider developing a new rule to protect workers from repetitive-motion injuries. Others, however, believe that the Congressional Review Act precludes OSHA from issuing a new ergonomics rule without new legislation authorizing it to do so.

Judicial Review and the Regulatory Process (pp. 183-191)

As noted in the casebook, the major federal environmental statutes specifically authorize judicial review of agency action. Thus, when EPA issues new regulations or modifies existing regulations, their validity may be challenged in court. However, EPA frequently acts not by adopting regulations, but by issuing "guidance documents" that are not the product of notice-and-comment rulemaking. The agency maintains that these documents are not intended to change any legal obligations imposed on the regulated community, but rather to provide clarification concerning how EPA interprets existing regulations. Thus, EPA long has argued that positions it takes in guidance documents are not the kind of final agency action that is subject to judicial review.

In the *Appalachian Power* case, which is excerpted below, industry groups challenged EPA's "Periodic Monitoring Guidance" for permits issued under Title V of the Clean Air Act. The industry petitioners argued that the guidance effectively amended regulations issued by EPA in 1992 to implement the Title V permit program. EPA claimed that the guidance was not binding, final agency action and thus did not require the agency to conduct notice-and-comment rulemaking. The decision below is widely viewed as representing a major challenge to

Chapter 2. Structural Overview

EPA's practice of issuing guidance documents without conducting rulemaking proceedings.

Appalachian Power Co. v. EPA,
208 F.3d 1015 (D.C. Cir. 2000)

RANDOLPH, Circuit Judge:

These consolidated petitions for judicial review, brought by electric power companies, and trade associations representing the nation's chemical and petroleum industry, challenge the validity of portions of an EPA document entitled "Periodic Monitoring Guidance," released in 1998. In the alternative, petitioners seek review of a 1992 EPA rule implementing Title V of the Clean Air Amendments of 1990.

I.

Title V of the 1990 amendments to the Clean Air Act altered the method by which government regulated the private sector to control air pollution. Henceforth, stationary sources of air pollution, or of potential air pollution, must obtain operating permits from State or local authorities administering their EPA-approved implementation plans. The States must submit to EPA for its review all operating permits and proposed and final permits. *See* 42 U.S.C. § 7661d. EPA has 45 days to object; if it does so, "the permitting authority may not issue the permit," *id.* § 7661d(b)(3). Congress instructed EPA to pass regulations establishing the "minimum elements of a permit program to be administered by any air pollution control agency," including "Monitoring and reporting requirements." 42 U.S.C. § 7661a(b). Under Title V, the Governor of each State could submit to EPA a permit program by November 15, 1993, to comply with Title V and with whatever regulations EPA had promulgated in the interim. *See* 42 U.S.C. § 7661a(d). This was to be accompanied by a legal opinion from the State's attorney general that the laws of the State contained sufficient authority to authorize the State to implement the program. *Id.* If a State decided not to participate, or if EPA disapproved the State's program, federal sanctions would kick in, including a cut-off of federal highway funds and an EPA takeover of permit-issuing authority within the State. *See Commonwealth of Virginia v. Browner,* 80 F.3d 869, 873-74 (4th Cir.1996).

Chapter 2. Structural Overview

EPA promulgated rules implementing the Title V permit program in 1992. The rules list the items each State permit program must contain, including this one:

(3) *Monitoring and related record-keeping and reporting requirements.*

(i) Each permit shall contain the following requirements with respect to monitoring:

(A) All monitoring and analysis procedures or test methods required under applicable monitoring and testing requirements, including part 64 of this chapter and any other procedures and methods that may be promulgated pursuant to sections 114(a)(3) or 504(b) of the Act. If more than one monitoring or testing requirement applies, the permit may specify a streamlined set of monitoring or testing provisions provided the specified monitoring or testing is adequate to assure compliance at least to the same extent as the monitoring or testing applicable requirements that are not included in the permit as a result of such streamlining;

(B) Where the applicable requirement does not require periodic testing or instrumental or noninstrumental monitoring (which may consist of record-keeping designed to serve as monitoring), periodic monitoring sufficient to yield reliable data from the relevant time period that are representative of the source's compliance with the permit, as reported pursuant to paragraph(a)(3)(iii) of this section. Such monitoring requirements shall assure use of terms, test methods, units, averaging periods, and other statistical conventions consistent with the applicable requirement. Recordkeeping provisions may be sufficient to meet the requirements of this paragraph (a)(3)(i)(B) of this section; and

(C) As necessary, requirements concerning the use, maintenance, and, where appropriate, installation of monitoring equipment or methods. . . .

40 C.F.R. § 70.6(a)(3).

Chapter 2. Structural Overview

The key language—key because this dispute revolves around it—is in the first sentence of § 70.6(a)(3)(i)(B). Permits contain terms and conditions with which the regulated entities must comply. Some of the terms and conditions—in regulatory lingo, "applicable requirements" (*see* § 70.6(a)(3)(i)(B))—consist of emission limitations and standards, State and federal. Experts in the field know that federal emission standards, such as those issued for hazardous air pollutants and new stationary sources, contain far more than simply limits on the amount of pollutants emitted.

[The court then describes examples of other regulations that establish specific monitoring requirements].

On one thing the parties are in agreement. If an applicable State emission standard contains no monitoring requirement to ensure compliance, EPA's regulation requires the State permitting agency to impose on the stationary source some sort of "periodic monitoring" as a condition in the permit or specify a reasonable frequency for any data collection mandate already specified in the applicable requirement. According to petitioners this sort of gap-filling is all §70.6(a)(3)(i)(B)—the so-called periodic monitoring rule—requires of State permit programs. By petitioners' lights, if a federal or State emission standard already contains some sort of requirement to do testing from time to time, this portion of the standard must be incorporated in the permit, not changed by the State to conform to EPA's imprecise and evolving notion of what constitutes "periodic monitoring." Otherwise, State authorities will wind up amending federal emission standards in individual permits, something not even EPA could do without conducting individual rulemakings to amend the regulations containing the federal standards. And with respect to State standards, the State agency will in effect be revising its implementation plan at EPA's behest, without going through the procedures needed to accomplish this. *See, e.g.,* 42 U.S.C. § 7410(k)(5) & (*l*).

In a document entitled "Periodic Monitoring Guidance for Title V Operating Permits Programs," released in September 1998, EPA took a sharply different view of § 70.6(a)(3) than do petitioners. The "Guidance" was issued over the signature of two EPA officials—the Director of the Office of Regulatory Enforcement, and the Director of the Office of Air Quality Planning and Standards. It is narrative in form, consists of 19 single-spaced, typewritten pages, and is available on EPA's internet web site (www.epa.gov). "Periodic monitoring," the Guidance states, "is required for each emission point at a source subject to title V of the Act that is subject to an applicable requirement, such as a Federal regulation or a SIP emission limitation." Periodic Monitoring Guidance for Title V Operating Permits Program (hereinafter "Guidance") at 5. New source performance standards, and national emission standards for hazardous pollutants, if EPA promulgated the standards after November 15, 1990, the effective date of the Clean Air Act amendments, are "presumed to have adequate monitoring." *Id.* Also, for "emission units subject to the acid rain requirements," EPA has determined that its "regulations contain sufficient monitoring for the acid rain requirements." *Id.* Outside of these categories and one other, the Guidance states that "periodic monitoring is required . . . when the applicable requirement does not require . . . monitoring sufficient to yield reliable data from the relevant time period that are representative of the source's compliance with the permit." *Id.* at 6. How to determine this? Clearly, according to the Guidance, if an "applicable requirement imposes a one-time testing requirement, periodic monitoring is not satisfied . . . ," presumably because one time is not from time to time, which is what periodic means. *Id.*

II.

The phenomenon we see in this case is familiar. Congress passes a broadly worded statute. The agency follows with regulations containing broad language, open-ended phrases, ambiguous standards and the like. Then as years pass, the agency issues circulars or guidance or memoranda, explaining, interpreting, defining and often expanding the commands in the regulations. One guidance document may yield another and then another and so on. Several words in a regulation may spawn hundreds of pages of text as the agency offers more and more detail regarding what its regulations demand of regulated entities. Law is made, without notice and comment, without public participation, and without publication in the Federal Register or the Code of Federal Regulations. With the advent of the Internet, the agency does not need these official publications to ensure widespread circulation; it can inform those affected simply by posting its new guidance or memoranda or policy statement on its web site. An agency operating in this way gains a large advantage. "It can issue or amend its real rules, i.e., its interpretative rules and policy statements, quickly and inexpensively without following any statutorily prescribed procedures." Richard J. Pierce, Jr., *Seven Ways to Deossify Agency Rulemaking*, 47 Admin. L. Rev. 59, 85 (1995). The agency may also think there is another advantage—immunizing its lawmaking from judicial review.

A.

EPA tells us that its Periodic Monitoring Guidance is not subject to judicial review because it is not final, and it is not final because it is not "binding." Brief of Respondent at 30. *See* Guidance at 19. It is worth pausing a minute to consider what is meant by "binding" in this context. Only "legislative rules" have the force and effect of law. *See Chrysler Corp. v. Brown*, 441 U.S. 281, 302-03 & n. 31 (1979). A "legislative rule" is one the agency has duly promulgated in compliance with the procedures laid down in the statute or in the Administrative Procedure Act. If this were all that "binding" meant, EPA's Periodic Monitoring Guidance could not possibly qualify: it was not the product of notice and comment rulemaking in accordance with the Clean Air Act, 42 U.S.C. § 7607(d), and it has not been published in the Federal Register. But we have also recognized that an agency's other pronouncements can, as a practical matter, have a binding effect. *See, e.g., McLouth Steel Prods. Corp. v. Thomas*, 838 F.2d 1317, 1321 (D.C.Cir.1988). If an agency acts as if a document issued at headquarters is controlling in the field, if it treats the document in the same manner as it treats a legislative rule, if it bases enforcement actions on the policies or interpretations formulated in the document, if it leads private parties or State permitting authorities to believe that it will declare permits invalid unless they comply with the terms of the document, then the agency's document is for all practical purposes "binding." *See* Robert A. Anthony, *Interpretative Rules, Policy Statements, Guidances, Manuals, and the Like—Should Federal Agencies Use Them to Bind the Public?*, 41 Duke L.J. 1311, 1328-29 (1992), and cases there cited.

For these reasons, EPA's contention must be that the Periodic Monitoring Guidance is not binding in a practical sense. Even this, however, is not an accurate way of putting the matter. Petitioners are not challenging the Guidance in its entirety. Under the Administrative Procedure Act, a "rule" may consist of "part of an agency statement of general or particular applicability and future effect. . . ." 5 U.S.C. § 551(4); *see* 5 U.S.C. §§ 551(13), 702. "Interpretative rules" and "policy statements" may be rules within the meaning of the APA and the Clean Air Act, although neither type of "rule" has to be promulgated through notice and comment rulemaking. *See* 42 U.S.C. § 7607(d)(1), referring to 5 U.S.C. § 553(b)(A) & (B). EPA claims, on the one hand, that the Guidance is a policy statement, rather than an interpretative rule, and is not binding. On the other hand, EPA agrees with petitioners that "the Agency's position on the central legal issue here—the appropriateness of a sufficiency review of all Title V monitoring requirements—indeed is settled. . . ." Brief of Respondent at 32. In other words, whatever EPA may think of its Guidance generally, the elements of the Guidance petitioners challenge consist of the agency's settled position, a position it plans to follow in reviewing State-issued permits, a position it will insist State and local authorities comply with in setting the terms and conditions of permits issued to petitioners, a position EPA officials in the field are bound to apply. . . .

Of course, an agency's action is not necessarily final merely because it is binding. Judicial orders can be binding; a temporary restraining order, for instance, compels compliance but it does not finally decide the case. In the administrative setting, "two conditions must be satisfied for agency action to be 'final': First, the action must mark the 'consummation' of the agency's decisionmaking process, *Chicago & Southern Air Lines, Inc. v. Waterman S.S. Corp.,* 333 U.S. 103, 113 (1948)—it must not be of a merely tentative or interlocutory nature. And second, the action must be one by which 'rights or obligations have been determined,' or from which 'legal consequences will flow,' *Port of Boston Marine Terminal Assn. v. Rederiaktiebolaget Transatlantic,* 400 U.S. 62, 71 (1970)." *Bennett v. Spear,* 520 U.S. 154, 178 (1997). The first condition is satisfied here. The "Guidance," as issued in September 1998, followed a draft circulated four years earlier and another, more extensive draft circulated in May 1998. This latter document bore the title *"EPA Draft Final Periodic Monitoring Guidance."* On the question whether States must review their emission standards and the emission standards EPA has promulgated to determine if the standards provide enough monitoring, the Guidance is unequivocal— the State agencies must do so. *See* Guidance at 6-8. On the question whether the States may supersede federal and State standards and insert additional monitoring requirements as terms or conditions of a permit, the Guidance is certain—the State agencies must do so if they believe existing requirements are inadequate, as measured by EPA's multi-factor, case-by-case analysis set forth in the Guidance. *See* Guidance at 7-8.

EPA may think that because the Guidance, in all its particulars, is subject to change, it is not binding and therefore not final action. There are suggestions in its brief to this effect. *See, e.g.,* Brief of Respondent at 3, 33 n.30. But all laws are subject to change. Even that most enduring of documents, the Constitution of the United States, may be amended from time to time. The fact that a law may be altered in the future has nothing to do with whether it is subject to judicial review at the moment. *See McLouth Steel Prods. Corp. v. EPA,* 838 F.2d at 1320.

On the issue whether the challenged portion of the Guidance has legal consequences, EPA points to the concluding paragraph of the document, which contains a disclaimer: "The policies set forth in this paper are intended solely as guidance, do not represent final Agency action, and cannot be relied upon to create any rights enforceable by any party." Guidance at 19. This language is boilerplate; since 1991 EPA has been placing it at the end of all its guidance documents. *See* Robert A. Anthony, *supra,* 41 Duke L.J. at 1361; Peter L. Strauss, Comment, *The Rulemaking Continuum,* 41 Duke L.J. 1463, 1485 (1992) (referring to EPA's notice as "a charade, intended to keep the proceduralizing courts at bay"). Insofar as the "policies" mentioned in the disclaimer consist of requiring State permitting authorities to search for deficiencies in existing monitoring regulations and replace them through terms and conditions of a permit, "rights" may not be created but "obligations" certainly are—obligations on the part of the State regulators and those they regulate. At any rate, the entire Guidance, from beginning to end—except the last paragraph—reads like a ukase. It commands, it requires, it orders, it dictates. Through the Guidance, EPA has given the States their "marching orders" and EPA expects the States to fall in line, as all have done, save perhaps Florida and Texas. *See Natural Resources Defense Council, Inc. v. Thomas,* 845 F.2d 1088, 1094 (D.C.Cir.1988); *Community Nutrition Inst. v. Young,* 818 F.2d 943, 947-48 (D.C.Cir.1987). . . .

The short of the matter is that the Guidance, insofar as relevant here, is final agency action, reflecting a settled agency position which has legal consequences both for State agencies administering their permit programs and for companies like those represented by petitioners who must obtain Title V permits in order to continue operating.

B.

As to the validity of the Guidance, petitioners' arguments unfold in the following sequence. First, they contend that the Guidance amended the "periodic monitoring rule" of § 70.6(a)(3)(i)(B). Although the rule only allowed State authorities to fill in gaps, that is, to require periodic monitoring when the applicable State emission standard contained no monitoring requirement, a one-time startup test, or provided no frequency for monitoring, the Guidance applies across the board, charging State authorities with the duty of assessing the sufficiency of all State and federal standards. With the Guidance in place, regional EPA offices have solid legal grounds for objecting to State-issued permits if the State authorities refuse to bend to EPA's will. Therefore, as petitioners see it, the Guidance is far more than a mere interpretation of the periodic monitoring rule and it is far more than merely a policy statement. In practical effect, it creates a new regime, a new legal system governing permits, and as such it should have been, but was not, promulgated in compliance with notice and comment rulemaking procedures. Petitioners say that if they are wrong about this, if the Guidance represents a valid interpretation of the periodic monitoring rule in § 70.6(a)(3)(i)(B), then the rule itself is invalid. Congress did not authorize EPA to require States, in issuing Title V permits, to make revisions to monitoring requirements in existing federal emission standards.

The case is presented to us in pure abstraction. Neither side cites any specific federal or State emission standard. Although petitioners complain that State officials will revise federal standards promulgated before November 1990, petitioners' briefs identify no specific federal standard potentially subject to revision. Which, if any, federal standards are susceptible to State revision in a permit for lack of periodic monitoring is thus something about which we can only guess. The same is true regarding State emission standards.

Perhaps petitioners should not be faulted. They disagree with EPA's general principle, with the agency's position that it can give State permit officials the authority to substitute new monitoring requirements in place of existing State or federal emission standards already containing some sort of monitoring requirements. The validity of that general principle does not turn on the specifics of any particular emission standard, although its application does. Besides, EPA is currently developing even more detail in far more extensive "guidance" using concrete examples of what would, and would not, constitute "periodic monitoring" in EPA's opinion. *See* Draft—Periodic Monitoring Technical Reference Document (Apr. 30, 1999).

It is well-established that an agency may not escape the notice and comment requirements (here, of 42 U.S.C. § 7607(d)) by labeling a major substantive legal addition to a rule a mere interpretation. *See Paralyzed Veterans v. D.C. Arena L.P.,* 117 F.3d 579, 588 (D.C.Cir.1997); *American Mining Congress v. MSHA,* 995 F.2d 1106, 1109-10 (D.C.Cir.1993). "We must still look to whether the interpretation itself carries the force and effect of law, . . . or rather whether it spells out a duty fairly encompassed within the regulation that the interpretation purports to construe." (citations and internal quotations omitted). *See Paralyzed Veterans,* 117 F.3d at 588. With that in mind, we will deal first with petitioners' claim that the Guidance significantly expanded the scope of the periodic monitoring rule. Section 70.6(a)(3)(i)(B) tells us that "periodic monitoring" must be made part of the permit when the applicable State or federal standard does not provide for "periodic testing or instrumental or noninstrumental monitoring." If "periodic" has its usual meaning, this signifies that any State or federal standard requiring testing from time to time—that is yearly, monthly, weekly, daily, hourly—would be satisfactory. The supplementing authority in § 70.6(a)(3)(i)(B) therefore would not be triggered; instead, the emission standard would simply be incorporated in the permit, as EPA acknowledged in the rule's preamble. On the other hand, if the State or federal standard contained merely a one-time startup test, specified no frequency for monitoring or provided no compliance method at all, §70.6(a)(3)(i)(B) would require the State authorities to specify that some testing be performed at regular intervals to give assurance that the company is complying with emission limitations. . .

The short of the matter is that the regulatory history EPA offers fails to demonstrate that §70.6(a)(3)(i)(B) initially had the broad scope the Guidance now ascribes to it. Nothing on the face of the regulation or in EPA's commentary at the time said anything about giving State authorities a roving commission to pore over existing State and federal standards, to decide which are deficient, and to use the permit system to amend, supplement, alter or expand the extent and frequency of testing already provided. In fact, EPA's promise in the 1992 rulemaking—that if federal standards were found to be inadequate in terms of monitoring it would open rulemaking proceedings—is flatly against EPA's current position. (EPA makes no attempt to square this promise with the argument it makes today.)

Furthermore, we attach significance to EPA's recognition, in its 1992 permit regulations, that "Title V does not impose substantive new requirements," 40 C.F.R. §70.1(b). Test methods and the frequency of testing for compliance with emission limitations are surely "substantive" requirements; they impose duties and obligations on those who are regulated. Federal testing requirements contained in emissions standards are promulgated after notice and comment rulemaking. Testing requirements in emission standards in State standards are presumably adopted by the State's legislature or administrative agency, and approved by EPA as part of the State's implementation plan. We have recognized before that changing the method of measuring compliance with an emission limitation can affect the stringency of the limitation itself. *Portland Cement Ass'n v. Ruckelshaus,* 486 F.2d 375, 396-97 (D.C.Cir.1973), *discussed in Clean Air Implementation Project v. EPA,* 150 F.3d at 1203. In addition, monitoring imposes costs. Petitioners represent that a single stack test can "cost tens of thousands of dollars, and take a day or more to complete," which is why "stack testing is limited to once or twice a year (at most)." Brief of Petitioners at 22 n.75. If a State agency, acting under EPA's direction in the Guidance, devised a permit condition increasing a company's stack test obligation (as set forth in a State or federal standard) from once a year to once a month, no one could seriously maintain that this was something other than a substantive change.

There is still another problem with EPA's position. Although its Guidance goes to great lengths to explain what is meant by the words "periodic monitoring," it almost completely neglects a critical first step. On the face of § 70.6(a)(3)(i)(B), "periodic monitoring" is required if and only if "the applicable requirement does not require periodic testing or instrumental or noninstrumental monitoring (which may consist of record-keeping designed to serve as monitoring)." While the Guidance is quick to say that all Title V permits must contain "periodic monitoring," it never explains what constitutes "periodic testing" or what constitutes "instrumental or noninstrumental monitoring." Instead, throughout the Guidance, EPA either yokes these three items together, or treats the terms as synonymous, without saying why. Yet if "periodic testing" and "instrumental or noninstrumental monitoring" mean the same thing as "periodic monitoring," there is no accounting for why § 70.6(a)(3)(i)(B) was written as it was. The regulation could simply have said "periodic monitoring" is required for all permits, period. . . .

In sum, we are convinced that elements of the Guidance—those elements petitioners challenge—significantly broadened the 1992 rule. The more expansive reading of the rule, unveiled in the Guidance, cannot stand. In directing State permitting authorities to conduct wide-ranging sufficiency reviews and to enhance the monitoring required in individual permits beyond that contained in State or federal emission standards even when those standards demand some sort of periodic testing, EPA has in effect amended § 70.6(a)(3)(i)(B). This it cannot legally do without complying with the rulemaking procedures required by 42 U.S.C. § 7607(d). *See Alaska Professional Hunter's Ass'n v. FAA,* 177 F.3d 1030, 1034 (D.C.Cir.1999); *Caruso v. Blockbuster-Sony Music Entertainment Centre,* 174 F.3d 166, 176-78 (3d Cir.1999); *Paralyzed Veterans,* 117 F.3d at 585-86.

For the reasons stated, we find setting aside EPA's Guidance to be the appropriate remedy. Though petitioners challenge only portions of the Guidance, partial affirmance is not an option when, as here, "there is 'substantial doubt' that the agency would have adopted the severed portion on its own." *Davis County Solid Waste Management v. EPA,* 108 F.3d 1454, 1458 (D.C.Cir.1997) (quoting *North Carolina v. FERC,* 730 F.2d 790, 795-96 (D.C.Cir.1984)). In view of the intertwined nature of the challenged and unchallenged portions of the Guidance, the Guidance must be set aside in its entirety. *See* 42 U.S.C. § 7607. State permitting authorities therefore may not, on the basis of EPA's Guidance or 40 C.F.R. § 70.6(a)(3)(i)(B), require in permits that the regulated source conduct more frequent monitoring of its emissions than that provided in the applicable State or federal standard, unless that standard requires no periodic testing, specifies no frequency, or requires only a one-time test.

NOTES AND QUESTIONS

1. The Administrative Procedure Act defines a "rule" in pertinent part as "the whole or a part of an agency statement of general or particular applicability and future effect designed to implement, interpret, or prescribe law or policy or describing the organization, procedure, or practice requirements of an agency . . .." 5 U.S.C. § 551(4). What features of the EPA guidance convinced the court that it constituted a rule that could not be adopted without conducting rulemaking proceedings? Will the court's decision significantly constrain EPA's ability to provide guidance to states and the regulated community?

2. Why would EPA have decided not to conduct notice-and-comment rulemaking proceedings before issuing the guidance? If EPA had employed notice-and-comment rulemaking as a vehicle for adopting the guidance, would the guidance have been upheld in court?

3. The court rejected EPA's arguments that its guidance document was not subject to judicial review because it was not "final" and not "binding." How does the court define "binding" for purposes of this case? What features of the guidance convince the court that it constitutes final agency action?

4. In Barrick Goldstrike Mines v. Browner, 215 F.3d 45 (D.C. Cir. 2000), the D.C. Circuit reversed a district court's decision dismissing another challenge to EPA guidance. A mining company challenged EPA guidance stating that chemicals in waste rock from metal mining are not eligible for the de minimis exception from reporting under the Emergency Planning and Community Right-to-Know's "toxic release inventory" program. The court held that the guidance was "final agency action" and ripe for judicial review, and that the same was true of EPA's position that mining companies can be considered to "manufacture" a "toxic chemical" when, in the course of extracting gold from ore, trace amounts of naturally occurring metal compounds change form. The court noted that there was no indication that EPA's position was anything other than firm and conclusive and that "legal consequences flow from [it]—Barrick must keep records and report to EPA unless it wishes to risk an enforcement action." The court noted that it "presents a pure question of law and withholding review has sufficient adverse effects on Barrick's business" to warrant a determination that the claim was ripe for review. Thus, it returned the matter to the district court to consider the merits of the company's challenge.

- 3 -
Waste Management and Pollution Prevention

What Substances Are "Solid Wastes"?
(pp. 218-32)

In 2000 the U.S. Court of Appeals for the D.C. Circuit issued two decisions that focused on the question whether material had been "discarded," subjecting it to regulation as waste under RCRA. In Association of Battery Recyclers v. EPA, 208 F.3d 1047 (D.C. Cir. 2000), the court held that EPA improperly classified secondary and residual materials generated in mining and mineral processing operations as solid waste for purposes of RCRA. The agency had done so when it promulgated Phase IV of its regulations limiting land disposal of hazardous waste. EPA argued that the materials could be regulated as wastes because they were not immediately reintroduced into the production process. However, the court rejected the notion that temporary storage of the materials even "for a few minutes" subjected them to regulation as solid waste.

Referring to its 1987 decision in *American Mining Congress v. EPA*, 824 F.2d 1177 (casebook, p. 220), the court asserted that "[l]ater cases in this court do not limit *AMC*," noting that none of the decisions subsequent to *American Mining Congress* undermined the notion that material must be discarded before it can be regulated as a waste. The court distinguished American Petroleum Institute v. EPA, 906 F.2d 729 (D.C. Cir. 1990) (casebook, p. 229) as involving the taking of waste from one industry for reclamation in another. It distinguished *AMC II* (American Mining Congress v. EPA, 907 F.2d 1179 (D.C. Cir. 1990) (casebook, p. 229)) as involving a situation where it was not clear whether or not the waste ultimately would be recycled because the defendants had asserted only that they "may" reclaim the material at some time in the future.

In American Petroleum Institute v. EPA, 216 F.3d 50 (D.C. Cir. 2000), the court vacated part of a RCRA regulation that sought to subject oil-bearing wastewaters generated by the petroleum refining industry to regulation as a solid waste. While recognizing that wastewaters eventually become waste as they progress through later phases of treatment, the court held that EPA had not adequately explained why it had determined that wastewaters should be considered discarded even before they had received primary treatment.

These decisions suggest that secondary materials that are stored for beneficial reuse may not be considered to be solid waste even if they are not immediately reused. However, it still is probably the case that secondary materials accumulated for excessive periods of time can be regulated as solid wastes. EPA has taken the position that material "accumulated speculatively" for possible reuse may be regulated as a solid waste – the agency's regulations require that 75 percent of the secondary material be reused within a calendar year. A more difficult issue involves material that is accumulated for reuse by another company at another site in another industry. *Association of Battery Recyclers* dealt with "closely related" materials intended for reuse at the same site where they were generated. While there are indications that EPA believes the impact of the decision is limited to such materials, other disagree. See Donald J. Paterson, Jr., The Definition of Solid Waste: Discerning the "Intelligible Principle," in Proceedings of the ABA 30th Annual Conference on Environmental Law, March, 2001, at 99, 106.

RCRA "Mixture" and "Derived-From" Rules (p. 233)

As discussed in the text (p. 233), for nearly a decade EPA has been considering whether to retain its "mixture" and "derived-from" rules for determining whether listed hazardous wastes remain hazardous when mixed with other solid waste or when converted into another material. This reconsideration was a product of the decision in Shell Oil Co. v. EPA, 950 F.2d 741 (D.C. Cir. 1991). In spring 2001, EPA adopted a final rule that retains the mixture and derived-from rules while expanding some exclusions from them. 66 Fed. Reg. 27266 (May 16, 2001). The mixture rule provides that any mixture of a waste listed as hazardous under RCRA with another solid waste is itself considered to be a hazardous waste unless specifically delisted by EPA. The derived-from rule provides that any wastes derived from the treatment, storage, or disposal of a listed waste are deemed to be hazardous wastes unless specifically delisted by EPA. The revisions adopted by EPA narrow the scope of the mixture and derived-from rules, in an effort to tailor the rules to more specifically match the risks posed by particular wastes. The first revision is an expanded exclusion for mixtures and/or derivatives of wastes listed solely for the ignitability, corrosivity, and/or reactivity characteristics. The second revision is a new conditional exemption from the mixture and derived-from rules for mixed wastes (that is, wastes that are both hazardous and radioactive).

CERCLA Liability of Generators: the Superfund Recycling Equity Act (pp. 295-305)

In 1999 Congress amended CERCLA by adopting the Superfund Recycling Equity Act, 42 U.S.C. § 127. This legislation adds § 127 to CERCLA, 42 U.S.C. § 9627, which exempts from CERCLA liability as arrangers or transporters those who arrange for recycling of recyclable material. "Recyclable material" is defined by §127(b) to include "scrap paper, scrap plastic, scrap glass, scrap textiles, scrap rubber (other than whole tires), scrap metal, or spent lead-acid, spent nickel-cadmium, and other spent batteries . . ." It does not include shipping containers that contain hazardous substances or items with PCBs at concentrations greater than 50 parts per million. To qualify for the exemption, recyclers must demonstrate that there was a market for the recyclable material, that a substantial portion of it was made available for use for new products, and that the arranger exercised reasonable care to determine that the facility managing the material was in compliance with the environmental laws. The exemption is not available if the arranger had an objectively reasonable basis to believe that the material would not be recycled or would be incinerated or if hazardous materials have been added to the recyclable material for purposes other than processing or recycling. It also is unavailable if the arranger failed to exercise reasonable care with respect to the management and handling of the material. The exemption does not affect the liability of current or past owners and operators under §§107(a)(1) or (2). In Gould, Inc. v. A & M Battery & Tire Service, 232 F.3d 162 (3d Cir. 2000), the

U.S. Court of Appeals for the Third Circuit held that the Act's exemption applies retroactively . Thus, it vacated a judgment against suppliers of spent batteries for recycling in a contribution action brought by a site owner.

Strict, Joint and Several Liability and Allocation of Liability Under CERCLA (pp. 305-25)

The following decision is the latest in the two-decade-long saga of the Vertac Superfund site. This decision follows a judgment by the district court in the allocation of liability phase of a Section 113(f) contribution action, which had found had found Hercules to be responsible for 97.4% , and Uniroyal for 2.6% of nearly 90 million dollars of response costs incurred by EPA. United States v. Vertac Chem. Co., 79 F.Supp. 2d 1034 (E.D. Ark. 1999), vacated on other grounds, United States. v. Hercules, 247 F.3d 706 (8th Cir., 2001). As a predicate for this allocation, the district court had earlier rejected Hercules's arguments that the harm at the site was divisible. On appeal from the final allocation, the court of appeals ruled that the district court had not properly addressed the question of divisibility. The following excerpt is limited to the court's discussion of this question.

United States v. Hercules, 247 F.3d 706 (8th Cir., 2001)

WOLLMAN, Chief Judge.

Hercules, Inc. (Hercules) and Uniroyal Chemical Co. (Uniroyal) raise various claims arising from a series of decisions made by the district court over the past decade finding them jointly and severally liable to the United States for environmental cleanup costs and allocating such costs between them pursuant to [Superfund] We affirm in part and reverse and remand in part.

I. BACKGROUND

A. Factual History

This case involves the Vertac Chemical Plant site, a ninety-three acre tract of land in Jacksonville, Arkansas (the Jacksonville site or the site), that was originally developed by the federal government in the 1930s as a munitions factory. In the late 1940s the site was sold to a now-defunct company called Reasor-Hill Corporation (Reasor-Hill), which at first manufactured various pesticides but in 1958 began to make herbicides including dichlorophenoxyacetic acid (2,4-D) and trichlorophenoxyacetic acid (2,4,5-T), synthetic hormones that kill weeds or brush by accelerating growth to the point of natural death. Although these herbicides rapidly biodegrade into harmless substances, the manufacture of 2,4,5-T (but not of 2,4-D) creates a byproduct, 2,3,7,8-tetrachlorodibenzo-p-dioxin (dioxin), that is now viewed as hazardous to humans. While Reasor-Hill operated the site, an unknown quantity of these and other untreated chemical wastes from the production process flowed through cooling ponds on the west side of the plant into a nearby stream. Other wastes were stored in numerous drums stacked in a field on the site.

Hercules bought the site from Reasor-Hill in 1961 and continued to manufacture herbicides, including 2,4-D and 2,4,5-T, at the plant until 1971. During this period Hercules sold the bulk of its product to the United States Department of Defense as the defoliant Agent Orange, a herbicide used in Vietnam to clear jungle undergrowth. Soon after Hercules took over the site it buried the deteriorating drums of chemical waste left by Reasor-Hill in unlined trenches on the site. Hercules did not learn of the toxicity of dioxin until March of 1965, when a scientific study found that it could cause chloracne, a particularly persistent and disfiguring form of acne that typically affects the face, neck, and shoulders. Dioxin was subsequently linked to cancer.

Later in 1965, Hercules instituted a "toluene extraction" process designed to remove organic impurities from 2,4,5-T products. This process yielded residue ("stillbottoms") containing extremely high levels of dioxin. Hercules placed this residue in drums, some of which it buried at the site and some of which it disposed of at two nearby landfills. Although Hercules has acknowledged numerous leaks and spills during its operation of the site, the record indicates that Hercules generally improved the safety and cleanliness of the site and complied with environmental regulations between 1961 and 1971.

In 1971, Hercules ceased production at the site and leased the facility to Transvaal, Inc., which later became Vertac Chemical Corp. (Vertac). When Hercules ceased operations at the cite, it cleaned out all of its equipment and production vessels, buried its waste, and shipped empty drums off-site. . . .

In 1976, Hercules sold the site to Vertac, which continued its operations until 1986 and abandoned the site altogether when it went into receivership in 1987. By then there were nearly 29,000 waste-filled drums at the site that contained waste materials including 2,4-D, 2,4,5-T, and dioxin. Many of these drums had corroded and leaked, contaminating more soil, groundwater, and buildings at the site. Contamination was also found in other areas of the site, at the landfills, in nearby neighborhoods, and in grounds adjacent to the site. . . .

Vertac was the last operator of the Jacksonville site. After it abandoned the plant, the United States Environmental Protection Agency (EPA) took over the site, closed down all operations, and assumed cleanup responsibilities that have cost well over $100 million to date.

B. Procedural History

. . .

Beginning in 1993, the district court issued a number of decisions that are the subject of the instant appeal. On October 12, 1993, it entered an order of partial summary judgment in favor of the United States. . . . The court found Hercules jointly and severally liable under CERCLA for the release of hazardous substances at the Jacksonville site, landfills, neighborhoods, and off-site areas, and rejected Hercules's argument that the harm at the site was divisible. . . .

The remaining claims in the case went to trial on November 3, 1993, before an advisory jury, [all of whose decisions were endorsed by the district court, save one]. . . .

Finally, on December 28, 1999, the district court addressed the issue of allocation of costs between Hercules and Uniroyal [another PRP] for the more than $89 million for which they were both jointly and severally liable. Acknowledging that "Uniroyal and Hercules are left 'holding the bag' for Vertac [because Vertac was insolvent], who at least arguably caused the greatest amount of harm,". . . the court determined that Hercules's share of the response costs should be 97.4 percent and Uniroyal's share should be 2.6 percent. . . .

Chapter 3. Waste Management and Pollution Prevention

II. CERCLA

A. Background

. . . To establish that a party is liable, CERCLA section 9607(a) requires the government to prove that there has been a release or threat of release of a hazardous substance at a "facility," as a result of which the United States incurred response costs that were necessary and consistent with the NCP, and that the defendant falls within one of four listed categories of responsible parties. 42 U.S.C. § 9607(a). . . . The categories are: (1) current owners or operators of a site at which a release or threatened release occurred; (2) owners or operators of such a site at the time of disposal of hazardous material; (3) generators who arranged for disposal at such a site; and (4) transporters of hazardous waste to such a site. *Id.* CERCLA liability attaches "[n]otwithstanding any other provision or rule of law, and subject only to" three narrowly defined defenses. 42 U.S.C. § 9607(a) & (b). Liability is strict and is typically joint and several. . . . Where multiple defendants are involved, the initial liability finding is followed by a contribution proceeding to allocate damages among responsible parties.

B. Divisibility of Harm

One aspect of CERCLA that has long vexed courts is the role of causation in the statutory scheme. . . . This is because, "[a]lthough the simplistic slogan 'make the polluter pay' may have helped propel CERCLA into law, the statutory scheme does not take a simplistic view of who is and who is not a 'polluter.' " *Westfarm Assoc. Ltd. Partnership v. Washington Suburban Sanitary Comm'n,* 66 F.3d 669, 681 (4th Cir.1995). Indeed, at least at the liability stage, the language of the statute does not require the government to prove as part of its prima facie case that the defendant caused any harm to the environment. . . . Rather, once the requisite connection between the defendant and a hazardous waste site has been established (because the defendant fits into one of the four categories of responsible parties), it is enough that response costs resulted from "a" release or threatened release—not necessarily the defendant's release or threatened release. 42 U.S.C. § 9607(a)(4). Thus, the government need not trace or "fingerprint" a defendant's wastes in order to recover under CERCLA. Considerations of causation explicitly enter into the statutory liability scheme only as part of the three statutory defenses not at issue in this case. 42 U.S.C. § 9607(b).

Many courts, however, have recognized the defense of divisibility of harm, a "special exception to the absence of causation requirement" that in effect brings causation principles "back into the case—through the backdoor, after being denied entry at the front door." *United States v. Alcan Alum. Corp.*, 990 F.2d 711, 722 (2d Cir.1993) (*Alcan II*); *see United States v. Township of Brighton*, 153 F.3d 307, 317-19 (6th Cir.1998); *Bell*, 3 F.3d at 894-902 [see page 317]; *Alcan I*, 964 F.2d at 268-69 [see page 317]; *O'Neil v. Picillo*, 883 F.2d 176, 178-79 (1st Cir.1989) [see pp. 307-314]; *Monsanto*, 858 F.2d at 171-73. . . .

The universal starting point for divisibility of harm analyses in CERCLA cases is the Restatement (Second) of Torts, which provides for the apportionment of damages among two or more parties when at least one is able to show either (1) "distinct harms" or (2) a "reasonable basis for determining the contribution of each cause to a single harm." Restatement (Second) of Torts § 433A (1965); *see Township of Brighton*, 153 F.3d at 318; *Bell*, 3 F.3d at 895; *Chem-Dyne*, 572 F.Supp. at 810. We will follow the Restatement, however, only to the extent that it is compatible with the provisions of CERCLA. *See O'Neil*, 883 F.2d at 179 n. 4 (describing the Restatement as "one source for us to consult"). Thus, for example, although the Restatement contemplates that plaintiffs bear the burden of proving causation, in a CERCLA case, once the government has established the four essential elements of liability the burden shifts to the defendant to demonstrate, by a preponderance of the evidence, that there exists a reasonable basis for divisibility. . . .

We have previously observed that proving divisibility is a "very difficult proposition," . . . and the Restatement recognizes that some harms, "by their nature, are normally incapable of any logical, reasonable, or practical division." Restatement (Second) of Torts § 433A cmt. to subsection (2) (1965), *quoted in Bell*, 3 F.3d at 896. Where this is the case, the Restatement cautions against making an "arbitrary apportionment for its own sake." Id. . . . When a defendant is successful in demonstrating a reasonable basis for apportionment, approaches to divisibility will vary tremendously depending on the facts and circumstances of each case. Evidence of divisibility will focus on determining the amount of harm caused by the defendant. . . .Our description below of some of the most common approaches is by no means intended to be exhaustive, for "we know that we cannot define for all time what is a reasonable basis for divisibility and what is not." *Township of Brighton,* 153 F.3d at 319.

"Distinct harms" are those that may properly be regarded as separate injuries. *See* Restatement (Second) of Torts § 433A (1965); *Bell,* 3 F.3d at 895. Defendants may be able to demonstrate that harms are distinct based on geographical considerations, such as where a site consists of "non-contiguous" areas of soil contamination, *Akzo Coatings, Inc. v. Aigner Corp.,* 881 F.Supp. 1202, 1210 (N.D.Ind.1994), *clarified on reconsid.,* 909 F.Supp. 1154 (N.D.Ind.1995), or separate and distinct subterranean "plumes" of groundwater contamination, *United States v. Broderick Investment Co.,* 862 F.Supp. 272, 277 (D.Colo.1994).

Other cases, by contrast, involve a "single harm" that is nonetheless divisible because it is possible to discern the degree to which different parties contributed to the damage. *Id.* The basis for division in such situations is that "it is clear that each [defendant] has caused a separate amount of harm, limited in time, and that neither has any responsibility for the harm caused by the other," such as where "two defendants, independently operating the same plant, pollute a stream over successive periods of time." *Bell,* 3 F.3d at 895. Single harms may also be "treated as divisible in terms of degree," based, for example, on the relative quantities of waste discharged into the stream. *Id.* at 895-96. Divisibility of this type may be provable even where wastes have become cross-contaminated and commingled, for "commingling is not synonymous with indivisible harm." *Alcan II,* 990 F.2d at 722; *see also Bell,* 3 F.3d at 903.

Evidence supporting divisibility must be concrete and specific. *See United States v. Alcan Alum. Corp.,* 892 F.Supp. 648, 657 (M.D.Pa.1995) (*Alcan III*) (rejecting divisibility argument on remand because defendant took "all or nothing approach," presenting no new evidence beyond what court of appeals had already considered), *aff'd,* 96 F.3d 1434 (3d Cir.1996) (table). The preliminary issue of whether the harm to the environment is capable of apportionment among two or more causes is a question of law. *Bell,* 3 F.3d at 902. Then, "[o]nce it has been determined that the harm is capable of being apportioned among the various causes of it, the actual apportionment of damages is a question of fact." *Id.* at 896.

We also observe that the divisibility doctrine is conceptually distinct from contribution or allocation of damages. . . . At the allocation phase, the only question is the extent to which a defendant's liability may be offset by the liability of another; the inquiry at this stage is an equitable one and courts generally take into account the so-called "Gore factors." . . . The divisibility of harm inquiry, by contrast, is guided not by equity — specifically, not by the Gore factors — but by principles of causation alone. . . . Thus, where causation is unclear, divisibility is not an opportunity for courts to "split the difference" in an attempt to achieve equity. . . . Rather, "[i]f they are in doubt, district courts should not settle on a compromise amount that they think best approximates the relative responsibility of the parties." *Id.* In such circumstances, courts lacking a reasonable basis for dividing causation should avoid apportionment altogether by imposing joint and several liability. *Id.*

III. ANALYSIS

. . . Hercules challenges the district court's imposition of joint and several liability, raising various divisibility arguments that are specific to certain areas of the site, off-site areas, neighborhoods, and landfills. In some of these arguments Hercules urges us to reverse outright the entry of summary judgment against it and instruct the district court to deduct from the final judgment all response costs pertinent to the area at issue; in others it asks us to hold simply that there is a reasonable basis for divisibility and remand to the district court to apportion the harm. We review the district court's October, 1993, summary judgment decision (*Vertac V*) de novo, viewing the evidence in the light most favorable to the nonmoving party. *Dico,* 136 F.3d at 578. We will affirm only if we conclude that there are no genuine issues of material fact and that the United States is entitled to judgment as a matter of law. . . .

We believe that the district court's analysis of Hercules's divisibility arguments reflects a fundamental misunderstanding of the doctrine of divisibility. These legal errors clouded the court's view of the evidence supporting divisibility. For example, when the district court discussed divisibility in *Vertac V,* it did so in summary fashion, stating merely that "Hercules has not set forth any facts establishing that the harm is clearly divisible, or that Hercules' waste did not, or could not, contribute to the release and the resulting response costs at the site." *Vertac V,* Dist. Ct. Order at 4 (Oct. 12, 1993). The proper standard for determining divisibility, however, is that the defendant show either distinct harms or a "reasonable basis" for apportioning causation for a single harm. Restatement (Second) of Torts § 433A (1965). A defendant need not prove that its "waste did not, or could not, contribute" to any of the harm at a CERCLA site in order to establish divisibility, because it is also possible to prove divisibility of single harms based on volumetric, chronological, or other types of evidence. *Bell,* 3 F.3d at 895-96. A site may also be divisible if a defendant can establish that it consists of "non-contiguous" areas of contamination. *Akzo,* 881 F.Supp. at 1210; *Broderick,* 862 F.Supp. at 277.

Accordingly, we reverse the summary judgment against Hercules on the issue of liability (*Vertac V*) and remand so that the district court can address the evidence supporting divisibility in light of the proper legal standards. In so holding, we reject the EPA's suggestion that evidence adduced subsequent to summary judgment—specifically, evidence presented against Uniroyal at the 1993 liability trial and evidence from the 1998 allocation trial—incontrovertibly demonstrates that Hercules cannot prevail on any of its divisibility arguments. By the same token, we deny Hercules's request that we reverse the district court's decision outright and hold that certain harms were divisible, for we conclude that the question of divisibility is one to be determined in the first instance by the district court. . . .

The summary judgment against Hercules on the issue of liability is reversed. On remand, the district court should address Hercules's divisibility arguments. The judgment[] of contribution (*Vertac X*) [is] vacated; these issues should be revisited by the district court following further proceedings consistent with this opinion.

NOTES AND QUESTIONS

1. *Aceto* **Revisited** In a portion of the opinion not included above, Uniroyal had separately challenged the district court's ruling that it was a PRP at all, claiming that its relationship as a customer of Vertac in the 1970s did not bring it within any of the four categories of poten-

tially responsible parties under Section 107. Uniroyal's difficulties arose from the fact that in 1978, Vertac had told Uniroyal that it lacked sufficient funds to purchase the TCB necessary to complete Vertac's contract with Uniroyal for the production of 2,4, 5 -T. Uniroyal agreed to purchase enough TCB for Vertac to complete production of 1.3 million pounds of 2,4,5-T for Uniroyal. The nature of the finanical transaction Uniroyal entered into for delivery of the TCB resulted in its retaining legal ownership of the TCB, never transferring it to Vertac. The 2,4,5-T that was produced with Uniroyal's TCB represents less than one percent of the more than 150 million pounds of 2,4-D and 2,4,5-T that were manufactured at the site over the course of its operation.

The district court found Uniroyal to be an arranger based on its conclusion that these facts closely paralleled those of the *Aceto* decision (casebook, page 296), and hence that Uniroyal was liable as an arranger. In affirming that ruling, the 8th Circuit characterized its earlier *Aceto* opinion as one in which "(1) the suppliers retained an ownership interest in the materials throughout the formulation process as well as in the finished product, (2) the generation of wastes was inherent in the formulation process, and (3) wastes were in fact generated and disposed." at 247 F.3d at 720. Uniroyal argued that the district court had focused too much on bare legal ownership of the TCB, and that arranger liability at a minimum required the authority to control the waste disposal operations, which Uniroyal argued it lacked. The court disagreed, stating that in the context of a totality of the circumstances, "control . . . is not a necessary factor in every case of arranger liability." Id.

2. **The Last Act of the Superfund Drama: Allocation of Liability** If a PRP establishes the basis for a division of the harm, its liability becomes several, and the court must then determine what share of the entire response costs was *caused* by that PRP's actions. If the PRP fails to establish such a basis, liability is joint and several. Any PRP who subsequently pays a greater share of the response costs than it believes constitutes its fair share of liability may bring a contribution action against other PRPs. In this proceeding, the court makes an allocation of liability on the basis of equitable considerations not limited to issues of causation alone. This is typically the last stage of litigation over responsiblity for a Superfund site.

It was just such a contribution action that the court of appeals reversed in the principal case above. The district court had been trying to bring to a close one of the oldest pieces of Superfund litigation, a case which had actually been begun by the government under RCRA and the CWA prior to CERCLA's enactment. The CERCLA counts were added soon after the bill became law. There are now roughly a dozen reported decisions in the district court and the eighth circuit court of appeals involving Vertac. Together, they decribe the evolutionary of CERCLA litigation in general, as the statute and practice under it have matured over the years. Vertac's reaching the allocation of liability stage provides a good signal that the part of the CERCLA clean-up and liability scheme under the most intense litigation pressure has moved from initial questions of constitutionality, retroactivity, and definitions of PRPs to the final allocation-of-liability issues. See Williams D Evans, Jr., Turn Out the Lights, The Party's Over: The Emerging Consensus on CERCLA Salvage Litigation Issues, 29 Envtl. L. Rcp. 10203 (1999) (noting the relative shift from litigation over the liability of PRPs to the secondary suits for contribution among liable PRPs).

3. *Vertac* **Revisited** Even though the decision has been vacated on other grounds, the district court's ruling in the Vertac contribution action provides a good example of some of the issues litigants and courts face in determining the ultimate allocation of liability. In reading the following excerpt, note the many different considerations each party uses to urge adoption of an allocation favorable to it.

United States v. Vertac Chemical Corp., 79 F. Supp. 2d 1034 (E.D. Ark. 1999)

GEORGE HOWARD, Jr., District Judge.

. . . As can be expected, Hercules and Uniroyal each advance different arguments. On the one hand, Uniroyal relies primarily on the relative involvement of the liable parties. It contends that its role as an arranger was minimal. It asserts that the Court should use a volumetric calculation, which can be calculated based on the evidence presented at the hearing. Based on Uniroyal's calculations, a volumetric calculation would result in an initial allocation of 1.58% to Uniroyal and 98.42% to Hercules. In addition to its volumetric calculation, Uniroyal argues that it is then entitled to a "downward departure." Hercules, on the other hand, attempts to divvy up the site, so that it ends up with an allocation in which Uniroyal would be about 70 percent liable. In particular, Hercules advances a division in which it has no connection with the drummed waste, the EPA's single largest expenditure.

Hercules' attempt to limit its responsibility for response costs to about 30 percent is, on its face, absurd. Hercules operated or owned the plant from 1961 to 1976. It had the greatest presence, by far, of any of the responsible parties. The problem is that Uniroyal and Hercules are left "holding the bag" for Vertac, who at least arguably caused the greatest amount of harm.

Resolution of contribution claims under CERCLA is governed by 42 U.S.C. § 9613(f). It provides: "In resolving contribution claims, the court may allocate response costs among liable parties using such equitable factors as the court determines are appropriate." 42 U.S.C. § 9613(f)(1). The statute does not limit the courts to any particular factors, but grants the court "broad discretion to balance the equities in the interest of justice." *Bedford Affiliates v. Sills,* 156 F.3d 416, 429 (2d Cir.1998). In an attempt to find an equitable resolution to what is at times a complex problem, the courts have employed a number of approaches. *See* David G. Mandelbaum, *Toward A Superfund Cost Allocation Principle,* 3 Envtl. Law. 117, 124 (1996) (noting the difficulty in allocating costs). Most have looked to the what are referred to as the "Gore factors," proposed by then Senator Albert Gore as a method to apportion joint and several liability. These factors are:

(1) the ability of the parties to demonstrate that their contribution to a discharge, release, or disposal of a hazardous waste can be distinguished;
(2) the amount of hazardous waste involved;
(3) the degree of toxicity of the hazardous waste;
(4) the degree of involvement of the parties in the generation, transportation, treatment, storage, or disposal of the hazardous waste;
(5) the degree of care exercised by the parties with respect to the hazardous waste concerned, taking into account the characteristics of such hazardous waste; and
(6) the degree of cooperation by the parties with Federal, State, or local officials to prevent any harm to the public health or the environment.

The factors are neither an exhaustive nor exclusive list. . . . The primary emphasis is placed on the harm each party causes the environment and care on the part of the parties. . . .

Divisibility of harm is not a defense to a contribution action under § 113(f), although the Court may consider separate harms caused by different parties in allocating costs. . . . . *But see Acushnet Co. v. Mohasco Corp.,* 191 F.3d 69, 77 (1st Cir.1999) (party may avoid liability for response costs in contribution action "if it demonstrates that its share of hazardous waste deposited at the site constitutes no more than background amounts of such substances in the environment and cannot concentrate with other wastes to produce higher amounts.")

Hercules seeks to divide the Site into various areas, or "harms." The Court has previously rejected Hercules' attempt to divide the Site into "mini-sites." The Court, however, is not persuaded that the "mini-sites" represent "distinct" harms on which the Court can allocate costs. The history of this site reveals a commingling of the wastes. Furthermore, Hercules' proposed division is, at best, arbitrary, and couched in terms to reduce Hercules' liability. As the First Circuit recently noted in rejecting a quantitative minimum at which a party could be held responsible, the task of tracing chemical waste to particular sources in particular amounts "is often technologically infeasible due to the fluctuating quantity and varied nature of the pollution at a site over the course of many years." *Acushnet Co. v. Mohasco Corp.,* 191 F.3d at 77.

The problem noted in *Acushnet* is illustrated by Hercules' argument regarding the costs associated with the incineration of the drummed wastes. When the State ordered Vertac to shut down in the summer of 1979, there were approximately 2700 drums of 2,4,5-T still bottoms stored on-site. Workers spent much of the summer placing those 55-gallon drums into larger drums, shoveling up contaminated soil, and placing that soil into the larger overpack drums. When Vertac resumed production in the fall of 1979, it produced only 2,4-D and eventually accumulated about 26,000 drums of 2,4-D waste. This waste was accumulated between 1979 and 1986, when Hercules had no involvement or presence at the Site.

Hercules argues that no dioxin is produced in the 2,4-D manufacturing process. Thus, according to Hercules, none of the 2,4-D waste drums should have contained dioxin. Furthermore, Hercules presented expert testimony to demonstrate that there should not have been cross contamination of the 2,4-D waste with the 2,4,5-T wastes. According to Hercules, none of the 2,4-D wastes should have had any detectable concentration of dioxin from the fall of 1979 onward, when Vertac ceased manufacturing 2,4,5-T.

Hercules states that it had no involvement in management of the drummed wastes and should not be responsible for the costs of incineration of the drummed waste. Of course, Uniroyal, as an arranger, also did not have any involvement.

The Court has previously found that there was cross-contamination and commingling of the wastes at the entire Site. During the years Hercules operated the plant, Hercules generated hazardous substances which were disposed of at the Site through "leaks, spills, drum burial, and other releases into the environment. . . .The Hercules operation resulted in contamination of soil, groundwater, equipment, tanks, sewer lines, the sewage treatment plants, and sediments and flood plains in Rocky Branch Creek and Bayou Meto." *United States v. Vertac Chemical Corp.*, 966 F.Supp. 1491, 1494-95 (E.D.Ark.1997).

Furthermore, as noted in previous decisions, dioxin was found in the 2,4-D wastes. *See United States v. Vertac Chemical Corp.*, 33 F.Supp.2d at 780. The Court will not second guess the studies and find that they are incorrect or unreliable, as requested by Hercules. Additionally, Hercules admitted that some degree of dioxin contamination found in the 2,4-D drums could have come from contaminated soil being placed in the drums. That soil was contaminated by years of production.

Thus, the Court is not persuaded that Hercules has established "separate harms" on which to allocate responsibility.

The Court has considered carefully the arguments of the parties, the voluminous record and reviewed a large number of decisions and articles in an attempt to reach an equitable resolution to the problem. Allocation of costs between the two remaining parties is difficult, given the particular circumstances of this case where one of the major polluters is insolvent, a number of parties have settled, and the remaining parties' involvement at the site are quite different. *See Browning-Ferris Industries of Ill. v. Ter Maat,* 13 F.Supp.2d 756, 777-78 (N.D.Ill.1998), *rev'd on other grounds,* 195 F.3d 953 (7th Cir.1999) (discussing difficulty in allocating response costs and stating that allocation in the case would be a "best guess" proposition).

At first glance, Uniroyal's argument that it is responsible for about 1 percent of the costs seems inequitable. It would amount to less than $1 million dollars, when the overall cleanup effort for which Uniroyal was held jointly and severally liable was almost $90 million. Nevertheless, it is clear that Hercules' "responsibility as an owner and operator, who was deeply involved in the daily operations of the waste-producing enterprise," should far exceed that of Uniroyal, whose involvement with the Vertac Site was indirect and for a limited time. *See Bedford Affiliates,* 156 F.3d at 430. The question, of course, is how much responsibility to assign in light of the circumstances.

As discussed above, Uniroyal argues for strictly a volumetric approach. In this instance, the Court is persuaded that volumetrics is the most significant factor and should be the starting point at which to assess each party's contribution. However, the Court is not persuaded that volume alone should be the measure of allocation.

Uniroyal presented evidence of the volumes of product produced at the plant during the various ownership periods. The rates of production were based on production records and other documents. Hercules does not dispute the production rates presented by Uniroyal's expert, Steven Michael Quigley. Reasor-Hill was estimated to have produced 6,240,000 pounds of 2,4-D and 2,4,5- T. Hercules produced about 33,231,400 pounds of 2,4,-D, 2,4,5 -T and 2,4,5-TP during the time it owned and operated the site. During the time Transvaal leased the Site from Hercules (1971-1976), it produced approximately 43,004,255 pounds of 2,4,-D, 2,4,5-T and 2,4,5-TP. Vertac produced 71,183,140 pounds of 2,4,-D, 2,4,5-T, and 2,4,5-TP between 1976 and 1987. Of that, Vertac produced 1,344,000 pounds of 2,4,5-T for sale to Uniroyal. In all, about 153,658,795 pounds of 2,4-D, 2,4,5-T and 2,4,5-TP were produced at the plant site during its years of operation.

If Uniroyal's share of the total production was considered, it would amount to 0.87 percent. The more equitable approach, however, is to calculate the amount of Uniroyal's share in comparison to that of Hercules. Production during the years Hercules owned or operated the plant was 76,235,655 pounds of 2,4-D, 2,4,5-T and 2,4,5-TP. Uniroyal's production is 1.76 percent of that of Hercules.

Hercules argues that the volumes of the parties cannot be compared because Hercules produced the majority of its 2,4-D and 2,4,5-T to fulfill Agent Orange contracts during the 1960's. According to Hercules, only 2 million pounds of 2,4-D and 1 million pounds of 2,4,5-T or 2,4,5-TP were produced for "commercial customers." Uniroyal, by comparison, produced 1.34 million pounds of 2,4,5-T for commercial customers through its tolling arrangement with Vertac.

The Court has already discussed the Agent Orange contracts in *United States v. Vertac Chemical Corp.,* 841 F.Supp. 884 (E.D.Ark.1993), *aff'd,* 46 F.3d 803 (8th Cir.1995), *cert. denied,* 515 U.S. 1158 (1995). In that decision, the Court noted that Hercules bid on the contracts, and profited from them. 841 F.Supp. at 890. The Court cannot find that Hercules' production of Agent Orange which was used as part of the country's military effort in Vietnam should be given any consideration.

Hercules also argues that Uniroyal's predecessor developed a process that led to the creation of the 2,4,5-T still bottoms which should be considered in determining each party's contribution. This argument requires the Court to find causation based on a tenuous thread. The Court refuses to impose greater costs on Uniroyal based on a process developed in the 1960's which Hercules purchased and used.

As stated above, production volume is the most significant factor in allocating the costs in this case. The volumetric approach takes into account the relative involvement of the parties at the Site and their contribution to the harm created. Uniroyal argues that it is entitled to a "downward departure" because of its limited involvement. Uniroyal was neither an operator nor owner. Hercules was an operator of the Site for nine years, an owner of the plant for fourteen years and a lessor for five years, during which it had the authority to control the lessee's operations. The Court is not persuaded, however, that Uniroyal's "lack of involvement" warrants a downward departure. The Court has already considered Uniroyal's relatively minor degree of involvement in looking at volumetrics. The Court is also not persuaded that Uniroyal is completely uninvolved, as it would have the Court find. It arranged for production of hazardous materials through a tolling arrangement, and it was aware of the production of hazardous wastes that would be produced as a result of the product. It benefitted from the production of hazardous materials at the Site.

It is, therefore, not inequitable to place a larger percentage of costs on Uniroyal than just what the difference in volume would support. In *Browning-Ferris Industries of Illinois, Inc. v. Ter Maat,* 195 F.3d 953 (7th Cir.1999), the court found that allocating a larger share of responsibility to one responsible party who had operated the landfill for fewer years and dumped less waste in it than other parties was equitable. The court found that the polluter's conduct was a sufficient though not necessary condition of the clean up. Similarly, here, the production of 2,4,5-T for Uniroyal which resulted in the production of hazardous wastes was a sufficient condition for the clean up. The Court previously found that some of the drums and tanks contained dioxin contaminated waste from the production of Uniroyal's 2,4,5-T. That is, but for the production of 2,4,5-T for Uniroyal, there would not be a certain amount of wastes left and ultimately stored in the drums that had to be incinerated.

The Court finds that an "upward departure" is warranted in this instance. The percentage will be small given Uniroyal's limited involvement with the Site, but takes into account Uniroyal's role in the generation of hazardous material.

The Court has also given consideration to the parties' cooperation with government officials. Hercules responded to EPA's Orders under Section 106 of CERCLA and undertook extensive remediation. Hercules' efforts arguably had some effect on reducing the costs of remediation, and therefore Uniroyal's liability. Uniroyal did not respond, taking the position that it had cause to disregard Section 106 Orders because the Court did not find it liable until 1997. The Court notes, however, that the case on which it relied for finding Uniroyal liable as an arranger, *United States v. Aceto Agricultural Chemicals Corp.,* 872 F.2d 1373 (8th Cir.1989), had been decided several years before the first 106 Order. Thus, the Court finds that the sixth Gore factor also justifies finding Uniroyal to be responsible for more than the 1.76 percent and that Uniroyal and Hercules should share, pro rata, the orphan shares of Reasor-Hill and Vertac.

Hercules points to a number of other factors that the Court should consider in allocating the costs to reduce its costs. For example, Hercules introduced evidence that Vertac was not as concerned about safety and cleanliness as Hercules and that the plant went downhill under Vertac.

There is no doubt that Hercules' safety and environmental programs are to be commended. However, the degree of care used in Hercules in handling the waste does not have any weight in allocating the costs between Uniroyal and Hercules. Hercules owned and operated the plant, and therefore was in a position to oversee the care used at plant site. As discussed above, Hercules' safety and maintenance programs are laudatory; however, that being so does not mean that Uniroyal should assume more of the costs. Uniroyal was in no position to manage the disposal of any hazardous materials.

Hercules also introduced evidence regarding the knowledge the scientific community had of the problems with dioxin at the time Hercules manufactured the herbicides and pesticides. Although Hercules learned of the presence of dioxin by the mid-1960s, the technology did not exist at that time to adequately analyze the presence of dioxin in the soil or water during the years that Hercules operated the plant. Furthermore, the possibility of a link of dioxin to cancer did not surface until the mid to late 1970s.

The evidence regarding the state of knowledge of dioxin is interesting but irrelevant to this proceeding. It does not negate that the Court has found hazardous materials at the Site. . . .

In sum, after consideration of all the evidence, the Court finds that Uniroyal should be responsible for 2.6 percent of the costs for which it is jointly and severally liable. This includes the orphan shares. Thus, the parties are entitled to contribution from one another consistent with the allocation findings expressed herein.

The parties are directed to consult with each other, and the EPA regarding the offsets from other PRPs, the interest calculations, and the allocations as set forth in this Order. If the parties can agree on the amount, they should submit a proposed precedent for judgment within twenty days of the date of this Order. If not, each party should submit a proposed precedent setting forth its position.

NOTES AND QUESTIONS

1. **Who Can Blame Them?** PRPs raise diverse considerations in a contribution action, limited only by their anticipation of what might be a plausible appeal to the equitable discretion of the trial judge. In a case such as Vertac, where each percentage point of liabiilty is worth nearly $1 million, PRPs are perhaps not be criticized for the diversity of considerations that they bring to the court's attention.

2. **The Gore Factors.** Do the Gore factors make more sense when the court is trying to allocate liability among generators of wastes than they do when trying to allocate liability between a group of generators and an owner? Consider a group of generators representing 70% of the total wastes shipped to the site, none of whom played any active role in disposing or monitoring the waste once it reached the site. The previous site owner generated no waste, but failed to dispose of it properly. Once the current owner found out about the waste, she took immediate measures to contain the contamination and cooperated fully with government authorities. How do the Gore factors apply?

3. **Equitable Factors.** Courts have refused to limit the equitable factors that they are able to consider, treating this as a matter of case-by-case judgment. They can consider several factors or only one (e.g., volumetric allocation with equal weighting of all wastes; duration of ownership when allocating among owners). One court recently identified a list of (sometimes overlapping) factors relevant to other courts' holdings: "(1) the parties' relative fault or culpability, (2) the ability of the parties to demonstrate that their contribution to a discharge, release or disposal of a hazardous waste can be distinguished, (3) the amount of hazardous waste involved, (4) the degree of toxicity, (5) the degree of involvement of the parties in the generation, transportation, treatment, storage or disposal of the hazardous waste, (6) the degree of care exercised by the parties with respect to the hazardous waste, (7) the degree of cooperation by the parties with government agencies to pre-

vent harm to the public health or the environment, (8) financial resources or economic status, (9) economic benefits received by the parties from contaminating activities or remediation, (10) knowledge and/or acquiescence of the parties in the contaminating activities, and (11) contracts between the parties." Waste Management of Alameda Cty. v. East Bay Regional Park Dist., 135 F.Supp. 2d. 1071 (N.D. Cal., 2001).

4. **Zero Allocation for De Minimis Contributors.** The amount of clean-up attributable to Uniroyal's arranging was calculated by it to be 1.58% by volume. Is there a level of contribution so minor that a PRP ought to bear none of the costs of clean up? In Acushnet Co. v. Mohasco Corp., 191 F.3d 69, 77 (1st Cir.1999), cited by the Vertac district court, the First Circuit upheld grants of summary judgment and judgments according to law to three small contributors to a site prior to a full allocation trial. One PRP had offered uncontradicted testimony that the cresote soaked telephone poles that it had disposed of at the site could not leach polycyclic aromatic hydrocarbons (PAHs) into the ground water at concentrations greater than the background level. Three others had deposited wastes that were minuscule in quantity compared to the entire site – in one case the court speculated that the PRP's contribution would equate to a 1 in 500,000th share. Acushnet v. Coaters, 948 F.Supp. 128 (D. Mass, 1996). The district court acknowledged that the fact that the linchpin of a contribution action is a holistic consideration of all the relevant equitable factors, so that it was impossible to identify any single bright-line criterion for granting summary dismissal to de minimis PRPs. Nonetheless, the court concluded that in a contribution action, the plaintiff bore a burden of proving a "minimum standard of significance of [a] defendant's responsibility as a source of one or more hazardous substances at the site." One determinant of that threshold-of-significance was a showing that "reasons for court intervention that outweigh the public interest against recognizing causes of action the enforcement of which exceed the added resources that would be tapped for waste-site remediation." Id. at 136. The court seems to say, in other words, plaintiffs needed to show that they are reasonably likely to recover more from a PRP than the public and private resources required to adjudicate that liability.

The First Circuit affirmed the district court decision, although it concluded that insofar as any element of the district court's decision turned on a conclusion that a PRP's contribution to the site had not caused the plaintiff to incur any response costs was inappropriate and out of place in a Section 113(f) contribution action. 191 F.3d at 72. There is no "minimum quantity of hazardous waste before liability may be imposed [under CERCLA] . . . [A]ny reasonable danger of release, however insignificant, would seem to give rise to liability." Id. at 76. However, while de minimis PRPS are to be held joint and severally liable at the liability stage of the trial, unless they can show divisibility, "[t]his does not mean, however, that the de minimis polluter must necessarily be held liable for all response costs. . . . [A] defendant may avoid . . . liability for response costs in a contribution action under § 113(f) if it demonstrates that its share of hazardous waste deposited at the site constitutes no more than background amounts of such substances in the environment and cannot concentrate with other wastes to produce higher amounts. This rule is not based on CERCLA's causation requirement, but it is logically derived from § 113(f)'s express authorization that a court take equity into account when fixing each defendant's fair share of response costs. We caution, however, that not every de minimis polluter will elude liability in this way. As always, an equitable determination must be justified by the record....On the whole, the costs and inherent unfairness in saddling a party who has contributed only trace amounts of hazardouse waste with joint and several liability for all costs incurred outweigh the public interest in requiring full contribution from de minimis polluters." Id. at 77-79.

5. **Allocating Orphan Shares.** PRPs who have gone out of business, been declared insolvent, or cannot be located leave behind "orphan shares" of liability. Superfund liability is joint and several, so that any or all of the remaining PRPs can be held liable for 100% of response costs, including the orphan shares. How should those orphan shares be dealt with in a contribution action, where the ruling concept is equitable allocation? Consider a site in which the site owner (O) has paid 100% of the cleanup expenses, totaling $1 million. O then brings a contribution action against another PRP, G. The contribution court allocates responsibility 20% to O, 20% to G, and 60% to D, a defunct corporation with no remaining assets. If liability among the contribution action defendants remained joint and several, G would end up paying 80%. If liability were several and allocated among all the PRPs, G would end up paying 20%, with O retaining 80% of the liability. Both of these inequitable results are avoided if the contribution court divides up all the liability among the solvent plaintiff and defen-

dant only. In that case, each end up bearing 50% of the clean up costs, including the orphan shares. The burden of the orphan shares is shared among them in proportion to their comparative degrees of responsibility. This result is consistent with the Restatement of Torts § 886A(2), and followed in a number of CERCLA decisions. E.g., Pinal Creek Group v. Newmont Mining Corp., 118 F.3d 1298, 1301-06 (9th Cir., 1997).

6. **Settlements.** Does this same principle work in cases where the plaintiff has settled with some of the PRPs, or simply has not sued all of them for contribution? Suppose that D was not solvent, but had settled with O for $100,000. How should the court allocate liability? Should the court continue to limit its allocation just to the parties before the court according to their comparative degrees of responsibility? Should it first subtract D's settlement and then divide 50/50 between O and G? If so, O will end up receiving $550,000 from G, instead of the $500,000 G would pay were D's share an orphan. Should O bear the responsibilty for allowing D to make a "sweetheart" settlement with O? Would it matter if comparative responsibility had been completely unclear at the time of the settlement? The following decision bears on these questions.

AKZO Nobel Coatings, Inc. v. Aigner Corp., 197 F.3d 302 (7th Cir., 1999)

EASTERBROOK, Circuit Judge.

[This is an appeal from a contribution action brought by Akzo against a consortium of other PRPs, including Aigner and about 50 others, all generators of hazardous wastes. After hearing arguments on other equitable allocation formulas, the district court settled on dividing liability among the plaintiff and defendants on the basis of the volume of hazardous waste disposed on at the site, named Fisher-Calo, with all wastes being weighted equally.]

Having decided that all gallons of solvents shipped to Fisher-Calo count equally, the court then ordered Akzo to pay approximately one third more than equal-weighting implies. Akzo generated approximately 9% by volume of all solvents that Fisher-Calo processed, but the court ordered Akzo to reimburse Aigner for approximately 13% of the costs that Aigner has incurred or will expend in completing the cleanup. Aigner and the other firms in its consortium sent about 71% of the total volume of solvents to the Fisher-Calo site, so Akzo's shipments are approximately 13% of the Akzo + Aigner total; other shipments and shippers were ignored because they are not parties to this suit.

According to the district court, this outcome is required by the Uniform Comparative Fault Act. The district court read § 2 and § 6 of the UCFA to provide that the responsibility of non-parties must be disregarded, even if they are financially able to pay (indeed, even if they already *have* paid) their share of the cleanup. To take a simple example, suppose Firm A is responsible for 40% of the pollutants, Firm B for 10%, and Firm C for 50%. Firm A agrees with the EPA to perform the cleanup and sues B for contribution. On the district court's reading of the UCFA, B must pay 20% of the total cleanup costs, because B sent 20% of the pollutants that A and B generated jointly. That C is able to pay its 50% share—indeed, that C has *already* paid 50%, and that the outcome of the suit between A and B will leave A bearing only 30% of the total costs—is irrelevant on the district court's (and Aigner's) understanding of the UCFA. A polluter that agreed to clean up a Superfund site could turn a tidy profit if this were so. Suppose that ten firms, A through J, sent 10% each, and that A, having agreed to do the cleanup work, sues B for contribution. Firms A and B are responsible for equal volumes of wastes, so the court would order B to pay 50% of the total cleanup costs. Next A sues C and recovers another 50%. If all of Firms B through J were good for the judgments, then A would recover 450% of its total outlay for pollution control. Even if the court set a cap of 100%, to prevent A from making a profit, the upshot would be that of ten equally responsible polluters, B and C would pay 50% each, and the other eight would pay nothing. That is not a sensible outcome of a process that is supposed to yield an "equitable" allocation of expenses.

Akzo contends that the UCFA requires the district court to undertake a global assessment of responsibility, so that Akzo cannot be required to pay anything until every shipper's share has been determined. That might take years of trial time. Akzo would be happy to skip the trial and chip in 9%, but that would leave Aigner holding the bag if the other shippers were unable to pay their shares. Aigner, for its part, contends that the UCFA requires courts to ignore non-parties just as the district court concluded. None of these approaches is sound. Akzo's would either complicate an already difficult allocation process or saddle firms such as Aigner with excess costs. The Supreme Court has cautioned against the adoption of any contribution rule that would complicate litigation. . . . Aigner's approach would lead to disproportionate liability, with contribution shares turning not on actual responsibility (or on the actual collections of the party performing the cleanup) but on litigation strategy. It is of course possible that both sides are wrong, and that the UCFA requires the inclusion of either pollution shares of, or the actual recoveries from, the additional parties with which Aigner has reached settlements. But we resist all temptation to give the UCFA a close reading—and this despite the fact that Akzo and Aigner agreed in the district court that it supplies the rule of decision. Section 113(f)(1) provides otherwise: "Such claims [for contribution] shall be brought in accordance with this section and the Federal Rules of Civil Procedure, and shall be governed by Federal law." The UCFA is not a federal law, and we are not bound by the parties' agreement to an inapplicable body of legal rules. . . .

Although federal law governs, it is possible and often desirable to borrow a rule from state law, when the alternative is judicial invention. . . . The reference to "Federal law" in § 113(f)(1) implies that the law should be nationally uniform, rather than varying according to each state's idea of appropriate contribution. Yet the UCFA would not be an attractive national rule. Unlike the Uniform Commercial Code [upon which the Supreme Court has looked for guidance in other contexts], the UCFA has not been adopted throughout the United States. Only two states (Iowa and Washington) have enacted the UCFA; eleven have adopted the Uniform Contribution Among Tortfeasors Act, which supplies a different approach to contribution; the rest resolve contribution issues through the common law or non-uniform statutes. When one of the litigants has settled with a third party, the UCFA reduces other shares by the percentage of total fault of the person released in the settlement (UCFA § 2); this is the source of Akzo's contention that the district court must hold a comprehensive trial to determine every shipper's share of liability. The UCATA, by contrast, reduces liability only by the dollar amount of third-party settlements (UCATA § 4). These competing approaches can produce substantial differences in incentives to settle and in the complexity of litigation. . . . To the extent language in § 113 speaks to the issue, it prefers the approach of the UCATA: A settlement with the United States or a state "does not discharge any of the other potentially liable persons unless its terms so provide, but it reduces the potential liability of the others by the amount of the settlement." Section 113(f)(2), 42 U.S.C. § 9613(f)(2). Adopting the UCFA as a federal rule would undermine that decision.

As a proposition of federal law, the district court's approach has nothing to recommend it, for it produces disparities in liability when third parties have settled. We assume, with the district court, that the proportionate share of the parties is a good starting point. Suppose that Akzo and Aigner were the only two financially sound parties responsible for the pollution. Then the final contribution shares properly would reflect only their relative responsibility, and the 13% share for Akzo would stand. But they are not. Aigner has settled with some other firms that sent solvents to Fisher-Calo and with some past owner-operators of portions of the site. It has claims pending against still more potentially responsible parties. It is very unlikely that 13% is an accurate estimate of Akzo's share among the financially sound firms that will eventually chip in.

[McDermott v. AmClyde, 511 U.S. 202 (1994)] considered at length the proper treatment of settling parties under a body of federal law that includes contribution—the law of admiralty. The Court deemed two approaches "closely matched" (511 U.S. at 217): claim reduction (also known as "proportionate share"), see *Restatement (2d) of Torts* § 886A Comment m(3), and reduction *pro tanto* by the actual amounts recovered in settlements, see *Restatement* § 886A Comment m(2). The claim-reduction approach requires the court to determine the responsibility of all firms that have settled, as well as those still involved in the litigation, and to ignore any firms that have not settled. To return to the ten-firm hypothetical above, if Firm A had settled with C and D, then their shares of responsibility (and the corresponding cleanup costs) would be excluded from the calculation. In a contribution suit between A and B, Firm B would be ordered to pay 50% of the costs after excluding C and D, or 40% of the total costs of restoring the site. It would not matter how much A actually had recovered from C and D. By contrast, under the *pro tanto* approach, anything A recovered from C and D in settlement would be deducted from the total cleanup costs, and the court would order A and B to bear the remaining costs equally. In *McDermott* the Court adopted claim reduction, deeming it most compatible with the way related issues in admiralty have been handled.

If as *McDermott* explained the choice between the *pro tanto* approach and claim reduction is a tossup, 511 U.S. at 217, then it is best to match the handling of settlements with the way intersecting principles of law work. For admiralty that meant claim reduction. For CERCLA the most closely related rule of law is § 113(f)(2), which reduces third-party claims by the actual cash value of settlements reached with governmental bodies. Extending the *pro tanto* approach of § 113(f)(2) to claims under § 113(f)(1) enables the district court to avoid what could be a complex and unproductive inquiry into the responsibility of missing parties. The extended litigation between Akzo and Aigner well illustrates the difficulties of fixing responsibility for wastes sent years (if not decades) ago to a firm that did not keep good records and contaminated a wide area. Excluding only actual collections from third parties enables the court to conserve its resources.

On remand, the district court should determine how much Aigner has collected from third parties in settlement, then require Akzo to pay 12.56% of the costs net of those recoveries, rather than of Aigner's total outlay. The total must be reduced not only by collections Aigner has realized to date, but also by future third-party payments. Phrasing Akzo's liability as "12.56% of the cleanup cost net of third-party collections" or some similar formula will avoid any need to reopen the judgment under Fed.R.Civ.P. 60(b)(5) to account for the outcome of litigation now pending or to be filed in the future.

If some of Aigner's settlements provide for percentage-of-cost payments rather than cash payments, then the district court should exclude that percentage from the pool. (To this extent the *pro tanto* approach works like claim reduction, but without the need for the court to determine the responsibility of the settling parties.) Even if, as Akzo believes, Aigner settled for too little with any of these third parties, it is not free to bring its own contribution actions against them. *McDermott* labeled "clearly inferior" the possibility of collecting more from parties who reached private settlements in good faith. 511 U.S. at 211. A potentially responsible party (PRP in CERCLA jargon) that wants to guard against inadequate collections from third parties must either intervene in the suits against them or challenge the *bona fides* of the settlements immediately after they are reached. *Id.* at 212-14. . . .

Chapter 3. Waste Management and Pollution Prevention

The judgment is vacated to the extent it quantifies Akzo's contribution liability, and the case is remanded for further proceedings consistent with this opinion.

Has Superfund Worked? (pp. 326-30)

In July 2001 a major report commissioned by Congress found that the Superfund program had succeeded in cleaning up or removing environmental threats caused by more than half of the sites on EPA's national priority list (NPL). The report by Resources for the Future found that 57 percent of the 1,280 sites on the NPL (excluding sites on federal property) had been designated as "construction complete" to indicate that threats to humans from toxic exposure had been removed. Resources for the Future, Superfund's Future: What Will It Cost? (July 2001). The report found that if current trends continue the number of sites on the NPL will continue to grow by nearly 50 per year and that the federal government would have to continue to spend approximately $1.5 billion per year to operate the program at current levels. Efforts to reauthorize the program have stalled in Congress, which currently is focusing on brownfields legislation. A bill to encourage states to clean up more brownfields areas passed the Senate on April 25, 2001, by a vote of 99 to 0. The House currently is considering its own version of the legislation. Eric Pianin, Superfund Cleanup Effort Shows Results, Study Reports, Wash. Post, July 10, 2001, p. A19.

The Dormant Commerce Clause and State Restrictions on Interstate Waste Disposal (pp. 331-51)

State efforts to restrict waste imports continue to generate considerable litigation in the federal courts which continue to use the dormant commerce clause to strike them down. As states become more astute in designing regulatory programs to avoid facial discrimination against waste originating out-of-state, the courts are taking a closer look at the actual impact of state regulations before deciding their constitutionality. This is illustrated by Waste Management Holdings v. Gilmore, 252 F.3d 316 (4th Cir. 2001).

91

Chapter 3. Waste Management and Pollution Prevention

The case arose as a result of Virginia's response to efforts by New York City to ship large volumes of its trash to landfills in Virginia. Declaring that "the home state of Washington, Jefferson, and Madison has no intention o[f] becoming New York's dumping ground," Virginia Governor James Gilmore proposed legislation to discourage such imports. The legislation adopted by the Virginia General Assembly imposed a host of restrictions on waste disposal and transportation, which were challenged by a waste disposal company. These included a cap on the amount of waste that large landfills, which primarily receive the out-of-state waste, may accept, and limits on shipping waste by barge and on trucks with four or more axles. The district court granted summary judgment to the company challenging the restrictions, finding that they violated the dormant commerce clause and that a ban on shipping waste by barge on three Virginia rivers violated the Supremacy Clause in light of existing federal regulation of maritime commerce. The Commonwealth appealed the decision to the Fourth Circuit, which found that the district court had been too quick to grant summary judgment to the plaintiffs on some aspects of the restrictions.

Waste Management Holdings, Inc. v. Gilmore, 252 F.3d 316 (4ᵗʰ Cir. 2001)

HAMILTON, Senior Circuit Judge:

In March and April 1999, the Commonwealth of Virginia's (Virginia) General Assembly, its legislative body, enacted and the Governor of Virginia signed into law five statutory provisions, which, collectively, cap the amount of municipal solid waste (MSW) that may be accepted by landfills located in Virginia and restrict the use of barges and trucks to transport such waste in Virginia. *See* Va.Code Ann. §§ 10.1-1408.1(Q); 10.1-1408.3; 10.1-1454.1(A); 10.1-1454.2; 10.1-1454.3 (Michie Supp.2000). The first statutory provision (the Cap Provision) caps the amount of waste that any landfill located in Virginia may accept. Va.Code Ann. § 10.1-1408.3. The second statutory provision (the Stacking Provision) requires Virginia's Waste Management Board (the Board) to promulgate regulations governing the transport of MSW by ship, barge, or other vessel, as well as the loading and unloading of such waste. Va.Code Ann. § 10.1-1454.1(A). This statutory provision requires that such regulations, which have yet to be issued, prohibit stacking containerized waste on a barge more than two containers high. *Id.* The third statutory provision (the Three Rivers' Ban), which pertains to barges, prohibits "the commercial transport of hazardous or nonhazardous solid waste . . . by ship, barge or other vessel upon the navigable waters of the Rappahanock, James and York Rivers, to the fullest extent consistent with limitations posed by the Constitution of the United States." Va.Code Ann. § 10.1-1454.2. The fourth statutory provision (the Trucking Certification Provision) prohibits landfill operators from accepting MSW from a vehicle with four or more axles "unless the transporter of the waste provides certification, in a form prescribed by the Board, that the waste is free of substances not authorized for acceptance at the facility." Va.Code Ann. § 10.1-1408.1(Q). Finally, the fifth statutory provision (the Four or More Axle Provision) requires the Board to develop regulations governing the "commercial transport" of MSW by "any tractor truck semitrailer combination with four or more axles." Va.Code Ann. § 10.1-1454.3(A), (D). Among other things, the Four or More Axle Provision provides that the new regulations require, as a condition of carrying MSW on Virginia roads, the owners of such trucks to make financial assurances that trucks having less than four axles or carrying other cargo need not make. *Id.* § 10.1-1454.3(A)(2).

Following the enactment of these statutory provisions, several Virginia landfill operators and transporters of MSW and one Virginia county (collectively the Plaintiffs) commenced this 42 U.S.C. § 1983 action in the United States District Court for the Eastern District of Virginia against the following individuals, in their official capacities: (1) Virginia's Governor, James Gilmore; (2) Virginia's Secretary of Natural Resources, John Paul Woodley; and (3) Virginia's Director of the Department of Environmental Control, Dennis Treacy. The Plaintiffs' action challenges the five Virginia statutory provisions on the basis that they are violative of the dormant Commerce, Contract, and Equal Protection Clauses of the United States Constitution. The action seeks declaratory and injunctive relief. . . .

I.

MSW "generally includes solid waste generated by households, commercial activities, institutions, and non-process waste from industries." (J.A. 249). The Virginia Department of Environmental Quality (DEQ) reported that as of November 1998, there were seventy active landfills in Virginia accepting MSW. Although the parties disagree over how many of those landfills accept MSW from other states, the record is clear that seven "regional" landfills account for ninety-seven percent of the out-of-state waste deposited in Virginia. Approximately sixty-one "local" landfills accept no out-of-state waste at all. DEQ also reported that for the calendar year ending December 31, 1998, New York, Maryland, North Carolina, and Washington, D.C. exported the largest quantities of MSW into Virginia compared to other states or jurisdictions.

The regional landfills, which are privately operated and have substantially greater disposal capacity than their local counterparts, have been sited and constructed over the past decade in order to comply with strict state and federal regulations. Pursuant to a "host agreement" with the county in which it is located, each regional landfill pays the host county a fee based upon the volume of waste (excluding the host's waste) deposited at that location. These agreements also require the regional landfills to perform certain services for their host communities, such as providing free waste disposal and recycling services and/or funding the closing of any local landfills which do not meet state and federal regulations. The construction of these regional landfills has required tens of millions of dollars in private investment, and the landfills face high operation and maintenance costs in addition to the sizeable host fees.

To meet their revenue needs and remain economically viable, each regional landfill relies heavily on the disposal of MSW generated outside Virginia. In fact, MSW generated outside Virginia comprises seventy-five percent of the MSW accepted at the five regional landfills operated by Waste Management and almost one-hundred percent of the MSW accepted at Brunswick's regional landfill.

Under its host agreements, Waste Management is permitted to dispose of over 2,000 tons of MSW per day at all but one of its regional landfills. Prior to enactment of the statutory provisions at issue, Waste Management expected to exceed that level in 1999. Waste Management further expected that three of its five regional landfills would accept substantially more waste in 1999 than they had in 1998. The Charles City County Landfill, for instance, accepted approximately 2,849 tons of MSW per day in 1999, compared to less than 2,000 tons per day in 1998. Likewise, Brunswick accepted approximately 2,400 tons per day in 1998, and accepted more than 2,800 tons per day in 1999. Before the enactment of the statutory provisions at issue, Brunswick had expected to reach 5,000 tons per day by the end of the year 2000. By contrast, not one of the sixty-one landfills located in Virginia that accept only Virginia-generated MSW has ever accepted more than 2,000 tons per day, and only one or two of those might ever be expected to reach that level in the future.

For several decades, New York City has disposed of its residential MSW at the Fresh Kills Landfill in Staten Island. In 1997, New York Governor George Pataki and New York City Mayor Rudolph Giuliani announced that the Fresh Kills Landfill would cease accepting waste in December 2001. The New York City Department of Sanitation, therefore, began to negotiate interim disposal contracts in order to phase out its dependency on the Fresh Kills Landfill. Waste Management has been awarded two of those contracts, and much of the MSW handled under those two contracts has been deposited at its regional landfills in Virginia. In March 1999, it bid on a third contract, which also contemplates the disposal of New York-generated MSW in Virginia. More significantly, Waste Management has bid on, and is a primary contender for, a twenty-year contract to dispose of all or part of 12,000 tons of residential waste per day from Manhattan, Queens, Brooklyn, and the Bronx. New York City's Department of Sanitation's Request For Proposal expresses a preference that any waste removed under this contract be transported by barge and/or rail, rather than by truck.

Waste Management's response contemplates sending sixty percent of the New York City residential MSW to Virginia landfills, particularly the Charles City County Landfill. It also contemplates that most of this waste will be containerized and transported by barge along the James River for off-loading at the James River Facility. In addition to the residential MSW covered by existing and pending contracts, Waste Management also removes significant quantities of commercial waste per day from New York City and surrounding communities. Waste Management had transported a substantial portion of this MSW to its regional landfills in Virginia by tractor trailer, but in 1998 began planning to transport much of the waste by barge. In furtherance of this plan, it negotiated a contract with Hale, whereby Hale would lease to Waste Management four barges for five years at a fixed price, with an option to lease an additional two barges. Each barge is capable of carrying 5,000 tons of MSW in specially constructed containers that can be stacked five high.

Hale and Waste Management expected that barging would commence in March or April 1999, that Waste Management would transport 2,500 to 3,000 tons of MSW per day from Brooklyn to the James River Facility, and that this waste would then be unloaded and delivered to the Charles City County Landfill for disposal. Toward this end, Waste Management has agreed to purchase 400 American Bureau of Shipping-approved, double steel walled containers at a cost of $10,000 per container. It has also invested more than $5,000,000 in improvements at the James River facility and has guaranteed payment on two cranes for off-loading containers that together are worth more than $5,000,000. Only a small amount of MSW generated inside Virginia is transported to Virginia landfills by water. . . .

Governor Gilmore . . . expressed concern about the increased flow of MSW generated outside Virginia into landfills located in Virginia. On September 29, 1998, he announced that he was dispatching his top environmental officials to meet with their counterparts from other states "to ensure that Virginia does not drown in a regional sea of garbage." (J.A. 597). In November 1998, Governor Gilmore imposed a moratorium on new landfill development and instructed Secretary Woodley to recommend legislation to deal with the problem. Furthermore, in his January 13, 1999 State of the Commonwealth address, Governor Gilmore proposed such legislation. Specifically referring to Waste Management's intentions, he noted that "[j]ust two days ago, a major company announced plans to import four thousand more tons of New York City trash into Virginia per day." (J.A. 630). To combat this increase, he announced that he would ask Virginia's General Assembly to take the following steps: (1) to prohibit the use of barges for transporting MSW on Virginia's waterways; (2) to impose new permit requirements for landfills located in Virginia; (3) to cap the amount of waste that may be deposited in Virginia landfills; and (4) to increase inspections of waste being hauled by truck or other means. And when New York City Mayor Giuliani suggested that Virginia might have an obligation to accept New York City's MSW, Governor Gilmore responded that "the home state of Washington, Jefferson, and Madison has no intention o[f] becoming New York's dumping grounds." (J.A.

635). Meanwhile, numerous Virginia lawmakers and other state officials announced their support for Senator Bolling and the Governor's efforts, frequently couching their positions in anti-out-of-state MSW terms.

In March and April 1999, Virginia's General Assembly approved and Governor Gilmore signed into law the five statutory provisions at issue in this case. The present civil action followed. . . .

[The court rejected Virginia's claim that the action was barred by the Eleventh Amendment, finding that it fit within the exception recognized in *Ex Parte Young*, 239 U.S. 123, which permits certain suits in federal court against state officers. However, it ruled that Governor Gilmore should be dismissed as a party because he lacks a specific duty to enforce the challenged restrictions. The court also rejected Virginia's defense that the plaintiff lacked standing.]

V.

We now turn to address the merits of the Plaintiffs' dormant Commerce Clause challenge to the statutory provisions at issue. The Commerce Clause provides that "[t]he Congress shall have Power . . . [t]o regulate Commerce . . . among the several States. . . ." Art. I, § 8, cl. 3. Supreme Court precedent has long recognized that although phrased as a grant of regulatory power to Congress, the Commerce Clause inherently "denies the States the power unjustifiably to discriminate against or burden the interstate flow of articles of commerce." *Oregon Waste Sys. v. Department of Envtl. Quality*, 511 U.S. 93, 98 (1994).

We apply the following two-tier approach in determining the constitutionality of a statutory provision challenged under the dormant Commerce Clause:

The first tier, a virtually *per se* rule of invalidity, applies where a state law discriminates facially, in its practical effect, or in its purpose. In order for a law to survive such scrutiny, the state must prove that the discriminatory law is demonstrably justified by a valid factor unrelated to economic protectionism, and that there are no nondiscriminatory alternatives adequate to preserve the local interests at stake. . . .

The second tier applies if a statute regulates evenhandedly and only indirectly affects interstate commerce. In that case, the law is valid unless the burdens on commerce are clearly excessive in relation to the putative local benefits.

Envtl. Tech. Council v. Sierra Club, 98 F.3d 774, 785 (4th Cir.1996) (internal quotation marks and citations omitted); *see also Eastern Kentucky Resources v. Fiscal Court of Magoffin County,* 127 F.3d 532, 540 (6th Cir.1997) ("A statute can discriminate against out-of-state interests in three different ways: (a) facially, (b) purposefully, or (c) in practical effect.").

A.

Here, the parties are in agreement that the statutory provisions at issue are not facially discriminatory against MSW generated outside Virginia. Thus, we must determine whether the statutory provisions at issue would discriminate against MSW generated outside Virginia in their practical effect or were enacted for the purpose of discriminating against MSW generated outside Virginia. Quite obviously, both inquiries present questions of fact. If the answer to either question is yes, we apply strict scrutiny analysis.

B.

1. The Plaintiffs offer the following evidence in support of their contention that the Cap Provision would discriminate against MSW generated outside Virginia in its practical effect. First, the Plaintiffs rely upon a November 1998 report issued by DEQ, reporting that, with respect to the MSW received by the seven large regional landfills in Virginia, approximately ninety-seven percent is MSW generated outside Virginia, while only two of the sixty-three small local landfills in Virginia accepted the remaining approximately three percent. Second, the Plaintiffs rely upon a sworn statement by Lee Wilson that he has personal knowledge that all seven of the large regional landfills in Virginia, except for the Gloucester County landfill, which operates under a local cap of 2,000 tons per day, have disposed of more than 2,000 tons per day of MSW in the past or can reasonably be expected to do so in the future. By contrast, he further stated, none of the approximately sixty-three landfills that receive principally Virginia-generated MSW receive any amount of MSW close to 2,000 tons per day of MSW. The Plaintiffs argue that from this evidence, a reasonable juror could only find that if the Cap Provision is allowed to take effect, it will impose a

real and substantial burden on MSW generated outside Virginia while barely, if at all, impacting MSW generated in Virginia. Specifically, the burden is less access to permanent disposal.

In response, the Defendants argue that the Plaintiffs' evidence is legally insufficient because Lee Wilson did not identify a basis for his testimony and provided no reason to believe that he had personal knowledge of this information. Furthermore, the Defendants argue that Lee Wilson's testimony is contradicted by their evidence that the Southeastern Public Authority Landfill (SPA Landfill), which accepts exclusively Virginia MSW, operates near the cap already and expects to reach that level soon. Moreover, the Defendants argue, the effect of the Cap Provision on the SPA Landfill is demonstrated by the fact that prior to the injunction against enforcement of the Cap Provision, the SPA Landfill applied for an increased tonnage allotment under the Cap Provision.

The Plaintiffs argue in response that Lee Wilson had ample basis for his testimony based upon his knowledge and experience in the MSW industry and based upon DEQ's November 1998 report. With regard to the SPA Landfill, the Plaintiffs note that on December 30, 1998, DEQ reported to Senator Bolling that the SPA Landfill receives 1,540 tons of MSW per day and that when the SPA Landfill applied for an increase in tonnage allotment, it made clear that it expected to exceed the cap only on the "rare" occasions when its waste-to-energy plant is shutdown for repairs. (J.A. 1002).

After reviewing the evidence and arguments offered by both sides on this issue, we conclude that a genuine issue of material fact exists regarding whether the Cap Provision discriminates in its practical effect against MSW generated outside Virginia. Thus, the Plaintiffs are not entitled to summary judgment in their favor with respect to this issue.

2. With respect to the Stacking Provision and the Three Rivers' Ban, the Defendants do not dispute that a far greater amount of MSW generated outside Virginia, as compared to MSW generated inside Virginia, is shipped in specialized containers on barges on Virginia's waterways for ultimate disposal in landfills located in Virginia. Likewise, the Defendants do not dispute that Hale and Waste Management had

serious proposals, prior to the enactment of the statutory provisions at issue, whereby Hale would lease four barges for five years to Waste Management, which Waste Management in turn would use in transporting MSW generated in New York to Virginia on Virginia waterways for disposal in landfills located in Virginia. Finally, the Defendants do not dispute that enforcement of the Stacking Provision would more than double the cost of shipping MSW by barge on Virginia waterways.

Nevertheless, the Defendants argue that the Plaintiffs' evidence is insufficient to establish that the Stacking Provision and the Three Rivers' Ban discriminates in practical effect against MSW generated outside Virginia because the Plaintiffs failed to present any evidence establishing that there is not, never has been, and never would be any interest in barging MSW generated inside Virginia. The Defendants offer no citation of authority for this argument and we understand why. The obvious focus of the practical effect inquiry is upon the discernable practical effect that a challenged statutory provision has or would have upon interstate commerce as opposed to intrastate commerce. Logic dictates that for this purpose, the Plaintiffs are only required to show how the Stacking Provision and the Three Rivers' Ban, if enforced, would negatively impact interstate commerce to a greater degree than intrastate commerce. This they have done, and the Defendants have not created a genuine issue of material fact on the issue.

3. According to the Plaintiffs, the Trucking Certification Provision and the Four or More Axle Provision, if enforced, would have a discriminatory impact upon MSW generated outside Virginia because virtually all MSW generated outside Virginia is delivered to landfills in vehicles with four or more axles, while the majority of MSW generated inside Virginia is delivered to landfills in vehicles with less than four axles. We have reviewed both the evidence offered by the Plaintiffs in support of this assertion and the evidence offered by the Defendants in contest in the light most favorable to the Defendants. It suffices to say that the record reflects a genuine issue of material fact regarding whether the Trucking Certification Provision and the Four or More Axle Provision, if enforced, would discriminate against MSW generated outside Virginia in practical effect

Chapter 3. Waste Management and Pollution Prevention

C.

We now ask whether, viewing the evidence in the record in the light most favorable to the Defendants, and drawing all reasonable inferences in their favor, reasonable jurors could find that Virginia's General Assembly enacted the statutory provisions at issue without a discriminatory purpose.

> Several factors have been recognized as probative of whether a decisionmaking body was motivated by a discriminatory intent, including: (1) evidence of a "consistent pattern" of actions by the decisionmaking body disparately impacting members of a particular class of persons; (2) historical background of the decision, which may take into account any history of discrimination by the decisionmaking body or the jurisdiction it represents; (3) the specific sequence of events leading up to the particular decision being challenged, including any significant departures from normal procedures; and (4) contemporary statements by decisionmakers on the record or in minutes of their meetings.

Sylvia Dev. Corp. v. Calvert County, 48 F.3d 810, 819 (4th Cir.1995).

We conclude the record in this case establishes that no reasonable juror could find that in enacting the statutory provisions at issue Virginia's General Assembly acted without a discriminatory purpose. Furthermore, the record in this case establishes that no reasonable juror could find that in signing the statutory provisions at issue into law Governor Gilmore acted without a discriminatory purpose.

Our conclusions rest upon the historical background of and sequence of events leading up to the General Assembly's enactment of and Governor Gilmore's signing into law the statutory provisions at issue. In 1998, the General Assembly and Governor Gilmore learned that, as of 1997, Virginia had become the nation's second largest importer of MSW. Next came the widely reported news that New York City was planning to close the Fresh Kills landfill and begin exporting more of its MSW. Then came reports that Waste Management was making a $20,000,000 investment in the James River facility. At this point, the wheels of a political movement to curb the flow of MSW generated outside Virginia from entering the borders of Virginia began to turn. The movement was co-spearheaded by Senator Bolling and Governor Gilmore. . . .

[The court then reviewed several statements issued by Senator Bolling and Governor Gilmore decrying the import of waste from New York City].

. . . [T]he Governor announced in another press release that he was proposing, and that Senator Bolling would be the chief patron of, legislation intended to prevent Virginia from becoming the nation's dumping ground. Specifically, the Governor stated:

> The home state of Washington, Jefferson, and Madison has no intention of becoming the nation's dumping grounds.... That is *why* I've asked Senator Bolling to sponsor these bills that will increase state regulations on landfills, cap daily landfill deposits, and ban trash barges on Virginia's waterways.

(J.A. 635) (emphasis added).

. . . The record also contains transcripts of speeches on the floor of the General Assembly by two delegates to the General Assembly and the general reaction of fellow delegates. The transcripts establish the General Assembly's general antipathy toward MSW generated outside Virginia. First, one delegate to the General Assembly queried: "'Do we want to be known as the capital of garbage?'" (J.A. 1007). His query was met with a chorus of nos. He then queried: "'Maybe we need a new bumper sticker-instead of Virginia is for lovers, what about Virginia is for garbage? Or how about a special license plate with a dumpster on it.'" *Id.* Again, the record shows a chorus of nos. Finally, Delegate Williams lamented before the General Assembly: "'What a message we are sending, buy a home, live in the great Commonwealth, the number one importer of garbage.'" *Id.* . . .

The evidence just outlined shows unmistakably the legislative and gubernatorial opposition to further increases in the volume of MSW generated outside Virginia crossing the borders of Virginia for ultimate placement in Virginia's seven regional landfills. No reasonable juror could find the statutory provisions at issue had a purpose other than to reduce the flow of MSW generated outside Virginia into Virginia for disposal. Indeed, the very purpose the Defendants proffer in this litigation for the enactment of the statutory provisions at issue -- to alleviate or at least reduce health and safety threats to Virginia's citizens and environment created by the importation of MSW from states with less

Chapter 3. Waste Management and Pollution Prevention

strict limitations upon the content of MSW than Virginia fully supports our conclusion. This is because an inherent component of the Defendants' proffered purpose of Virginia's enactment of the statutory provisions at issue is discrimination against MSW generated outside Virginia. Whether Virginia has a constitutionally valid reason for engaging in such discrimination is the focus of the strict scrutiny inquiry.

The Defendants contend the record shows that a genuine issue of material fact exists with respect to whether the statutes at issue were enacted with discriminatory intent or for neutral reasons. In support, the Defendants direct our attention to a post-enactment statement in a sworn declaration by Senator Bolling to the effect that he sponsored the statutory provisions at issue because of his concern over the rapid growth in the volume of MSW being deposited in Virginia landfills "regardless of the source" of that MSW. (J.A. 1228).

This statement is not sufficient to create a genuine issue of material fact on the issue of intent, because other statements by Senator Bolling in the same sworn declaration flatly contradict his "regardless of the source" phrase. Specifically, Senator Bolling admitted that MSW generated outside Virginia presented "increased concerns" on account of "the rapidly increasing volume and our perception that we in the Commonwealth have less control over the content of that waste and our ability to enforce Virginia regulations as to that waste stream." (J.A. 1229). In enacting the statutory provisions at issue, Senator Bolling further explained: "We were aware that the solid waste regulations of other states were not as stringent as those of the Commonwealth." *Id.* These latter quoted statements of Senator Bolling unequivocally show that the volume of MSW generated outside Virginia flowing into Virginia triggered *more concern* on the part of Virginia's General Assembly than the volume of MSW generated in Virginia being deposited in landfills located in Virginia. It is true that other portions of Senator Bolling's sworn declaration stress that Virginia intended the challenged statutes to regulate evenhandedly without regard to the source of the waste; however, the Defendants cannot create a genuine issue of material fact by presenting conflicting sworn statements as they have done with respect to the issue of discriminatory intent. *Barwick v. Celotex Corp.*, 736 F.2d 946, 960 (4th Cir.1984) ("A genuine issue of material fact is not created where the only issue of fact is to determine which of the two conflicting versions of the plaintiff's testimony is correct.").

D.

We must next consider whether, viewing the evidence in the light most favorable to the Defendants, the Defendants have proffered sufficient evidence for reasonable jurors to find, with respect to each statutory provision at issue, that the provision is demonstrably justified by a valid factor unrelated to economic protectionism, and that no nondiscriminatory alternatives exist that are adequate to preserve the local interests at stake. *Environmental Technology Council,* 98 F.3d at 785.

1. The Defendants argue that all of the statutory provisions at issue are demonstrably justified because "solid waste streams generated in trash exporting states raise health and safety concerns not presented by Virginia waste." (the Defendants' Br. at 56). In this regard, the Defendants stress that the problem is particularly acute with respect to exporting states that do not have laws as strict as Virginia's laws governing regulated medical waste and certain types of hazardous waste. By analogy, the Defendants rely upon *Maine v. Taylor,* 477 U.S. 131 (1986). In that case, Maine demonstrated that all out-of-state baitfish were subject to parasites foreign to in-state baitfish. This difference posed a threat to Maine's natural resources, and absent a less discriminatory means of protecting the environment—and none was available—the importation of baitfish from any state could properly be banned. *Id.* at 140.

The Plaintiffs do not quarrel with the Defendants' position that the health and safety of Virginia citizens is a legitimate local interest. Neither do we. Nevertheless, in order to survive the Plaintiffs' motion for summary judgment with respect to the first prong of strict scrutiny analysis, the Defendants must carry their burden of showing that MSW generated outside Virginia is more dangerous than MSW generated in Virginia. *Chemical Waste Management, Inc. v. Hunt,* 504 U.S. 334, 343-44 (1992) (recognizing that while the health and safety of the citizens of Alabama may be a legitimate local interest, Alabama offered no evidence that hazardous waste generated outside Alabama is more dangerous than hazardous waste generated in Alabama; therefore, Alabama failed to carry its burden of showing that the Alabama statute imposing an additional fee on all hazardous waste generated outside Alabama and disposed of at Alabama facilities was demonstrably justified by a valid factor unrelated to economic protectionism).

In this regard, the Defendants have offered evidence demonstrating, when viewed in the light most favorable to them: (1) that certain materials in MSW can be hazardous to human health; (2) that each state has its own definition of MSW; (3) that "[w]hile one state may find it appropriate to regulate strictly a certain type of solid waste, another state may not be as aware of or concerned about the risks posed by that type of item into the MSW stream," (J.A. 356); (4) that Virginia law completely prohibits potentially infectious items such as blood and urine from being disposed of as MSW, while Maryland and North Carolina allow disposal of blood and urine as MSW under limited circumstances; (5) that Virginia law prohibits urine from being disposed of as MSW while New York allows its disposal as MSW without limitation; (6) that Maryland and New York allow hazardous waste generated at less than 100 kilograms per month to be disposed of as MSW while Virginia does not; and (7) that unlike Virginia, Maryland and New York do not impose manifesting or tracking requirements on hazardous waste from small quantity generators.

From this evidence, a reasonable juror could infer that, as a whole, MSW generated outside Virginia poses health and safety risks not posed by MSW generated inside Virginia. Such a finding would satisfy the Defendants' burden of establishing that the statutory provisions at issue are justified by a reason other than economic protectionism.

2. With respect to the second prong of the strict scrutiny test, the Defendants must prove that the statutory provisions at issue are the least discriminatory means of addressing Virginia's concern that MSW generated outside Virginia poses health and safety risks not posed by MSW generated inside Virginia.

a. The Defendants assert that any plan for improving state police powers over MSW must begin with and be linked to limiting the volume of MSW to a level where waste can be screened adequately. In support of this assertion, the Defendants rely on the following sworn statements by Virginia's Director of Program Coordination for DEQ:

The cap statute is a necessary and appropriate response to the MSW volume crisis faced by the Commonwealth. The problem is particularly acute with regard to out-of-state MSW. While out-of-state MSW poses more of a threat than Virginia MSW, the Commonwealth has less ability to police the out-of-state loads. Any plan for improving state police powers over MSW must begin with and be linked to controlling the volume to a level where waste can be adequately screened. The disposal cap statute allows the Commonwealth to better protect health and safety within the Commonwealth by controlling daily levels of MSW to a volume that reasonably can be managed and policed. . . .

(J.A. 1159-61).

In response, the Plaintiffs primarily argue that the Defendants have failed to meet the second prong because the Cap Provision does not use the least discriminatory means of addressing the alleged health and safety concern about the composition of MSW generated outside Virginia. The Plaintiffs point out that the Cap Provision makes no effort to distinguish between the MSW of states according to an individual state's level of MSW regulation. According to the Plaintiffs, interstate commerce would be burdened less if Virginia only capped the amount of waste that can be imported from states with MSW regulatory schemes less restrictive than Virginia. Additionally, the more closely a state's MSW regulatory scheme tracks that of Virginia, the higher the cap should be.

At first blush, the Plaintiffs' argument seems more discriminatory against MSW generated outside Virginia than the across the board cap in the Cap Provision. However, when one carefully considers the Plaintiffs' argument, its logic is clear. If a state enacts a statute that purposely discriminates against interstate commerce in an effort to address a concern other than economic or resource protectionism, the second prong of the strict scrutiny test requires that the statute impose the least burden possible on interstate commerce. In other words, rather than discriminating against MSW from every state other than Virginia, Virginia's cap should only target the MSW from states that have lesser health and safety standards regarding MSW than Virginia. Because the Defendants have presented no evidence as to why a narrower capping statute would not adequately address the identified health and safety concerns for Virginia citizens, the Defendants fail to survive the Plaintiffs' motion for summary judgment with respect to the second prong of the strict scrutiny test as it pertains to the Cap Provision. [10]

b. The Defendants argue that they have submitted sufficient evidence to create a genuine issue of material fact regarding whether the Stacking Provision and the Three Rivers' Ban are the least discriminatory alternatives available for protecting the health and safety of Virginia citizens against the toxic contamination of its rivers from unintended spills. We agree. Notwithstanding the Plaintiffs' protestations to the contrary, the Defendants have submitted sufficient evidence in this regard to create genuine issues of material fact that need to be resolved by the trier of fact. For example, the Defendants have submitted the sworn statement of DEQ Director Dennis Treacy that based upon his knowledge and experience, the Stacking Provision and Three Rivers' Ban are necessary to protect the health and safety of Virginia citizens. Treacy outlines in a sworn declaration why and how barge transport of MSW presents serious and unique health and safety threats to Virginia's citizens that cannot be alleviated absent enforcement of the Stacking Provision and the Three Rivers' Ban. Furthermore, the record contains Hale's answers to interrogatories in which Hale admits: (1) in 1993, it lost thirty-three containers containing general merchandise overboard on a barge it owned due to improper lashing; and (2) in 1994, a fire resulted in the partial destruction of cargo on board a barge it owned. These incidents certainly suggest the potential for a health and environmental disaster on a Virginia waterway presented by the barge transport of MSW.

c. As for the Trucking Certification Provision and the Four or More Axle Provision, the Defendants fail to offer any affirmative evidence of the non-existence of less burdensome alternatives on interstate commerce. Instead, the Defendants rely on the deference that is traditionally given state legislation in the area of highway safety. The traditional deference that is due state legislation in the area of highway safety

> derives in part from the assumption that where such regulations do not discriminate on their face against interstate commerce, their burden usually falls on local economic interests as well as other States' economic interest, thus insuring that a State's own political processes will serve as a check against unduly burdensome regulations. Less deference to the legislative judgment is due . . . where the local regulation bears disproportionately on out- of-state residents and businesses.

Kassel v. Consolidated Freightways Corp., 450 U.S. 662, 675-76 (1981).

Chapter 3. Waste Management and Pollution Prevention

While all the parties agree that the Trucking Certification Provision and the Four or More Axle Provision are not facially discriminatory against MSW generated outside Virginia, and we have already determined that a genuine issue of material fact exists regarding whether these statutory provisions discriminate in their practical effect against MSW generated outside Virginia, the Defendants' argument that we are required to give deference to the legislative judgment of the General Assembly in applying the second prong of the strict scrutiny analysis (to the Trucking Certification Provision and the Four or More Axle Provision) is without merit. This is because we have also determined that no reasonable juror could find that in enacting these two statutory provisions Virginia's General Assembly acted without a discriminatory purpose. Such a discriminatory purpose wholly undercuts the notion that Virginia's political process served as a check against unduly burdensome regulations. Without such a check, the rationale for owing deference to the legislative judgment of Virginia's General Assembly in the area of highway safety is completely lacking.

With no deference owed to the legislative judgment of Virginia's General Assembly in enacting the Trucking Certification Provision and the Four or More Axle Provision, and with absolutely no evidence showing that less burdensome alternatives do not exist on interstate commerce, these two statutory provisions do not survive the second prong of the strict scrutiny test. Accordingly, we affirm the district court's grant of summary judgment in favor of the Plaintiffs with respect to their dormant Commerce Clause challenge in regard to the Trucking Certification Provision and the Four or More Axle Provision. . . .

[The court then rejected Virginia's arguments that it could favor its citizens because it was acting as a "market participant", that Subtitle D of RCRA authorized Virginia to discriminate against waste generated outside of the state, and that New York had itself interfered with the free flow of commerce by discouraging disposal of waste within its own state].

VI.

Lastly, the Defendants challenge the district court's holding that the Three Rivers' Ban and the Stacking Provision violate the Supremacy Clause. The Supremacy Clause provides that the "Constitution, and the Laws of the United States which shall be made in Pursuance thereof

... shall be the supreme Law of the Land; and the Judges in every State shall be bound thereby, any Thing in the Constitution or Laws of any State to the Contrary notwithstanding." U.S. Const., art. VI, cl. 2.

> Thus, federal legislation, if enacted pursuant to Congress' constitutionally delegated authority, can nullify conflicting state or local actions. Consideration of issues arising under the Supremacy Clause start[s] with the assumption that the historic police powers of the States [are] not to be superseded by ... Federal Act unless that [is] the clear and manifest purpose of Congress. The ultimate touchstone of preemption analysis is the intent of Congress. Even when Congress' intent is unclear, state law must nevertheless yield when it conflicts with federal law. In making the determination of whether state law conflicts with federal law, the test to apply is whether it is impossible to comply with both state and federal law or whether the state law stands as an obstacle to the accomplishment of the full purposes and objectives of the relevant federal law.

National Home Equity Mortg. Assoc. v. Face, 239 F.3d 633, 636-37 (4th Cir.2001).

The Supremacy Clause claim at issue in this appeal principally relies on the federal documentation provisions governing the use of vessels in the coastwise trade. *See* 46 U.S.C. § 12103 (describing prerequisites for issuance of a "certificate of documentation") and § 12106 (describing criteria for endorsing a certificate of documentation with a "coastwise endorsement"). According to the record, each barge that Hale plans to supply Waste Management for the transportation of MSW has a valid federal Certificate of Documentation authorizing it to engage in "coastwise trade" and a valid Coast Guard Certificate of Inspection.

The Supreme Court has held that a federal license confers upon the licensee a right to operate freely in each state's waters, subject only to legitimate exercises of the state's police power. *Douglas v. Seacoast Prods., Inc.*, 431 U.S. 265, 281 (1977). Thus, "[s]tates may impose upon federal licensees reasonable, nondiscriminatory conservation and environmental protection measures otherwise within their police power." *Id.* at 277. Precedent is clear, however, that a state statute that completely excludes federally licensed commerce upon such state's waterways is unconstitutional. *Id.* 283.

Here, the Three Rivers' Ban completely excludes federally licensed barges from transporting any type or amount of MSW on the Rappahanock, James and York Rivers in Virginia. The reasonableness of such a complete ban is simply not supported by the evidence in the record, even when viewed in the light most favorable to the Defendants. The issue of whether federal preemption of the Stacking Provision exists is far less clear. Indeed, genuine issues of material fact exist regarding the health and environmental risks associated with stacking sealed shipping containers containing MSW more than two high on barges. Accordingly, the district court erred in concluding as a matter of law that the Stacking Provision violates the Supremacy Clause.

VII.

In conclusion, we affirm the district court's grant of summary judgment in favor of the Plaintiffs with respect to their dormant Commerce Clause challenges to the Cap Provision, the Trucking Certification Provision, and the Four or More Axle Provision. We also affirm the district court's grant of summary judgment in favor of the Plaintiffs with respect to Hale's Supremacy Clause challenge to the Three Rivers' Ban. However, we vacate the district court's grant of summary judgment in favor of the Plaintiffs with respect to their dormant Commerce Clause challenge to the Three Rivers' Ban and the Stacking Provision and remand for further proceedings consistent with this opinion. We also vacate the district court's grant of summary judgment in favor of Hale with respect to Hale's claim that the Stacking Provision violates the Supremacy Clause and remand for further proceedings consistent with this opinion. Finally, we vacate the district court's entry of judgment against Governor Gilmore and remand with instructions that the district court dismiss him as a party in this action.

AFFIRMED IN PART, VACATED IN PART, AND REMANDED.

NOTES AND QUESTIONS

1. Virginia's law capped the amount of municipal waste a landfill could accept at the greater of 2,000 tons per day or the average daily amount accepted by the landfill in 1998. It provided for variances if Virginia's Waste Management Board determined that additional capacity was needed and that it could be handled safely. Would Virginia

have had an easier time defending its legislation if the Governor and state legislators had not made it obvious that the purpose of the legislation was to protect against waste imports from New York? What effect did these statements have on Virginia's defense?

2. Virginia argued that other states did not regulate municipal solid waste as stringently as Virginia did. The court expresses some sympathy for the notion that out-of-state waste may pose greater health risks than wastes generated within Virginia. Virginia maintained that inspection procedures for municipal waste were inadequate to protect the health and safety of citizens of Virginia from wastes generated in states with less stringent regulations. Why is this not a sufficient basis for upholding Virginia's regulations?

3. How did Virginia try to demonstrate that there were no non-discriminatory alternatives available for protecting legitimate state interests? Why did this effort fail?

4. What should Virginia try to prove on remand to salvage the portions of its regulations that were not struck down?

5. Suppose that you were asked by Virginia's legislators to redesign Virginia's law to accomplish the purposes sought by the state without running into constitutional problems. What would you advise?

"Flow Control" Ordinances, the Dormant Commerce Clause, and the Rationale for the Nondiscrimination Rule (pp. 351-60)

In C & A Carbone, Inc. v. Town of Clarkstown, 511 U.S. 383 (1994) (casebook, p. 352), the Supreme Court struck down a "flow control" ordinance that sought to ensure that all waste in a municipality was processed first in a local waste transfer station. The Court held that the ordinance discriminated against out-of-state waste processors. In response to this decision, many local governments have adopted what have been called "bifurcated" flow control ordinances which attempt to get around *Carbone* by providing that only waste haulers who do not use an out-of-state disposal facility are required to send their waste to a particular local facility. Others simply have announced that they will not enforce their flow control ordinances against those sending their waste out of state.

The *Carbone* opinion is reproduced on pp. 352-359 of the case. On page 353 of the casebook, immediately before the last full paragraph on that page (which starts with "Clarkstown protests . . ."), we edited out a paragraph of the Court's opinion that some professors have found helpful in explaining the rationale for the nondiscrimination rule. The paragraph is as follows:

> The central rationale for the rule against discrimination is to prohibit state or municipal laws whose object is local economic protectionism, laws that would excite those jealousies and retaliatory measures the Constitution was designed to prevent. See The Federalist No. 22, pp. 143-145 (C. Rossiter ed. 1961) (A. Hamilton); Madison, Vices of the Political System of the United States, in 2 Writings of James Madison 362-363 (G. Hunt ed. 1901). We have interpreted the Commerce Clause to invalidate local laws that impose commercial barriers or discriminate against an article of commerce by reason of its origin or destination out of State. See, *e.g., Philadelphia, supra* (striking down New Jersey statute that prohibited the import of solid waste); *Hughes v. Oklahoma,* 441 U.S. 322, 99 S.Ct. 1727, 60 L.Ed.2d 250 (1979) (striking down Oklahoma law that prohibited the export of natural minnows).

511 U.S. at 390.

Siting Controversies: In re Louisiana Energy Services (pp. 361-372)

Following the Nuclear Regulatory Commission's ruling referenced in the text, LES abandoned its plans for the Claiborne Enrichment Center and asked the NRC to withdraw its application. On April 30, 1998, the NRC granted the motion to withdraw the application and terminated the proceedings. (See the discussion on p. 1 of this supplement).

- 4 -
Regulation of Toxic Substances

Chemical Hazard Data Availability (pp. 375-77)

EDF's "Toxic Ignorance" study (p. 376) has helped to spur the chemical industry to launch a massive voluntary testing program of high-production volume chemicals. By the end of the year 2000, EPA had obtained commitments from 403 companies to voluntarily test 2,011 chemicals for potential health and environmental effects. This High Production Volume Chemical Challenge Program is expected to provide the public with basic toxicity information about chemicals manufactured or imported in quantities greater than one million pounds per year.

In December 2000 EPA launched a Voluntary Children's Chemical Evaluation Program to obtain health effects and exposure information on 23 pilot chemicals to which children are believe to be disproportionately exposed. If no companies agree to sponsor voluntary Tier I testing for a particular chemical, EPA will consider issuing a test rule for the chemical under Section 4 of TSCA.

Environmental Releases of Toxic Substances: The National Report on Human Exposure to Environmental Chemicals (pp. 377-78)

In March 2001 the U.S. Centers for Disease Control (CDC) released the first National Report on Human Exposure to Environmental Chemicals. The report, available online at http://www.cdc.gov/nced/dls/report, provides the first comprehensive data on actual levels of 27 environmental chemicals in humans. These chemicals include metals (e.g., lead and mercury), pesticide metabolites, phthalate metabolites, and cotinine (which tracks exposure to tobacco smoke). Levels of these chemicals were measured in blood and urine samples collected from participants in CDC's National Health and Nutrition Examination Survey (NHANES) — an ongoing national health survey of the U.S. population.

The report found a continued decline in levels of lead in children's blood, which could be a product of the phaseout of leaded gasoline. The report found that the geometric mean blood lead level for children aged 1-5 years in 1999 had decreased to 2.0 micrograms per deciliter (mg/dL), from 2.7 mg/dL, the geometric mean for the period 1991-1994. The report also found a surprising 75% decrease in levels of the nicotine byproduct cotinine in nonsmokers, suggesting that measures restricting smoking in public places have dramatically reduced non-smokers' exposure to environmental tobacco smoke. The report also provided important new data on levels of mercury in blood levels among children 1 to 5 years old and among women of childbearing age (16-49 years old). The geometric mean of blood mercury levels among children (0.3 mg/L) was about 25% of the geometric mean of blood mercury levels among women of childbearing age (1.2 mg/L). The report also found higher levels of human absorption of phthalates, a common ingredient in plastics and cosmetics, which is prompting further study to determine how these compounds are absorbed.

CDC plans to continue to monitor human exposure to the 27 substances while eventually expanding the report to provide information about 100 chemicals. CDC also will be reporting exposure levels for more specific population groups (e.g., children, minority populations, or women of childbearing age) and data from studies of people exposed from localized or point-source exposures (e.g., data on levels of mercury in people who eat mercury-contaminated fish from a polluted river).

Principal Provisions of FIFRA (p. 435)

The provision in section 6(a) of FIFRA that provides for automatic cancellation of a pesticide's registration after five years unless the registrant requests that it be continued was repealed when FIFRA was amended by the 1996 Food Quality Protection Act. We are grateful to Professor Shi-Ling Hsu of the George Washington University Law School for bringing this to our attention.

Chapter 4. Regulation of Toxic Substances

The Uncertainties of Risk Assessment
(pp. 444-53)

One of the recurring industry criticisms of EPA is that it fails to rely upon sound science in its regulatory decisions, a criticism that EPA vigorously resists. As the casebook states, science and scientific data are almost always incomplete and evolving with respect to the questions that risk assessment tries to answer. Commenters on EPA rules quite often introduce alternative scientific theories, data and conclusions in commenting upon those rules. In deciding what to do, then, EPA often has to elect to follow the conclusions of one approach versus another, or to rely upon some data and not others. Courts typically recognize that "it is not for the judicial branch to undertake comparative evaluations of conflicting scientific evidence," International Fabricare Inst. v. EPA, 972 F.2d 384, 398 (D.C. Cir. 1992), and they give EPA wide latitude to decide questions on the frontiers of science. See Schroeder and Glicksman, Chevron, State Farm and EPA in the Courts of Appeals During the 1990s, 31 Env. L. Rptr. 10371, 10392-412 (2001).

A provision of the Safe Drinking Water Act (SDWA) requires maximum contaminant level goals to be set on the basis of the "best available . . . science." 42 U.S.C. § 300g-1(b)(3)(A). The entire SDWA statutory scheme is described at pages 479-485. Litigation under this statute has produced one of the infrequent cases in which a court has reversed an EPA choice among different scientific conclusions. The decision came in response to EPA regulations setting a maximum contaminant level goal (MCGL) of zero for chloroform in drinking water under the Safe Drinking Water Act. Chloroform is a chemical byproduct of the chlorination of water. Water is deliberately chlorinated by public health authorities to eliminate microbial pathogens (germs).

Chlorine Chemistry Council v. EPA,
206 F.3d 1286 (D.C. Cir. 2000)

STEPHEN F. WILLIAMS, Circuit Judge:

The Safe Drinking Water Act ("SDWA" or the "Act") directs the Environmental Protection Agency to set standards for the regu-

115

lation of covered drinking water contaminants. For each EPA sets a "maximum contaminant level goal" ("MCLG"), defined as "the level at which no known or anticipated adverse effects on the health of persons occur and which allows an adequate margin of safety." 42 U.S.C. § 300g-1(b)(4)(A). The MCLG is somewhat aspirational. After having set it, EPA is to promulgate an enforceable standard, known as a maximum contaminant level ("MCL"), which takes practical considerations into account while remaining "as close to the [MCLG] as is feasible." *Id*. § 300g-1(b)(4)(B).

In March 1998 EPA concluded that chloroform, a drinking water contaminant, exhibits a "nonlinear mode of carcinogenic action." Notice of Data Availability: National Primary Drinking Water Regulations: Disinfectants and Disinfection Byproducts, 63 Fed.Reg. 15,674, 15,686/1 (1998). In other words, exposures to chloroform below some threshold level pose no risk of cancer. But in promulgating the MCLG it retained the existing standard of zero, which was based on the previously held assumption that there was no safe threshold. Final Rule: National Primary Drinking Water Regulations: Disinfectants and Disinfection Byproducts, 63 Fed.Reg. 69,390, 69,398/3 (1998) ("Final Rule"). EPA justified its action on a variety of grounds, including an alleged need to consult the report of its Science Advisory Board ("SAB"), which would not be available until after the statutory deadline for rulemaking had expired. Petitioners, including the Chlorine Chemistry Council, a trade association comprised of chlorine and chlorine product manufacturers, petitioned this court for review, arguing that EPA violated its statutory mandate to use the "best available" evidence when implementing the provisions of the Safe Drinking Water Act. 42 U.S.C. § 300g-1(b)(3)(A). We agree. . . .

On July 29, 1994 EPA issued a proposed rule on disinfectants and disinfection byproducts in water. This included a zero MCLG for chloroform, based on EPA's finding of an *absence* of data to suggest a threshold level below which there would be no potential carcinogenic effects. *Id*. The Agency's default method of inferring risk at exposure levels for which it has no adequate data is linear extrapolation from cancer incidence inferred at exposures for which it does have data. See EPA's Proposed Guidelines for Carcinogen Risk Assessment, 61 Fed.Reg. 17,960, 17,968/3 (1996). Thus, either if the evidence supports linearity, *or* if there is "insufficient" evidence of nonlinearity,

Chapter 4. Regulation of Toxic Substances

EPA assumes that if a substance causes cancer at *any* exposure it will do so at *every* non-zero exposure (though with cancer incidence declining with exposure). But EPA acknowledges its authority "to establish nonzero MCLGs for carcinogens if the scientific evidence" indicates that a "safe threshold" exists. See Final Rule, 63 Fed.Reg. at 69,401/2. And petitioners here assume the validity of the linear default assumption. . . .

On the basis of [a SDWA scientific advisory committee's] findings and recommendations, EPA in November 1997 published a Notice of Data Availability ("NODA"). . . . Among the findings it discussed were those arrived at by a panel of experts organized by the International Life Sciences Institute. The panel, whose work was subject to independent peer review and was convened under the auspices of the EPA, concluded on the basis of chloroform's mode of action that although it was "a likely carcinogen to humans above a certain dose range, [it was] unlikely to be carcinogenic below a certain dose range." *Id.* at 15,685/1. The panel recommended "the nonlinear[ ] or margin of exposure approach [as] the preferred approach to quantifying the cancer risk associated with chloroform exposure." *Id.* at 15,686/1.

EPA agreed. It said that "[a]lthough the precise mechanism of chloroform carcinogenicity is not established," nevertheless "the chloroform dose-response should be considered nonlinear." *Id.* at 15,685/3. Rather than operating through effects on DNA, which is consistent with linearity, chloroform evidently works through "cytotoxicity" (i.e., damage to the cells) followed by regenerative cell proliferation. *Id.* Employing the threshold approach that it found was entailed by chloroform's mode of action, EPA then calculated an MCLG of 600 parts per billion ("ppb"), based solely on carcinogenicity. *Id.* at 15,686/2. This level built in a 1000-fold margin of error in relation to the maximum safe dosage implied from the animal studies used by EPA. *Id.* But because even lower chlorine doses cause liver toxicity (a non-cancer effect), EPA proposed an MCLG of 300 ppb. *Id.*

When EPA came to promulgate its final rule in December 1998, however, its MCLG was again zero. Final Rule, 63 Fed.Reg. at 69,398/3. It stuck with 1994's zero level despite its explicit statement that it now "believe[d] that the underlying science for using a nonlinear extrapolation approach to evaluate the carcinogenic risk from chloroform is well founded." *Id*. at 69,401/1. It justified the action on the basis that "additional deliberations with the Agency's SAB on the analytical approach used" and on the underlying scientific evidence were needed "prior to departing from a long-held EPA policy." *Id*. at 69,399-69,401. It could not complete such additional deliberations by the November 1998 statutory deadline, and, moreover, the rulemaking would not affect the enforceable MCL for TTHMs.

After briefing on the petition for review at issue here, but before oral argument, EPA moved for a voluntary remand to consider the SAB report on chloroform that would soon be available. But EPA made no offer to vacate the rule; thus EPA's proposal would have left petitioners subject to a rule they claimed was invalid. We denied the motion.

On February 11, 2000, the day of oral argument, EPA released a draft report by the SAB on chloroform. See Draft, Chloroform Risk Assessment Review, February 10, 2000 (visited March 27, 2000) <http://www.epa.gov/science1/chlod00x.pdf>. The report concluded that chloroform exhibits a "cytotoxic" mode of action. Such a mode of action (unlike a "genotoxic" mechanism, which acts directly on a cell's DNA) involves no carcinogenic effects at low doses; thus a nonlinear approach is "scientifically reasonable." *Id*. at 17. After consideration of the draft SAB report, EPA stated that it "no longer believes that it should continue to defend its original decision," and moved that this court vacate the MCLG. Motion for Vacatur, at 2 (February 24, 2000).

[The court denied EPA's motion to vacate, and proceeded to the merits, because in its motion EPA had not committed itself to promulgate a nonzero MCLG for chloroform, which was the specific relief sought by petitioners.]

Petitioners argue that EPA's decision to adopt a zero MCLG in the face of scientific evidence establishing that chloroform is a threshold carcinogen was inconsistent with the Safe Drinking Water Act. Section 300g-1(b)(3)(A) of the Act states unequivocally that "to the degree that an Agency action is based on science, the Administrator shall use . . . the best available, peer-reviewed science and supporting studies conducted in accordance with sound and objective scientific practices."

Chapter 4. Regulation of Toxic Substances

In promulgating a zero MCLG for chloroform EPA openly overrode the "best available" scientific evidence, which suggested that chloroform is a threshold carcinogen.

EPA provides several arguments in defense of its action. First, it argues that to establish a non-zero MCLG would be a "precedential step," that represents "a major change in the substance of regulatory decisions related to chloroform." EPA's Br. at 28-29. We do not doubt that adopting a nonzero MCLG is a significant step, one which departs from previous practice. But this is a change in result, not in policy. The change in outcome occurs simply as a result of steadfast application of the relevant rules: first, the statutory mandate to set MCLGs at "the level at which no known or anticipated adverse effect on the health of persons occur," 42 U.S.C. § 300g-1(b)(4)(A), as determined on the basis of the "best available" evidence; and second, EPA's Carcinogen Risk Assessment guidelines, stating that when "adequate data on mode of action show that linearity is not the most reasonable working judgment and provide sufficient evidence to support a nonlinear mode of action," the default assumption of linearity drops out. Proposed Guidelines for Carcinogen Risk Assessment, 61 Fed.Reg. at 17,969/1. The fact that EPA has arrived at a novel, even politically charged, outcome is of no significance either for its statutory obligation or for fulfillment of its adopted policy.

Second, and similarly, EPA supports its action on the basis that "it could not complete the deliberations with the SAB" before the November 1998 deadline. EPA's Br. at 29; Final Rule, 63 Fed.Reg. at 69,399/1. But however desirable it may be for EPA to consult an SAB and even to revise its conclusion in the future, that is no reason for acting against its own science findings in the meantime. The statute requires the agency to take into account the "best *available*" evidence. 42 U.S.C. § 300g-1(b)(3)(A) (emphasis added). EPA cannot reject the "best available" evidence simply because of the possibility of contradiction in the future by evidence unavailable at the time of action—a possibility that will *always* be present. . . .

Finally, EPA argues that its statements in the 1998 Notice of Data Availability do not represent its "ultimate conclusions" with respect to chloroform, and thus in adopting a zero MCLG it did not reject what it considered to be the "best available" evidence. In fact, the zero MCLG merely represented an "interim risk management decision" pending the final SAB report. EPA's Br. at 35. We find these semantic somersaults pointless. First, whether EPA has adopted its 1998 NODA as its "ultimate conclusion" is irrelevant to whether it represented the "best available" evidence. All scientific conclusions are subject to some doubt; future, hypothetical findings always have the potential to resolve the doubt (the new resolution itself being subject, of course, to falsification by later findings). What is significant is Congress's requirement that the action be taken on the basis of the best available evidence *at the time* of the rulemaking. The word "available" would be senseless if construed to mean "expected to be available at some future date." Second, EPA cannot avoid this result by dubbing its action "interim." The statute applies broadly to any "[a]gency action"; whether the action is interim is irrelevant. . . .

[W]e vacate the rule.

So ordered.

Corrosion Proof Fittings and Efforts to Ban Asbestos (pp. 458-76)

While the *Corrosion Proof Fittings* decision (p. 458) derailed EPA's efforts to ban asbestos in the United States, a growing number of countries throughout the world are enacting asbestos bans. In September 2000, the World Trade Organization (WTO) rejected a challenge by Canada to France's decision to ban imports of chrysotile asbestos. When Spain banned asbestos on July 3, 2001, it became the thirteenth out of fifteen members of the European Union to ban the import and use of the substance. Chile banned asbestos in July 2001 despite a personal plea not to do so by Canadian Prime Minister Jean Chetrien. Argentina followed suit in August 2001. Australia, Saudi Arabia, and Brazilian cities and states accounting for 70 percent of Brazil's market also have banned asbestos use. El Salvador banned asbestos in the mid-1980s.

Chapter 4. Regulation of Toxic Substances

Example: The Safe Drinking Water Act
(pp. 479-84)

See the *Chlorine Chemistry Council* decision on page 115, above.

Case Study: Regulation of Arsenic in
Drinking Water (pp. 479-84)

Controversy over the Bush administration's reconsideration of lower limits on arsenic in drinking water, issued in the closing days of the Clinton administration, also provides an excellent illustration of the uncertainties that surround risk assessment. Inorganic arsenic is a naturally occurring element in the Earth's crust. Arsenic is released into ground water that travels through underground rocks and soil. Erosion can deposit arsenic in water bodies and the metal also can be absorbed by animals and plants. Consumption of food and water are the major sources of arsenic exposure for the majority of U.S. citizens. People also may be exposed from industrial sources, as arsenic is used in semiconductor manufacturing, petroleum refining, wood preservatives, animal feed additives, and herbicides.

Arsenic can combine with other elements to form inorganic and organic arsenicals. In general, inorganic derivatives are regarded as more toxic than the organic forms. While food contains both inorganic and organic arsenicals, primarily inorganic forms are present in water. Exposure to arsenic at high levels poses serious health effects as it is a known human carcinogen. In addition, it has been reported to affect the vascular system in humans and has been associated with the development of diabetes. Water from wells often has higher concentrations of arsenic than does surface water such as lakes and streams. Arsenic also can be found in plants, fish, and shellfish. Serious health problems associated with very high levels of arsenic in drinking water have surfaced in India and Bangladesh.

The World Health Organization's International Standards for Drinking-Water were established in 1958. Arsenic initially was classified as a toxic contaminant and 200 micrograms per liter (μg/L), or parts per billion (ppb), was set as an allowable concentration for arsenic in drinking water. In 1963 the World Health Organization (WHO) reevaluated its arsenic standard and reduced it to 50 ppb, though no specific reasons were given for this change. When WHO again updated its drinking water standards in 1971, it kept arsenic in the toxic substances category and reaffirmed the 50 ppb standard. While concluding that it would be prudent to keep levels of arsenic in drinking water as low as possible, the WHO noted that levels of arsenic up to 20 ppb were not known to have caused health problems. Epidemiological studies suggested that arsenic is carcinogenic but the WHO noted that there was no real proof of its carcinogenicity to humans.

In 1984 the WHO adopted Guidelines for Drinking-Water Quality. These were intended to influence the development of national drinking water regulations around the world. Arsenic was listed by WHO as one of the inorganic constituents of significance to health. WHO recommended 50 ppb as a guideline value with the explanation that, based on available human health data, this concentration had not been associated with any adverse health effects. In 1993, WHO lowered its guideline for arsenic in drinking water to 10 ppb. The WHO noted the fact that inorganic arsenic compounds are classified by the International Agency for Research on Cancer (IARC) in Group 1 (carcinogenic to humans) on the basis of sufficient evidence for carcinogenicity in humans and limited evidence for carcinogenicity in animals. Based on data from Taiwan and using an EPA risk assessment, WHO estimated the lifetime risk of skin cancer to be greater than 1 in 100,000 even in a population ingesting far less than 10 ppb of arsenic. However, because 10 ppb was deemed the practical quantification limit for arsenic in drinking water, it was selected as the guideline level even though skin cancer risks at this level of exposure were estimated to be 6 in 10,000.

In a number of countries, the WHO provisional guideline of 10 ppb has been adopted as the standard. Japan adopted this standard in 1993. The European Union endorsed it in 1998. Australia has a standard of 7 ppb. Many other countries have retained the earlier WHO guideline of 50 ppb as their national standard, including China, India, and Bangladesh. Canada's standard is 25 ppb.

In the United States, EPA established the current maximum contaminant level (MCL) for arsenic in drinking water at 50 ppb as an interim standard in 1975, following enactment of the Safe Drinking Water Act (SDWA). This initial standard was set at the level recommended by the Public Health Service in 1943. While EPA in 1985 proposed to adopt 50 ppb as a permanent standard, it had not taken final action on this proposal when the 1986 Amendments to the Safe Drinking Water Act converted the interim standard into a national primary drinking water regulation, which was to be revised within three years. EPA missed the 1989 deadline for revising the arsenic standard, in part due to disagreements over agency risk assessments for arsenic. A citizen suit, which was filed to require EPA to revise the standard, was settled by consent decree, which extended the deadline to 1995 as controversy continued over EPA's assessments of arsenic risks.

The Wall Street Journal reports that mining companies made extensive efforts to influence scientific assessments of arsenic risks during the 1990s. Peter Waldman, All Agree Arsenic Kills; The Question Is How Much It Takes to Do So, Wall St. J., April 19, 2001, p. A1. Faced with billions of dollars in cleanup costs under the Superfund program, the mining industry hired numerous scientists in an effort to demonstrate that there was a safe threshold for human exposure to arsenic. In 1990 Professor Richard Wilson of Harvard was hired by Atlantic Richfield (ARCO), owner of the Anaconda mining complex, to demonstrate that low levels of arsenic were not carcinogenic to humans. However, after he encountered epidemiological data linking arsenic exposures to lung, bladder, and kidney cancers, he recommended that EPA set more stringent limits on arsenic. ARCO then canceled the research project and barred Wilson and others from publishing their results. Id., at A8. Corporate interests then helped fund an arsenic task force within the Society of Environmental Geochemistry and Health, which sponsored biannual international conferences on arsenic beginning in 1993. Although EPA co-sponsored the task force, some independent scientists viewed it as an industry effort to disrupt the regulatory process. Id. In an effort to counter epidemiological data from Taiwan, an industry consultant published a paper in 1995 ostensibly co-authored by the author of the previous Taiwanese studies. Dr. Chien-Jen Chen, the author of the Taiwanese studies "was shocked . . . to learn that his data had been improperly manipulated in a paper under his own name," id. In 1996 after new epidemiological data from Chile showed high risks from human exposure to arsenic, ARCO sought unsuccessfully to hire the Chilean researchers "to do research to show the EPA that the impact of arsenic was not as high as was claimed." Id.

In August 1996, Congress enacted the Safe Drinking Water Act Amendments of 1996. As discussed in the casebook (p. 479), these amendments significantly qualified the SDWA's feasibility-limited approach to regulation by directing EPA to analyze the costs and benefits of proposed MCLs and by permitting the agency to deviate from the maximum feasible level in setting MCLs if the agency finds that their benefits "would not justify the costs of complying with the level." 42 U.S.C. § 300g-1(b)(6)(A). In such circumstances EPA is authorized to set the MCL at the level "that maximizes health risk reduction benefits at a cost that is justified by the benefits." Id.

The 1996 SDWA Amendments required EPA to promulgate a new national primary drinking water regulation for arsenic by June 22, 2001. 42 U.S.C. § 300g-1(b)(12). Recognizing that considerable uncertainty surrounded estimates of human health risks from exposure to arsenic, Congress directed EPA, in consultation with the National Academy of Sciences (NAS), first to develop a comprehensive plan of study "to reduce the uncertainty in assessing health risks associated with exposure to low levels of arsenic." The amendments required the EPA Administrator to propose a national primary drinking water regulation for arsenic by January 1, 2000, and to promulgate final regulations by January 1, 2001.

EPA asked the NAS to conduct a study of the human health risks associated with low levels of arsenic in drinking water. On March 23, 1999, the NAS's National Research Council released its report. National Research Council, Arsenic in Drinking Water (1999). The report recommended that EPA develop a stricter standard for allowable levels of arsenic in the nation's drinking water as soon as possible. The report noted that while arsenic in drinking water has been associated with skin cancer and other disorders, recent studies suggest that it also can lead to bladder and lung cancer, which are more likely to be fatal.

The committee examined clinical studies and epidemiological data from several international studies, including research from Taiwan, Argentina, and Chile. These studies show that in addition to causing skin, bladder, and lung cancer, consuming arsenic in drinking water also can cause skin lesions, anemia, nerve damage, and circulatory problems. Studies examining males who daily consume water that contains 50 micrograms of arsenic per liter show that they have about a 1 in 1,000 risk of developing bladder cancer. However, the choice of models used to estimate risks posed by arsenic can significantly affect risk estimates. Linear dose-response models assume that there is some risk at every level of exposure, but some scientists believe that small amounts of arsenic actually could be beneficial to humans. However, the NRC report noted that arsenic has not been tested as an essential nutrient for humans, and no evidence suggests that arsenic is required for any human biochemical processes.

Arsenic is readily absorbed from the gastrointestinal tract to the blood. The mechanisms through which arsenic causes cancer are not well-understood, but data suggest that arsenic probably causes chromosomal abnormalities that lead to cancer. Sensitivity to arsenic's toxic effects — including carcinogenic effects — varies with each individual and appears to be influenced by such factors as nutrition and genetic susceptibility. No human studies of sufficient scope in the United States have directly examined whether regular consumption of arsenic in drinking water at EPA's current standard increases the risk of cancer or other adverse health effects. Rather, the NRC committee's characterization of risk was based on findings from the international studies, experimental data on the mechanisms through which arsenic causes cancer, and available information on human susceptibility.

However, the committee noted that there were problems in applying the data from the international studies. The studies measured exposure to arsenic in drinking water regionally, rather than assessing the amount of arsenic to which each individual was exposed. Moreover, most people in these studies were exposed to concentrations of more than 100 micrograms of arsenic per liter of water. While the committee concluded that more research is needed to assess how exposure to very small amounts of arsenic affects human health, these uncertainties did not change its finding that exposure to arsenic in drinking water increases risks for developing bladder and lung cancer.

In accordance with the requirements of the Safe Drinking Water

Amendments of 1996, EPA worked to develop a new standard for arsenic by focusing on the results of peer-reviewed health effects research, along with studies of treatment technologies, analytical methods, the costs and benefits of regulatory alternatives, and affordable technologies for small water supply systems. Long before the NRC report was issued, EPA had begun holding a series of public meetings with states, tribes, local governments, water utilities, and the public to solicit their views on how to develop a new standard for arsenic in drinking water. These included a two-day "stakeholder meeting" in September 1997, another meeting in February 1998 in San Antonio that immediately followed a two-day American Water Works Association (AWWA) workshop on inorganic contaminants, and a third meeting in Monterey, California in May 1998. At these meetings EPA outlined the requirements of the Safe Drinking Water Act Amendments, described its research activities, and discussed possible regulatory approaches and policy issues raised by the arsenic standard in order to solicit input and to obtain stakeholder involvement in the regulatory development process.

Following the issuance of the NRC report, EPA convened another two-day stakeholder meeting to discuss development of the arsenic standard in June 1999. EPA explained that it was scheduled to propose the arsenic rule by January 1, 2000, and to promulgate the final rule by January 1, 2001.

EPA missed the January 2000 deadline for proposing a new arsenic standard. In February 2000, the Natural Resources Defense Council issued a report entitled "Arsenic and Old Laws: A Scientific and Public Health Analysis of Arsenic Occurrence in Drinking Water, Its Health Effects, and EPA's Outdated Arsenic Tap Water Standard." The report, which is available at http://www.nrdc.org/water/drinking/arsenic/aolinx.asp estimated that more than 34 million Americans drink tap water supplied by systems containing average levels of arsenic that pose unacceptable cancer risks. While noting that drinking water provided by most water utility companies meets or falls below the current 50 ppb standard, NRDC argued that the standard was outdated because it was established in 1942, before health officials knew that arsenic causes cancer. Based on data in the NRC report, NRDC estimated the lifetime risks of dying of cancer from arsenic in tap water as indicated in Table 1 on page 127.

Table 1.
NRDC'S ESTIMATES OF LIFETIME RISKS OF
DYING OF CANCER FROM INGESTING
ARSENIC IN DRINKING WATER
BASED ON DATA IN
NATIONAL RESEARCH COUNCIL REPORT

Arsenic Level in Tap Water	Approximate Total Cancer Risk
0.5 ppb	1 in 10,000
1 ppb	1 in 5,000
3 ppb	1 in 1,667
4 ppb	1 in 1,250
5 ppb	1 in 1,000
10 ppb	1 in 500
20 ppb	1 in 250
25 ppb	1 in 200
50 ppb	1 in 100

EPA worked extensively with the U.S. Geological Survey (USGS) to gather data on levels of arsenic in ground water. Arsenic analyses were collected from approximately 18,500 sites throughout the U.S., including wells used for public supply, research, agriculture, industry and domestic supply (which are not necessarily current sources of drinking water). Approximately 12% of the samples were taken from public supplies as defined by USGS to include wells used for bottling, commercial, medicinal, or institutional purposes, as well as individual homeowner's and public water utility wells. In May 2000, the USGS released a report analyzing the concentrations of arsenic in groundwater throughout the United States. U.S. Geological Survey, A Retrospective Analysis on the Occurrence of Arsenic in Ground-Water Resources of the United States and Limitations in Drinking-Water-Supply Characterizations (2000). The report found that while the large majority of groundwater samples contained less than the WHO guideline level of 10 ppb arsenic, approximately 10 percent of the samples exceeded this level. The highest concentrations of arsenic were found throughout the West and in parts of the Midwest and Northeast.

Chapter 4. Regulation of Toxic Substances

On June 22, 2000, EPA proposed to establish the aspirational maximum contaminant level goal (MCLG) for arsenic in drinking water at zero and to set the enforceable maximum contaminant level (MCL) for it at 5 ppb. The agency requested comment on alternative MCL options of 3 ppb, 10 ppb and 20 ppb. 65 Fed. Reg. 38887 (2000). EPA explained that 3 ppb was the lowest technically feasible level, but that the agency did not believe that the benefits of regulating arsenic at this level would justify the costs. In August 2000, the agency convened another stakeholder meeting, attended by more than 140 people in person and 40 people who joined the meeting by conference call. In response to its proposed rule, EPA received more than 6,500 pages of comments from 1,100 commenters.

Although the Safe Drinking Water Act Amendments of 1996 had required EPA to issue a final arsenic rule by January 1, 2001, Congress extended the deadline until June 22, 2001, the date one year after EPA proposed its regulations. The vehicle for this extension was language inserted into the conference report on the VA-HUD appropriations bill for Fiscal Year 2001. In January 2001, days before the Clinton administration left office, outgoing EPA Administrator Carol Browner adopted final regulations for arsenic in drinking water. The regulations set the MCLG at zero, as EPA had proposed. However, they set the MCL at 10 ppb, a less stringent level than the 5 ppb the agency had proposed. 66 Fed. Reg. 6976 (2001). While EPA had proposed to give small public water suppliers (those serving 10,000 people or less) five years to meet the new standard and large suppliers three years, the final rule gave all water supply systems five years (until January 23, 2006) to comply.

EPA's decision to set the MCLG at zero was based on its conclusion that any level of exposure to arsenic in drinking water could cause harm to health. While some commenters had argued that there may be a safe threshold level of human exposure to arsenic, EPA concluded that the most scientifically valid approach, given the lack of critical data, was to use a linear approach to assessing the risks of arsenic. EPA noted that because the available data point to several potential carcinogenic modes of action for arsenic, the dose-response relationship may be sublinear. However, because the data do not provide any basis upon which EPA could reasonably construct a sublinear dose-response curve, EPA concluded that it could not depart from its assumption of linearity.

Chapter 4. Regulation of Toxic Substances

The agency cited the NRC report's findings that available data that could help determine the shape of the dose-response curve are inconclusive and do not meet EPA's stated criteria for departure from its default assumption of linearity.

Recall that EPA's decision to set a zero MCLG for chloroform was struck down in *Chlorine Chemistry Council* (above) as contrary to the SDWA's mandate to use the best available evidence. In its final arsenic rule, EPA distinguished arsenic from chloroform in the following manner:

> In the case of chloroform, there was sufficient information to describe key events and undertake mode of action analysis. In the case of arsenic, the postulated mode of action cannot be specifically described, the key events are unknown, and no analysis of the remaining elements of the mode of action framework can be made. Several possible influences of arsenic on the carcinogenic process have been postulated, but there are insufficient experimental data either to show that any one of the possible modes is the influence actually at work or to test the dimensions of its influence as the framework requires.

> For chloroform there are extensive data on metabolism that identify the likely active metabolite. The key events—cell toxicity followed by sustained cell proliferation and eventually tumor effects—have been extensively studied in many experiments. The key events have been empirically demonstrated to precede and consistently be associated with tumor effects. In sum, a very large number of studies have satisfied the requirements of the framework analysis. By contrast, the arsenic database fails to even be able to satisfy the first element of the framework; the key events are unknown. While there are a number of possible modes of action implied by existing data, none of them has been sufficiently studied to be analyzed under the Agency's framework. For this reason the comparison of the "best available, peer reviewed data" for arsenic and chloroform shows quite different results. There are not sufficient data on arsenic to describe a mode of action as there were for chloroform. This was also the conclusion of the SAB review of arsenic.

66 Fed. Reg. 6976 (2001).

Chapter 4. Regulation of Toxic Substances

In its final regulations, EPA justified its choice of a 10 ppb MCL based on its discretionary authority under 42 U.S.C. § 300g-1(b)(6)(A) to set the standard at a level that "maximizes health risk reduction benefits at a cost that is justified by the benefits." EPA estimated that its MCL of 10 ppb for arsenic would prevent between 37.4 and 55.7 cases of bladder and lung cancer per year, as indicated in Table 2 below. EPA also estimated that the standard would produce significant non-quantified benefits by reducing cancers affecting other parts of the body, including skin, kidney, liver, prostate, and nasal passages.

Table 2.
ESTIMATED ANNUAL TOTAL
QUANTIFIED CANCER CASES
(Lung & Bladder Cancer)
PREVENTED BY 10 ppb MCL

Arsenic Level (ppb)	Reduced Mortality Cases	Reduced Morbidity Cases	Total Lung/Bladder Cancers Avoided
3 ppb	32.6 to 74.1	24.6 to 64.2	57.2 to 138.3
5 ppb	29.1 to 53.7	22.0 to 46.5	51.1 to 100.2
10 ppb	21.3 to 29.8	16.1 to 25.9	37.4 to 55.7
20 ppb	10.2 to 11.3	8.5 to 8.8	19.0 to 19.8

SOURCE: 66 Fed. Reg. 7009.

EPA estimated that the quantified benefits of the 10 ppb MCL in reducing lung and bladder cancers would range from $140 million to $198 million annually, as indicated in Table 3 on page 131. It constructed this estimate by applying a value of $6.1 million to each death prevented and a value of $607,000 to each nonfatal cancer case prevented. The $607,000 figure was derived from surveys showing that this is the average amount people would pay to avoid a case of chronic bronchitis, which the agency acknowledged might understate the value of avoiding a nonfatal cancer. The $6.1 million figure is the current "value of a statistical life" employed by the agency in performing cost-benefit analyses (in 1999 dollars), a figure EPA now indicates should be increased to $6.77 million in light of the growth in real income over time. Table 3 below shows EPA's summary of the monetized benefits of each of the alternative standards.

Table 3.
EPA'S ESTIMATES OF THE QUANTIFIED AND POTENTIAL NON-QUANTIFIED HEALTH BENEFITS FROM REDUCING ARSENIC IN DRINKING WATER

[$ in millions, 1999]

MCL level(ppb)	Total quantified health benefits	Potential non-quantified health benefits
3	$213.8-$490.9	Reductions in Skin Cancer,Kidney
5	$191.1-$355.6	Cancer, Cancer of Nasal Passages,
10	$139.6-$197.7	Liver Cancer, Prostate Cancer
20	$66.2 -$75.3	Cardiovascular Effects, Pulmonary
		Effects, Immunological Effects,
		Neurological Effects, Endocrine Effects

EPA estimates that the overall cost of complying with its 10 ppb MCL would be approximately $200 million annually. This estimate includes total annual costs for community water systems (CWSs) of $172.3 million and total annual compliance costs for nontransient noncommunity water systems of $8.1 million, as indicated in the Table 4 on page 132.

Table 4.
TOTAL ANNUAL NATIONAL SYSTEM AND STATE COMPLIANCE COSTS FOR VARIOUS ARSENIC MCLS
[$ in millions, 1999]

	CWS Discount rate		NTNCWS Discount rate		Total Discount rate	
MCL = 3 µg/L	3 %	7 %	3 %	7 %	3 %	7 %
System Costs	$668.1	$759.5	$28.2	$31.0	$696.3	$790.4
Treatment	665.9	756.5	27.2	29.6	693.1	786.0
Monitoring/Administrative	2.2	3.0	1.0	1.4	3.2	4.4
State Costs	1.4	1.6	0.1	0.2	1.5	1.7
Total	$669.4	761.0	28.3	31.1	697.8	792.1
MCL = 5 µg/L						
System Costs	396.4	451.1	17.3	18.9	413.5	470.2
Treatment.	394.4	448.3	16.3	17.6	410.6	466.1
Monitoring/Administrative.	2.0	2.8	1.0	1.3	2.9	4.1
State Costs	1.1	1.3	0.1	0.2	1.2	1.4
Total	$397.5	452.5	17.3	19.1	414.8	471.7
Final MCL = 10 µg/L						
System Costs	171.4	195.5	7.9	8.9	179.4	204.4
Treatment	169.6	193.0	7.0	7.6	176.7	200.6
Monitoring/Administrative	1.8	2.5	0.9	1.3	2.7	3.8
State Costs	0.9	1.0	0.1	0.2	1.0	1.2
Total	$172.3	196.6	8.1	9.1	180.4	205.6
MCL = 20 µg/L						
System Costs	62.4	71.4	3.5	4.1	65.9	75.5
Treatment	60.7	69.0	2.6	2.8	63.3	71.8
Monitoring/Administrative	1.7	2.4	0.9	1.3	2.6	3.7
State Costs	0.7	0.8	0.1	0.2	0.9	1.0
Total	$63.2	72.3	3.6	4.2	66.8	76.5

SOURCE: 66 Fed. Reg. 7011

For alternative arsenic MCLs, EPA estimated the annual cost per cancer case avoided using two different discount rates. The agency's upper-bound and lower-bound estimates are shown in Table 5 below.

Table 5.
ESTIMATED ANNUAL COST
PER CANCER CASE AVOIDED
FOR VARIOUS ARSENIC MCLS
(Combined Bladder and Lung Cancer Cases)
[$ in millions, 1999]

Arsenic level (ppb)	Lower-bound estimate	Upper-bound estimate
3 % Discount Rate		
3	$12.2	$5.0
5	8.1	4.1
10	4.8	3.2
20	3.5	3.4
7 % Discount Rate		
3	$13.8	$5.7
5	9.2	4.7
10	5.5	3.7
20	4.0	3.9

SOURCE: 66 Fed. Reg. 7018.

The costs of complying with the new standard are not evenly distributed across the country. EPA estimates that roughly five percent, or 3,000, of community water systems, serving 11 million people, would have to take corrective action to lower their current levels of arsenic in drinking water. Five percent, or 1,100, of the water supply systems in schools, nursing homes, and factories, serving approximately 2 million people, also will need to take measures to meet the new arsenic standard. Of all of the systems affected by the new rule, 97 percent are small systems that serve fewer than 10,000 people each.

EPA estimates that for small community water systems (those serving fewer than 10,000 people), the new regulations would increase costs per customer between $38 and $327. For community water systems that serve greater than 10,000 people, annual household costs for water were expected to increase from $0.86 to $32. EPA offered to provide financial assistance for these systems through its drinking-water state revolving fund program, which had funded $3.6 billion in projects to improve the infrastructure of drinking water systems. EPA also offered to give compliance period extensions of up to 9 years (resulting in a total compliance period of 14 years) to small systems through an exemption process.

After analyzing the costs and benefits of alternative MCLs, EPA concluded "that, based on comparisons of cost and benefits (using the various benefit-cost comparison tools discussed), the monetized benefits of a regulatory level of 10 μg/L best justify the costs." EPA noted that "strict parity of monetized costs and monetized benefits is not required to find that the benefits of a particular MCL option are justified under the [SDWA]."

On March 20, 2001, the Bush administration stunned the environmental community when it announced that it would delay the effective date of EPA's new standard for arsenic in drinking water. EPA published a notice in the Federal Register delaying the effective date of the regulation from March 23, 2001 until May 22, 2001, in order to give the administration an opportunity to reconsider the standard. EPA did not seek public comment prior to suspending the regulations. The Agency stated that "seeking public comment is impracticable, unnecessary, and contrary to the public interest."

Both EPA Administrator Christine Whitman and President George W. Bush described the decision to suspend the new arsenic standard as an effort to ensure that the regulation is based on "sound science." Douglas Jehl, EPA to Abandon New Arsenic Limits for Water Supply, N.Y. Times, March 21, 2001, p. A1. Peter Waldman, All Agree Arsenic Kills; The Question Is How Much It Takes to Do So, Wall St. J., April 19, 2001, p. A1. The Bush administration had been heavily lobbied to block the new arsenic standard by the National Mining Association,

Chapter 4. Regulation of Toxic Substances

Republican Senator Pete Domenici of New Mexico, and Utah Governor Mike Leavitt, who personally lobbied Administrator Whitman at a reception during inaugural weekend. Jeanne Cummings and John Harwood, Arsenic Issue May Poison Bush's "Compassionate Conservatism," Wall St. J., April 20, 2001, p. A16. In a letter to Administrator Whitman, which argued that the regulation would place an "excruciating financial burden" on water users in New Mexico, Sen. Domenici added a hand-written postscript: "No benefits, huge costs." Id.

The decision to reconsider the arsenic rule provoked considerable public outrage. Public opinion polls showed that it was intensely unpopular. Editorial writers harshly denounced it. The Democratic Party quickly filmed a television commercial attacking the decision by having a small child ask her mother for more arsenic. The former EPA official responsible for the rule during the Clinton administration denounced the decision as an "action [that] will jeopardize the health of millions of Americans" and that "compromises literally a decade's worth of work on behalf of developing a public health standard." Douglas Jehl, EPA to Abandon New Arsenic Limits for Water Supply, N.Y. Times, March 21, 2001, p. A1.

Representatives of water suppliers and the mining and wood preserving industries had a very different reaction. Nebraska Attorney General Don Stenberg praised the decision, noting that it could have cost nearly $100 million for Nebraska communities to comply with the new regulations. "People in these communities have been drinking the exact same water for 50 to 100 years, and we're not aware of any health problems as a result." Peter Waldman and John Fialka, EPA's Move to Rescind Arsenic Standard Is Welcomed by Those Facing the Cleanup," Wall St. J., March 22, 2001, p. A2. A spokesperson for the National Mining Association also praised the decision: "The Clinton administration rushed this out in the midnight hour. We felt all along that it was really a political decision unsupported by the science." Id. A spokesman for the American Wood Preservers Institute expressed "delight" at the decision to block the new regulations. Id.

Responding to public criticism, the Bush administration explained that it only had instructed EPA to review the new standard to ensure that it was based on sound science and accurate cost and benefit estimates. However, moderate Republicans in the U.S. House of Representatives later joined Democrats in adopting an appropriations rider to bar EPA from spending any funds to block the Clinton administration's arsenic standard from going into effect. This action, while a stunning legislative defeat for the Bush administration, will remain largely symbolic unless a similar provision is adopted by the Senate and incorporated into legislation signed by President Bush.

On April 23, EPA requested public comment on a proposal to delay the effective date of the rule until February 22, 2002. On May 22, 2001, EPA announced that it would delay the effective date for the rule until February 22, 2002 to give it time to complete its reassessment process and to afford the public a full opportunity to provide further input. On July 19, 2001, EPA issued a proposal to request comment on whether the data and technical analyses associated with the January 2001 arsenic rule support setting the arsenic standard at 3 ppb, 5 ppb, 10 ppb, or 20 ppb. In addition, the Agency asked commenters to submit new information for review.

Both the National Academy of Sciences' (NAS) National Research Council's subcommittee on arsenic and EPA's Science Advisory Board (SAB) Arsenic Benefits Review Panel have been holding meetings to reassess the agency's estimates of the benefits of the new arsenic regulation. EPA's National Drinking Water Advisory Council, which was asked to reexamine EPA's analysis of the cost of implementing the arsenic rule, completed its reassessment on August 21. The working group concluded that EPA's previous estimate of compliance costs was credible given the constraints the agency was operating under. While noting that there are considerable uncertainties in the development of national cost estimates, the working group made a number of recommendations to improve future cost estimates.

After the June 22, 2001 statutory deadline for issuing a new arsenic standard expired, the Natural Resources Defense Council filed suit against EPA in federal district court in Washington, D.C. The suit charges that the EPA has failed to perform a non-discretionary duty required by law. "The Bush EPA's suspension of the arsenic [standard] is a distressing, unscientific and illegal threat to the health of millions of Americans," Erik D. Olson, a senior attorney with the environmental group, stated when the suit was filed. Joining NRDC as plaintiffs were six Democratic Senators: Barbara Boxer, D-California; Hillary Clinton,

Chapter 4. Regulation of Toxic Substances

D-New York; Harry Reid, D-Nevada; Jon Corzine, D-New Jersey; Charles Schumer, D-New York; and Paul Wellstone, D-Minnesota. EPA Administrator Christine Whitman maintains that the agency will adopt a new arsenic standard that will take effect no later than the standard that had been established by the Clinton administration.

NOTES AND QUESTIONS

1. Should the Bush administration have suspended the Clinton administration's stricter standard for arsenic in drinking water? Now that the standard is being reconsidered by the Bush administration, at what level should the MCL for arsenic be set?

2. Is it fair to characterize the Clinton administration's arsenic standard as a "midnight regulation"? The regulation had been under development for several years, but Congress has extended the deadline for promulgating it until June 22, 2001.

3. Is NRDC likely to win its lawsuit against EPA for failure to promulgate a new arsenic standard by the statutory deadline? Can EPA argue successfully that it did in fact meet the statutory deadline by promulgating a new regulation, but that it now is free to reconsider the regulation since there is nothing in the statute that would prohibit such a reconsideration?

4. One of the major difficulties faced by EPA in assessing the risks of arsenic is the problem of gathering reliable epidemiological information on the health effects of low levels of exposure. How reassuring is the comment by the Attorney General of Nebraska that: "People in these communities have been drinking the exact same water for 50 to 100 years, and we're not aware of any health problems as a result"?

5. Did the public overreact to the Bush administration's decision to suspend the new regulation because it involved a substance widely known to be poisonous at high levels of exposure? In a paper analyzing the dispute over the arsenic standard, Professor Cass Sunstein observes that people are "intuitive toxicologists" who tend to believe that substances that cause cancer are unsafe and should simply be banned. This reaction, according to Sunstein, "does not accommodate the judgment that low levels of admittedly carcinogenic substances should some-

times be tolerated, because the risks are low and the costs of eliminating them are high." Sunstein, The Arithmetic of Arsenic (Aug. 2001) (Working Paper 01-10 of the AEI/Brookings Joint Center for Regulatory Studies). Sunstein argues that cost-benefit analysis should be understood as a way of moving beyond this "intuitive toxicology" to one based on data.

6. After analyzing the cost-benefit analyses performed by EPA and by industry groups attacking the arsenic standard, Professor Sunstein concludes that plausible alternative assumptions can lead to cost-benefit analyses findings that the arsenic regulation has net costs of $210 million or net benefits of $3.15 billion. Id., at 35. Sunstein notes that this demonstrates the wide range of uncertainty that can prevail when costs and benefits of difficult regulatory policy choices are estimated. However, he concludes that cost-benefit analysis can play a highly useful role in regulatory decisions and he argues that courts should be highly deferential to agencies' estimates of costs and benefits.

7. Consider the uncertainties in extrapolating from the Taiwanese epidemiological studies of arsenic risks. Both the NRC and EPA's Science Advisory Board endorsed the use of the Taiwanese studies, citing the following advantages: "mortality data were drawn from a cancer registry; arsenic well water concentrations were measured for each of the 42 villages; there was a large, relatively stable study population that had life-time exposures to arsenic; there are limited measured data for the food intake of arsenic in this population; age- and dose-dependent responses with respect to arsenic in the drinking water were demonstrated; the collection of pathology data was unusually thorough; and the populations were quite homogeneous in terms of lifestyle." But the data also had the following problems: "the use of median exposure data at the village level; the low income and relatively poor diet of the Taiwanese study population (high levels of carbohydrates, low levels of protein, selenium and other essential nutrients); high exposure to arsenic via food and cooking water, . . . confounding factors that may have contributed to risk may not be adequately accounted for."

8. A epidemiological study often cited by opponents of stricter regulation of arsenic focused on Utah residents and was published in 1999. It did not find any excess bladder or lung cancer risks after exposure to arsenic at concentrations ranging from 14 to 166 ppm. The

study estimated excess risk by comparing cancer rates among the study population, in Millard County, Utah, to background rates in all of Utah. Here is why EPA did not find the data persuasive:

> the cancer rates observed among the study population, even those who consumed the highest levels of arsenic, were lower, in many cases significantly lower, than in all of Utah. This is evidence that there are important differences between the study and comparison populations besides their consumption of arsenic. One such differ- ence is that Millard County is mostly rural, while Utah as a whole contains some large urban populations. Another difference is that the subjects of the Utah study were all members of the Church of Jesus Christ of Latter Day Saints, who for religious reasons have relatively low rates of tobacco and alcohol use. For these reasons, the Agency believes that the comparison of the study population to all of Utah is not appropriate for estimating excess risks.

9. Why did EPA decide that the benefits of its proposed MCL of 5 ppb would not "justify" the costs of complying with that standard? Why did the agency find that the 10 ppb MCL would "best justify the costs"? Does EPA's decision reflect an implicit judgment concerning how much it is worth to save a human life?

Pesticides and the Food Quality Protection Act
(pp. 493-97)

EPA's Office of Pesticide Programs continues to implement provi- sions of the Food Quality Protection Act (FQPA). One of the most significant features of the FQPA was a statutory requirement that the allowable amounts of pesticides permissible on various food and non- food products (tolerances) be reassessed under the "reasonable cer- tainty of no harm" standard. As of October 2000, the EPA had reas- sessed 3,551 tolerances, out of a total of 8,961. The product of these reviews has been to raise 183 tolerances, leave 1,688 unchanged, lower 146, and revoke 1,487. Karen L. Werner, Pesticides: Agency Clears Half of Priority Chemicals; Announcement Planned on 2002 Sched- ule, BNA-Daily Environment Report, March 8, 2001.

The FQPA established a statutory schedule for reassessment of the entire universe of tolerances, and on August 3, 1999, the date by which EPA was required to have completed the first third, the NRDC sued the agency, claiming that it was not meeting the deadline. On January 19, 2001, the last full day of the Clinton administration, the government entered into a consent decree with the NRDC. Id. Industry groups have objected to the terms of the consent decree, arguing that tight deadlines operate to provide EPA with an excuse for proceeding without a firm basis in science. Bush administration lawyers at EPA and Justice, however, concluded that the consent decree amounted to a binding contract that could not be disavowed. Karen L. Werner, Pesticides: EPA Amends Agreement with NRDC Following Talks with Industry, Growers, BNA-Daily Environment Report, March 21, 2001. Nonetheless, the EPA subsequently negotiated modifications of the consent decree providing for the consideration of new data by EPA, including human clinical studies and agricultural worker exposure studies that would not become available until November 1, 2001. Id.

Informational Approaches to Regulation (pp. 516-20)

Congress currently is considering a proposal to require school districts to disclose to parents the use of pesticides on school grounds. The measure was attached to the Bush administration's education bill while it is under consideration in the U.S. Senate. It would require schools to improve their pest management practices and to notify parents three times per year about the use of pesticides on school grounds. The Republican leadership of the House has vowed to kill the provisions, arguing that it would discourage pest control and add to paperwork and potential liability problems for schools. Eric Pianin, School Pesticide Measure Is Attacked, Wash. Post, July 19, 2001, p. A3.

Hazardous Chemicals and Counterterrorism Activities (pp. 531-38)

As a result of the terrorist attacks on the United States on September 11, 2001, the question of how to balance the public's right to know about hazardous chemicals with efforts to ensure that terrorists will not be able to profit from such information undoubtedly will receive more attention. Companies are now required to disclose information about hazardous chemicals under various laws, including the Emergency Planning and Community Right-to-Know Act (EPCRA), the Occupational Safety and Health Act, and the Clean Air Act. Section 112(r) of the Clean Air Act requires chemical companies to develop risk management programs (RMPs). Concern that terorists may use information generated by this law or by EPCRA to learn about hazardous chemicals present at industrial sites led Congress in 1999 to enact the Chemical Safety Information, Site Security and Fuels Regulatory Relief Act, Pub. L. 106-40. This legislation, which was signed into law by President Clinton on August 5, 1999, amends section 112(r) of the Clean Air Act to limit access to information in companies' RMPs about the offsite consequences of chemical releases. Information about possible "worst case" chemical accidents is now available to the public only in limited-access reading rooms where it is easier to monitor who is accessing the information and for what purpose. The legislation also removes flammable fuels used as fuel from coverage under the RMP program. While the legislation required the Justice Department to report to Congress on the safety precautions undertaken at chemical plants to prevent terrorist attacks, this report is now more than one year overdue, with no signs that it has become a priority for the Department. Guy Gugliotta, Agencies Scrub Web Sites of Sensitive Chemical Data, Wash. Post, Oct. 4, 2001, at A29.

As a result of the September 11th terrorist attacks, several federal agencies voluntarily have removed information about hazardous chemicals from their websites. EPA removed information about RMPs from its website and the Department of Transportation removed maps of pipelines and a study describing risk profiles for certain chemicals. Id. The U.S. Centers for Disease Control removed a "Report on Chemical Terrorism" that described the chemical industry's vulnerabilities to a terrorist attack. The reading rooms that contain information about "worst case" chemical accidents have not experienced any suspicious activity in recent months. Id.

EPA is involved in efforts to prevent terrorists from releasing hazardous chemicals into the environment and to prepare for responding to such releases. Three Presidential Decision Directives (## 39, 62, and 63) require EPA to participate in a federal response program designed to prevent and to respond to terrorist incidents. In the wake of the destruction of the World Trade Center by terrorists, EPA has been monitoring the air and drinking water in lower Manhattan to assess levels of asbestos and other contaminants in them. While EPA has been directed to ensure that public drinking water supplies are secure from terrorist attack, efforts to implement this program reportedly are years behind schedule. Greg Winter, E.P.A. Years Behind Timetable On Guarding Water From Attack, N.Y. Times, Oct. 4, 2001, at B7.

Expansion of the TRI to Nonmanufacturing Operations (p. 537)

In Note 3 on page 537 of the casebook there is a typographical error. At the end of the first sentence of Note 3, the words "toxic chemicals" should be struck and the sentence should continue with "major nonmanufacturing operations" as part of the same sentence. Thus, the first sentence of Note 3 should read: "The TRI initially did not cover major nonmanufacturing operations that release large quantities of toxics (such as incinerators, electric utilities, TSDs, the transportation industry, and mining operations)." As its name (Toxics Release Inventory) implies, the TRI at all times *did* cover releases of toxic chemicals.

- 5 -
Air Pollution Control

Problem Exercise: A Short-Term SO₂ NAAQS to Protect Asthmatics? (pp. 559-63)

EPA has not made a new decision on whether to adopt a short-term SO2 NAAQS to protect asthmatics, despite the agency's previous pledge to decide by December 2000. Because the Supreme Court was reviewing the D.C. Circuit's decision in the *American Trucking* case (p. 564), which had substantial implications for the agency's promulgation of any NAAQS, the American Lung Association agreed to extend the time for EPA to respond to the remand of the *American Lung Association* case (p. 563).

In January 2001, EPA published an informational notice in the Federal Register, 66 Fed. Reg. 1665 (2001), describing its progress in reconsidering a short-term NAAQS for SO2 The agency reported that it had received relatively little additional monitoring data from states on five-minute peak SO2 levels despite its request for such information. It pledged to intensify its efforts to collect such data and to encourage states to improve their ability to monitor short-term bursts of SO2. EPA noted that "the results of the data analyses completed to date continue to suggest that there may be a number of locations in the country where repeated exposures to 5-minute peak SO2 levels of 0.60 ppm and above could pose a risk of significant health effects."

The agency stated that it anticipated making a final decision on its proposed "intervention level program" (ILP) as an alternative to a short-term NAAQS during summer 2001. The proposed ILP would "assist States in determining whether 5-minute peak concentrations of SO2 posed a significant health risk in the local population, and if so, to identify appropriate remedial measures." EPA's proposed ILP would establish a concern level of 0.6 parts per million (ppm), 5-minute aver-age SO2 concentration, and an endangerment level of 2.0 ppm, 5-minute average. The agency's proposed ILP would require that state and tribal SIPs "contain the authority to take whatever action is necessary to prevent further exceedances of such concern and endangerment levels when the State/tribe determines that intervention is appropriate." EPA emphasized that decision will be made separately from the agency's response to the remand in *American Lung Association*.

Asthmatics and the American with Disabilities Act: The *Save Our Summers* Litigation (p. 562)

On June 15, 2001, the *Save Our Summers* litigation (casebook Question 8, p. 562) was dismissed by federal district judge Robert H. Whaley. The judge found that there was ample evidence indicating that agricultural burning disproportionately affected the plaintiff children because of their disabilities. However, he concluded that the state's failure to control or eliminate the burning did not constitute discrimination against the plaintiffs on the basis of their disabilities. Save Our Summers v. Washington Dept. of Ecology, NO. CS-99-269 (E.D. Wash. June 15, 2001).

> "The fact that disabled persons are disproportionately harmed by agricultural burning carried out by private individuals does not establish that Defendants are discriminating against these persons; instead, it just establishes that different people react to burning in different ways. Stated differently, the fact that Plaintiffs were harmed does not mean that this harm is the result of discrimination. Neither the Americans with Disabilities Act nor the Rehabilitation Act create a right in disabled persons to be free from the adverse health effects of private action. Instead, these statutes only create a right to equal treatment under the law. The only evidence in the record that Defendants treat Plaintiffs differently than non-disabled persons is that Plaintiffs are being injured by burning; there is no evidence that this disparate impact is caused by discriminatory animus or any other deliberate or reckless action taken because Plaintiffs are disabled. The Court concludes that this evidence is not sufficient to support a claim under the Americans with Disabilities Act or the Rehabilitation Act and, accordingly, grants summary judgement."

Id. at 2.

The court found that the plaintiff children "are deprived of meaningful access to public services and programs (such as roads, parks, and school) when burning occurs," but it found that this denial of access was caused by third party conduct and not by the state's own conduct. The court essentially determined that the state had no duty under the Americans with Disabilities Act and Rehabilitation Act to regulate polluting "activity to a level at which disabled persons were not harmed." The plaintiffs are appealing the district court's decision to the U.S. Court of Appeals for the Ninth Circuit.

[*Note to professors*: In the Teacher's Manual (p. 225), the answer given for Question Seven on page 562 of the casebook actually is the answer to Question Six. The answer given for Question Eight, which deals with the Washington state litigation brought by Save Our Summers, actually is the answer to Question Seven. The answer given in the Teacher's Manual for Question Six actually responds to a question that appeared in the second edition of the casebook, but which has been deleted in the third edition.]

Non-Delegation and the NAAQS:
The *American Trucking* Decision (pp. 563-70)

The casebook includes an excerpt from the D.C. Circuit's decision in American Trucking Associations v. EPA (p. 564). *American Trucking* involved challenges to national air quality standards issued by EPA under the Clean Air Act in 1997. The standards were struck down by the D.C. Circuit not because it found them to be unreasonable, but because it found that Congress had not been specific enough in telling EPA how to set them. The court's surprising rationale — that the Clean Air Act's directive to provide an "adequate margin of safety" could unconstitutionally delegate legislative power to the EPA — threatened to invalidate many other federal regulatory schemes.

When EPA appealed the decision to the Supreme Court., opponents of the standards argued that the Court could avoid deciding the non-delegation issue by reinterpreting the Clean Air Act to require EPA to set standards on the basis of cost-benefit analysis. In their view cost-benefit analysis could provide the "intelligible principle" the D.C.

Circuit had found lacking to constrain EPA's discretion and avoid non-delegation problems. However, for decades, the D.C. Circuit had interpreted the Clean Air Act not to permit EPA to consider costs when it set air quality standards to protect public health. That feature of the Act seemed so clear that even the D.C. Circuit judges who struck down the standards had quickly dismissed the claim that the EPA should consider costs when setting air quality standards.

Undaunted by legal precedent, industry groups assembled a legal *Who's Who* to author Supreme Court briefs assailing the Clean Air Act. Amicus General Electric hired Harvard constitutional law professor Laurence Tribe, who authored an impassioned plea for the Court to strike down the Act on non-delegation grounds. Dozens of the nation's most eminent economists filed an unusual amicus brief urging the Court to find a way to rewrite the law to require cost-benefit analysis.

However, on February 27, 2001, the Court unanimously rejected the legal assault on the Clean Air Act and reversed the D.C. Circuit in the decision reproduced below. The Court ruled that Section 109(b)(1) of the Clean Air Act was not an unconstitutional delegation of legislative power to EPA. In his majority opinion for the unanimous Court, Justice Scalia found that the "scope of discretion" afforded EPA by the Clean Air Act was "well within the outer limits of our nondelegation precedents." The Court affirmed the lower court's decision that the EPA Administrator may not consider costs in establishing or revising national ambient air quality standards (NAAQSs). Justice Scalia noted that "Were it not for the hundreds of pages of briefing respondents have submitted on the issue, one would have thought it fairly clear that this text does not permit the EPA to consider costs in setting standards." The decision thus confirms the agency's long-standing interpretation of Section 109 of the Act as requiring NAAQSs to be based solely on considerations of health. While the Court rejected EPA's interpretation of a portion of the Act (Part D of Title I) governing the schedule for implementing a revised ozone NAAQS in nonattainment areas, it remanded this aspect of the case back to the agency to develop a new interpretation of the provision.

Chapter 5. Air Pollution Control

Whitman v. American Trucking Associations,
531 U.S. 457 (2001)

Justice SCALIA delivered the opinion of the Court.

These cases present the following questions: (1) Whether §109(b)(1) of the Clean Air Act (CAA) delegates legislative power to the Administrator of the Environmental Protection Agency (EPA). (2) Whether the Administrator may consider the costs of implementation in setting national ambient air quality standards (NAAQS) under §109(b)(1). (3) Whether the Court of Appeals had jurisdiction to review the EPA's interpretation of Part D of Title I of the CAA, 42 U.S.C. § 7501-7515, with respect to implementing the revised ozone NAAQS. (4) If so, whether the EPA's interpretation of that part was permissible.
. . .

II

In *Lead Industries Assn., Inc.* v. *EPA, supra,* at 1148, the District of Columbia Circuit held that "economic considerations [may] play no part in the promulgation of ambient air quality standards under Section 109" of the CAA. In the present cases, the court adhered to that holding, 175 F.3d, at 1040-1041, as it had done on many other occasions. See, *e.g., American Lung Assn.* v. *EPA*, 134 F.3d 388, 389 (1998); *NRDC* v. *Administrator, EPA*, 902 F.2d 962, 973 (1990), vacated in part on other grounds, *NRDC* v. *EPA*, 921 F.2d 326 (CADC 1991); *American Petroleum Institute* v. *Costle*, 665 F.2d 1176, 1185 (1981). Respondents argue that these decisions are incorrect. We disagree; and since the first step in assessing whether a statute delegates legislative power is to determine what authority the statute confers, we address that issue of interpretation first and reach respondents' constitutional arguments in Part III, *infra.*

Section 109(b)(1) instructs the EPA to set primary ambient air quality standards "the attainment and maintenance of which . . . are requisite to protect the public health" with "an adequate margin of safety." 42 U.S.C. § 7409(b)(1). Were it not for the hundreds of pages of briefing respondents have submitted on the issue, one would have thought it fairly clear that this text does not permit the EPA to consider costs in setting the standards. The language, as one scholar has noted, "is absolute." D. Currie, Air Pollution: Federal Law and Analysis 4-15 (1981). The EPA, "based on" the information about health effects contained in the technical "criteria" documents compiled under §108(a)(2), 42 U.S.C. § 7408(a)(2), is to identify the maximum airborne concentration of a pollutant that the public health can tolerate, decrease the concentration to provide an "adequate" margin of safety, and set the standard at that level. Nowhere are the costs of achieving such a standard made part of that initial calculation.

Against this most natural of readings, respondents make a lengthy, spirited, but ultimately unsuccessful attack. They begin with the object of §109(b)(1)'s focus, the "public health." When the term first appeared in federal clean air legislation–in the Act of July 14, 1955 (1955 Act), 69 Stat. 322, which expressed "recognition of the dangers to the public health" from air pollution–its ordinary meaning was "[t]he health of the community." Webster's New International Dictionary 2005 (2d ed. 1950). Respondents argue, however, that §109(b)(1), as added by the Clean Air Amendments of 1970 (1970 Act), 84 Stat. 1676, meant to use the term's secondary meaning: "[t]he ways and means of conserving the health of the members of a community, as by preventive medicine, organized care of the sick, etc." *Ibid.* Words that can have more than one meaning are given content, however, by their surroundings, *FDA* v. *Brown & Williamson Tobacco Corp.,* 529 U.S. 120, 132-133 (2000); *Jones* v. *United States,* 527 U.S. 373, 389 (1999), and in the context of §109(b)(1) this second definition makes no sense. Congress could not have meant to instruct the Administrator to set NAAQS at a level "requisite to protect" "the art and science dealing with the protection and improvement of community health." Webster's Third New International Dictionary 1836 (1981). We therefore revert to the primary definition of the term: the health of the public.

Even so, respondents argue, many more factors than air pollution affect public health. In particular, the economic cost of implementing a very stringent standard might produce health losses sufficient to offset the health gains achieved in cleaning the air – for example, by closing down whole industries and thereby impoverishing the workers and consumers dependent upon those industries. That is unquestionably true, and Congress was unquestionably aware of it. Thus, Congress had commissioned in the Air Quality Act of 1967 (1967 Act) "a detailed estimate of the cost of carrying out the provisions of this Act; a comprehensive study of the cost of program implementation by affected units of government; and a comprehensive study of the economic impact of air quality standards on the Nation's industries, communities, and other contributing sources of pollution." §2, 81 Stat. 505. The 1970 Congress, armed with the results of this study, see The Cost of Clean Air, S. Doc. No. 91-40 (1969) (publishing the results of the study), not only anticipated that compliance costs could injure the public health, but provided for that precise exigency. Section 110(f)(1) of the CAA permitted the Administrator to waive the compliance deadline for stationary sources if, *inter alia,* sufficient control measures were simply unavailable and "the continued operation of such sources is *essential . . . to the public health* or welfare." 84 Stat. 1683 (emphasis added). Other provisions explicitly permitted or required economic costs to be taken into account in implementing the air quality standards. Section 111(b)(1)(B), for example, commanded the Administrator to set "standards of performance" for certain new sources of emissions that as specified in §111(a)(1) were to "reflec[t] the degree of emission limitation achievable through the application of the best system of emission reduction which (taking into account the cost of achieving such reduction) the Administrator determines has been adequately demonstrated." Section 202(a)(2) prescribed that emissions standards for automobiles could take effect only "after such period as the Administrator finds necessary to permit the development and application of the requisite technology, giving appropriate consideration to the cost of compliance within such period." 84 Stat. 1690. See also §202(b)(5)(C) (similar limitation for interim standards); §211(c)(2) (similar limitation for fuel additives); §231(b) (similar limitation for implementation of aircraft emission standards). Subsequent amendments to the CAA have added many more provisions directing, in explicit language, that the Administrator consider costs in performing various duties. See, *e.g.,* 42 U.S.C. § 7545(k)(1) (reformulate gasoline to "require the greatest reduction in emissions . . . taking into consideration the cost of achieving such emissions reductions"); §7547(a)(3) (emission reduction for nonroad vehicles to be set "giving appropriate consideration to the cost" of the standards). We have therefore refused to find implicit in ambiguous sections of the CAA an authorization to consider costs that has elsewhere, and so often, been expressly granted.

See *Union Elec. Co.* v. *EPA*, 427 U.S. 246, 257, and n. 5 (1976). Cf. *General Motors Corp.* v. *United States*, 496 U.S. 530, 538, 541 (1990) (refusing to infer in certain provisions of the CAA deadlines and enforcement limitations that had been expressly imposed elsewhere).

Accordingly, to prevail in their present challenge, respondents must show a textual commitment of authority to the EPA to consider costs in setting NAAQS under §109(b)(1). And because §109(b)(1) and the NAAQS for which it provides are the engine that drives nearly all of Title I of the CAA, 42 U.S.C. § 7401-7515, that textual commitment must be a clear one. Congress, we have held, does not alter the fundamental details of a regulatory scheme in vague terms or ancillary provisions—it does not, one might say, hide elephants in mouseholes. See *MCI Telecommunications Corp.* v. *American Telephone & Telegraph Co.*, 512 U.S. 218, 231 (1994); *FDA* v. *Brown & Williamson Tobacco Corp., supra*, at 159-160. Respondents' textual arguments ultimately founder upon this principle.

Their first claim is that §109(b)(1)'s terms "adequate margin" and "requisite" leave room to pad health effects with cost concerns. Just as we found it "highly unlikely that Congress would leave the determination of whether an industry will be entirely, or even substantially, rate-regulated to agency discretion—and even more unlikely that it would achieve that through such a subtle device as permission to 'modify' rate-filing requirements," *MCI Telecommunications Corp.* v. *American Telephone & Telegraph Co., supra*, at 231, so also we find it implausible that Congress would give to the EPA through these modest words the power to determine whether implementation costs should moderate national air quality standards. Accord *Christensen* v. *Harris County*, 529 U.S. 576, 590, n. (2000) (Scalia, J., concurring in part and concurring in judgment) ("The implausibility of Congress's leaving a highly significant issue unaddressed (and thus 'delegating' its resolution to the administering agency) is assuredly one of the factors to be considered in determining whether there is ambiguity" (emphasis deleted)).

The same defect inheres in respondents' next two arguments: that while the Administrator's judgment about what is requisite to protect the public health must be "based on [the] criteria" documents developed under §108(a)(2), see §109(b)(1), it need not be based *solely* on those criteria; and that those criteria themselves, while they must include "effects on public health or welfare which may be expected from the presence of such pollutant in the ambient air," are not necessarily *limited* to those effects. Even if we were to concede those premises, we still would not conclude that one of the unenumerated factors that the agency can consider in developing and applying the criteria is cost of implementation. That factor is *both* so indirectly related to public health *and* so full of potential for canceling the conclusions drawn from direct health effects that it would surely have been expressly mentioned in §§108 and 109 had Congress meant it to be considered. Yet while those provisions describe in detail how the health effects of pollutants in the ambient air are to be calculated and given effect, see §108(a)(2), they say not a word about costs.

Respondents point, finally, to a number of provisions in the CAA that *do* require attainment cost data to be generated. Section 108(b)(1), for example, instructs the Administrator to "issue to the States," simultaneously with the criteria documents, "information on air pollution control techniques, which information shall include data relating to the cost of installation and operation." 42 U.S.C. § 7408(b)(1). And §109(d)(2)(C)(iv) requires the Clean Air Scientific Advisory Committee to "advise the Administrator of any adverse public health, welfare, social, economic, or energy effects which may result from various strategies for attainment and maintenance" of NAAQS. 42 U.S.C. § 7409(d)(2)(C)(iv). Respondents argue that these provisions make no sense unless costs are to be considered in setting the NAAQS. That is not so. These provisions enable the Administrator to assist the States in carrying out their statutory role as primary *implementers* of the NAAQS. It is to the States that the Act assigns initial and primary responsibility for deciding what emissions reductions will be required from which sources. See 42 U.S.C. § 7407(a), 7410 (giving States the duty of developing implementation plans). It would be impossible to perform that task intelligently without considering which abatement technologies are most efficient, and most economically feasible—which is why we have said that "the most important forum for consideration of claims of economic and technological infeasibility is before the state agency formulating the implementation plan," *Union Elec. Co.* v. *EPA*, 427 U.S., at 266. Thus, federal clean air legislation has, from the very beginning, directed federal agencies to develop and transmit implementation data, including cost data, to the States. See 1955 Act, §2(b), 69 Stat. 322; Clean Air Act of 1963, amending §§3(a), (b) of the CAA, 77 Stat. 394; 1967 Act, §§103(a)-(d), 104, 107(c), 81 Stat. 486-488. That Congress chose to carry forward this research program to assist States in choosing the means through which they would implement the standards is perfectly sensible, and has no bearing upon whether cost considerations are to be taken into account in formulating the standards.

It should be clear from what we have said that the canon requiring texts to be so construed as to avoid serious constitutional problems has no application here. No matter how severe the constitutional doubt, courts may choose only between reasonably available interpretations of a text. See, *e.g., Miller* v. French, 530 U.S. 327, 341 (2000); *Pennsylvania Dept. of Corrections* v. *Yeskey,* 524 U.S. 206, 212 (1998). The text of §109(b), interpreted in its statutory and historical context and with appreciation for its importance to the CAA as a whole, unambiguously bars cost considerations from the NAAQS-setting process, and thus ends the matter for us as well as the EPA.[4] We therefore affirm the judgment of the Court of Appeals on this point.

III

Section 109(b)(1) of the CAA instructs the EPA to set "ambient air quality standards the attainment and maintenance of which in the judgment of the Administrator, based on [the] criteria [documents of §108] and allowing an adequate margin of safety, are requisite to protect the public health." 42 U.S.C. § 7409(b)(1). The Court of Appeals held that this section as interpreted by the Administrator did not provide an "intelligible principle" to guide the EPA's exercise of authority

---

4. Respondents' speculation that the EPA is secretly considering the costs of attainment without telling anyone is irrelevant to our interpretive inquiry. If such an allegation could be proved, it would be grounds for vacating the NAAQS, because the Administrator had not followed the law. See, *e.g., Chevron U. S. A. Inc.* v. *Natural Resources Defense Council, Inc.,* 467 U.S. 837, 842-843 (1984); *Atlantic Mut. Ins. Co.* v. *Commissioner,* 523 U.S. 382, 387 (1998). It would not, however, be grounds for this Court's changing the law.

in setting NAAQS. "[The] EPA," it said, "lack[ed] any determinate criteria for drawing lines. It has failed to state intelligibly how much is too much." 175 F.3d, at 1034. The court hence found that the EPA's interpretation (but not the statute itself) violated the nondelegation doctrine. *Id.*, at 1038. We disagree.

In a delegation challenge, the constitutional question is whether the statute has delegated legislative power to the agency. Article I, §1, of the Constitution vests "[a]ll legislative Powers herein granted ... in a Congress of the United States." This text permits no delegation of those powers, *Loving* v. *United States,* 517 U.S. 748, 771 (1996); see *id.*, at 776-777 (Scalia, J., concurring in part and concurring in judgment), and so we repeatedly have said that when Congress confers decisionmaking authority upon agencies *Congress* must "lay down by legislative act an intelligible principle to which the person or body authorized to [act] is directed to conform." *J. W. Hampton, Jr., & Co.* v. *United States,* 276 U.S. 394, 409 (1928). We have never suggested that an agency can cure an unlawful delegation of legislative power by adopting in its discretion a limiting construction of the statute. Both *Fahey* v. *Mallonee,* 332 U.S. 245, 252-253 (1947), and *Lichter* v. *United States,* 334 U.S. 742, 783 (1948), mention agency regulations in the course of their nondelegation discussions, but *Lichter* did so because a subsequent Congress had incorporated the regulations into a revised version of the statute, *ibid.*, and *Fahey* because the customary practices in the area, implicitly incorporated into the statute, were reflected in the regulations. 332 U.S., at 250. The idea that an agency can cure an unconstitutionally standardless delegation of power by declining to exercise some of that power seems to us internally contradictory. The very choice of which portion of the power to exercise—that is to say, the prescription of the standard that Congress had omitted—would *itself* be an exercise of the forbidden legislative authority. Whether the statute delegates legislative power is a question for the courts, and an agency's voluntary self-denial has no bearing upon the answer.

We agree with the Solicitor General that the text of §109(b)(1) of the CAA at a minimum requires that "[f]or a discrete set of pollutants and based on published air quality criteria that reflect the latest scientific knowledge, [the] EPA must establish uniform national standards at a level that is requisite to protect public health from the adverse effects of the pollutant in the ambient air." Tr. of Oral Arg. in No. 99-1257, p. 5. Requisite, in turn, "mean[s] sufficient, but not more than necessary." *Id.*, at 7. These limits on the EPA's discretion are strikingly similar to the ones we approved in *Touby* v. *United States,* 500 U.S. 160 (1991), which permitted the Attorney General to designate a drug as a controlled substance for purposes of criminal drug enforcement if doing so was " 'necessary to avoid an imminent hazard to the public safety.' " *Id.*, at 163. They also resemble the Occupational Safety and Health Act provision requiring the agency to " 'set the standard which most adequately assures, to the extent feasible, on the basis of the best available evidence, that no employee will suffer any impairment of health' "–which the Court upheld in *Industrial Union Dept., AFL-CIO* v. *American Petroleum Institute,* 448 U.S. 607, 646 (1980), and which even then-Justice Rehnquist, who alone in that case thought the statute violated the nondelegation doctrine, see *id.,* at 671 (opinion concurring in judgment), would have upheld if, like the statute here, it did not permit economic costs to be considered. See *American Textile Mfrs. Institute, Inc.* v. *Donovan,* 452 U.S. 490, 545 (1981) (Rehnquist, J., dissenting).

   The scope of discretion §109(b)(1) allows is in fact well within the outer limits of our nondelegation precedents. In the history of the Court we have found the requisite "intelligible principle" lacking in only two statutes, one of which provided literally no guidance for the exercise of discretion, and the other of which conferred authority to regulate the entire economy on the basis of no more precise a standard than stimulating the economy by assuring "fair competition." See *Panama Refining Co.* v. *Ryan,* 293 U.S. 388 (1935); *A. L. A. Schechter Poultry Corp.* v. *United States,* 295 U.S. 495 (1935). We have, on the other hand, upheld the validity of §11(b)(2) of the Public Utility Holding Company Act of 1935, 49 Stat. 821, which gave the Securities and Exchange Commission authority to modify the structure of holding company systems so as to ensure that they are not "unduly or unnecessarily complicate[d]" and do not "unfairly or inequitably distribute voting power among security holders." *American Power & Light Co.* v. *SEC,* 329 U.S. 90, 104 (1946). We have approved the wartime conferral of agency power to fix the prices of commodities at a level that " 'will be generally fair and equitable and will effectuate the [in some respects conflicting] purposes of th[e] Act.' " *Yakus* v. *United States,* 321 U.S. 414, 420, 423-426 (1944). And we have found an "intelligible principle" in various statutes authorizing regulation in the "public interest." See, *e.g., National Broadcasting Co.* v. *United States,* 319 U.S. 190, 225-226 (1943) (FCC's power to regulate airwaves); *New York Central Securities Corp.* v. *United States,* 287 U.S. 12, 24-25 (1932) (ICC's power to approve railroad consolidations). In short, we have "almost never felt qualified to second-guess Congress regarding the permissible degree of policy judgment that can be left to those executing or applying the law." *Mistretta* v. *United States,* 488 U.S. 361, 416 (1989) (Scalia, J., dissenting); see *id.,* at 373 (majority opinion).

It is true enough that the degree of agency discretion that is acceptable varies according to the scope of the power congressionally conferred. See *Loving* v. *United States, supra,* at 772-773; *United States* v. *Mazurie,* 419 U.S. 544, 556-557 (1975). While Congress need not provide any direction to the EPA regarding the manner in which it is to define "country elevators," which are to be exempt from new-stationary-source regulations governing grain elevators, see §7411(i), it must provide substantial guidance on setting air standards that affect the entire national economy. But even in sweeping regulatory schemes we have never demanded, as the Court of Appeals did here, that statutes provide a "determinate criterion" for saying "how much [of the regulated harm] is too much." 175 F.3d, at 1034. In *Touby,* for example, we did not require the statute to decree how "imminent" was too imminent, or how "necessary" was necessary enough, or even – most relevant here – how "hazardous" was too hazardous. 500 U.S., at 165-167. Similarly, the statute at issue in *Lichter* authorized agencies to recoup "excess profits" paid under wartime Government contracts, yet we did not insist that Congress specify how much profit was too much. 334 U.S., at 783-786. It is therefore not conclusive for delegation purposes that, as respondents argue, ozone and particulate matter are "nonthreshold" pollutants that inflict a continuum of adverse health effects at any airborne concentration greater than zero, and hence require the EPA to make judgments of degree. "[A] certain degree of discretion, and thus of lawmaking, inheres in most executive or judicial action." *Mistretta* v. *United States, supra,* at 417 (Scalia, J., dissenting) (emphasis deleted); see 488 U.S., at 378-379 (majority opinion). Section 109(b)(1) of the CAA, which to repeat we interpret as requiring the EPA to set air quality standards at the level that is "requisite"– that is, not lower or higher than is necessary–to protect the public health with an adequate margin of safety, fits comfortably within the scope of discretion permitted by our precedent.

We therefore reverse the judgment of the Court of Appeals remanding for reinterpretation that would avoid a supposed delegation of legislative power. It will remain for the Court of Appeals – on the remand that we direct for other reasons – to dispose of any other preserved challenge to the NAAQS under the judicial-review provisions contained in 42 U.S.C. § 7607(d)(9).

IV

[The Court went on to find that EPA had misinterpreted the impact of provisions added to the Act in the 1990 Amendments (Subpart 2 of Part D of Title I) specifying implementation schedules for ozone nonattainment areas. The Court rejected EPA's claim that this issue was not properly before it because it found that EPA's "interim implementation policy" was sufficiently final and ripe for judicial review. Recognizing that some parts Subpart 2 may be "ill-fitted" for implementation of a revised ozone standard, the Court expressed doubt "that Congress clearly intended Subpart 2 to be the exclusive, permanent means of enforcing a revised ozone standard in nonattainment areas." In this respect the Court departed from the D.C. Circuit's interpretation of the impact of Subpart 2. However, while acknowledging the statute's ambiguity on this issue, the Court refused to defer to EPA's interpretation that Subpart 2 was entirely inapplicable to a revised ozone NAAQS because it deemed it unreasonable to think that Congress would let EPA render Subpart 2 nugatory simply by revising the ozone NAAQS. Thus the Court remanded this aspect of the case back to EPA "to develop a reasonable interpretation of the nonattainment implementation provisions" as applied to a revised ozone NAAQS.]

NOTES AND QUESTIONS

1. The Court unanimously rejects the D.C. Circuit's holding that an agency could cure an unconstitutional delegation of legislative power by developing an "intelligible principle" to confine its exercise of its discretion. In his opinion for the Court, Justice Scalia argues that "the prescription of the standard that Congress had omitted would itself be an exercise of the forbidden legislative authority." Noting that the Court

has only twice struck down statutes on nondelegation grounds, Justice Scalia found that the scope of discretion afforded EPA by §109(b)(1) is "well within the outer limits of [the Court's] nondelegation precedents." He did so even though he concludes that to avoid nondelegation problems Congress must provide more substantial guidance when it authorizes regulations that can affect the entire nation's economy. What such guidance does the Court find in §109(b)(1)? In light of this decision, what must EPA do in the future when deciding at what level to set the NAAQSs?

2. How does the Court compare the non-delegation issue in this case with the non-delegation challenge raised against OSHA's *Benzene* standard in *Industrial Union Dept., AFL-CIO* v. *American Petroleum Institute* (page 411 of the casebook)?

3. While the Court was unanimous in rejecting the notion that the Clean Air Act violated the non-delegation doctrine, some Justices had different views of how the doctrine should be interpreted. In a concurring opinion, Justice Stevens, joined by Justice Souter, argued that the Court should simply acknowledge that the power delegated to EPA is "legislative," but uphold the delegation as constitutional because it is adequately limited by the terms of the authorizing statute. Stevens and Souter maintained that neither Article I,§1, which vests "All legislative Powers" in the Congress, nor Article II, §1, which vests the "executive Power" in the President, purports to limit the authority of either to delegate authority to others. Thus, in their view, executive agency rulemaking "pursuant to a valid delegation from Congress is 'legislative,' but constitutional so "long as the delegation provides a sufficiently intelligible principle" for exercising that authority. By contrast, Justice Thomas argued in another concurrence that even delegations accompanied by intelligible principles may be struck down as unconstitutional if the significance of the decision is simply too great to enable it to be delegated constitutionally.

4. The Court apparently did not think that the question of whether costs may be considered in setting NAAQSs was even a close one. As Justice Scalia wryly noted, "Were it not for the hundreds of pages of briefing respondents have submitted on the issue, one would have thought it fairly clear that this text does not permit the EPA to consider costs in setting the standards." In a concurring opinion not joined by

any other Justice, Justice Breyer stressed that the Act does not require the elimination of all risk simply because it mandates a cost-blind standard-setting process. Citing the observation in Justice Stevens' plurality opinion in *Benzene* (page 411 of the casebook) that "the word 'safe' does not mean 'risk-free'," Justice Breyer argues that what is "requisite" to protect public health will "vary with background circumstances, such as the public's ordinary tolerance of the particular health risk in the particular context at issue." He maintains that the EPA Administrator has considerable discretion in standard-setting under the statute because she can consider estimates of comparative health risks, the severity of adverse effects, the number and distribution of people affected by a pollutant, and the uncertainties surrounding each estimate.

5. The *American Trucking* case was argued in the Supreme Court on November 7, 2000. While awaiting the Court's decision, EPA received significant support for its view of the scilished a study linking particulate levels to substantial increases in mortality rates. Laura Johannes, Study Shows Need for Tougher Air Rules, Wall St. J., Dec. 14, 2000, at B10. The study by Professor Jonathan Samet of Johns Hopkins University examined mortality rates in 20 U.S. cities following spikes in particulate pollution during the period from 1987 to 1994. It found that mortality rates increased immediately during the 24 hours following increases in particulate pollution. Unlike previous research, the study was able to isolate the effects of changes in particulate pollution from the effects of other pollutants.

6. The holding in Part IV, finding the relationship of the provisions governing implementation of revised standards and the provisions governing statutorily established compliance timetables to be ambiguous, is one of the few times Justice Scalia has ruled that a significant question of statutory interpretation was not clear, and hence could be decided at the first step of a *Chevron* analysis. The consequence of Part IV has been a remand to the agency to reconsider that relationship and promulgate a new approach to implementing the revised NAAQS. As of this writing, EPA is still engaged in that reconsideration.

7. Opponents of the revised NAAQS vigorously lobbied the incoming Bush Administration to reconsider the standards themselves, in addition to their implementation. In what one paper called "argu-

ably the biggest victory for environmentalists since President Bush took office," the President has signaled that it will retain the standards in their current form. Traci Watson, Bush to Keep Tough Air Rules, USA Today 1A (May 18, 2001).

8. The *American Trucking* decision indicates that the Court is loathe to extend its revival of dormant constitutional limits on regulatory authority to dismantle basic elements of the federal regulatory infrastructure. As the oldest, most established and arguably most successful federal environmental statute, the Clean Air Act was a particularly ill-chosen target for a non-delegation claim. The Court also was unimpressed with the tired old tactic of pitting the environment against the economy. Opponents of the Act argued that massive overregulation is inevitable if benefit-cost analysis is not used. However, when industry counsel told the Court at oral argument that "we can't live with" such a law, Chief Justice Rehnquist replied that we seem to have done pretty well with it for decades. The Court seems to have appreciated the notion that Congress intended for Clean Air standards to help stimulate the development of new pollution control technology when needed to protect public health.

SIP Calls, Section 126 Petitions and New Source Review Litigation (pp. 576-80 & 590-92)

The Environmental Protection Agency and the Northeastern States comprising the Northeastern Ozone Transport Commission (NOTC) continue to struggle with ways to lower ozone levels throughout the region. These efforts have illustrated the resourcefulness of the EPA in utilizing a variety of provisions of the Clean Air Act to address a single interstate pollution goal. One strategy was a NOx SIP call, which followed EPA's announcement of lower ozone NAAQS. See casebook, page 580. A second strategy involved responding affirmatively to petitions brought by some of the northeastern states under Section 126, which allows EPA to regulate directly upwind point sources that significantly contribute to air quality exceedances in other states. Id. A third involved bringing enforcement lawsuits against old utility power plants whose less stringent emission controls had been grandfathered under the original Clean Air Act Amendments of 1970, in part out of the expectation that they would be replaced by newer facilities subject

Chapter 5. Air Pollution Control

to New Source Performance Standards. Over the years, however, the owners of many of the older plants had repowered them, replacing old equipment with new, without going through the new source review process that would have subjected them to the stringent NSPS. As indicated on page 592, the EPA had long distinguished ordinary maintenance from the modifications that to an existing facility that would trigger NSR, and the utilities had relied upon that distinction in repowering their older facilities. There have been significant developments in each of these areas.

NOx SIP Call (p. 580). As mentioned in the casebook on page 580, the D.C. Circuit temporarily suspended the EPA's SIP call in light of its decision in American Trucking Ass'n remanding the ozone standard to the agency. The D.C. Circuit subsequently lifted its stay, and upheld most aspects of EPA's SIP call. Michigan v. EPA, 213 F.3d 663 (D.C. Cir. 2000). In order to achieve reductions in ozone in the NOTC, EPA had required that some twenty-two states revise their SIPs so as to reduce nitrogen by the amount that could be accomplished by applying to major NOx point sources controls EPA found capable of removing NOx at a cost of $2000 or less per ton. In Michigan v. EPA the court rejected industry claims that EPA could not call for the SIP revisions without convening a transport commission; that EPA failed to undertake a sufficiently state-specific determination of ozone contribution; that EPA unlawfully overrode past precedent regarding "significant" contribution; that EPA's consideration of the cost of NOx reduction violated the statute; that EPA's scheme of uniform controls is arbitrary and capricious; and that CAA § 110(a)(2)(D)(i)(I) as construed by EPA violates the non-delegation doctrine. However, the court did hold that the record did not support including Wisconsin in the SIP call, or in creating NOx budgets based on the entire emissions of Missouri or Georgia.

SIP Calls and Section 126 Petitions (p. 580). As noted on page 580, several northeastern states had filed petitions under Section 126, alleging that many of the same sources that are now subject to the NOx SIP call were causing ozone exceedances in the northeastern states, and hence were subject to regulation under Section 126. Originally, EPA chose to postpone final action on these petitions so that that action could be coordinated with the SIP call. Once the D.C. Circuit stayed the NOx SIP call, however, EPA revised its approach to the petitions

Chapter 5. Air Pollution Control

and proceeded to final action on them. The EPA established a cap and trade NOx reduction program, similar to the Title IV acid rain program, see pages 592-604, assigning NOx allowances to major sources and overall NOx budgets to each of twelve states plus the District of Columbia, based upon application of the same "highly effective controls" which EPA had included in the SIP call. The D.C. Circuit has upheld the vast bulk of EPA's 126 rulings. Appalachian Power Co. v. EPA, 249 F.3d 1032 (D.C. Cir. 2001). Petitioners had argued that the cooperative federalism approach of the Clean Air Act meant that EPA needed to give the states the opportunity to respond to the SIP call before EPA could directly regulate sources within the state. The court, however, found that the instructions of Section 126 were clear. A state's power to determine how to meet the NAAQS, which was recognized in Viriginia v. EPA (casebook, pp. 577 ff), was thus not "absolute in the face of Section 126, which contemplates that in at least some circumstances the EPA will directly regulate sources within a state." Id. Thus, while

> both the SIP call and the Section 126 rulemaking are directly linked to the requirement . . . that SIPs contain provisions prohibiting 'any source or other type of emissions activity within the State from emitting any air pollutant in amounts which will . . . contribute significantly to nonattainment' . . . the necessary determinations are different in at least two material respects. First, whereas the SIP call exercise yielded a total amount of NOx cutback for each state, which the state was then free to achieve however it might, . . . here the mandate applies directly to sources. Second, whereas [Section 110's] broad reference to 'any source or other type of emissions activity' supported SIP call findings based on aggregate emissions from within each regulated state, Section 126 demands that the significant contribution come from a 'major source or group of *stationary* sources.' (emphasis added) Appalachian Power Co. v. EPA, 249 F.3d at 1049.

The court then upheld EPA's basic methodology for determining whether emissions from single or groups of stationary sources were in violation of Section 126, although it did find that certain projections EPA had made for growth in electric power generation were unsupported by the record, and that EPA had failed to justify adequately why

161

it has chosen to classify facilities that co-generated both energy used in some industrial activity and electricity for sale to the grid as electrical generating units instead of nonelectrical generating units.

NSR Litigation (pp. 590-592). As noted in the casebook on page 592, EPA and the state of New York have filed lawsuits against several electric utilities, charging that the utilities modified coal-fired power plants without complying with the NSR and NSPS requirements. The utilities have strenuously contested EPA's interpretation of plant alterations that trigger NSR, claiming that it contradicts long-standing understandings by advancing "regulatory interpretations during litigation that are found nowhere in the statute or implementing regulations or even in guidance documents...The new source review enforcement cases [by introducing novel interpretations in litigation engage in] an enforcement strategy best described as 'lawmaking by litigation'." Peter E. Seley, Lawmaking Through Litigation: EPA's Gamble on New Source Review, 15 Nat. Res. & Env. 260, 260 (2001). Nothwithstanding, EPA has had a number of successes. In the closing months of the Clinton Administration, several utility defendants had reached agreements on the principles (AOP) of settlements with EPA. Virginia Electric Power Company (VEPCO) agreed to reduce significantly emissions of NOx and sulfur dioxide at a capital cost of $1.2 billion in addition to paying fines and underwriting supplemental environmental projects. Air Pollution: Virginia Utility Agrees to Major Reductions in NOx and Sulfur Dioxide at Eight Plants to Cut Transport, BNA, Daily Env. Rep. (Nov. 17, 2000). Under a phased-in, ten-year schedule, VEPCO said it will reduce its NOx emissions from 105,000 tons per year (tpy) to 30,000 tpy. Installation of modern scrubbers will also reduce sulfur dioxide emissions from a current level of 263,000 tpy to 82,000 tpy. Cinergy Corporation, a Cincinnati-based utility, subsequently reached a similar settlement agreement. In addition to paying fines and underwriting supplemental environmental agreements, Cinergy said it will spend $1.4 billion installing up-to-date pollution reduction equipment. BNA Daily Env. Rep. (Dec. 27, 2000). Both Cinergy and VEPCO also will convert several coal-fired plants to natural gas. Other utilities continue to contest the lawsuits. Duke Power Claims EPA Is Changing Definition of "Routine" Maintenance Unfairly, BNA Daily Env. Rep. (Dec. 28, 2000).

Industry insists that the NSR strategy has brought efficiency-improving maintenance to a halt, costing the nation significant amounts of additional electrical power. They sought to have the Administration's review of national energy policy include relaxation of the NSR strategy as one of its recommendations. The policy, released in May 2001, did not make such a recommendation, but EPA Administrator Whitman has been asked to head a group to review the NSR litigation enforcement and litigation strategy. Darren Samuelson, Air Pollution: New Interpretation in EPA's Court, Greenwire (Vol. 10, No. 9, May 10, 2001). The settlement negotiations proceeding under the AOPs that have been reached will probably not be concluded until the industry understands what the final position of the Bush administration will be on the strategy. Except for a concluded settlement with Tampa Electric, all of the cases EPA has filed are either in settlement negotiations after AOPs, or are awaiting court dates. Id.

In its May 2001 regulatory agenda, EPA expressed its intention to revise its NSR regulations to exclude from major NSR program requirements those activities that have little environmental impact and to give State, local, and tribal permitting agencies more flexibility. EPA expects that this will decrease the number of activities that are subject to NSR requirements and expedite the permitting process for those sources that are subject to NSR, reducing the regulatory burden over all industries. While the Bush administration expected to complete its review of NSR requirements in August 2001, it has postponed a decision until September, reportedly because of a split within the administration. EPA Administrator Christie Whitman reportedly favors continuing some of the NSR litigation initiated by the Clinton administration, while Energy Secretary Spencer Abraham wants the government to withdraw from at least some of the lawsuits. See Richard Perez-Pena, Possible Federal Pullout Clouds Northeast States' Pollution Suits, N.Y. Times, Aug. 20, 2001, p. A1.

Fuel Content (pp. 611-14)

After initially blocking Clinton administration regulations to reduce levels of sulfur in diesel fuels, the Bush administration announced in late February 2001 that it would let the regulations take effect. The new standards are designed to reduce pollution from heavy-duty trucks and buses by 95 percent, preventing an estimated 8,300 premature deaths and tens of thousands of cases of bronchitis each year. Producers of diesel fuel will be required virtually to eliminate sulfur from the fuel by the year 2010. Christopher Marquis, Whitman Backs Clinton Rules Designed to Cut Diesel Pollution, N.Y. Times, March 1, 2001, p. A15.

Alternative Vehicles (pp. 614-18)

As noted in the casebook (p. 615), California decided in December 1995 to suspend its requirement that 2% of the automobiles sold in its state be zero-emission vehicles (ZEVs) by 1998. In Association of International Automobile Manufacturers v. Commissioner, Massachusetts Dept. of Envt'l Protection, 208 F.3d 1 (1st Cir. 2000), the First Circuit struck down Massachusetts's ZEV regulations because they were no longer identical to California's in light of California's repeal of its ZEV mandate. The court held that the state regulations no longer fell within the Clean Air Act's preemption exception for standards identical to California's program.

- 6 -
Water Pollution Control

The Scope of Federal Authority
to Regulate Water Pollution (pp. 644-61)

In *Solid Waste Agency of Northern Cook County v. U.S. Army Corps of Engineers (SWANCC)* the Court considered whether Congress has the constitutional authority to regulate isolated wetlands used by migratory birds. The provision of the Army Corps of Engineers' definition of "waters of the United States" that extends § 404 jurisdiction on the basis of the use of waters by migratory birds was challenged in this case, which was an outgrowth of the Court's decision in *United States v. Lopez*, 514 U.S. 549 (1995). *Lopez* (casebook, pp. 129-30) had held that an intrastate activity must "substantially affect" interstate commerce before Congress could regulate it under its commerce powers. Relying on *Lopez*, the petitioner in *SWANCC* argued that Congress could not require it to obtain a federal permit under § 404(a) of the Clean Water Act before it filled an abandoned sand and gravel pit to create a landfill. The Seventh Circuit had upheld application of §404(a) to the isolated wetland, finding that because it served as habitat for migratory birds, substantial effects on interstate commerce could be inferred from the millions of hunters and bird watchers who travel interstate in pursuit of birds (casebook p. 661).

SWANCC involved land that had been used as a sand and gravel pit mine prior to 1960. Subsequently, the excavation trenches became permanent and seasonal ponds, and the entire area was overgrown. The county solid waste agency proposed to convert the site into a landfill. The Corps initially disclaimed having 404 jurisdiction over the site because it contained no wetlands. Later, it reversed its position upon learning that the site was visited by over 100 species of migratory birds. The Seventh Circuit found for the Corps in a challenge to the Corps' jurisdiction, and the solid waste agency sought and was granted certiorari in the Supreme Court. In the following 5-4 decision, the Supreme Court reversed.

165

Chapter 6. Water Pollution Control

Solid Waste Agency of Northern Cook County v. U.S. Army Corps of Engineers, 531 U.S. 159 (2001)

CHIEF JUSTICE REHNQUIST delivered the opinion of the Court.
. . .

Section 404(a) grants the Corps authority to issue permits "for the discharge of dredged or fill material into the navigable waters at specified disposal sites." Ibid. The term "navigable waters" is defined under the Act as "the waters of the United States, including the territorial seas." § 1362(7). The Corps has issued regulations defining the term "waters of the United States" to include "waters such as intrastate lakes, rivers, streams (including intermittent streams), mudflats, sandflats, wetlands, sloughs, prairie potholes, wet meadows, playa lakes, or natural ponds, the use, degradation or destruction of which could affect interstate or foreign commerce . . . ."

33 CFR § 328.3(a)(3) (1999).

In 1986, in an attempt to "clarify" the reach of its jurisdiction, the Corps stated that § 404(a) extends to instrastate waters:

a. Which are or would be used as habitat by birds protected by Migratory Bird Treaties; or
b. Which are or would be used as habitat by other migratory birds which cross state lines; or
c. Which are or would be used as habitat for endangered species; or
d. Used to irrigate crops sold in interstate commerce.

51 Fed.Reg. 41217. This last promulgation has been dubbed the "Migratory Bird Rule.". . .

Congress passed the CWA for the stated purpose of "restor[ing] and maintain[ing] the chemical, physical, and biological integrity of the Nation's waters." 33 U.S.C. § 1251(a). In so doing, Congress chose to "recognize, preserve, and protect the primary responsibilities and rights of States to prevent, reduce, and eliminate pollution, to plan the development and use (including restoration, preservation, and enhancement) of land and water resources, and to consult with the Administrator in the exercise of his authority under this chapter." § 1251(b). Relevant here, § 404(a) authorizes respondents to regulate the discharge of fill material into "navigable waters," 33 U.S.C. § 1344(a), which the statute defines as "the waters of the United States, including the territorial seas," § 1362(7). Respondents have interpreted these words to cover the abandoned gravel pit at issue here because it is used as habitat for migratory birds. We conclude that the "Migratory Bird Rule" is not fairly supported by the CWA.

This is not the first time we have been called upon to evaluate the meaning of § 404(a). In United States v. Riverside Bayview Homes, Inc., 474 U.S. 121 (1985), we held that the Corps had § 404(a) jurisdiction over wetlands that actually abutted on a navigable waterway. In so doing, we noted that the term "navigable" is of "limited import" and that Congress evidenced its intent to "regulate at least some waters that would not be deemed 'navigable' under the classical understanding of that term." Id., at 133. But our holding was based in large measure upon Congress' unequivocal acquiescence to, and approval of, the Corps' regulations interpreting the CWA to cover wetlands adjacent to navigable waters. See id., at 135-139. We found that Congress' concern for the protection of water quality and aquatic ecosystems indicated its intent to regulate wetlands "inseparably bound up with the 'waters' of the United States." Id., at 134.

It was the significant nexus between the wetlands and "navigable waters" that informed our reading of the CWA in Riverside Bayview Homes. Indeed, we did not "express any opinion" on the "question of the authority of the Corps to regulate discharges of fill material into wetlands that are not adjacent to bodies of open water . . . ." Id., at 131-132, n. 8. In order to rule for respondents here, we would have to hold that the jurisdiction of the Corps extends to ponds that are not adjacent to open water. But we conclude that the text of the statute will not allow this.

[The Corps' original interpretation of its jurisdiction under the 1972 Act — restricted to navigable waters — is inconsistent with its current view.]

Respondents next contend that whatever its original aim in 1972, Congress charted a new course five years later when it approved the more expansive definition of "navigable waters" found in the Corps' 1977 regulations. In July 1977, the Corps formally adopted 33 CFR § 323.2(a)(5) (1978), which defined "waters of the United States" to include "isolated wetlands and lakes, intermittent streams, prairie potholes, and other waters that are not part of a tributary system to interstate waters or to navigable waters of the United States, the degradation or destruction of which could affect interstate commerce." Respondents argue that Congress was aware of this more expansive interpretation during its 1977 amendments to the CWA. Specifically, respondents point to a failed House bill, H.R. 3199, that would have defined "navigable waters" as "all waters which are presently used, or are susceptible to use in their natural condition or by reasonable improvement as a means to transport interstate or foreign commerce." 123 Cong. Rec. 10420, 10434 (1977). They also point to the passage in § 404(g)(1) that authorizes a State to apply to the Environmental Protection Agency for permission "to administer its own individual and general permit program for the discharge of dredged or fill material into the navigable waters (other than those waters which are presently used, or are susceptible to use in their natural condition or by reasonable improvement as a means to transport interstate or foreign commerce . . . including wetlands adjacent thereto) within its jurisdiction . . . ." 33 U.S.C. § 1344(g)(1). The failure to pass legislation that would have overturned the Corps' 1977 regulations and the extension of jurisdiction in § 404(g) to waters "other than" traditional "navigable waters," respondents submit, indicate that Congress recognized and accepted a broad definition of "navigable waters" that includes nonnavigable, isolated, intrastate waters.

Although we have recognized congressional acquiescence to administrative interpretations of a statute in some situations, we have done so with extreme care. "[F]ailed legislative proposals are 'a particularly dangerous ground on which to rest an interpretation of a prior statute'." Central Bank of Denver, N.A. v. First Interstate Bank of Denver, N. A., 511 U.S. 164, 187 (1994) (quoting Pension Benefit Guaranty Corporation v. LTV Corp., 496 U.S. 633, 650 (1990)). A bill can be proposed for any number of reasons, and it can be rejected for just as many others. The relationship between the actions and inactions of the 95th Congress and the intent of the 92d Congress in passing § 404(a) is also considerably attenuated. Because "subsequent history is less illuminating than the contemporaneous evidence," Hagen v. Utah, 510 U.S. 399, 420 (1994), respondents face a difficult task in overcoming the plain text and import of § 404(a).

We conclude that respondents have failed to make the necessary showing that the failure of the 1977 House bill demonstrates Congress' acquiescence to the Corps' regulations or the "Migratory Bird Rule," which, of course, did not first appear until 1986. Although respondents cite some legislative history showing Congress' recognition of the Corps' assertion of jurisdiction over "isolated waters," as we explained in *Riverside Bayview Homes*, "[i]n both Chambers, debate on the proposals to narrow the definition of navigable waters centered largely on the issue of wetlands preservation." 474 U.S., at 136. Beyond Congress' desire to regulate wetlands adjacent to "navigable waters," respondents point us to no persuasive evidence that the House bill was proposed in response to the Corps' claim of jurisdiction over nonnavigable, isolated, intrastate waters or that its failure indicated congressional acquiescence to such jurisdiction.

Section 404(g) is equally unenlightening. In *Riverside Bayview Homes* we recognized that Congress intended the phrase "navigable waters" to include "at least some waters that would not be deemed 'navigable' under the classical understanding of that term." Id., at 133. But § 404(g) gives no intimation of what those waters might be; it simply refers to them as "other . . . waters." Respondents conjecture that "other . . . waters" must incorporate the Corps' 1977 regulations, but it is also plausible, as petitioner contends, that Congress simply wanted to include all waters adjacent to "navigable waters," such as nonnavigable tributaries and streams. The exact meaning of § 404(g) is not before us and we express no opinion on it, but for present purposes it is sufficient to say, as we did in *Riverside Bayview Homes*, that " § 404(g)(1) does not conclusively determine the construction to be placed on the use of the term 'waters' elsewhere in the Act (particularly in § 502(7), which contains the relevant definition of 'navigable waters') . . ." Id., at 138, n. 11.

We thus decline respondents' invitation to take what they see as the next ineluctable step after *Riverside Bayview Homes*: holding that isolated ponds, some only seasonal, wholly located within two Illinois counties, fall under § 404(a)'s definition of "navigable waters" because they serve as habitat for migratory birds. As counsel for respondents conceded at oral argument, such a ruling would assume that "the use of the word navigable in the statute . . . does not have any independent significance." Tr. of Oral Arg. 28. We cannot agree that Congress' separate definitional use of the phrase "waters of the United States" constitutes a basis for reading the term "navigable waters" out of the statute. We said in *Riverside Bayview Homes* that the word "navigable" in the statute was of "limited effect" and went on to hold that § 404(a) extended to nonnavigable wetlands adjacent to open waters. But it is one thing to give a word limited effect and quite another to give it no effect whatever. The term "navigable" has at least the import of showing us what Congress had in mind as its authority for enacting the CWA: its traditional jurisdiction over waters that were or had been navigable in fact or which could reasonably be so made. See, e.g., United States v. Appalachian Elec. Power Co., 311 U.S. 377, 407-408 (1940).

Respondents—relying upon all of the arguments addressed above— contend that, at the very least, it must be said that Congress did not address the precise question of § 404(a)'s scope with regard to non-navigable, isolated, intrastate waters, and that, therefore, we should give deference to the "Migratory Bird Rule." See, e.g., Chevron U.S.A. Inc. v. Natural Resources Defense Council, Inc., 467 U.S. 837 (1984). We find § 404(a) to be clear, but even were we to agree with respondents, we would not extend *Chevron* deference here.

Where an administrative interpretation of a statute invokes the outer limits of Congress' power, we expect a clear indication that Congress intended that result. See Edward J. DeBartolo Corp. v. Florida Gulf Coast Building & Constr. Trades Council, 485 U.S. 568, 575 (1988). This requirement stems from our prudential desire not to needlessly reach constitutional issues and our assumption that Congress does not casually authorize administrative agencies to interpret a statute to push the limit of congressional authority. See ibid. This concern is heightened where the administrative interpretation alters the federal-state framework by permitting federal encroachment upon a traditional state power. See United States v. Bass, 404 U.S. 336, 349 (1971) ("[U]nless Congress conveys its purpose clearly, it will not be deemed to have significantly changed the federal-state balance"). Thus, "where an otherwise acceptable construction of a statute would raise serious constitutional problems, the Court will construe the statute to avoid such problems unless such construction is plainly contrary to the intent of Congress." DeBartolo, supra, at 575.

Twice in the past six years we have reaffirmed the proposition that the grant of authority to Congress under the Commerce Clause, though broad, is not unlimited. See United States v. Morrison, 529 U.S. 598 (2000); United States v. Lopez, 514 U.S. 549 (1995). Respondents argue that the "Migratory Bird Rule" falls within Congress' power to regulate intrastate activities that "substantially affect" interstate commerce. They note that the protection of migratory birds is a "national interest of very nearly the first magnitude," Missouri v. Holland, 252 U.S. 416, 435 (1920), and that, as the Court of Appeals found, millions of people spend over a billion dollars annually on recreational pursuits relating to migratory birds. These arguments raise significant constitutional questions. For example, we would have to evaluate the precise object or activity that, in the aggregate, substantially affects interstate commerce. This is not clear, for although the Corps has claimed jurisdiction over petitioner's land because it contains water areas used as habitat by migratory birds, respondents now, *post litem motam*, focus upon the fact that the regulated activity is petitioner's municipal landfill, which is "plainly of a commercial nature." Brief for Federal Respondents 43. But this is a far cry, indeed, from the "navigable waters" and "waters of the United States" to which the statute by its terms extends.

These are significant constitutional questions raised by respondents' application of their regulations, and yet we find nothing approaching a clear statement from Congress that it intended § 404(a) to reach an abandoned sand and gravel pit such as we have here. Permitting respondents to claim federal jurisdiction over ponds and mudflats falling within the "Migratory Bird Rule" would result in a significant impingement of the States' traditional and primary power over land and water use. See, e.g., Hess v. Port Authority Trans-Hudson Corporation, 513 U.S. 30, 44 (1994) ("[R]egulation of land use [is] a function traditionally performed by local governments"). Rather than expressing a desire to readjust the federal-state balance in this manner, Congress chose to "recognize, preserve, and protect the primary responsibilities and rights of States . . . to plan the development and use . . . of land and water resources . . ." 33 U.S.C. § 1251(b). We thus read the statute as written to avoid the significant constitutional and federalism questions raised by respondents' interpretation, and therefore reject the request for administrative deference.

We hold that 33 CFR § 328.3(a)(3) (1999), as clarified and applied to petitioner's balefill site pursuant to the "Migratory Bird Rule," 51 Fed.Reg. 41217 (1986), exceeds the authority granted to respondents under § 404(a) of the CWA. The judgment of the Court of Appeals for the Seventh Circuit is therefore

Reversed.

JUSTICE STEVENS, with whom JUSTICE SOUTER, JUSTICE GINSBURG, and JUSTICE BREYER join, dissenting.

. . .

It is fair to characterize the Clean Water Act as "watershed" legislation. The statute endorsed fundamental changes in both the purpose and the scope of federal regulation of the Nation's waters. In § 13 of the Rivers and Harbors Appropriation Act of 1899 (RHA), 30 Stat. 1152, as amended, 33 U.S.C. § 407, Congress had assigned to the Army Corps of Engineers (Corps) the mission of regulating discharges into certain waters in order to protect their use as highways for the transportation of interstate and foreign commerce; the scope of the Corps' jurisdiction under the RHA accordingly extended only to waters that were "navigable." In the CWA, however, Congress broadened the Corps' mission to include the purpose of protecting the quality of our Nation's waters for esthetic, health, recreational, and environmental uses. The scope of its jurisdiction was therefore redefined to encompass all of "the waters of the United States, including the territorial seas." § 1362(7). That definition requires neither actual nor potential navigability.

The Court has previously held that the Corps' broadened jurisdiction under the CWA properly included an 80-acre parcel of low-lying marshy land that was not itself navigable, directly adjacent to navigable water, or even hydrologically connected to navigable water, but which was part of a larger area, characterized by poor drainage, that ultimately abutted a navigable creek. United States v. Riverside Bayview

Chapter 6. Water Pollution Control

Homes, Inc., 474 U.S. 121 (1985). [Our broad finding in *Riverside Bayview* that the 1977 Congress had acquiesced in the Corps' understanding of its jurisdiction applies equally to the 410-acre parcel at issue here. Moreover, once Congress crossed the legal watershed that separates navigable streams of commerce from marshes and inland lakes, there is no principled reason for limiting the statute's protection to those waters or wetlands that happen to lie near a navigable stream.

In its decision today, the Court draws a new jurisdictional line, one that invalidates the 1986 migratory bird regulation as well as the Corps' assertion of jurisdiction over all waters except for actually navigable waters, their tributaries, and wetlands adjacent to each. Its holding rests on two equally untenable premises: (1) that when Congress passed the 1972 CWA, it did not intend "to exert anything more than its commerce power over navigation," ante, at 7, n. 3; and (2) that in 1972 Congress drew the boundary defining the Corps' jurisdiction at the odd line on which the Court today settles.

As I shall explain, the text of the 1972 amendments affords no support for the Court's holding, and amendments Congress adopted in 1977 do support the Corps' present interpretation of its mission as extending to so-called "isolated" waters. Indeed, simple common sense cuts against the particular definition of the Corps' jurisdiction favored by the majority.

I

The significance of the FWPCA Amendments of 1972 is illuminated by a reference to the history of federal water regulation, a history that the majority largely ignores. Federal regulation of the Nation's waters began in the 19th century with efforts targeted exclusively at "promot[ing] water transportation and commerce." Kalen, Commerce to Conservation: The Call for a National Water Policy and the Evolution of Federal Jurisdiction over Wetlands, 69 N.D.L.Rev. 873, 877 (1993). This goal was pursued through the various Rivers and Harbors Acts, the most comprehensive of which was the RHA of 1899. Section 13 of the 1899 RHA, commonly known as the Refuse Act, prohibited the discharge of "refuse" into any "navigable water" or its tributaries, as well as the deposit of "refuse" on the bank of a navigable water "whereby navigation shall or may be impeded or obstructed" without first obtaining a permit from the Secretary of the Army. 30 Stat. 1152.

During the middle of the 20th century, the goals of federal water regulation began to shift away from an exclusive focus on protecting navigability and toward a concern for preventing environmental degradation. Kalen, 69 N.D.L.Rev., at 877-879, and n. 30. This awakening of interest in the use of federal power to protect the aquatic environment was helped along by efforts to reinterpret § 13 of the RHA in order to apply its permit requirement to industrial discharges into navigable waters, even when such discharges did nothing to impede navigability. See, e.g., United States v. Republic Steel Corp., 362 U.S. 482, 490-491, (1960) (noting that the term "refuse" in § 13 was broad enough to include industrial waste). Seeds of this nascent concern with pollution control can also be found in the FWPCA, which was first enacted in 1948 and then incrementally expanded in the following years. . . .

Section 404 of the CWA resembles § 13 of the RHA, but, unlike the earlier statute, the primary purpose of which is the maintenance of navigability, § 404 was principally intended as a pollution control measure. A comparison of the contents of the RHA and the 1972 Act vividly illustrates the fundamental difference between the purposes of the two provisions. The earlier statute contains pages of detailed appropriations for improvements in specific navigation facilities, 30 Stat. 1121-1149, for studies concerning the feasibility of a canal across the Isthmus of Panama, id., at 1150, and for surveys of the advisability of harbor improvements at numerous other locations, id., at 1155-1161. Tellingly, § 13, which broadly prohibits the discharge of refuse into navigable waters, contains an exception for refuse "flowing from streets and sewers . . . in a liquid state." Id., at 1152.

The 1972 Act, in contrast, appropriated large sums of money for research and related programs for water pollution control, 86 Stat. 816-833, and for the construction of water treatment works, id., at 833?844. Strikingly absent from its declaration of "goals and policy" is any reference to avoiding or removing obstructions to navigation. Instead, the principal objective of the Act, as stated by Congress in § 101, was "to restore and maintain the chemical, physical, and biological integrity of the Nation's waters." 33 U.S.C. § 1251. Congress therefore directed federal agencies in § 102 to "develop comprehensive programs for preventing, reducing, or eliminating the pollution of the navigable waters and ground waters and improving the sanitary condition of surface and underground waters." 33 U.S.C. § 1252. The CWA commands federal agencies to give "due regard," not to the interest of unobstructed navigation, but rather to "improvements which are necessary to conserve such waters for the protection and propagation of fish and aquatic life and wildlife [and] recreational purposes." Ibid.

Because of the statute's ambitious and comprehensive goals, it was, of course, necessary to expand its jurisdictional scope. Thus, although Congress opted to carry over the traditional jurisdictional term "navigable waters" from the RHA and prior versions of the FWPCA, it broadened the definition of that term to encompass all "waters of the United States." § 1362(7). Indeed, the 1972 conferees arrived at the final formulation by specifically deleting the word "navigable" from the definition that had originally appeared in the House version of the Act. The majority today undoes that deletion.

The Conference Report explained that the definition in § 502(7) was intended to "be given the broadest possible constitutional interpretation." S. Conf. Rep. No. 92-1236, p. 144 (1972), reprinted in 1 Leg. Hist. 327. The Court dismisses this clear assertion of legislative intent with the back of its hand. Ante, at 7, n. 3. The statement, it claims, "signifies that Congress intended to exert [nothing] more than its commerce power over navigation." Ibid.

The majority's reading drains all meaning from the conference amendment. By 1972, Congress' Commerce Clause power over "navigation" had long since been established. The Daniel Ball, 10 Wall. 557 (1871); Gilman v. Philadelphia, 3 Wall. 713 (1866); Gibbons v. Ogden, 9 Wheat. 1 (1824). Why should Congress intend that its assertion of federal jurisdiction be given the "broadest possible constitutional interpretation" if it did not intend to reach beyond the very heartland of its commerce power? The activities regulated by the CWA have nothing to do with Congress' "commerce power over navigation." Indeed, the goals of the 1972 statute have nothing to do with navigation at all.

As we recognized in *Riverside Bayview*, the interests served by the statute embrace the protection of " 'significant natural biological functions, including food chain production, general habitat, and nesting, spawning, rearing and resting sites' " for various species of aquatic wildlife. 474 U.S., at 134-135. For wetlands and "isolated" inland lakes, that interest is equally powerful, regardless of the proximity of the swamp or the water to a navigable stream. Nothing in the text, the stated purposes, or the legislative history of the CWA supports the conclusion that in 1972 Congress contemplated—much less commanded— the odd jurisdictional line that the Court has drawn today.

The majority accuses respondents of reading the term "navigable" out of the statute. Ante, at 11. But that was accomplished by Congress when it deleted the word from the § 502(7) definition. After all, it is the definition that is the appropriate focus of our attention. Babbitt v. Sweet Home Chapter, Communities for Great Ore., 515 U.S. 687, 697-698, n. 10 (1995) (refusing to be guided by the common-law definition of the term "take" when construing that term within the Endangered Species Act of 1973 and looking instead to the meaning of the terms contained in the definition of "take" supplied by the statute). Moreover, a proper understanding of the history of federal water pollution regulation makes clear that—even on respondents' broad reading—the presence of the word "navigable" in the statute is not inexplicable. The term was initially used in the various Rivers and Harbors Acts because (1) at the time those statutes were first enacted, Congress' power over the Nation's waters was viewed as extending only to "water bodies that were deemed 'navigable' and therefore suitable for moving goods to or from markets," Power 513; and (2) those statutes had the primary purpose of protecting navigation. Congress' choice to employ the term "navigable waters" in the 1972 Clean Water Act simply continued nearly a century of usage. Viewed in light of the history of federal water regulation, the broad § 502(7) definition, and Congress' unambiguous instructions in the Conference Report, it is clear that the term "navigable waters" operates in the statute as a shorthand for "waters over which federal authority may properly be asserted."

II

. . .

Even if the majority were correct that Congress did not extend the Corps' jurisdiction in the 1972 CWA to reach beyond navigable waters and their nonnavigable tributaries, Congress' rejection of the House's efforts in 1977 to cut back on the Corps' 1975 assertion of jurisdiction clearly indicates congressional acquiescence in that assertion. Indeed, our broad determination in *Riverside Bayview* that the 1977 Congress acquiesced in the very regulations at issue in this case should foreclose petitioner's present urgings to the contrary. The majority's refusal in today's decision to acknowledge the scope of our prior decision is troubling. Compare *Riverside Bayview*, at 136 ("Congress acquiesced in the [1975] administrative construction [of the Corps' jurisdiction]"), with ante, at 9 ("We conclude that respondents have failed to make the necessary showing that the failure of the 1977 House bill demonstrates Congress' acquiescence to the Corps' regulations . . ."). Having already concluded that Congress acquiesced in the Corps' regulatory definition of its jurisdiction, the Court is wrong to reverse course today. See Dickerson v. United States, 530 U.S. 428 (2000) (REHNQUIST, C.J.) ("[T]he doctrine [of stare decisis] carries such persuasive force that we have always required a departure from precedent to be supported by some 'special justification'").

More important than the 1977 bill that did not become law are the provisions that actually were included in the 1977 revisions. Instead of agreeing with those who sought to withdraw the Corps' jurisdiction over "isolated" waters, Congress opted to exempt several classes of such waters from federal control. § 67, 91 Stat. 1601, 33 U.S.C. § 1344(f). For example, the 1977 amendments expressly exclude from the Corps' regulatory power the discharge of fill material "for the purpose of construction or maintenance of farm or stock ponds or irrigation ditches, or the maintenance of drainage ditches," and "for the purpose of construction of temporary sedimentation basins on a construction site which does not include placement of fill material into the navigable waters." Ibid. The specific exemption of these waters from the Corps' jurisdiction indicates that the 1977 Congress recognized that similarly "isolated" waters not covered by the exceptions would fall within the statute's outer limits. . . .

III

Although it might have appeared problematic on a "linguistic" level for the Corps to classify "lands" as "waters" in Riverside Bayview, 474 U.S., at 131-132, we squarely held that the agency's construction of the statute that it was charged with enforcing was entitled to deference under Chevron U.S.A. Inc. v. Natural Resources Defense Council, Inc., 467 U.S. 837 (1984). Today, however, the majority refuses to extend such deference to the same agency's construction of the same statute, see ante, at 11-13. This refusal is unfaithful to both Riverside Bayview and Chevron. For it is the majority's reading, not the agency's, that does violence to the scheme Congress chose to put into place.

Contrary to the Court's suggestion, the Corps' interpretation of the statute does not "encroac[h]" upon "traditional state power" over land use. Ante, at 12. "Land use planning in essence chooses particular uses for the land; environmental regulation, at its core, does not mandate particular uses of the land but requires only that, however the land is used, damage to the environment is kept within prescribed limits." California Coastal Comm'n v. Granite Rock Co., 480 U.S. 572, 587 (1987). The CWA is not a land-use code; it is a paradigm of environmental regulation. Such regulation is an accepted exercise of federal power. Hodel v. Virginia Surface Mining & Reclamation Assn., Inc., 452 U.S. 264, 282 (1981).

It is particularly ironic for the Court to raise the specter of federalism while construing a statute that makes explicit efforts to foster local control over water regulation. Faced with calls to cut back on federal jurisdiction over water pollution, Congress rejected attempts to narrow the scope of that jurisdiction and, by incorporating § 404(g), opted instead for a scheme that encouraged States to supplant federal control with their own regulatory programs. S.Rep. No. 95-370, at 75, reprinted in 4 Leg. Hist. of CWA 708 ("The committee amendment does not redefine navigable waters. Instead, the committee amendment intends to assure continued protection of *all the Nation's waters*, but allows States to assume the primary responsibility for protecting those lakes, rivers, streams, swamps, marshes, and other portions of the navigable waters outside the [C]orps program in the so-called phase I waters" (emphasis added)). Because Illinois could have taken advantage of the opportunities offered to it through § 404(g), the federalism concerns to which the majority adverts are misplaced. The Corps' interpretation of the statute as extending beyond navigable waters, tributaries of navigable waters, and wetlands adjacent to each is manifestly reasonable and therefore entitled to deference. . . .

Because I would affirm the judgment of the Court of Appeals, I respectfully dissent.

NOTES AND QUESTIONS

1. How did the Court distinguish *Riverside Bayview Homes*? Compare the approach to statutory construction used in *Riverside Bayview* with the approach used in *SWANCC*. Why does the Court find that wetlands adjacent to navigable waters are covered by § 404 in *Riverside Bayview*, but that the isolated wetlands in *SWANCC* are not? Does the statutory language make any distinction between these two? The U.S. Army Corps of Engineers argued in its brief that the term "isolated wetlands" is potentially misleading. The Corps noted that while the term is used to refer to waters that are remote from and lack a surface connection to navigable waters, isolated waters may have other hydrologic connections to, and affect the quality of, traditional navigable waters, e.g., through groundwater connections and by playing important roles in flood and erosion control. Thus, the Corps maintained that its regulation "reflects an effort to identify categories of waters the degradation of which can be expected to have significant interstate effects, making protection of the relevant waters an appropriate subject of federal concern."

2. Why did the Court reject the Corps' argument for *Chevron* deference to its interpretation of the scope of its authority? Is the Court's use of *Chevron* in *SWANCC* consistent with its treatment in *Riverside Bayview*? See Michael P. Healy, Textualism's Limits on the Administrative State: Of Isolated Waters, Barking Dogs, and *Chevron*, 31 Env. L. Rep. 10928 (2001) (discussing the Court's use of *Chevron* in *Riverside Bayview* and *SWANCC*).

3. *SWANCC* was decided by the same 5-4 lineup that prevailed in *Lopez*. While the Court declined to reach the *Lopez* question by refusing to decide whether Congress had the constitutional authority to regulated isolated wetlands, how did the constitutional question affect the Court's ultimate holding in *SWANCC*? Does this provide any indication concerning how the Court would rule if it had to decide the constitutional issue?

4. Ironically, while the Court appears concerned about the federal government encroaching on state authority to regulate land use, the attorneys general of seven states (Iowa, Maine, New Jersey, Oklahoma, Oregon, Vermont and Washington) filed an amicus brief supporting the Corps' position in this case. Their brief argued that Congress had the constitutional authority to apply § 404 to isolated wetlands because

the placement of dredged or fill material in such waters was an economic activity that Congress had a rational reason to conclude substantially affects interstate commerce. While an amicus brief filed by the U.S. Chamber of Commerce portrayed the migratory bird rule as a federal intrusion on a quintessential state function – land use regulation – the attorneys general characterized it as an environmental regulation that protects states from the interstate impacts of wetlands degradation.

5. To avoid what it described as "significant constitutional and federalism questions," the Court held that §404(a)'s jurisdictional predicate — "waters of the United States" – did not include isolated wetlands where migratory birds are present. *SWANCC* thus narrows the reach of the federal Clean Water Act, while leaving important questions unanswered concerning the ultimate effect of *Lopez* on federal authority to protect the environment. It remains unclear how the "substantially affects" test is to be applied and whether Congress has lesser constitutional authority to protect the environment from destruction by noncommercial activities than by commercial ones. The Court appears reluctant to address these questions, for it declined to review two other important decisions narrowly rejecting similar constitutional challenges to the Endangered Species Act — Gibbs v. Babbitt, 214 F.3d 483 (4th Cir. 2000) (reproduced in the Teacher's Manual at pp. 318-27) and National Association of Home Builders v. Babbitt, 130 F. 3d 1041 (D.C. Cir. 1997) (casebook, pp. 912-23).

6. What is the practical impact of the Court's decision? There are at least two important aspects to this question. One is its effect on the scope of jurisdiction of the federal 404 program. A memorandum issued by the Association of State Wetlands Managers (which is available online at http://www.aswm.org/swancc/gis-swan.htm) notes that the impact of SWANCC on 404 jurisdiction depends upon subsequent interpretation of the decision. If the Corps and EPA were to continue to have authority to regulate navigable waters and their adjacent wetlands plus tributaries and wetlands adjacent to those tributaries, they estimate that the program would cover 40% to 60% of the nation's wetlands. The ASWM memorandum, which is available on-line, refers to this as the interpretation suggested by Justice Stevens's dissent and "the most reasonable interpretation of the decision." Do you agree? ASWM notes that the above estimate would be in the 60% range if "tributary" and "adjacent" are interpreted liberally, and in the 40% range if they are not.

7. The second important aspect of assessing the decision's impact is the extent to which states and localities have or can put in place their own wetlands programs, and how protective these programs will be. ASWM reports that fourteen states currently provide "considerable protection" for isolated freshwater wetlands, although a significant percentage of these programs are limited in their jurisdiction by wetland size (e.g., 12.4 acres in New York, 5 acres in Michigan). Little state or local protection is currently in place for some of the states with the largest percentages of the nation's isolated wetlands.

8. On January 19, 2001, the last full day of the Clinton Administration, EPA issued a guidance memorandum regarding the impact of the decision. This document is available online at: http://www.epa.gov/owow/wetlands/swancc-ogc.html.

9. Recall that the Court's justification for preempting the federal common law of interstate nuisance in City of Milwaukee v. Illinois, 451 U.S. 304 (1981) was that Congress "has occupied the field through the establishment of a comprehensive regulatory program supervised by an expert administrative agency." Id. at 317. If pollution of isolated wetlands causes harm to interstate waters, is the Court's rationale still valid? At oral argument, counsel for SWANCC sought to convince the Court that the decision in favor of his client would not have adverse environmental effects because isolated wetlands are extensively regulated by the states. He stated that a 50,000-page record had been compiled while his client tried to obtain state approval for filling the wetlands over which the Corps ultimately had asserted jusridiction.

10. After *SWANCC* was decided, the corporate defendant in United States v. Wilson, 133 F.3d251 (4th Cir. 1997) (casebook, pp. 651-59) sought to have its criminal conviction for intentionally violating § 404 overturned on the ground that § 404 no longer could be applied to the conduct for which it was convicted. In United States v. Interstate General Company, 2001 U.S. Dist. LEXIS 8061 (D. Md. 2001), the federal district court refused the company's request for a writ of error coram nobis. The court explained:

> The Defendants wish to have *SWANCC* read as having drawn a new jurisdiction line under the CWA. The Defendants believe that the Government's jurisdiction should now be limited to (1) navigable waters, as traditionally defined by the 1974 act, and (2) wetlands and other waters that are immediately adjacent to navigable

waters. Based on this new jurisdictional definition, the Defendants posit that the parcels of land in question located in Charles County, Maryland are not within the Government's jurisdiction as provided for by the CWA. The Defendants rely primarily on language in the *SWANCC* decision that addresses the states' rights in regulating its own land. Furthermore, the Defendants latch on to language by the court expressing a concern that the expanded definition of "waters of the United States" is rendering the definition of "navigable" meaningless. The Court rejects this interpretation of *SWANCC*.

The Government in their continued pursuit of the Defendants for prosecution, relied solely on their primary theory of the case (the adjacent/abutting land theory of tributaries impacting on navigable waters) which involved *33 CFR § 328.3 (a)(1)*, (a)(5), and (a)(7). The *SWANCC* case is a narrow holding in that only *33 CFR § 328.3 (a)(3)*, as applied to the Corps creation of the Migratory Bird Rule, is invalid pursuant to a lack of congressional intent. The *SWANCC* court specifically states that, "we conclude that the 'Migratory Bird Rule' is not fairly supported by the CWA." *121 S. Ct. at 680.* The *SWANCC* court chose not to determine the exact meaning of "navigable waters" as used in § 404(g) of the CWA. In doing so, the Supreme Court stated, ". . . it is also plausible, as petitioner contends, that Congress simply wanted to include all waters adjacent to "navigable waters," such as *nonnavigable tributaries and streams*. The exact meaning of § 404(g) is not before us and we express no opinion on it." *Id.* at 682. (Emphasis added). Because the Supreme Court only reviewed *33 CFR § 328.3(a)(3)*, it would be improper for this Court to extend the *SWANCC* Court's ruling any farther than they clearly intended.

Id.

Defining "Point Sources" Subject to NPDES Permit Requirements (pp. 662-79)

EPA has withdrawn a proposal it made in 1999 that would have amended its regulatory interpretation of the term "point source" to include some silvicultural activities that generate pollution. 66 Fed. Reg. 4550 (2001). EPA's proposal would have given the agency the authority to decide on a case-by-case basis whether activities associated with timber harvesting would require NPDES permits.

Chapter 6. Water Pollution Control

In December 2000, EPA issued proposed reviews to its NPDES permit regulations applicable to confined animal feeding operations (CAFOs). 66 Fed. Reg. 2960 (2001). The proposed regulations would extend NPDES permit requirements to a larger number of facilities by reducing the number of animals necessary to subject an operation to permit requirements, by co-permitting poultry processors who exert substantial control over growers and by applying permit requirements to poultry facilities that handle dry manure. CAFOs have been the target of many lawsuits under the Clean Water Act and state laws. In December 2000, a coalition of environmental organizations launched a coordinated campaign to force the corporate hog farming industry to comply with environmental standards.

Total Maximum Daily Loadings (TMDLs) (pp. 729-33)

In July 2000, EPA promulgated its final regulations governing the TMDL program, 65 Fed. Reg. 43586 (2000), shortly before an appropriations rider was enacted in an effort to bar the agency from spending any money to issue or to implement such regulations. The appropriations rider expires on October 1, 2001. The regulations issued by EPA were modified to remove some of the agency's most controversial proposals. These included a proposal to create an offset requirement prohibiting new or increased discharges into impaired waters by sources who failed to obtain offsetting reductions in discharges from other sources. Much of the EPA regulations focus on setting priorities for developing TMDLs, recognizing that the process will take a very long time to implement fully. States are required to develop lists of impaired waters using all existing and readily available water quality data and to set priorities and a schedule for issuing TMDLs. TMDLs are to be established for all impaired waters within 10 years of listing, though the state can get a five-year extension of this deadline if meeting it becomes impracticable. States must develop implementation plans, subject to EPA review and approval (as are the lists of impaired waters). If states fail to act, EPA is required to establish its own TMDLs for them. See Mark T. Pifher, TMDLs: A new rule? 32 Trends (March/April 2001), p. 1.

Chapter 6. Water Pollution Control

The Bush administration has targeted the TMDL regulations for reconsideration. On July 16, 2001, new EPA Administrator Christie Whitman proposed to delay the effective date of the TMDL regulations by 18 months (until April 2003) while she convenes a "consensus-building process" to reconsider the TMDL program. On August 3, 2001, EPA released a study estimating that it would cost between $900 million and $4.3 billion annually to implement the Clinton administration's TMDL regulations. The cost study is available on EPA's website at http://www.epa.gov/owow/tmdl/coststudy/coststudy.pdf The study follows a National Academy of Sciences Report issued on June 19, 2001, which would that many states lack sufficient data to develop TMDLs for all of their impaired waters.

In March 2000, a federal district court ruled that EPA has the authority under § 303(d) of the Clean Water Act to set TMDLs for all navigable waters impaired by pollution, including those where pollutants come from nonpoint sources. Pronsolino v. Marcus, 91 F.Supp. 2d 1337 (N.D. Cal. 2000). The court explained:

> In summary, the Clean Water Act called for a comprehensive set of water-quality standards for every navigable river and water in America. For every substandard navigable river or water, Congress sought a determination whether the central innovation of the 1972 Act – technology-driven limits on effluent – would be sufficient to achieve compliance. If not, the river or water was required to go on a list of unfinished business and a TMDL calculation was required. The TMDL was to quantify the load improvements necessary to meet standards. If EPA disagreed with a state's list or any TMDL as inconsistent with the purposes of the Act, then EPA was required to revise the list or the TMDL. No substandard river or water was immune by reason of its sources of pollution. The process was made just as mandatory for wild but ruined rivers as it was for urban-blighted rivers.

> Once the TMDLs were prepared, they were intended to be applied to point and nonpoint sources differently. As to point sources, the TMBLs were to be taken into account in further restricting effluent, under NPDES permits, as authorized by 301(b)(1)(C). As to nonpoint sources of pollution, the TMDLs were to be incorporated into the continuing planning processes of the states. This con-

ferred a large degree of discretion on the state in how and to what extent to implement the TMDLs for nonpoint sources. A state could even refuse to implement a TMDL, eschewing best management practices if it wishes, although to do so might provoke EPA to curtail or to deny grant money to the state. But as to whether TMDLs were authorized in the first place for all substandard rivers and waters, there is no doubt. They plainly were and remain so today – without regard to the sources of pollution.

Id.

Wetlands Protection and the Tulloch Rule
(pp. 736-45)

As a result of the decision in *National Mining Association v. Army Corps of Engineers* (casebook, p. 736), which held that "incidental fallback" is not regulated under § 404 of the Clean Water Act, it is estimated that at least 20,000 wetland acres have been degraded or destroyed, and 150 miles of streams channelized without environmental review or mitigation. To combat this problem, the Clinton administration issued new rules clarifying what types of activities are likely to result in a discharge of dredged material requiring a permit under § 404 of the Clean Water Act. The new regulations were issued jointly by EPA and the U.S. Army Corps of Engineers on January 17, 2001. 66 Fed. Reg. 4549 The regulations modify the definition of "discharge of dredged material" by clarifying what types of activities EPA and the Corps of Engineers believe typically result in regulable discharges, based on the nature of the equipment used and agency experience. The rules create a rebuttable presumption that the use of mechanized earth moving equipment to conduct landclearing, ditching, channelization, in-stream mining, or other earth-moving activity in waters of the U.S. result in a discharge of dredged material, unless project-specific evidence shows that the activity results in only "incidental fallback." The regulations also provide a definition of what constitutes non-regulable incidental fallback that is consistent with the Court decision. Copies of the regulations can be found at: www.epa.gov/owow/wetlands/dredgedmat/dredmat.html.

The Bush administration initially delayed the effective date of the regulations for 60 days, from February 16, 2001 to April 17, 2001. 66 Fed. Reg. 10367. On April 16, 2001, acting on behalf of the Bush Administration, Environmental Protection Agency Administrator Christie Todd Whitman strongly endorsed the new rules and announced that they would be allowed to take effect. While noting that the rules are an important step toward protecting the Nation's wetlands, the EPA Administrator observed that no regulatory action that can fully close the loophole in the Clean Water Act opened by the *National Mining Association* decision, which only Congress can correct.

Nationwide 40 Replaces Nationwide 26
(pp. 744-45)

In Note 7 on pp. 744-45 of the casebook, we report on proposed changes to Nationwide Permit #26, a general permit that allowed development of projects of less than three acres of wetlands without obtaining an individual § 404 permit so long as the U.S. Army Corps of Engineers was notified of any development affecting more than one-third acre. In March 2000 EPA adopted final rules reducing the acreage of wetlands that may be disturbed without obtaining an individual permit from three acres to one-half acre. 65 Feb. Reg. 12,818 (2000). The Corps now must be notified of any activity that will destroy more than one-tenth of an acre of wetlands, instead of the one-third acre threshold in the prior regulations.

Watershed Management Policies (pp. 755-58)

In June 2000 EPA issued a document providing a "Draft Framework for Watershed-Based Trading," designed to encourage emissions trading among sources of water pollution. The draft framework provides that emissions trading within watersheds will not be allowed to result in any violations of water quality standards. It emphasizes that development of watershed-based trading programs could become an important incentive for reducing pollution from nonpoint sources that now are not directly subject to regulatory controls.

- 7 -
Land Use Regulation and Regulatory Takings

Land Use and the Environment:
The Spread of Sprawl (pp. 760-62)

A study released by the Brookings Institution in July 2001 reports that land development in the United States is significantly outstripping population growth. Approximately 25 million acres of agricultural lands and open space have been developed between 1982 and 1997 due to the expansion of metropolitan areas, according to the report entitled "Who Sprawls Most? How Growth Patterns Differ Across the United States." All but 17 of the nation's 281 metropolitan areas are experiencing declines in population density, with the western states the only part of the United States bucking this trend. Atlanta has suffered some of the worst sprawl, growing 81.5% in area during the 15 years, while the city's population grew by 60.8%. The Pittsburgh metropolitan area's developed surface area grew by 42.6% even though its population declined 8%. Toledo increased in area by 30% while its population grew only 0.3%. Peter Grant, Sprawl Thins Populations of Older Suburbs, Wall St. J., July 9, 2001. The report found that metropolitan areas with large shares of foreign-born residents have higher population densities and less sprawl.

While the Brookings report notes that sprawl is progressing at very different rates in different parts of the country, another report suggests that sprawl has not been as bad as previously believed. The U.S. Department of Agriculture reported in January 2001 that a software error led it to greatly overestimate the amount of farmland developed during the period from 1992 to 1997. While the Department had reported that 16 million acres of farmland was developed during this period, the correct figure should have been 11.2 million acres, a rate of sprawl nearly a million acres per year less than previously reported. Paul Leavitt, Government Admits Overestimating Urban Sprawl, USA Today, January 11, 2001, p. 6A.

Chapter 7. Land Use Controls and Regulatory Takings

Land Use Controls and Regulatory Takings
(pp. 780-829)

On June 28, 2001, the final day of its October 2000 Term, the U.S. Supreme Court issued what is likely to be one of its most significant regulatory takings decisions. In *Palazollo v. Rhode Island*, 121 S.Ct. 2448 (2001), the Court, by a 5-4 vote, rejected the notion that acquisition of property after the enactment of regulations restricting its development automatically bars claims that the preexisting regulations effect a regulatory taking. Excerpts from this important decision, which produced six separate opinions, are reproduced below.

Palazzolo v. Rhode Island, 121 S.Ct. 2448 (2001)

JUSTICE KENNEDY delivered the opinion of the Court.

Petitioner Anthony Palazzolo owns a waterfront parcel of land in the town of Westerly, Rhode Island. Almost all of the property is designated as coastal wetlands under Rhode Island law. After petitioner's development proposals were rejected by respondent Rhode Island Coastal Resources Management Council (Council), he sued in state court, asserting the Council's application of its wetlands regulations took the property without compensation in violation of the Takings Clause of the Fifth Amendment, binding upon the State through the Due Process Clause of the Fourteenth Amendment. Petitioner sought review in this Court, contending the Supreme Court of Rhode Island erred in rejecting his takings claim. . . .

I

The town of Westerly is on an edge of the Rhode Island coastline. . . .Westerly today has about 20,000 year-round residents, and thousands of summer visitors come to enjoy its beaches and coastal advantages.

One of the more popular attractions is Misquamicut State Beach, a lengthy expanse of coastline facing Block Island Sound and beyond to the Atlantic Ocean. The primary point of access to the beach is Atlantic Avenue, a well-traveled 3-mile stretch of road running along the coast-

188

line within the town's limits. At its western end, Atlantic Avenue is something of a commercial strip, with restaurants, hotels, arcades, and other typical seashore businesses. The pattern of development becomes more residential as the road winds eastward onto a narrow spine of land bordered to the south by the beach and the ocean, and to the north by Winnapaug Pond, an intertidal inlet often used by residents for boating, fishing, and shellfishing.

In 1959 petitioner, a lifelong Westerly resident, decided to invest in three undeveloped, adjoining parcels along this eastern stretch of Atlantic Avenue. To the north, the property faces, and borders upon, Winnapaug Pond; the south of the property faces Atlantic Avenue and the beachfront homes abutting it on the other side, and beyond that the dunes and the beach. To purchase and hold the property, petitioner and associates formed Shore Gardens, Inc. (SGI). After SGI purchased the property petitioner bought out his associates and became the sole shareholder. In the first decade of SGI's ownership of the property the corporation submitted a plat to the town subdividing the property into 80 lots; and it engaged in various transactions that left it with 74 lots, which together encompassed about 20 acres. During the same period SGI also made initial attempts to develop the property and submitted intermittent applications to state agencies to fill substantial portions of the parcel. Most of the property was then, as it is now, salt marsh subject to tidal flooding. The wet ground and permeable soil would require considerable fill— as much as six feet in some places—before significant structures could be built. SGI's proposal, submitted in 1962 to the Rhode Island Division of Harbors and Rivers (DHR), sought to dredge from Winnapaug Pond and fill the entire property. The application was denied for lack of essential information. A second, similar proposal followed a year later. A third application, submitted in 1966 while the second application was pending, proposed more limited filling of the land for use as a private beach club. These latter two applications were referred to the Rhode Island Department of Natural Resources, which indicated initial assent. The agency later withdrew approval, however, citing adverse environmental impacts. SGI did not contest the ruling.

No further attempts to develop the property were made for over a decade. Two intervening events, however, become important to the issues presented. First, in 1971, Rhode Island enacted legislation creat-

189

ing the Council, an agency charged with the duty of protecting the State's coastal properties. 1971 R.I. Pub. Laws ch. 279, § 1 *et seq.* Regulations promulgated by the Council designated salt marshes like those on SGI's property as protected "coastal wetlands," Rhode Island Coastal Resources Management Program (CRMP) § 210.3 (as amended, June 28, 1983), on which development is limited to a great extent. Second, in 1978 SGI's corporate charter was revoked for failure to pay corporate income taxes; and title to the property passed, by operation of state law, to petitioner as the corporation's sole shareholder.

In 1983 petitioner, now the owner, renewed the efforts to develop the property. An application to the Council, resembling the 1962 submission, requested permission to construct a wooden bulkhead along the shore of Winnapaug Pond and to fill the entire marsh land area. The Council rejected the application, noting it was "vague and inadequate for a project of this size and nature." App. 16. The agency also found that "the proposed activities will have significant impacts upon the waters and wetlands of Winnapaug Pond," and concluded that "the proposed alteration . . . will conflict with the Coastal Resources Management Plan presently in effect." *Id.,* at 17. Petitioner did not appeal the agency's determination.

Petitioner went back to the drawing board, this time hiring counsel and preparing a more specific and limited proposal for use of the property. The new application, submitted to the Council in 1985, echoed the 1966 request to build a private beach club. The details do not tend to inspire the reader with an idyllic coastal image, for the proposal was to fill 11 acres of the property with gravel to accommodate "50 cars with boat trailers, a dumpster, port-a-johns, picnic tables, barbecue pits of concrete, and other trash receptacles." *Id.,* at 25.

The application fared no better with the Council than previous ones. Under the agency's regulations, a landowner wishing to fill salt marsh on Winnapaug Pond needed a "special exception" from the Council. CRMP § 130. In a short opinion the Council said the beach club proposal conflicted with the regulatory standard for a special exception. To secure a special exception the proposed activity must serve "a compelling public purpose which provides benefits to the public as a whole as opposed to individual or private interests." CRMP § 130A(1). This time petitioner appealed the decision to the Rhode Island courts, challenging the Council's conclusion as contrary to principles of state administrative law. The Council's decision was affirmed.

Petitioner filed an inverse condemnation action in Rhode Island Superior Court, asserting that the State's wetlands regulations, as applied by the Council to his parcel, had taken the property without compensation in violation of the Fifth and Fourteenth Amendments. The suit alleged the Council's action deprived him of "all economically beneficial use" of his property, *ibid.*, resulting in a total taking requiring compensation under *Lucas v. South Carolina Coastal Council*, 505 U.S. 1003 (1992). He sought damages in the amount of $3,150,000, a figure derived from an appraiser's estimate as to the value of a 74-lot residential subdivision. The State countered with a host of defenses. After a bench trial, a justice of the Superior Court ruled against petitioner, accepting some of the State's theories.

The Rhode Island Supreme Court affirmed. 746 A.2d 707 (2000). Like the Superior Court, the State Supreme Court recited multiple grounds for rejecting petitioner's suit. The court held, first, that petitioner's takings claim was not ripe, *id.*, at 712-715; second, that petitioner had no right to challenge regulations predating 1978, when he succeeded to legal ownership of the property from SGI, *id.*, at 716; and third, that the claim of deprivation of all economically beneficial use was contradicted by undisputed evidence that he had $200,000 in development value remaining on an upland parcel of the property, *id.*, at 715. In addition to holding petitioner could not assert a takings claim based on the denial of all economic use the court concluded he could not recover under the more general test of *Penn Central Transp. Co. v. City New York*, 438 U.S. 104 (1978). On this claim, too, the date of acquisition of the parcel was found determinative, and the court held he could have had "no reasonable investment-backed expectations that were affected by this regulation" because it predated his ownership, 746 A.2d, at 717; see also *Penn Central, supra*, at 124.

We disagree with the Supreme Court of Rhode Island as to the first two of these conclusions; and, we hold, the court was correct to conclude that the owner is not deprived of all economic use of his property because the value of upland portions is substantial. We remand for further consideration of the claim under the principles set forth in *Penn Central*.

Chapter 7. Land Use Controls and Regulatory Takings

II

... Since [*Pennsylvania Coal Co. v.*] *Mahon*, [260 U.S. 393 (1922)], we have given some, but not too specific, guidance to courts confronted with deciding whether a particular government action goes too far and effects a regulatory taking. First, we have observed, with certain qualifications, that a regulation which "denies all economically beneficial or productive use of land" will require compensation under the Takings Clause. *Lucas*, 505 U.S., at 1015; see also *id.*, at 1035 (Kennedy, J., concurring); *Agins v. City of Tiburon*, 447 U.S. 255, 261 (1980). Where a regulation places limitations on land that fall short of eliminating all economically beneficial use, a taking nonetheless may have occurred, depending on a complex of factors including the regulation's economic effect on the landowner, the extent to which the regulation interferes with reasonable investment-backed expectations, and the character of the government action. *Penn Central, supra*, at 124. These inquiries are informed by the purpose of the Takings Clause, which is to prevent the government from "forcing some people alone to bear public burdens which, in all fairness and justice, should be borne by the public as a whole." *Armstrong v. United States*, 364 U.S. 40, 49 (1960).

Petitioner seeks compensation under these principles. At the outset, however, we face the two threshold considerations invoked by the state court to bar the claim: ripeness, and acquisition which postdates the regulation.

A

In *Williamson County Regional Planning Comm'n v. Hamilton Bank of Johnson City*, 473 U.S. 172 (1985), the Court explained the requirement that a takings claim must be ripe. The Court held that a takings claim challenging the application of land-use regulations is not ripe unless "the government entity charged with implementing the regulations has reached a final decision regarding the application of the regulations to the property at issue." *Id.*, at 186. A final decision by the responsible state agency informs the constitutional determination whether a regulation has deprived a landowner of "all economically beneficial use" of the property, see *Lucas, supra*, at 1015, or defeated the reasonable investment-backed expectations of the landowner to the extent that a taking has occurred, see *Penn Central, supra*, at 124. These matters cannot be resolved in definitive terms until a court knows "the extent of permitted development" on the land in question. *MacDonald, Sommer & Frates v. Yolo County,* 477 U.S. 340, 351 (1986). Drawing on these principles, the Rhode Island Supreme Court held that petitioner had not taken the necessary steps to ripen his takings claim.

The central question in resolving the ripeness issue, under *Williamson County* and other relevant decisions, is whether petitioner obtained a final decision from the Council determining the permitted use for the land. As we have noted, SGI's early applications to fill had been granted at one point, though that assent was later revoked. Petitioner then submitted two proposals: the 1983 proposal to fill the entire parcel, and the 1985 proposal to fill 11 of the property's 18 wetland acres for construction of the beach club. The court reasoned that, notwithstanding the Council's denials of the applications, doubt remained as to the extent of development the Council would allow on petitioner's parcel. We cannot agree.

The court based its holding in part upon petitioner's failure to explore "any other use for the property that would involve filling substantially less wetlands." 746 A.2d, at 714. It relied upon this Court's observations that the final decision requirement is not satisfied when a developer submits, and a land use authority denies, a grandiose development proposal, leaving open the possibility that lesser uses of the property might be permitted. See *MacDonald, supra,* at 353, n. 9, 106 S.Ct. 2561. The suggestion is that while the Council rejected petitioner's effort to fill all of the wetlands, and then rejected his proposal to fill 11 of the wetland acres, perhaps an appliation to fill (for instance) 5 acres would have been approved. Thus, the reasoning goes, we cannot know for sure the extent of permitted development on petitioner's wetlands.

This is belied by the unequivocal nature of the wetland regulations at issue and by the Council's application of the regulations to the subject property. Winnapaug Pond is classified under the CRMP as a Type 2 body of water. See CRMP § 200.2. A landowner, as a general rule, is prohibited from filling or building residential structures on wetlands adjacent to Type 2 waters, see *id.,* Table 1, p. 22, and § 210.3(C)(4), but may seek a special exception from the Council to engage in a prohibited use, see *id.,* § 130. The Council is permitted to allow the exception, however, only where a "compelling public purpose" is served.

Id., § 130A(2). The proposal to fill the entire property was not accepted under Council regulations and did not qualify for the special exception. The Council determined the use proposed in the second application (the beach club) did not satisfy the "compelling public purpose" standard. There is no indication the Council would have accepted the application had petitioner's proposed beach club occupied a smaller surface area. To the contrary, it ruled that the proposed activity was not a "compelling public purpose." App. 27; cf. *id.,* at 17 (1983 application to fill wetlands proposed an "activity" conflicting with the CRMP).

Williamson County 's final decision requirement "responds to the high degree of discretion characteristically possessed by land-use boards in softening the strictures of the general regulations they administer." *Suitum v. Tahoe Regional Planning Agency,* 520 U.S. 725, 738 (1997). While a landowner must give a land-use authority an opportunity to exercise its discretion, once it becomes clear that the agency lacks the discretion to permit any development, or the permissible uses of the property are known to a reasonable degree of certainty, a takings claim is likely to have ripened. The case is quite unlike those upon which respondents place principal reliance, which arose when an owner challenged a land-use authority's denial of a substantial project, leaving doubt whether a more modest submission or an application for a variance would be accepted. See *MacDonald, supra,* at 342 (denial of 159-home residential subdivision); *Williamson County,* 473 U.S., at 182 (476-unit subdivision); cf. *Agins v. City of Tiburon,* 447 U.S. 255 (1980) (case not ripe because no plan to develop was submitted).

These cases stand for the important principle that a landowner may not establish a taking before a land-use authority has the opportunity, using its own reasonable procedures, to decide and explain the reach of a challenged regulation. Under our ripeness rules a takings claim based on a law or regulation which is alleged to go too far in burdening property depends upon the landowner's first having followed reasonable and necessary steps to allow regulatory agencies to exercise their full discretion in considering development plans for the property, including the opportunity to grant any variances or waivers allowed by law. As a general rule, until these ordinary processes have been followed the extent of the restriction on property is not known and a regulatory taking has not yet been established. See *Suitum, supra,* at 736, and n. 10 (noting difficulty of demonstrating that "mere enactment" of regulations restricting land use effects a taking). Government authorities, of course, may not burden property by imposition of repetitive or unfair land-use procedures in order to avoid a final decision. *Monterey v. Del Monte Dunes at Monterey, Ltd.*, 526 U.S. 687 (1999).

With respect to the wetlands on petitioner's property, the Council's decisions make plain that the agency interpreted its regulations to bar petitioner from engaging in any filling or development activity on the wetlands, a fact reinforced by the Attorney General's forthright responses to our questioning during oral argument in this case. The rulings of the Council interpreting the regulations at issue, and the briefs, arguments, and candid statements by counsel for both sides, leave no doubt on this point: On the wetlands there can be no fill for any ordinary land use. There can be no fill for its own sake; no fill for a beach club, either rustic or upscale; no fill for a subdivision; no fill for any likely or foreseeable use. And with no fill there can be no structures and no development on the wetlands. Further permit applications were not necessary to establish this point.

As noted above, however, not all of petitioner's parcel constitutes protected wetlands. The trial court accepted uncontested testimony that an upland site located at the eastern end of the property would have an estimated value of $200,000 if developed. App. While Council approval is required to develop upland property which lies within 200 feet of protected waters, see CRMP § 100.1(A), the strict "compelling public purpose" test does not govern proposed land uses on property in this classification, see *id.*, § 110, Table 1A, § 120. Council officials testified at trial, moreover, that they would have allowed petitioner to build a residence on the upland parcel. . . .So there is no genuine ambiguity in the record as to the extent of permitted development on petitioner's property, either on the wetlands or the uplands.

The state court . . . did not rely upon state law ripeness or exhaustion principles in holding that petitioner's takings claim was barred by virtue of his failure to apply for a 74 lot subdivision; it relied on *Williamson County*. As we have explained, *Williamson County* and our other ripeness decisions do not impose further obligations on petitioner, for the limitations the wetland regulations imposed were clear from the Council's denial of his applications, and there is no indication that any use involving any substantial structures or improvements would have been allowed. Where the state agency charged with enforcing a challenged land use regulation entertains an application from an owner and its denial of the application makes clear the extent of development permitted, and neither the agency nor a reviewing state court has cited non-compliance with reasonable state law exhaustion or pre- permit processes, see *Felder v. Casey,* 487 U.S. 131, 150-151 (1988), federal ripeness rules do not require the submission of further and futile applications with other agencies.

B

We turn to the second asserted basis for declining to address petitioner's takings claim on the merits. When the Council promulgated its wetlands regulations, the disputed parcel was owned not by petitioner but by the corporation of which he was sole shareholder. When title was transferred to petitioner by operation of law, the wetlands regulations were in force. The state court held the postregulation acquisition of title was fatal to the claim for deprivation of all economic use, 746 A.2d, at 716, and to the *Penn Central* claim, *id.,* at 717. While the first holding was couched in terms of background principles of state property law, see *Lucas,* 505 U.S., at 1015, and the second in terms of petitioner's reasonable investment-backed expectations, see *Penn Central,* 438 U.S., at 124, the two holdings together amount to a single, sweeping, rule: A purchaser or a successive title holder like petitioner is deemed to have notice of an earlier- enacted restriction and is barred from claiming that it effects a taking.

The theory underlying the argument that post-enactment purchasers cannot challenge a regulation under the Takings Clause seems to run on these lines: Property rights are created by the State. See, *e.g., Phillips v. Washington Legal Foundation,* 524 U.S. 156, 163 (1998). So, the argument goes, by prospective legislation the State can shape and define property rights and reasonable investment-backed expectations, and subsequent owners cannot claim any injury from lost value. After all, they purchased or took title with notice of the limitation.

The State may not put so potent a Hobbesian stick into the Lockean bundle. The right to improve property, of course, is subject to the reasonable exercise of state authority, including the enforcement of valid zoning and land-use restrictions. See *Pennsylvania Coal Co.,* 260 U.S., at 413 ("Government hardly could go on if to some extent values incident to property could not be diminished without paying for every such change in the general law"). The Takings Clause, however, in certain circumstances allows a landowner to assert that a particular exercise of the State's regulatory power is so unreasonable or onerous as to compel compensation. Just as a prospective enactment, such as a new zoning ordinance, can limit the value of land without effecting a taking because it can be understood as reasonable by all concerned, other enactments are unreasonable and do not become less so through passage of time or title. Were we to accept the State's rule, the postenactment transfer of title would absolve the State of its obligation to defend any action restricting land use, no matter how extreme or unreasonable. A State would be allowed, in effect, to put an expiration date on the Takings Clause. This ought not to be the rule. Future generations, too, have a right to challenge unreasonable limitations on the use and value of land.

Nor does the justification of notice take into account the effect on owners at the time of enactment, who are prejudiced as well. Should an owner attempt to challenge a new regulation, but not survive the process of ripening his or her claim (which, as this case demonstrates, will often take years), under the proposed rule the right to compensation may not by asserted by an heir or successor, and so may not be asserted at all. The State's rule would work a critical alteration to the nature of property, as the newly regulated landowner is stripped of the ability to transfer the interest which was possessed prior to the regulation. The State may not by this means secure a windfall for itself. See *Webb's Fabulous Pharmacies, Inc. v. Beckwith*, 449 U.S. 155, 164 (1980) ("[A] State, by *ipse dixit*, may not transform private property into public property without compensation"); cf. Ellickson, Property in Land, 102 Yale L.J. 1315, 1368-1369 (1993) (right to transfer interest in land is a defining characteristic of the fee simple estate). The proposed rule is, furthermore, capricious in effect. The young owner contrasted with the older owner, the owner with the resources to hold contrasted with the owner with the need to sell, would be in different positions. The Takings Clause is not so quixotic. A blanket rule that purchasers with notice have no compensation right when a claim becomes ripe is too blunt an instrument to accord with the duty to compensate for what is taken.

Direct condemnation, by invocation of the State's power of eminent domain, presents different considerations than cases alleging a taking based on a burdensome regulation. In a direct condemnation action, or when a State has physically invaded the property without filing suit, the fact and extent of the taking are known. In such an instance, it is a general rule of the law of eminent domain that any award goes to the owner at the time of the taking, and that the right to compensation is not passed to a subsequent purchaser. See *Danforth v. United States,* 308 U.S. 271, 284 (1939); 2 Sackman, Eminent Domain, at § 5.01[5][d][i] ("It is well settled that when there is a taking of property by eminent domain in compliance with the law, it is the owner of the property *at the time of the taking* who is entitled to compensation"). A challenge to the application of a land-use regulation, by contrast, does not mature until ripeness requirements have been satisfied, under principles we have discussed; until this point an inverse condemnation claim alleging a regulatory taking cannot be maintained. It would be illogical, and unfair, to bar a regulatory takings claim because of the post-enactment transfer of ownership where the steps necessary to make the claim ripe were not taken, or could not have been taken, by a previous owner.

There is controlling precedent for our conclusion. *Nollan v. California Coastal Comm'n,* 483 U.S. 825 (1987), presented the question whether it was consistent with the Takings Clause for a state regulatory agency to require oceanfront landowners to provide lateral beach access to the public as the condition for a development permit. The principal dissenting opinion observed it was a policy of the California Coastal Commission to require the condition, and that the Nollans, who purchased their home after the policy went into effect, were "on notice that new developments would be approved only if provisions were made for lateral beach access." *Id.,* at 860 (Brennan, J., dissenting). A majority of the Court rejected the proposition. "So long as the Commission could not have deprived the prior owners of the easement without compensating them," the Court reasoned, "the prior owners must be understood to have transferred their full property rights in conveying the lot." *Id.,* at 834, n.2.

It is argued that *Nollan*'s holding was limited by the later decision in *Lucas v. South Carolina Coastal Council,* 505 U.S. 1003 (1992). In *Lucas* the Court observed that a landowner's ability to recover for a government deprivation of all economically beneficial use of property is not absolute but instead is confined by limitations on the use of land which "inhere in the title itself." *Id.,* at 1029. This is so, the Court reasoned, because the landowner is constrained by those "restrictions that background principles of the State's law of property and nuisance already place upon land ownership." *Id.,* at 1029.. It is asserted here that *Lucas* stands for the proposition that any new regulation, once enacted, becomes a background principle of property law which cannot be challenged by those who acquire title after the enactment.

We have no occasion to consider the precise circumstances when a legislative enactment can be deemed a background principle of state law or whether those circumstances are present here. It suffices to say that a regulation that otherwise would be unconstitutional absent compensation is not transformed into a background principle of the State's law by mere virtue of the passage of title. This relative standard would be incompatible with our description of the concept in *Lucas,* which is explained in terms of those common, shared understandings of permissible limitations derived from a State's legal tradition, see *Lucas, supra,* at 1029-1030. A regulation or common-law rule cannot be a background principle for some owners but not for others. The determination whether an existing, general law can limit all economic use of property must turn on objective factors, such as the nature of the land use proscribed. See *Lucas, supra,* at 1030. ("The 'total taking' inquiry we require today will ordinarily entail . . . analysis of, among other things, the degree of harm to public lands and resources, or adjacent private property, posed by the claimant's proposed activities"). A law does not become a background principle for subsequent owners by enactment itself. *Lucas* did not overrule our holding in *Nollan,* which, as we have noted, is based on essential Takings Clause principles.

For reasons we discuss next, the state court will not find it necessary to explore these matters on remand in connection with the claim that all economic use was deprived; it must address, however, the merits of petitioner's claim under *Penn Central.* That claim is not barred by the mere fact that title was acquired after the effective date of the state-imposed restriction.

III

As the case is ripe, and as the date of transfer of title does not bar petitioner's takings claim, we have before us the alternative ground relied upon by the Rhode Island Supreme Court in ruling upon the merits of the takings claims. It held that all economically beneficial use was not deprived because the uplands portion of the property can still be improved. On this point, we agree with the court's decision. Petitioner accepts the Council's contention and the state trial court's finding that his parcel retains $200,000 in development value under the State's wetlands regulations. He asserts, nonetheless, that he has suffered a total taking and contends the Council cannot sidestep the holding in *Lucas* "by the simple expedient of leaving a landowner a few crumbs of value." Brief for Petitioner 37.

Assuming a taking is otherwise established, a State may not evade the duty to compensate on the premise that the landowner is left with a token interest. This is not the situation of the landowner in this case, however. A regulation permitting a landowner to build a substantial residence on an 18-acre parcel does not leave the property "economically idle." *Lucas, supra*, at 1019.

In his brief submitted to us petitioner attempts to revive this part of his claim by reframing it. He argues, for the first time, that the upland parcel is distinct from the wetlands portions, so he should be permitted to assert a deprivation limited to the latter. This contention asks us to examine the difficult, persisting question of what is the proper denominator in the takings fraction. See Michelman, Property, Utility, and Fairness: Comments on the Ethical Foundations of "Just Compensation Law," 80 Harv. L.Rev. 1165, 1192 (1967). Some of our cases indicate that the extent of deprivation effected by a regulatory action is measured against the value of the parcel as a whole, see, *e.g., Keystone Bituminous Coal Assn. v. DeBenedictis,* 480 U.S. 470, 497 (1987); but we have at times expressed discomfort with the logic of this rule, see *Lucas, supra*, at 1016- 1017, n. 7, a sentiment echoed by some commentators, see, *e.g.,* Epstein, Takings: Descent and Resurrection, 1987 Sup.Ct. Rev. 1, 16-17 (1987); Fee, Unearthing the Denominator in Regulatory Takings Claims, 61 U. Chi. L.Rev. 1535 (1994). Whatever the merits of these criticisms, we will not explore the point here. Petitioner did not press the argument in the state courts, and the issue was not presented in the petition for certiorari. The case comes to us on the premise that petitioner's entire parcel serves as the basis for his takings claim, and, so framed, the total deprivation argument fails. . . .

For the reasons we have discussed, the State Supreme Court erred in finding petitioner's claims were unripe and in ruling that acquisition of title after the effective date of the regulations barred the takings claims. The court did not err in finding that petitioner failed to establish a deprivation of all economic value, for it is undisputed that the parcel retains significant worth for construction of a residence. The claims under the *Penn Central* analysis were not examined, and for this purpose the case should be remanded.

The judgment of the Rhode Island Supreme Court is affirmed in part and reversed in part, and the case is remanded for further proceedings not inconsistent with this opinion.

JUSTICE O'CONNOR, concurring.

I join the opinion of the Court but with my understanding of how the issues discussed in Part II-B of the opinion must be considered on remand.

Part II-B of the Court's opinion addresses the circumstance, present in this case, where a takings claimant has acquired title to the regulated property after the enactment of the regulation at issue. As the Court holds, the Rhode Island Supreme Court erred in effectively adopting the sweeping rule that the preacquisition enactment of the use restriction *ipso facto* defeats any takings claim based on that use restriction. Accordingly, the Court holds that petitioner's claim under *Penn Central Transp. Co. v. City of New York,* 438 U.S. 104 (1978), "is not barred by the mere fact that title was acquired after the effective date of the state-imposed restriction." *Ante,* at 2464.

The more difficult question is what role the temporal relationship between regulatory enactment and title acquisition plays in a proper *Penn Central* analysis. Today's holding does not mean that the timing of the regulation's enactment relative to the acquisition of title is immaterial to the *Penn Central* analysis. Indeed, it would be just as much error to expunge this consideration from the takings inquiry as it would be to accord it exclusive significance. Our polestar instead remains the principles set forth in *Penn Central* itself and our other cases that govern partial regulatory takings. Under these cases, interference with investment-backed expectations is one of a number of factors that a court must examine. Further, the regulatory regime in place at the time the claimant acquires the property at issue helps to shape the reasonableness of those expectations.

The Fifth Amendment forbids the taking of private property for public use without just compensation. We have recognized that this constitutional guarantee is "'designed to bar Government from forcing some people alone to bear public burdens which, in all fairness and justice, should be borne by the public as a whole.'" *Penn Central, supra,* at 123-124 (quoting *Armstrong v. United States,* 364 U.S. 40, 49 (1960)). The concepts of "fairness and justice" that underlie the Takings Clause, of course, are less than fully determinate. Accordingly, we have eschewed "any 'set formula' for determining when 'justice and fairness' require that economic injuries caused by public action be compensated by the government, rather than remain disproportionately concentrated on a few persons." *Penn Central, supra,* at 124 (quoting *Goldblatt v. Hempstead,* 369 U.S. 590, 594 (1962)). The outcome instead "depends largely 'upon the particular circumstances [in that] case.'"*Penn Central, supra,* at 124 (quoting *United States v. Central Eureka Mining Co.,* 357 U.S. 155, 168 (1958)).

We have "identified several factors that have particular significance" in these "essentially ad hoc, factual inquiries." *Penn Central,* 438 U.S., at 124. Two such factors are "[t]he economic impact of the regulation on the claimant and, particularly, the extent to which the regulation has interfered with distinct investment-backed expectations." *Ibid.* Another is "the character of the governmental action." *Ibid.* The purposes served, as well as the effects produced, by a particular regulation inform the takings analysis. *Id.,* at 127 ("[A] use restriction on real property may constitute a 'taking' if not reasonably necessary to the effectuation of a substantial public purpose, [citations omitted], or perhaps if it has an unduly harsh impact upon the owner's use of the property"); see also *Yee v. Escondido,* 503 U.S. 519, 523 (1992) (Regulatory takings cases "necessarily entai[l] complex factual assessments of the purposes and economic effects of government actions"). *Penn Central* does not supply mathematically precise variables, but instead provides important guideposts that lead to the ultimate determination whether just compensation is required.

The Rhode Island Supreme Court concluded that, because the wetlands regulations predated petitioner's acquisition of the property at issue, petitioner lacked reasonable investment-backed expectations and hence lacked a viable takings claim. 746 A.2d 707, 717 (2000). The court erred in elevating what it believed to be "[petitioner's] lack of reasonable investment-backed expectations" to "dispositive" status. *Ibid.* Investment-backed expectations, though important, are not talismanic under *Penn Central.* Evaluation of the degree of interference with investment-backed expectations instead is *one* factor that points toward the answer to the question whether the application of a particular regulation to particular property "goes too far." *Pennsylvania Coal Co. v. Mahon,* 260 U.S. 393, 415 (1922).

Further, the state of regulatory affairs at the time of acquisition is not the only factor that may determine the extent of investment-backed expectations. For example, the nature and extent of permitted development under the regulatory regime vis-a-vis the development sought by the claimant may also shape legitimate expectations without vesting any kind of development right in the property owner. We also have never held that a takings claim is defeated simply on account of the lack of a personal financial investment by a postenactment acquirer of property, such as a donee, heir, or devisee. Cf. *Hodel v. Irving,* 481 U.S. 704, 714-718 (1987). Courts instead must attend to those circumstances which are probative of what fairness requires in a given case.

If investment-backed expectations are given exclusive significance in the *Penn Central* analysis and existing regulations dictate the reasonableness of those expectations in every instance, then the State wields far too much power to redefine property rights upon passage of title. On the other hand, if existing regulations do nothing to inform the analysis, then some property owners may reap windfalls and an important indicium of fairness is lost. * As I understand it, our decision today does not remove the regulatory backdrop against which an owner takes title to property from the purview of the *Penn Central* inquiry. It simply restores balance to that inquiry. Courts properly consider the effect of existing regulations under the rubric of investment-backed expectations in determining whether a compensable taking has occurred. As before, the salience of these facts cannot be reduced to any "set formula." *Penn Central,* 438 U.S., at 124. The temptation to adopt what amount to *per se* rules in either direction must be resisted. The Takings Clause requires careful examination and weighing of all the relevant circumstances in this context. The court below therefore must consider on remand the array of relevant factors under *Penn Central* before deciding whether any compensation is due.

JUSTICE SCALIA, concurring.

I write separately to make clear that my understanding of how the issues discussed in Part II-B of the Court's opinion must be considered on remand is not Justice O'Connor's.

The principle that underlies her separate concurrence is that it may in some (unspecified) circumstances be "[un]fai[r]," and produce unacceptable "windfalls," to allow a subsequent purchaser to nullify an unconstitutional partial taking (though, inexplicably, not an unconstitutional total taking) by the government. The polar horrible, presumably, is the situation in which a sharp real estate developer, realizing (or indeed, simply gambling on) the unconstitutional excessiveness of a development restriction that a naive landowner assumes to be valid, purchases property at what it would be worth subject to the restriction, and then develops it to its full value (or resells it at its full value) after getting the unconstitutional restriction invalidated.

This can, I suppose, be called a windfall — though it is not much different from the windfalls that occur every day at stock exchanges or antique auctions, where the knowledgeable (or the venturesome) profit at the expense of the ignorant (or the risk averse). There is something to be said (though in my view not much) for pursuing abstract "fairness" by requiring part or all of that windfall to be returned to the naive original owner, who presumably is the "rightful" owner of it. But there is nothing to be said for giving it instead to the *government*—which not only did not lose something it owned, but is both the *cause* of the miscarriage of "fairness" and the only one of the three parties involved in the miscarriage (government, naive original owner, and sharp real estate developer) which *acted unlawfully*—indeed *unconstitutionally*. Justice O'Connor would eliminate the windfall by giving the malefactor the benefit of its malefaction. It is rather like eliminating the windfall that accrued to a purchaser who bought property at a bargain rate from a thief clothed with the indicia of title, by making him turn over the "unjust" profit *to the thief.*

In my view, the fact that a restriction existed at the time the purchaser took title (other than a restriction forming part of the "background principles of the State's law of property and nuisance," *Lucas
v. South Carolina Coastal Council*, 505 U.S. 1003, 1029 (1992)) should
have no bearing upon the determination of whether the restriction is so
substantial as to constitute a taking. The "investment-backed expectations" that the law will take into account do not include the assumed
validity of a restriction that in fact deprives property of so much of its
value as to be unconstitutional. Which is to say that a *Penn Central*
taking, see *Penn Central Transp. Co. v. City of New York*, 438 U.S. 104
(1978), no less than a total taking, is not absolved by the transfer of
title.

[JUSTICE STEVENS, in an opinion concurring in part and dissenting in part, agreed with the majority only that the case was ripe for
review. Citing Justice Kennedy's concurrence in *Lucas*, Stevens concluded that "even a newly adopted regulation that diminishes the value
of property does not produce a significant Takings Clause issue if it (1)
is generally applicable and (2) is directed at preventing a substantial
public harm." He deemed it "quite likely that a regulation prohibiting
the filling of wetlands meets those criteria." Stevens maintained that
Palazzolo had no standing to make a takings claim because he was not
the owner of the property at the time the regulations were adopted. "If
the regulations are invalid, either because improper procedures were
followed when they were adopted, or because they have somehow gone
'too far,' *Pennsylvania Coal Co. v. Mahon*, 260 U.S. 393, 415 (1922),
petitioner may seek to enjoin their enforcement, but he has no right to
recover compensation for the value of property taken from someone
else."]

[JUSTICE GINSBURG, joined by JUSTICE SOUTER and JUS-
TICE BREYER dissented. They argued that Palazollo's takings claim
was not ripe for review because the record was ambiguous concerning
the extent of permissible development on Palazzolo's land. In a footnote citing Justice O'Connor's concurring opinion, they expressed
agreement with the notion "that transfer of title can impair a takings
claim."]

[JUSTICE BREYER filed a separate dissent in which he agreed
with Justice O'Connor "that the simple fact that a piece of property has

changed hands (for example, by inheritance) does not always and *automatically* bar a takings claim." Justice Breyer stated that "without in any way suggesting that Palazzolo has any valid takings claim, I believe his postregulatory acquisition of the property (through automatic operation of law) by itself should not prove dispositive." However, he observed that reasonable investment-backed expectations ordinarily "will diminish in force and significance – rapidly and dramatically – as property changes hands over time," a factor that can be taken into account under *Penn Central* to prevent takings doctrine from rewarding strategic property transfers.]

NOTES AND QUESTIONS

1. While the Court in *Palazzolo* did not hold that Rhode Island's actions constituted a regulatory taking, its decision that post-regulation transfer of title does not automatically bar takings claims could spawn an avalanche of new takings litigation. Under what circumstances can property owners now premise takings claims on regulations that predate their acquisition of title? Will such claims be limited to owners like Palazzolo who acquired the property by operation of law from those who owned the property when the regulations were adopted? Will it be limited to owners who acquired the property from parties who were unable to litigate taking claims to final judgment? Or will all subsequent purchasers be able to assert takings claims?

2. What justifications does the Court offer for its holding? Isn't the Court right that if takings claims may only be asserted by those who own property at the time of regulatory transitions, these owners still are disadvantaged by their inability to transfer their full pre-regulation interests in land? Is Justice Kennedy right when he asserts that states effectively could "put an expiration date on the Takings Clause" if post-enactment transfer of title bars takings claims?

3. In his partial dissent, Justice Stevens argued that only owners of property at the time regulations were adopted had standing to challenge the regulations as regulatory takings. He argued that "[i]f the existence of valid land-use regulations does not limit the title that the first postenactment purchaser of the property inherits, then there is no reason why such regulations should limit the rights of the second, the third, or the thirtieth purchaser." Is he right? Is there any temporal limit on the ability of subsequent purchasers to bring takings claims?

4. How should *Palazzolo* be decided on remand? The Court remanded the case for reconsideration of Palazzolo's takings claim under the *Penn Central* test. *Penn Central* (casebook, p. 782) focuses on the economic effect of regulation on the landowner, the extent of interference with reasonable investment-backed expectations, and the character of the government action. What relevance, if any, should it have for this analysis that Palazzolo acquired the property in his individual capacity only after the state regulations limiting development in wetlands areas were adopted? Compare Justice O'Connor's concurrence with that of Justice Scalia. Justice O'Connor maintains that postregulation acquisition of property is one factor to consider in assessing the reasonableness of investment-backed expectations under *Penn Central*. Justice Scalia vehemently disagrees. He argues that it would be better for litigious subsequent purchasers to reap "windfalls" from landowners who naively accept unreasonable regulations than to reward the government for acting as a "thief."

5. Suppose that David Lucas, the plaintiff in *Lucas v. South Carolina Coastal Council*, had sold his undeveloped South Carolina property for a token sum rather than pursuing his takings claim. Could the purchaser have successfully challenged the Coastal Council's development restrictions as a regulatory taking prior to *Palazzolo*? Could he do so now?

6. Has *Palazzolo* moved the focus of regulatory takings jurisprudence toward the reasonableness of land use regulation rather than the reasonableness of developer expectations? In his majority opinion Justice Kennedy notes that some regulations are simply "unreasonable and do not become less so through passage of time or title." He notes that it made no difference in *Nollan v. California Coastal Commission* (casebook, p. 788) that the Nollans purchased their home after the Coastal Commission had adopted a requirement that oceanfront landowners provide lateral beach access to the public as a condition for obtaining development permits. How should the reasonableness of land use regulation be assessed when considering regulatory takings claims? *Nollan* involved a regulatory exaction of a physical easement. Could *Palazzolo* presage extension to regulatory takings claims of the kind of "rough proportionality" analysis used to assess the reasonableness of regulatory exactions?

7. Citing *Lucas*, Justice Kennedy suggests that what is reasonable "is explained in terms of those common, shared understandings of permissible limitations derived from a State's legal tradition." What factors should govern assessments of the reasonableness of regulations that respond to new information or changed circumstances? Recall Justice Kennedy's discussion of this issue in *Lucas* (casebook, page 797). Have Kennedy's views changed?

8. Review the Post-*Lucas* decisions discussed in the casebook at pages 805-808. Could *Palazzolo* change the result in any of these cases?

Upcoming in the Supreme Court: Are Development Moratoria Temporary Takings? (pp. 823-829)

When the U.S. Supreme Court opened its October 2001 Term, the only environmental case on its docket was a takings case, *Tahoe-Sierra Preservation Council, Inc. v. Tahoe Regional Planning Agency*, No. 00-1167. The question before the Court is whether a temporary moratorium on land development constitutes a regulatory taking for which compensation must be paid under the Takings Clause of the Fifth Amendment of the U.S. Constitution.

As noted in the casebook (p. 775), the Tahoe Regional Planning Compact sought to protect Lake Tahoe by establishing the Tahoe Regional Planning Agency (TRPA) to control development around the lake. While the TRPA was developing its initial land-use regulations, it imposed a temporary moratorium on most residential and all commercial construction on environmentally sensitive land nearly streams and wetlands. The moratorium, which first became effective on August 24, 1981, was to last only until the new land-use regulations became effective. However, after lawsuits challenging the regulations resulted in an injunction, their effective date ultimately was delayed from 1984 until 1987. A group of 450 landowners brought suit, claiming that the moratorium constituted a temporary taking of their property rights.

In Tahoe-Sierra Preservation Council, Inc. v. Tahoe Regional Planning Agency, 216 F.3d 764 (9th Cir. 2000), the Ninth Circuit rejected the property owners' temporary takings claim. The court noted that a contrary decision "would risk converting every temporary planning moratorium into a categorical taking" that "would deprive state and local governments of an important land-use planning tool with a well-established tradition." The court observed that moratoria prevent a race-to-development by preserving the status quo during the time it takes to develop a regulatory scheme. It concluded that a temporary moratorium would not constitute a taking unless it was designed to be in effect for so long that it effectively deprived property owners of all economically beneficial use of their land.

Although the Ninth Circuit denied the Council's petition for a re-hearing en banc, five judges dissented from this decision. Tahoe-Sierra Preservation Council, Inc. v. Tahoe Regional Planning Agency, 228 F.3d 998 (9th Cir. 2000). Judge Alex Kozinski argued that the panel's decision is directly contrary to *First English Evangelical Lutheran Church v. County of Los Angeles* (casebook p. 788) and Tabb Lakes, Ltd. v. United States, 10 F.3d 796 (Fed. Cir. 1993), which stated that "a taking, even for a day, without compensation is prohibited by the Constitution." Id. at 800. The U.S. Supreme Court then granted review limited to the question "whether the Court of Appeals properly determined that a temporary moratorium on land development does not constitute a taking of property requiring compensation under the Takings Clause of the United States Constitution?"

Students may wish to follow the progress of this case in the Supreme Court. The case is likely to be argued in January 2002. The Court will issue its decision before it adjourns for the summer at the end of June 2002. Excerpts from the Ninth Circuit's panel decision and the dissent from the denial of rehearing en banc are reproduced below.

Tahoe-Sierra Preservation Council, Inc. v. Tahoe Regional Planning Agency, 216 F.3d 764, rehearing en banc denied, 228 F.3d 998 (9th Cir. 2000)

REINHARDT, Circuit Judge:

This case involves approximately 450 plaintiffs who own property in the Lake Tahoe Basin. The lead plaintiff, Tahoe-Sierra Preservation Council, Inc. (TSPC), is an association of Tahoe-area property owners. Each individual property owner has alleged, *inter alia,* that each of several land-use regulations enacted in the 1980's by the Tahoe Regional Planning Agency (TRPA) constituted a "taking" of his property under the Fifth and Fourteenth Amendments. The principal question on this appeal is whether a temporary planning moratorium, enacted by TRPA to halt development while a new regional land-use plan was being devised, effected a taking of each plaintiff's property under the standard set forth in *Lucas v. South Carolina Coastal Council,* 505 U.S. 1003 (1992). . . .

The plaintiffs contend that, for purposes of determining whether the regulations constitute a categorical taking under *Lucas,* we should not treat the plaintiffs' properties as the fee interests that they are. Instead, they argue, we should define narrowly, as a separate property interest, the temporal "slice" of each fee that covers the time span during which Ordinance 81-5 and Resolution 83-21 were in effect. It is this carved-out piece of each plaintiff's property interest, the plaintiffs assert, that has been "taken" by the regulations.

> "Because our test for regulatory taking requires us to compare the value that has been taken from the property with the value that remains in the property, one of the critical questions is determining how to define the unit of property 'whose value is to furnish the denominator of the fraction.' "

Keystone Bituminous Coal Ass'n, 480 U.S. at 497 (quoting Frank I. Michelman, *Property, Utility, and Fairness: Comments on the Ethical Foundations of "Just Compensation" Law,* 80 Harv. L.Rev. 1165, 1192 (1967)). In other words, for purposes of determining whether a "taking" of the plaintiffs' "property" has occurred, the proper inquiry is what constitutes the relevant "property"? Is it the fee interest that must be "taken," or is it some lesser unit of property? Property interests may have many different dimensions. For example, the dimensions of a property interest may include a physical dimension (which describes the size and shape of the property in question), a functional dimension (which describes the extent to which an owner may use or dispose of the property in question), and a temporal dimension (which describes the duration of the property interest). At base, the plaintiffs' argument is that we should conceptually sever each plaintiff's fee interest into discrete segments in at least one of these dimensions—the temporal one—and treat each of those segments as separate and distinct property interests for purposes of takings analysis. Under this theory, they argue that there was a categorical taking of one of those temporal segments.

While Supreme Court precedent has not over the years been entirely uniform in its treatment of the conceptual severance question, *compare Pennsylvania Coal Co. v. Mahon,* 260 U.S. 393 (1922) (employing conceptual severance) *with Keystone Bituminous Coal Ass'n v. DeBenedictis,* 480 U.S. 470 (1987) (rejecting conceptual severance in the identical context), most modern case law rejects the invitation of property holders to engage in conceptual severance, except in cases of physical invasion or occupation. Several cases illustrate the Court's refusal to employ this concept in other types of circumstances. In *Penn Central Transportation Company v. City of New York,* the Penn Central Transportation Company entered into a contract for the construction and lease of an office building above its Grand Central Terminal in New York City. 438 U.S. at 116. When the City denied two alternate building plans on the ground that they would destroy the architectural appeal of the historic landmark, Penn Central filed suit, claiming that the rejection of the building plans constituted a taking. *Id.* at 117-18. In affirming the denial of its takings claim, the Court explicitly rejected Penn Central's proposal to consider the airspace above the Terminal as a property interest separate from the rest of the Terminal site. The Court explained:

> "Taking" jurisprudence does not divide a single parcel into discrete segments and attempt to determine whether rights in a particular segment have been entirely abrogated. In deciding whether a particular governmental action has effected a taking, this Court focuses rather both on the character of the action and on the nature and extent of the interference with rights in *the parcel as a whole*-here, the city tax block designated as the "landmark site."

Id. (emphasis added); *see also MacLeod v. County of Santa Clara,* 749 F.2d 541, 547 (9th Cir.1984). . . .

In fact, the Supreme Court has already once rejected conceptual severance in the temporal dimension of property rights. In *Agins v.*

Tiburon, the city of Tiburon had instituted condemnation proceedings against the plaintiffs' property, but abandoned the proceedings a year later. The plaintiffs brought suit, contending, *inter alia,* "that the city's aborted attempt to acquire the land through eminent domain had destroyed the use of the land during the pendency of the condemnation proceedings." *Agins,* 447 U.S. at 258 n. 3. The Supreme Court rejected the plaintiffs' claim, holding:

> The State Supreme Court correctly rejected the contention that the municipality's good faith planning activities, which did not result in the successful prosecution of an eminent domain claim, so burdened the appellants' enjoyment of their property so as to constitute a taking. Even if the appellants' ability to sell their property was limited during the pendency of the condemnation proceeding, the appellants were free to sell or develop their property when the proceedings ended. *Mere fluctuations in value during the process of governmental decisionmaking, absent extraordinary delay, are "incidents of ownership. They cannot be considered as a 'taking' in the constitutional sense."*

447 U.S. at 263 n. 9 (citations omitted) (emphasis added) (quoting *Danforth v. United States,* 308 U.S. 271, 285 (1939)). In rejecting the takings claim, the Court relied only on the fact that the plaintiffs were able to sell or develop their property after the city abandoned its condemnation claim. By relying on the temporary nature of the restriction, the Court rejected the invitation to carve out, as a separate property interest, a temporal "slice" of the parcel that existed for the time period during which the condemnation proceedings were in progress. For, had the Court considered the plaintiffs' rights in their property during that time period as a separate interest, the plaintiffs' ability to sell or develop their property *after* the time period ended would have been irrelevant to the Court's takings analysis. Only the ability to sell or develop the property during the condemnation period would have mattered.

Agins 's rejection of conceptual severance in the temporal dimension is consistent with the Court's rejection of other forms of conceptual severance in *Penn Central* and *Andrus.* It would make little sense to accept temporal severance and reject spatial or functional severance. A planning regulation that prevents the development of a parcel for a temporary period of time is conceptually no different than a land-use

212

restriction that permanently denies all use on a discrete portion of property, or that permanently restricts a type of use across all of the parcel. *See* Margaret Jane Radin, *The Liberal Conception of Property: Cross Currents in the Jurisprudence of Takings,* 88 Colum.L.Rev. 1667, 1674-78 (1988). Each of these three types of regulation will have an impact on the parcel's value, because each will affect an aspect of the owner's "use" of the property—by restricting *when* the "use" may occur, *where* the "use" may occur, or *how* the "use" may occur. Prior to *Agins,* the Court had already rejected takings challenges to regulations eliminating all "use" on a portion of the property, and to regulations restricting the type of "use" across the breadth of the property. *See Penn Central,* 438 U.S. at 130-31; *Keystone Bituminous Coal Ass'n,* 480 U.S. at 498-99; *Village of Euclid v. Ambler Realty Co.,* 272 U.S. 365, 384, 397 (1926) (75% diminution in value caused by zoning law); *see also William C. Haas & Co. v. City & County of San Francisco,* 605 F.2d 1117, 1120 (9th Cir.1979) (value reduced from $2,000,000 to $100,000). In those cases, the Court "uniformly reject[ed] the proposition that diminution in property value, standing alone, can establish a 'taking.' " *Penn Central,* 438 U.S. at 131; *see also Concrete Pipe and Products, Inc. v. Construction Laborers Pension Trust,* 508 U.S. 602, 645 (1993). There is no plausible basis on which to distinguish a similar diminution in value that results from a temporary suspension of development.

To not reject the concept of temporal severance, we would risk converting every temporary planning moratorium into a categorical taking. *See Penn Central,* 438 U.S. at 130; *Stern v. Halligan,* 158 F.3d 729, 734 (3rd Cir.1998); Michelman, *supra,* at 1193. Such a result would run contrary to the Court's explanation that it is "relatively rare" that government "regulation denies all economically beneficial or productive use of land." *Lucas,* 505 U.S. at 1015.

More important, the widespread invalidation of temporary planning moratoria would deprive state and local governments of an important land-use planning tool with a well-established tradition. Land-use planning is necessarily a complex, time-consuming undertaking for a community, especially in a situation as unique as this. In several ways, temporary development moratoria promote effective planning. First, by preserving the status quo during the planning process, temporary moratoria ensure that a community's problems are not exacerbated during the time it takes to formulate a regulatory scheme. *See* Elizabeth A. Garvin & Martin L. Leitner, *Drafting Interim Development Ordinances: Creating Time to Plan,* Land Use Law and Zoning Digest, June 1996, at 3, 3; *Schafer v. City of New Orleans,* 743 F.2d 1086, 1090 (5th Cir.1984). Relatedly, temporary development moratoria prevent developers and landowners from racing to carry out development that is destructive of the community's interests before a new plan goes into effect. Such a race-to- development would permit property owners to evade the land-use plan and undermine its goals. *See id.; Miller v. Board of Public Works,* 195 Cal. 477, 234 P. 381, 388 (1925). Finally, the breathing room provided by temporary moratoria helps ensure that the planning process is responsive to the property owners and citizens who will be affected by the resulting land-use regulations. *See* Robert H. Freilich, *Interim Development Controls: Essential Tools for Implementing Flexible Planning and Zoning,* 49 J. Urb. Law 65, 79 (1971). Absent the pressure of trying to out-speed developers who are attempting to circumvent the planning goals, the "planning and implementation process may be permitted to run its full and natural course with widespread citizen input and involvement, public debate, and full consideration of all issues and points of view." Garvin and Leitner, *supra,* at 3. Given the importance and long-standing use temporary moratoria, courts should be exceedingly reluctant to adopt rulings that would threaten the survival of this crucial planning mechanism.

In opposition to the overwhelming legal and logical support for not conceptually severing fee interests into small temporal pieces, the plaintiffs argue (and the district court below decided) that the Court's decision in *First English Evangelical Lutheran Church v. County of Los Angeles,* 482 U.S. 304 (1987), compels such conceptual severance of the property rights in this case. The plaintiffs contend that *First English* holds that conceptual severance of the temporal dimension of property interests is generally required. This argument is flatly incorrect.

First English is not even a case about what constitutes a taking. In *First English,* property owners challenged an ordinance that prevented the development of property located on a flood plain; they sought "damages for the uncompensated taking of all use" of the property. *See id.* at 309. The California Court of Appeal rejected their claims on the ground that, regardless of whether a taking occurred, the claimants could not recover damages during the period running from the time of enactment of the ordinance to the time when it was finally declared unconstitutional. *See id.* Because the question presented to the Supreme Court related only to the remedy available *once a taking had been proven*, the Court stated explicitly that it was not addressing whether the ordinance constituted a taking. *See id.* at 313 ("We accordingly have no occasion to decide whether the ordinance at issue actually denied appellant all use of its property. . . ."). According to the Court, it was resolving only the question whether, *once a taking is established,* "abandonment [of that taking] by the government requires payment of compensation for the period of time during which regulations" that constitute a taking are in effect. *Id.* at 318; *see also id.* at 311 (noting that the "disposition of the case [by the California court on the assumption that a taking occurred] isolates the remedial question for our consideration"); Michelman, *supra,* at 1617 & n. 81.

It is true that *First English* holds that, when a *taking* has occurred, the government must compensate property owners, even if the taking is "temporary." Contrary to the plaintiffs' suggestion, however, the Court's holding in *First English* was not that temporary moratoria are "temporary takings." In fact, the opposite is true. The *First English* Court very carefully defined " 'temporary' regulatory takings [as] those regulatory takings which are ultimately invalidated by the courts." 482 U.S. at 310. What is "temporary," according to the Court's definition, is not the regulation; rather, what is "temporary" is the taking, which is rendered temporary only when an ordinance that effects a taking is struck down by a court. In other words, a *permanent* regulation leads to a *"temporary "* taking when a court invalidates the ordinance after the taking. *See id.* at 319 ("Invalidation of the ordinance or its successor ordinance after this period of time, though converting the taking into a 'temporary' one, is not a sufficient remedy to meet the demands of the Just Compensation Clause."); *id.* at 317 (discussing the fact "that the government may elect to abandon its intrusion or discontinue regulations," and thereby turn what would otherwise be a "permanent taking" into a " 'temporary' taking"). The Court's definition, therefore, does not comprehend temporary moratoria, which from the outset are designed to last for only a limited period of time. In short, we reject the plaintiffs' contentions that *First English* applies to temporary moratoria and that it works a radical change to takings law by requiring that property interests be carved up into finite temporal segments. . . .

Chapter 7. Land Use Controls and Regulatory Takings

Having determined that the property interest at stake is just what one would expect it to be—the plaintiffs' fee interests—we must evaluate whether Ordinance 81-5 and Resolution 83-21 effected a categorical taking of each plaintiff's property. For purposes of this analysis, two features of these provisions are relevant. First, the provisions effectively placed a moratorium on the development of the plaintiffs' property. The second relevant feature of the provisions is that the moratorium they effected was intended to be temporary—the regulations were designed to institute a temporary moratorium that would remain in effect *only* until a new regional land-use plan could be adopted. *See Union Oil Co. v. Morton*, 512 F.2d 743, 751 (9th Cir.1975) (describing a regulation as temporary if its "termination is conditioned [on] the occurrence of certain future events").

To determine whether the temporary moratorium instituted by TRPA's regulations denies "all economically beneficial or productive use" of the plaintiffs' land, we must first consider the meaning of the phrase "economically beneficial or productive use." The phrase's precise meaning is elusive, and has not been clarified by the Supreme Court. See, e.g., Lake Nacimiento Ranch Co. v. County of San Luis Obispo, 841 F.2d 872, 877 (9th Cir.1988). The central confusion over its meaning centers on the relationship between the "use" of property and its "value." Clearly, the economic value of property provides strong evidence of the availability of "economically beneficial or productive uses" of that property. Nevertheless, there are instances in which certain kinds of "value" may be poor measures of the existence of such uses. In any event, we need not resolve the sticky issues surrounding the meaning and proof of the existence of "economically beneficial or productive uses," because it is clear from the "general scope and dominant features" of Ordinance 81-5 and Resolution 83-21 that the temporary moratorium imposed by these regulations did not deprive the plaintiffs' land in the Lake Tahoe Basin of either all of its "value" or all of its "use." Garneau, 147 F.3d at 807.

First, as amici Cities and Counties of California note, basic principles of economics show that the moratorium did not render the plaintiffs' property valueless. See generally *Lucas*, 505 U.S. at 1020, 112 S.Ct. 2886 (assuming, as the basis for its decision, that the regulation at issue rendered Lucas's two beachfront lots "valueless"). The moratorium was temporary—it was designed to and did dissolve upon

216

the adoption of a new regional plan. Given that the ordinance and resolution banned development for only a limited period, these regulations preserved the bulk of the future developmental use of the property. This future use had a substantial present value.

Of course, were a temporary moratorium designed to be in force so long as to eliminate all present value of a property's future use, we might be compelled to conclude that a categorical taking had occurred. We doubt, however, that a true temporary moratorium would ever be designed to last for so long a period. Certainly, the moratorium at issue here was not. The temporary moratorium was designed to suspend development only until a new regional land-use plan could be formulated—a process that the 1980 Compact intended would take thirty months. While the completion of the regional plan actually took forty months (which led to the temporary moratorium remaining in effect for eight months longer than expected), the moratorium still was in effect for only thirty-two months.

Moreover, there is no evidence that owners or purchasers of property in the basin anticipated that the temporary moratorium would continue indefinitely. Nor would they have had reason to: the district court found that TRPA worked diligently to complete the regional plan as quickly as possible. See Tahoe-Sierra Preservation Council, 34 F.Supp.2d at 1250-51. Thus, while the temporary moratorium surely had a negative impact on property values in the basin, we cannot conclude that the interim suspension of development wiped out the value of the plaintiffs' properties.

Furthermore, the temporary moratorium did not deprive the plaintiffs of all "use" of their property. The "use" of the plaintiffs' property runs from the present to the future. (This is a simple corollary of our earlier conclusion that the plaintiffs' property interests may not be temporally severed.) By instituting a temporary development moratorium, TRPA denied the plaintiffs only a small portion of this future stream; the thirty-two months during which the moratorium was in effect represents a small fraction of the useful life of the Tahoe properties.

Because the temporary development moratorium enacted by TRPA did not deprive the plaintiffs of all of the value or use of their property, we hold that it did not effect a categorical taking. Indeed, given the above analysis, it is equally clear that the district court was correct to conclude that the moratorium did not constitute a taking under the Penn Central test. See Tahoe-Sierra Preservation Council, 34 F.Supp.2d at 1240- 42. Thus, while the district court was correct as to this latter point, we reverse its holding that a categorical taking occurred. In reaching this conclusion, we preserve the ability of local governments to do what they have done for many years—to engage in orderly, reasonable land-use planning through a considered and deliberative process. To do otherwise would turn the Takings Clause into a weapon to be used indiscriminately to penalize local communities for attempting to protect the public interest.

KOZINSKI, Circuit Judge, with whom Circuit Judges O'SCANNLAIN, TROTT, T.G. NELSON and KLEINFELD join, dissenting from the order denying the petition for rehearing en banc:

The panel does not like the Supreme Court's Takings Clause jurisprudence very much, so it reverses *First English Evangelical Lutheran Church v. County of Los Angeles,* 482 U.S. 304 (1987), and adopts Justice Stevens's *First English* dissent. Because we are not free to rewrite Supreme Court precedent, I urged our court to take this case en banc. By voting not to rehear, we have neglected our duty and passed the burden of correcting our mistake on to a higher authority.

For almost twenty years, Lake Tahoe property owners have battled the Tahoe Regional Planning Agency (TRPA), which has blocked the owners' efforts to build homes on their land. The primary issue on this appeal, the fourth in this interminable case, is a temporary moratorium that required owners to leave their land idle for almost three years. The moratorium is only one of a series of restrictions and regulations that have prevented the plaintiffs- largely families who purchased lots in the 1970s hoping to build vacation or retirement homes-from making any use whatsoever of their property. After a bench trial, the district court found that the regulation deprived the owners of the use of their property for three years, and so held they were entitled to compensation. The panel does not set aside the lower court's finding. Instead, it reverses the judgment because, in its view, a temporary regulation can *never* be a regulatory taking. . . .

The only difference between this case and *Lucas* is that the regulation here had a finite duration. It was originally supposed to expire after two years and then was extended for another eight months. (In fact, its prohibitions continue to this day under subsequent development plans.) So the question is whether there is something special about a finite moratorium that relieves the government from its duty to compensate. The Supreme Court answered that question in *First English* when it said that "'temporary' takings which, as here, deny a landowner all use of his property, are *not different in kind* from permanent takings, for which the Constitution clearly requires compensation." 482 U.S. at 318 (emphasis added).

First English concerned a temporary development moratorium that Los Angeles enacted in response to a flood in the Angeles National Forest. First English Church challenged the ordinance, which prevented it from rebuilding damaged buildings. The California courts ruled that the regulation could only be a taking if permanent; if, on the other hand, the county decided to rescind the regulation, it ceased to be a taking. The U.S. Supreme Court disagreed, holding that "where the government's activities have already worked a taking of all use of property, no subsequent action by the government can relieve it of the duty to provide compensation for the period during which the taking was effective." *Id.* at 321.

Justice Stevens dissented from *First English* because he disagreed with the Court's "conclu[sion] that all ordinances which would constitute takings if allowed to remain in effect permanently, necessarily also constitute takings if they are in effect for only a limited period of time." *Id.* at 322, 107 S.Ct. 2378 (Stevens, J., dissenting). Justice Stevens would have held that a temporary regulation cannot be a taking, even though it deprives the owner of all present uses, because the property retains value based upon its future uses. That reasoning, embraced by no other member of the Supreme Court, is adopted by the panel in this case. . . .

The panel opinion creates a conflict with *Tabb Lakes, Ltd. v. United States,* 10 F.3d 796 (Fed.Cir.1993), which followed the majority's reasoning in *First English.* In so doing, *Tabb Lakes* recognized that "a taking, even for a day, without compensation is prohibited by the Constitution." *Id.* at 800. Under the panel's ruling in our case, a taking for a day could *never* require compensation, because despite the temporary deprivation, the property would retain almost all of its value based upon its expected future uses.

One problem with the panel's theory, and the theory of Justice Stevens's dissent, is that it views the regulation's effect on a property's value as the taking itself, rather than as a test for whether the government has deprived the owner of the benefits of his property. A regulation is a taking not because it destroys value, but because "total deprivation of beneficial use is, from the landowner's point of view, *the equivalent of a physical appropriation.*" *Lucas,* 505 U.S. at 1017 (emphasis added). In the case of regulations without a sunset provision, the deprivations of value and use are one and the same because, where the government permanently prevents the owner from putting his property to any beneficial use, no potential buyer would offer a dime for it.

But this identity between value and use obviously does not hold true in the case of a temporary taking. The government can deprive the owner of all present use, but the property *might* still retain value based upon its future uses. I emphasize "might," because so-called temporary moratoria have a habit of living beyond their purported termination dates. In this case, a series of consecutive development moratoria has prevented the landowners from building any homes on their lots for the two decades since the start of this litigation. If a local government can evade its constitutional obligations by describing a regulation as "temporary," we create a sizable loophole to the Takings Clause. Why would a government enact a permanent regulation-and risk incurring an obligation to compensate-when it can enact one moratorium after another, perhaps indefinitely? Under the theory adopted by the panel, it's hard to see when a property owner would ever state a takings claim against such a scheme.

Consider also the effect of this theory on non-regulatory takings. Let's say the government decides to use your house as a warehouse for three years. You are locked out and the government has the run of the property for that period. Is there any doubt that you have suffered a taking for which you should be compensated? Of course not. Why should the case be any different if the government simply prohibits you from using your house for three years, but never does get around to using it as a warehouse?

Indeed, it's well-established that temporary physical takings require compensation. *See, e.g., Kimball Laundry Co. v. United States,* 338 U.S. 1 (1949); *United States v. Petty Motor Co.,* 327 U.S. 372 (1946); *United States v. General Motors Corp.,* 323 U.S. 373 (1945). The panel opinion dismisses these cases because they involved physical takings, rather than regulatory ones. *See Tahoe-Sierra,* 216 F.3d at 779 ("The fact that just compensation was required in these cases, however, has no bearing on the question before us."). But *First English* rejected that distinction and found that these cases provided "substantial guidance" for its holding that all temporary takings, including regulatory ones, required compensation. 482 U.S. at 318. Again, the panel substitutes its own view of takings law for that of the Supreme Court.

These are all big problems with the panel's theory. But, of course, the biggest problem is that *First English* rejected it. *First English* held that a taking occurs when the government deprives an owner of the use of his property, even temporarily. *See* 482 U.S. at 318 (" '[T]emporary' takings which, as here, deny a landowner all *use* of his property, are not different in kind from permanent takings, for which the Constitution clearly requires compensation." (emphasis added)); *see also Lucas,* 505 U.S. at 1033 (Kennedy, J., concurring) ("It is well established that temporary takings are as protected by the Constitution as are permanent ones."). Nothing in the opinion-or any other—suggests otherwise. By adopting Justice Stevens's dissent, the panel places itself in square conflict with the majority's opinion in *First English.*

Of course, the panel doesn't admit that its opinion aligns itself with Justice Stevens's dissent, so it must pretend *First English* said nothing relevant to this case. And so the panel does, claiming that *First English* does not address whether a temporary moratorium is a taking, because it was "not even a case about what constitutes a taking." *Tahoe-Sierra,* 216 F.3d at 777. It is true that *First English* did not have to determine whether there was a temporary taking, because it accepted the state court's conclusion that a regulation prohibiting all development was a taking while it was in effect. (The Supreme Court endorsed that result a few years later in *Lucas.*) But *First English* did decide that a temporary regulation is "not different in kind" from a permanent one: If either deprives the owner of all use of his property, then the owner is entitled to compensation for the taking. *First English,* 482 U.S. at 318.

The panel does not deny that the moratorium here, like the regulation in *Lucas*, deprived the owners of the use of their property for its duration. But it ignores *First English* 's requirement that the owners be compensated for a temporary taking.

The panel also takes shelter from *First English* in the Supreme Court's acknowledgment that it did " 'not deal with the quite different questions that would arise in the case of normal delays in obtaining building permits, changes in zoning ordinances, variances, and the like which are not before us.' " *Tahoe-Sierra*, 216 F.3d at 778 n. 17 (quoting *First English*, 482 U.S. at 321). But that language in *First English* hardly authorizes the panel to ignore the decision altogether. Rather, it recognizes that a temporary taking only occurs when there is in fact a taking. Delays in obtaining a building permit, changes in zoning ordinances, or other temporary restrictions will not require compensation unless they deprive the landowner of all economically beneficial uses of the property for their duration. Here, the three-year prohibition on construction does not compare with the inherent delay in obtaining a permit or the frictional delay in the permitting process. The regulation clearly blocked all construction during the moratorium period.

Justice Holmes noted long ago that "a strong public desire to improve the public condition is not enough to warrant achieving the desire by a shorter cut than the constitutional way of paying for the change." *Pennsylvania Coal*, 260 U.S. at 416. *First English* recognized that the costs its decision imposed upon local regulators "necessarily flow from any decision upholding a claim of constitutional right; many of the provisions of the Constitution are designed to limit the flexibility and freedom of governmental authorities, and the Just Compensation Clause of the Fifth Amendment is one of them." *First English*, 482 U.S. at 321. The panel's desire to ease local governance does not justify approving means that violate rights secured by the Fifth Amendment as authoritatively interpreted by the Supreme Court.

NOTES AND QUESTIONS

1. Is the Ninth Circuit panel's decision consistent with *First English Evangelical Lutheran Church v. County of Los Angeles* (casebook p. 788)? In *First English* the Supreme Court had decided that invalidation of a regulation does not automatically defeat a takings claim

because even temporary takings require payment of just compensation. But it did not address the question whether a regulation intended to be temporary from the start could be deemed to be a taking requiring payment of just compensation. Is this distinction unimportant, as the dissenters argue? Recall that in *First English* no taking was found on remand because the regulation that prevented rebuilding a summer camp in a flood plain was deemed to satisfy the nuisance exception.

2. If a temporary moratorium on development cannot give rise to a takings claim, can government entities insulate themselves from takings claims simply by pretending that regulations they adopt are temporary and that they ultimately will be revised?

3. If the Court rules that a moratorium on development can effect a temporary taking, what impact will such a decision have on land-use regulation? Will it still be possible to preserve the status quo to prevent a race-to-development during the time it takes to develop new land use regulations? How do the dissenters respond to the policy argument that moratoria are a crucial tool for land-use regulation?

- 8 -

Environmental Assessment and Biodiversity Protection

Environmental Assessment:
Problems of Timing (pp. 856-72)

Further whale hunting by the Makah has been halted by the success in the Ninth Circuit of the lawsuit referred to in the last paragraph of the Problem Exercise, page 30. Metcalf v. Daley, 214 F.3d 1135 (9th Cir., 2000). The opinion is excerpted below.

Metcalf v. Daley, 214 F.3d 1135 (9th Cir. 2000)

TROTT, Circuit Judge:

I

FACTUAL BACKGROUND

. . .Congress passed the Whaling Convention Act to implement domestically the International Convention for the Regulation of Whaling. . . The National Oceanic and Atmospheric Administration ("NOAA") and the National Marine Fisheries Service ("NMFS"), branches of the Department of Commerce, have been tasked with promulgating regulations to implement the provisions of the Whaling Convention Act. See id. § 916 et seq.; 50 C.F.R. § 230.1 (1998).

When the IWC was established on December 2, 1946, it took immediate action to protect the beleaguered mammal. Specifically, the IWC amended the Schedule to impose a complete ban on the taking or killing of gray whales. 62 Stat. at 1723. However, the IWC included an exception to the ban "when the meat and products of such whales are to be used exclusively for local consumption by the aborigines." Id. This qualification is referred to as the "aboriginal subsistence exception."

In addition to being shielded from commercial whaling under international law, the gray whale received increased protection in 1970 when the United States designated the species as endangered under the En-

225

dangered Species Conservation Act of 1969, the predecessor to the Endangered Species Act of 1973 ("ESA"). In 1993, however, NMFS determined that the eastern North Pacific stock of gray whales had recovered to near its estimated original population size and was no longer in danger of extinction. Endangered Fish and Wildlife, 58 Fed.Reg. 3121, 3135 (1993). As such, this stock of gray whales was removed from the endangered species list in 1994. Id. At that point, and as required by the ESA, NMFS began a five-year monitoring program to document and to evaluate the viability of the stock subsequent to delisting.

After these gray whales were removed from the endangered species list, the Makah decided to resume the hunting of whales who migrated through the [Olympic Coast National Marine Sanctuary ("Sanctuary"), which Congress established in 1993 in order to protect the marine environment in a pristine ocean and coastal area.] To execute this plan, the Makah turned to the United States government — the Department of Commerce, NOAA, and NMFS — for assistance. The Tribe asked representatives from the Department of Commerce to represent it in seeking approval from the IWC for an annual quota of up to five gray whales.

As evidenced in an internal e-mail message written by an NMFS representative, the United States agreed in 1995 to "work with" the Makah in obtaining an aboriginal subsistence quota from the IWC. It was too late, however, to present the Makah's request formally at the IWC annual meeting scheduled to take place in May 1995. Nevertheless, the United States took the opportunity at the annual meeting to inform the Commission that: (1) the Makah had expressed an interest in harvesting up to five gray whales for ceremonial and subsistence purposes; and (2) the United States intended to submit in the future a formal proposal requesting such a quota.

After the 1995 annual meeting, NOAA prepared an internal report evaluating the merits of the Tribe's proposal in order to determine whether the United States should support its request for a gray whale quota. In some respects, the report suggested that the United States should lend its support to the Tribe. For example, the report concluded that the Makah have a well-documented history of dependency on the gray whale, and that a return to whaling could benefit the Tribe. On the other hand, the report concluded also that allowing the Makah to whale could set a precedent for other tribes who had also expressed an interest in whaling. Despite these concerns, however, NOAA did not initiate the NEPA process by publishing a draft EA or EIS for public review.

In January 1996, Will Martin, an NOAA representative, sent an e-mail message to his colleagues informing them that "we now have interagency agreement to support the Makah's application in IWC for a whaling quota of 5 grey whales." Shortly thereafter, on March 22, 1996, NOAA entered into a formal written Agreement with the Tribe, which provided that "[a]fter an adequate statement of need is prepared [by the Makah], NOAA, through the U.S. Commissioner to the IWC, will make a formal proposal to the IWC for a quota of gray whales for subsistence and ceremonial use by the Makah Tribe." Furthermore, the Agreement provided for cooperation between NOAA and the Makah Tribal Council ("Council") in managing the harvest of gray whales. More specifically, NOAA agreed: (1) to monitor the hunt; (2) to assist the Council in collecting certain information (e.g., body length and sex of the landed whales; length and sex of any fetus in a landed whale; whether a whale that was struck, but not landed, suffered a potentially fatal wound from a harpoon or bomb emplacement); and (3) to collect specimen material from landed whales, including ovaries, ear plugs, baleen plates, stomach contents, and tissue samples. Finally, the Agreement provided that within thirty days of IWC approval of a quota, "NOAA will revise its regulations to address subsistence whaling by the Makah Tribe, and the Council will adopt a management plan and regulations to govern the harvest. . . ." The Agreement was signed by the Chairman of the Makah Tribal Council, Hubert Markishtum, and the Under Secretary for Oceans and Atmosphere, D. James Baker.

Pursuant to the Agreement, the Makah prepared an adequate statement of need, and the United States presented a formal proposal to the IWC for a quota of gray whales for the Tribe at the IWC annual meeting in June 1996. Several member nations supported the Makah whaling proposal, while others expressed concerns and indicated that they would vote against it. In short order, the proposal turned controversial. As the annual meeting was in progress, the United States House of Representatives Committee on Resources unanimously passed a resolution, introduced by Representatives Jack Metcalf (R-Washington) and

George Miller (D-California), opposing the proposal. Ultimately, the United States realized that it did not have the three-quarters majority required to approve it. Thus, after consulting with the Makah, the United States withdrew the proposal in order to give the Tribe an opportunity to address the delegates' concerns.

In June 1997, an attorney representing the organizations Australians for Animals and BEACH Marine Protection wrote a letter to NOAA and NMFS alleging that the United States Government had violated NEPA by authorizing and promoting the Makah whaling proposal without preparing an EA or an EIS. In response, the Administrator for NOAA wrote to Australians for Animals and BEACH Marine Protection on July 25, 1997, informing them that an EA would be prepared. Twenty-eight days later, on August 22, 1997, a draft EA was distributed for public comment.

On October 13, 1997, NOAA and the Makah entered into a new written Agreement, which, in most respects, was identical to the Agreement signed in 1996. Unlike the earlier Agreement, however, the 1997 Agreement required the Makah to "confin[e] hunting activities to the open waters of the Pacific Ocean outside the Tatoosh-Bonilla Line." Apparently, this provision was added to the Agreement in order to increase the probability that, although the whaling would occur in the Sanctuary, the Makah would hunt only the migratory whales, rather than the Sanctuary's "summer residents."[Editors' Note: A small subpopulation of gray whales, commonly referred to as "summer residents," lives in the Sanctuary throughout the entire year.] Four days later, and after the signing of this new Agreement, NOAA/NMFS issued, on October 17, 1997, a final EA and a Finding of No Significant Impact ("FONSI").

The 1997 IWC annual meeting was held on October 18, 1997, one day after the final EA had been issued. Before this meeting, however, the United States (representing the Makah) and the Russian Federation (representing a Siberian aboriginal group called the Chukotka) had met to discuss the possibility of submitting a joint proposal for a gray whale quota, as the IWC previously had granted a gray whale quota for the benefit of the Chukotka. After conferring, the United States and the Russian Federation decided to submit a joint proposal for a five-year block quota of 620 whales. The total quota of 620 assumed an average annual harvest of 120 whales by the Chukotka and an average annual harvest of four whales by the Makah. We note in passing that because "not every gray whale struck will be landed," the EA eventually concluded that the cumulative impact of the removal of injured gray whales by the Makah would total not just twenty whales over a five-year period, but forty-one. The EA makes no explicit mention of the decision to submit this joint proposal to the IWC, which would include a block quota of 620 whales for the Chukotka.

At the meeting, some delegates expressed doubts about whether the Makah qualified for the quota under the "aboriginal subsistence" exception. For this reason, these delegates suggested amending the joint proposal to allow the quota to be used only by aboriginal groups "whose traditional subsistence and cultural needs have been recognized by the International Whaling Commission." (emphasis added). Presumably, these delegates were attempting to amend the proposal in a manner that would allow the Chukotka to harvest gray whales, but would prohibit the Makah from doing so. However, the United States rejected this amendment on the grounds that the IWC did not have an established mechanism for recognizing such needs. Instead, the delegates agreed to amend the proposal to allow the quota to be used only by aboriginal groups "whose traditional subsistence and cultural needs have been recognized." Shortly thereafter, the quota was approved by consensus with no objections.

On April 6, 1998, NOAA issued a Federal Register Notice setting the domestic subsistence whaling quotas for 1998. See Notice of Aboriginal Subsistence Whaling Quotas, 63 Fed.Reg. 16,701 (1998). The Notice stated that the Makah's subsistence and cultural needs had been recognized by both the United States and the IWC. Id. at 16,704. Accordingly, the Notice allowed the Makah to engage in whaling pursuant to the IWC-approved quota and Whaling Convention Act regulations. Id.

II

PROCEDURAL BACKGROUND

On October 17, 1997, the same day as the release of the FONSI, appellants, including, inter alia, Congressman Metcalf, Australians for Animals, and BEACH Marine Protection, filed a complaint against the Federal Defendants in the United States District Court for the District of Columbia. Appellants alleged that the Federal Defendants had violated NEPA, the Whaling Convention Act, and the Administrative Procedures Act in connection with their support of the Makah whaling proposal. After granting the Makah's motion to intervene, the district court transferred the case to the Western District of Washington.

The Federal Defendants provided the district court with 172 documents that they claimed constituted the administrative record. However, material had been redacted from seventeen of these documents. Furthermore, pursuant to their request under the Freedom of Information Act, 5 U.S.C. § 552 (1996), appellants learned that NMFS possessed additional records relating to the Makah whaling proposal that had not been included in the administrative record. Because appellants believed the Federal Defendants were required to provide the court with the entire administrative record, they moved (1) to compel production of the materials that had been redacted from the administrative record, and (2) to supplement the administrative record with the additional documents discovered via the Freedom of Information Act request. The district court denied the first motion on the ground that the redacted material was protected by the "deliberative process privilege," which is an exception to the Freedom of Information Act, and it denied the second motion because appellants failed to establish that "the documents they sought would alter the summary judgment analysis."

Ultimately, the parties filed cross-motions for summary judgment on the merits, which were briefed and argued during the spring and summer of 1998. On September 21, 1998, the district court denied appellants' motion for summary judgment and granted the Federal Defendants' and the Makah's motions for summary judgment. . . .

IV

NEPA CLAIM

A.

NEPA sets forth a "national policy which will encourage productive and enjoyable harmony between man and his environment ... [and] promote efforts which will prevent or eliminate damage to the environment and biosphere and stimulate the health and welfare of man."

42 U.S.C.A. § 4321 (1994). NEPA does not set out substantive environmental standards, but instead establishes "action-forcing" procedures that require agencies to take a "hard look" at environmental consequences. See Robertson v. Methow Valley Citizens Council, 490 U.S. 332, 348, 109 S.Ct. 1835, 104 L.Ed.2d 351 (1989). We have characterized the statute as "primarily procedural," and held that "agency action taken without observance of the procedure required by law will be set aside." Save the Yaak, 840 F.2d at 717. In this respect, we have observed in connection with the preparation of an EA that "[p]roper timing is one of NEPA's central themes. An assessment must be 'prepared early enough so that it can serve practically as an important contribution to the decisionmaking process and will not be used to rationalize or justify decisions already made'." Id. at 718 (quoting 40 C.F.R. § 1502.5 (1987)).

The phrase "early enough" means "at the earliest possible time to insure that planning and decisions reflect environmental values." Andrus v. Sierra Club, 442 U.S. 347, 351, 99 S.Ct. 2335, 60 L.Ed.2d 943 (1979); see also 40 C.F.R. § 1501.2 (1999). The Supreme Court in referring to NEPA's requirements as "action forcing," Andrus, 442 U.S. at 350, 99 S.Ct. 2335, has embraced the rule that for projects directly undertaken by Federal agencies, environmental impact statements "shall be prepared at the feasibility analysis (go-no go) stage and may be supplemented at a later stage if necessary." Id. at 351 n. 3, 99 S.Ct. 2335; see also 40 C.F.R. § 1502.5(a) (1999).

All of these rules notwithstanding, NEPA does not require that agency officials be "subjectively impartial." Environmental Defense Fund v. Corps of Eng'rs of the U.S. Army, 470 F.2d 289, 295 (8th Cir.1972). The statute does require, however, that projects be objectively evaluated.

> NEPA assumes as inevitable an institutional bias within an agency proposing a project and erects the procedural requirements of § 102 to insure that "there is no way [the decisionmaker] can fail to note the facts and understand the very serious arguments advanced by the plaintiff if he carefully reviews the entire environmental impact statement."

Id. (quoting Environmental Defense Fund v. Corps of Eng'rs of the

U.S. Army, 342 F.Supp. 1211, 1218 (E.D.Ark.1972)).

In summary, the comprehensive "hard look" mandated by Congress and required by the statute must be timely, and it must be taken objectively and in good faith, not as an exercise in form over substance, and not as a subterfuge designed to rationalize a decision already made. As the Eighth Circuit observed in Environmental Defense Fund, "[t]he unequivocal intent of NEPA is to require agencies to consider and give effect to the environmental goals set forth in the Act, not just to file detailed impact studies which will fill governmental archives." Id. at 298.

NEPA requires that an EIS be prepared for all "major Federal actions significantly affecting the quality of the human environment." 42 U.S.C.A. § 4332(2)(C) (1994). However, if, as here, an agency's regulations do not categorically require the preparation of an EIS, then the agency must first prepare an EA to determine whether the action will have a significant effect on the environment. See 40 C.F.R. § 1501.4 (1999); Salmon River Concerned Citizens v. Robertson, 32 F.3d 1346, 1356 (9th Cir.1994). If, in light of the EA, the agency determines that its action will significantly affect the environment, then an EIS must be prepared; if not, then the agency issues a FONSI. See 40 C.F.R. §§ 1501.4, 1508.9 (1999); Salmon River, 32 F.3d at 1356. "If an agency decides not to prepare an EIS, it must supply a 'convincing statement of reasons' to explain why a project's impacts are insignificant." Blue Mountains, 161 F.3d at 1211 (quoting Save the Yaak, 840 F.2d at 717).

In this case, the Federal Defendants did (1) prepare an EA, (2) decide that the Makah whaling proposal would not significantly affect the environment, and (3) issue a FONSI, but they did so after already having signed two agreements binding them to support the Tribe's proposal. Appellants assert that, in so doing, the Federal Defendants violated NEPA in several ways. Appellants argue that, although NOAA/NMFS ultimately prepared an EA, they violated NEPA because they prepared the EA too late in the process. According to appellants, "by making a commitment to authorize and fund the Makah whaling plan, and then drafting a NEPA document which simply rubber-stamped the decision . . . , defendants eliminated the opportunity to choose among alternatives, . . . and seriously imped[ed] the degree to which their planning and decisions could reflect environmental values." Additionally, appellants contend that the Federal Defendants violated NEPA by preparing an inadequate EA, and by issuing a FONSI instead of preparing an EIS.

B.

We begin by considering appellants' argument that the Federal Defendants failed timely and in the proper sequence to comply with NEPA. As provided in the regulations promulgated to implement NEPA, "[a]gencies shall integrate the NEPA process with other planning at the earliest possible time to insure that planning and decisions reflect environmental values, to avoid delays later in the process, and to head off potential conflicts." 40 C.F.R. § 1501.2 (emphasis added); see also id. § 1502.5 ("An agency shall commence preparation of an [EIS] as close as possible to the time the agency is developing or is presented with a proposal. . . ."). Furthermore, this court has interpreted these regulations as requiring agencies to prepare NEPA documents, such as an EA or an EIS, "before any irreversible and irretrievable commitment of resources." Conner v. Burford, 848 F.2d 1441, 1446 (9th Cir.1988); see also EDF v. Andrus, 596 F.2d 848, 852 (9th Cir.1979). Thus, the issue we must decide here is whether the Federal Defendants prepared the EA too late in the decision-making process, i.e., after making an irreversible and irretrievable commitment of resources. We conclude that they did.

The purpose of an EA is to provide the agency with sufficient evidence and analysis for determining whether to prepare an EIS or to issue a FONSI. 40 C.F.R. § 1508.9. Because the very important decision whether to prepare an EIS is based solely on the EA, the EA is fundamental to the decision-making process. In terms of timing and importance to the goals of NEPA, we see no difference between an EA and an EIS in connection with when an EA must be integrated into the calculus. In the case at bar, the Makah first asked the Federal Defendants to help them secure IWC approval for a gray whale quota in 1995; however, NOAA/NMFS did not prepare an EA until 1997. During these two years, the United States and the Makah worked together toward obtaining a gray whale quota from the IWC. In January 1996, an NOAA representative informed his colleagues that "we now have interagency agreement to support the Makah's application in IWC for a whaling quota of 5 grey whales." More importantly, in March 1996, more than a year before the EA was prepared, NOAA entered into a contract with the Makah pursuant to which it committed to (1) making a formal proposal to the IWC for a quota of gray whales for subsistence and ceremonial use by the Makah and (2) participating in the management of the harvest. To demonstrate the firmness of this commitment, we need only to look at the EA, which says, "In early 1996, [NOAA and the Makah Tribal Council] signed an agreement in which the United States committed to make a formal request to the IWC. . . ."

The Federal Defendants did not engage the NEPA process "at the earliest possible time." Instead, the record makes clear that the Federal Defendants did not even consider the potential environmental effects of the proposed action until long after they had already committed in writing to support the Makah whaling proposal. The "point of commitment" in this case came when NOAA signed the contract with the Makah in March 1996 and then worked to effectuate the agreement. It was at this juncture that it made an "irreversible and irretrievable commitment of resources." As in Save the Yaak, the "contracts were awarded prior to the preparation of the EAs. . . . These events demonstrate that the agency did not comply with NEPA's requirements concerning the timing of their environmental analysis, thereby seriously impeding the degree to which their planning and decisions could reflect environmental values." Save the Yaak, 840 F.2d at 718-19. Although it could have, NOAA did not make its promise to seek a quota from the IWC and to participate in the harvest conditional upon a NEPA determination that the Makah whaling proposal would not significantly affect the environment.

Had NOAA/NMFS found after signing the Agreement that allowing the Makah to resume whaling would have a significant effect on the environment, the Federal Defendants would have been required to prepare an EIS, and they may not have been able to fulfill their written commitment to the Tribe. As such, NOAA would have been in breach of contract. Although the United States delegates to the 1996 IWC meeting ultimately withdrew their proposal for a Makah aboriginal subsistence whaling quota, they did so with the Tribe's approval and because the proposal did not have adequate support from other IWC delegations, not in order to reconsider environmental concerns. The firmness of the 1996 Agreement became even clearer and more resolute in 1997 when NOAA entered into a new, similar contract with the Tribe to pursue its whaling quota at the 1997 IWC meeting. This Agreement was signed four days before the final EA in this case was issued.

In the EA, the agencies referred to this second Agreement as having "renewed the cooperative Agreement" signed in 1996. This is strong evidence that NOAA and other agencies made the decision to support the Tribe's proposal in 1996, before the EA process began and without considering the environmental consequences thereof. By the time the Federal Defendants completed the final EA in 1997, the die already had been cast. The "point of commitment" to this proposal clearly had come and gone. ... the contracts here amounted to a surrender of the Government's right to prevent activity in the relevant area. Cf. Friends of Southeast's Future v. Morrison, 153 F.3d 1059, 1063 (9th Cir.1998) (holding that the Forest Service did not make an "irreversible and irretrievable commitment of resources" when it prepared a Tentative Operating Schedule because "the agency was free to follow the [Schedule] or alter it as conditions warrant").

It is highly likely that because of the Federal Defendants' prior written commitment to the Makah and concrete efforts on their behalf, the EA was slanted in favor of finding that the Makah whaling proposal would not significantly affect the environment. As the court below noted, "the longer the defendants worked with the Tribe toward the end of whaling, the greater the pressure to achieve this end. ... [A]n EA prepared under such circumstances might be subject to at least a subtle pro-whaling bias." The EA itself somewhat disingenuously claims in 1997 that the "decision to be made" is "whether to support the Makah Tribe in its effort to continue its whaling tradition," when in point of fact that decision had already been made in contract form. To quote the 1996 Agreement, "after an adequate statement of need is prepared, NOAA ... will make a formal proposal to the IWC for a quota of gray whales...." The Makah satisfied its part of the bargain in 1996, binding the Federal Defendants to deliver on theirs, as they did at the IWC meeting in June 1996. Also, NOAA/NMFS's statement in the EA that "[a]ny perception that the U.S. Government is trying to withdraw its support for Makah whaling would likely plunge the Tribe into a difficult controversy with the United States" strongly suggests that the Federal Defendants were predisposed to issue a FONSI.

NEPA's effectiveness depends entirely on involving environmental considerations in the initial decisionmaking process. See 40 C.F.R. §§ 1501.2, 1502.5; see also Methow Valley, 490 U.S. at 349 (explaining that NEPA "ensures that the agency, in reaching its decision, will have available, and will carefully consider, detailed information concerning significant environmental impacts"). Moreover, the Supreme Court has clearly held that treaty rights such as those at stake in this case "may be regulated . . . in the interest of conservation . . . , provided the regulation . . . does not discriminate against the Indians." Puyallup Tribe v. Department of Game of Wash., 391 U.S. 392, 398 (1968). Here, before preparing an EA, the Federal Defendants signed a contract which obligated them both to make a proposal to the IWC for a gray whale quota and to participate in the harvest of those whales. We hold that by making such a firm commitment before preparing an EA, the Federal Defendants failed to take a "hard look" at the environmental consequences of their actions and, therefore, violated NEPA.

Our decision in Thomas v. Peterson, 753 F.2d 754 (9th Cir.1985), supports this conclusion. In that case, the Forest Service planned to construct a road in order to facilitate timber sales. See id. at 756-57. The Forest Service wanted to build the road, and then prepare an EA/EIS to analyze the environmental impact of the timber sales. See id. at 757. However, the court explained that "[b]uilding the road swings the balance decidedly in favor of timber sales even if such sales would have been disfavored had road and sales been considered together before the road was built." Id. Accordingly, the Peterson court held that the Forest Service must prepare an EIS before deciding whether to approve the proposed road. Id. at 761. Similarly, we conclude that the Federal Defendants should not have fully committed to support the Makah whaling proposal before preparing the EA because doing so probably influenced their evaluation of the environmental impact of the proposal.

We want to make clear, however, that this case does not stand for the general proposition that an agency cannot begin preliminary consideration of an action without first preparing an EA, or that an agency must always prepare an EA before it can lend support to any proposal. We have discussed this distinction in Association of Pub. Agency Customers, Inc. v. Bonneville Power Admin., 126 F.3d 1158 (9th Cir.1997), where we pointed out that "an agency can formulate a proposal or even identify a preferred course of action before completing an EIS." Id. at 1184. We noted also that "Council on Environmental Quality ("CEQ") regulations actually encourage identification of a preferred course of action during the NEPA process. . . ." Id. at 1185 (citing 40 C.F.R. § 1502.14(e)). Rather, our holding here is limited to the unusual facts and circumstances of this case where the defendants already had made an "irreversible and irretrievable commitment of resources" — i.e., by entering into a contract with the Makah before they considered its environmental consequences and prepared the EA. . . .

V

REMEDY

Appellees argue that, even if the Federal Defendants did violate NEPA by preparing the EA after deciding to support Makah whaling, the issue is moot because the only relief that the court could order is the preparation of an adequate EA, which, appellees contend, already has been done. In making this argument, appellees rely on Realty Income Trust v. Eckerd, 564 F.2d 447 (D.C.Cir.1977), in which the court refused to remand to the district court because an adequate EIS had been prepared before any action was taken that might harm the environment. Id. at 457. The Eckerd court explained:

> The problem here, to repeat, was simply one of timing, that is, that there was not a timely filing of an EIS with Congress. No complaint remains on appeal that the statements in substance were inadequate in any way.

Id.

We conclude that the case at bar is distinguishable from Eckerd and, therefore, appellees' reliance on that case is misplaced. Unlike in Eckerd, appellants do not concede that the EA that ultimately was prepared is adequate. To the contrary, appellants contend that the EA is demonstrably suspect because the process under which the EA was prepared was fatally defective — i.e., the Federal Defendants were predisposed to finding that the Makah whaling proposal would not significantly affect the environment. We agree. Moreover, appellants vigorously maintain that the EA is deficient with respect to its content and conclusions.

Our conclusions about the EA in this case raise an obvious question: Having already committed in writing to support the Makah's whaling proposal, can the Federal Defendants now be trusted to take the clear-eyed hard look at the whaling proposal's consequences required by the law, or will a new EA be a classic Wonderland case of first-the-verdict, then-the-trial? In order to avoid this problem and to ensure that the law is respected, must we — and can we — set aside the

FONSI and require the Federal Defendants to proceed directly to the preparation of an Environmental Impact Statement? On reflection, and in consideration of our limited role in this process, we have decided that it is appropriate only to require a new EA, but to require that it be done under circumstances that ensure an objective evaluation free of the previous taint. Unlike many of the disputes we are called on to resolve, time here is not of the essence. Although the doctrine of laches cannot defeat Indian rights recognized in a treaty, see United States v. Washington, 157 F.3d 630, 649 (9th Cir.1998), the Makah's seventy year hiatus in connection with whale hunting suggests that a modest delay occasioned by the need to respect NEPA's commands will cause no harm. Cf. Forelaws on Bd. v. Johnson, 743 F.2d 677 (9th Cir.1984) (operation of contracts in third year of 20-year term not enjoined because of statutory mandate of implementation of a contractual system).

The manner of ensuring that the process for which we remand this case is accomplished objectively and in good faith shall be left to the relevant agencies. Should a new EA come back to the courts for additional scrutiny, however, the burden shall be on the Federal Defendants to demonstrate to the district court that they have complied with this requirement.

Accordingly, we REVERSE and REMAND to the district court. The district court is directed to order the Federal Defendants to set aside the FONSI, suspend implementation of the Agreement with the Tribe, begin the NEPA process afresh, and prepare a new EA.[4] Costs are awarded to Appellants Metcalf et al.

REVERSED and REMANDED.

[The dissent by Judge KLEINFELD is omitted].

NOTES AND QUESTIONS

1. The dissent raises two points against the majority opinion. First, the majority's recognition that it is permissible for an agency to have "an institutional bias" in favor of a project before preparing an EIS is inconsistent with its later objection that the EA/FONSI in this case was "slanted." Judge Kleinfeld argues that without having identified some aspect of the EIS that is inadequate, this is not a valid grounds to remand for further proceedings. How would you respond to this point?

2. The dissent also argues that the EA/FONSI was sufficiently timely because the agreement to promote the Makah petition before the IWC did not amount to an irretrievable commitment of resources: Even after IWC approval, further regulatory steps were necessary before the Makah could hunt. In Judge Kleinfeld's view, "there was no point in wasting the public's time and money on an environmental assessment until and unless the IWC made Makah whale hunting a possibility." How would you respond to this point?

3. As noted in Chapter One of this Supplement (p. 30), on July 13, 2001, the National Marine Fisheries Services released a new EA that endorsed resumption of the whaling. The new EA, which is 89 pages in length, finds that there is no biological reason for restricting the Makah hunt to the period from November through June when whales are migrating. It also recommends expanding the area where the hunt may occur. According to the EA, the population of gray whales is estimated to be around 26,000, the largest it has been since the mid-nineteenth century. The federal government now intends to develop a new cooperative agreement with the Makah that will allow the tribe to strike up to five whales per year until 2002 when the quota expires.

Determining the "Significance" of Action: Environmental Justice Concerns (p. 882)

Note 2 on page 882 of the casebook describes the ruling by the Nuclear Regulatory Commission's Atomic Safety and Licensing Board that environmental justice concerns must be addressed in the environmental impact statement (EIS) pertaining to the application by Louisiana Energy Services (LES) for the Claiborne Enrichment Center, a uranium enrichment facility near Homer, Louisiana. LES subsequently petitioned the full Nuclear Regulatory Commission (NRC) for a review of the Board's decision.

On April 3, 1998, the commission issued an Order that reversed the Board's requirement of further NRC staff investigation into racial discrimination, stating that the Board made "no finding one way or the other on whether intentional racism had tainted the decisional process." Furthermore, the commission said that while under the National Environmental Policy Act (NEPA), agencies are required to consider not only environmental impacts, but also social and economic impacts ancillary to them, "nothing in NEPA or in the cases interpreting it indicates that the statute is a tool for addressing problems of racial discrimination." The commission said the Board's proposed racial discrimination inquiry went "well beyond what NEPA has traditionally been interpreted to require," and "stretches NEPA to its breaking point."

The commission affirmed the Board's findings that the final EIS did not deal adequately with the "disparate impact" analysis. The Board ordered the NRC staff to revise the final EIS to deal with relocation of Parish Road 39 (road closures) and property value impacts. The commission agreed with the Board's disparate impact ruling, stating that "'disparate impact' analysis is our principal tool for advancing environmental justice under NEPA." The commission agreed that the NRC staff should provide a supplemental EIS with a more thorough analysis of the impacts of road closures and on local property values, and whether any actions can be taken to mitigate these impacts.

Despite the commission's ruling, LES abandoned its plans for the Claiborne Enrichment Center and asked NRC to withdraw its application noting that the project may linger indefinitely on these issues, and that the pace for LES to begin building the facility would be too slow to justify continued investment. On April 30, 1998, the commission granted the motion to withdraw the application, as well as terminate the proceedings.

Problem Exercise: Should the FCC Prepare an EIS Assessing the Cumulative Impact of Cellphone Tower Construction? (p. 883)

Construction of cellular, radio, television, and microwave communications towers in the United States has been growing at a rapid rate, estimated at 6 to 8 percent annually. As of September 2000, the Federal Communications Commission's Antenna Structure Registry included more than 74,000 towers, with 45,000 towers rising more than 199 feet above ground level.

In 2001, a pair of environmental groups – Friends of the Earth and the Forest Conservation Council – petitioned the Federal Communications Commission (FCC) to deny dozens of applications by telecommunications companies to build cellphone towers. The environmental groups argue that the FCC should not be allowed to approve any more applications to build new cellphone towers until it conducts an EIS that assesses the cumulative environmental effects of tower construction. The Commission requires companies to submit environmental impact studies with each application to build a new tower, but the environmental groups argue that none of these studies consider the cumulative environmental effects of the hundreds of cellphone towers that are erected each year with the FCC's approval. Yochi J. Dreazen, Cellular Towers Get Static From Environmentalists, Wall St. J., July 23, 2001, p. B1.

It has been well known since the nineteenth century that tall, lighted structures can pose significant hazards to birds, particularly to the 350 species of night-migrating birds. Cellular telephone towers usually are about 250 feet tall and the Federal Aviation Administration requires all towers more than 199 feet to display lights for aviation safety. The U.S. Fish and Wildlife Service (FWS) estimates that 4 to 5 million birds are killed every year as a result of collisions with communications towers. In addition to the millions of bird deaths that occur each year, environmental groups note that tower construction can damage wetlands and other environmentally sensitive areas. Towers also raise aesthetic concerns and there is considerable controversy over the potential health effects of the electromagnetic radiation they give off.

The telecommunications industry argues that estimates of bird deaths caused by towers are too high. Far more birds (hundreds of millions per year) are killed by collisions with windows and buildings and pesticides probably kill another 65 million birds annually. David Malakoff, Faulty Towers, Audubon Magazine, September 2001. The companies also argue that there is no conclusive data establishing that radiation emanating from cellphone towers causes health problems.

In November 1999, Jamie Clark, then the director of the FWS asked the chairman of the FCC to consider the cumulative environmental effects of cellphone tower construction. Clark noted that the towers were being built "with almost no environmental oversight by the FCC." The FCC refused to prepare a cumulative impact study. In September 2000 the FWS developed "Interim Guidelines for For Recommendation on Communications Tower Siting, Construction, Operation and Decommissioning" to help mitigate the risks of birds colliding with towers.

It could take more than a year to prepare an environmental impact statement of the cumulative effects of cellphone tower construction at a time when the telecommunications industry is rushing to offer new high-speed mobile access to the internet. The industry argues that it already is struggling to keep up with surging consumer demand for wireless services and that construction delays caused by environmental reviews could be devastating. Each month's delay in approving construction of a cellphone tower is estimated to cost a company $300,000 per tower in lost revenue. Id.

QUESTION ONE: How should the FCC rule on the petition by the environmental groups? Should the Commission consider the economic consequences of delaying cellphone tower construction when deciding whether or not to prepare an EIS of cumulative effects? Is the fact thatfar more birds are killed by other causes relevant to the decision?

QUESTION TWO: If the FCC refuses to prepare an EIS, what are the chances that the environmental groups can bring a successful lawsuit challenging the Commission's decision?

Supplementing EISs (pp. 897-900)

Two decisions by the U.S. Court of Appeals for the Ninth Circuit addressed agencies' duty to supplement environmental impact statements when new information becomes available. In Friends of the Clearwater v. Dombeck, 222 F.3d 552 (9th Cir. 2000), the court held that the issuance of supplemental information reports (SIRs) to explain why no supplemental EIS was necessary was a proper means for curing the Forest Service's failure to assess new information regarding sensitive wildlife species and old growth forest that might be affected by timber sales. However, in Idaho Sporting Congress, Inc. v. Alexander, 222 F.3d 1170 (9th Cir. 2000), the same Ninth Circuit panel held that SIRs could not be used to cure defects in the initial EIS by presenting and assessing information that was available, but not included, in it.

The Constitutional Reach of Federal Authority to Protect Endangered Species (pp. 912-23)

The Constitutional authority of Congress to protect endangered species was challenged in the case that follows. Citing United States v. Lopez, 514 U.S. 549 (1995), appellants argued that Congress did not have the authority to prohibit private action that harmed an experimental population of red wolves because it did not have a substantial effect on interstate commerce. Over a vigorous dissent, a panel of the Fourth Circuit rejected this argument. The Supreme Court declined to grant review of the Fourth Circuit's decision, despite Judge Luttig's vigorous dissent. The Bush administration's new Solicitor General, Theodore Olson, represented the plaintiffs in the case who sought Supreme Court review of the decision. The Court previously had declined to review the decision rejecting a similar challenge to the ESA in National Association of Home Builders v. Babbitt, 130 F.3d 1041 (D.C. Cir. 1997) (casebook pp. 912-23), despite Judge Sentelle's call to arms in dissent.

Gibbs v. Babbitt, 214 F.3d 483 (4th Cir. 2000)

Chief Judge WILKINSON wrote the majority opinion, in which Judge MICHAEL joined. Judge LUTTIG wrote a dissenting opinion.

WILKINSON, Chief Judge:

. . .

I.

A.

In response to growing concern over the extinction of many animal and plant species, Congress enacted the Endangered Species Act of 1973(ESA), Pub.L. 93-205, 81 Stat. 884 (codified as amended at 16 U.S.C. §§ 1531-44 (1994 & Supp. III 1997)). Congress found that many of the species threatened with extinction are of "esthetic, ecological, educational, historical, recreational, and scientific value to the Nation and its people." 16 U.S.C. § 1531(a)(3) (1994). Congress also found that "various species of fish, wildlife, and plants in the United States have been rendered extinct as a consequence of economic growth and development untempered by adequate concern and conservation." Id. § 1531(a)(1). To address these national concerns, the ESA sets forth a comprehensive regulatory scheme to conserve these species and the ecosystems upon which they depend. The Act provides, inter alia, for the listing of "endangered" and "threatened" species, id. § 1533, and various recovery plans for the "conservation and survival" of listed species, id. § 1533(f).

The cornerstone of the statute is section 9(a)(1), which prohibits the taking of any endangered species without a permit or other authorization. Id. § 1538(a)(1)(B). The term "take" is defined as "to harass, harm, pursue, hunt, shoot, wound, kill, trap, capture, or collect, or to attempt to engage in any such conduct." Id. § 1532(19). The ESA also authorizes the Fish and Wildlife Service (FWS) to issue any necessary regulations for the conservation of threatened species. Id. § 1533(d). Finally, in keeping with its commitment to species conservation, the ESA states that a state law may be more restrictive than the provisions of the Act, but not less. Id. § 1535(f).

In order to increase the Service's flexibility in reintroducing endangered species into portions of their historic range, Congress extensively amended the ESA in 1982, Pub.L. 97-304, 96 Stat. 1426. Prior to 1982, reintroduced species were treated the same as any other endangered species. See id. § 1536 & 1538(a) (providing for stringent consultation and reporting requirements and a near absolute prohibition on the taking of endangered species). These strict limits led to significant local opposition to the reintroductions. In response to these problems, Congress added section 10(j), which allows the FWS to designate as "experimental" some reintroduced populations of endangered or threatened species. Id. § 1539(j). Under the looser standards of section 10(j), members of an experimental population are generally to be treated as threatened rather than endangered. Id. § 1539(j)(2)(C). This means that protective regulations may be established for their conservation. See id. at 1533(d). By promulgating special rules for an experimental population the Service can determine which prohibitions and exceptions shall apply. See 50 C.F.R. § 17.82 (1998). . . .

B.

The red wolf, Canis rufus, is an endangered species whose protection is at issue in this case. The red wolf was originally found throughout the southeastern United States. It was once abundant in the "riverine habitats of the southeast," and was especially numerous near the "canebrakes" that harbored large populations of swamp and marsh rabbits, the primary prey of the red wolf. 51 Fed.Reg. 41,790, 41,791 (1986). The FWS found that "the demise of the red wolf was directly related to man's activities, especially land changes, such as the drainage of vast wetland areas for agricultural purposes . . . and predator control efforts at the private, State, and Federal levels." Id.

Ch. 8. Environmental Assessment/Biodiversity Protection

Activities such as wetlands drainage, dam construction, and hunting reduced the red wolf to such meager numbers that it was listed as endangered in 1976. See 32 Fed.Reg. 4001 (1976). Because of the paucity of animals left in the wild, their poor physical condition, and the threats posed by inbreeding, the FWS decided to trap the remaining red wolves in the mid-1970s and place them in a captive breeding program. See 51 Fed.Reg. at 41,791. The breeding program anticipated the eventual reintroduction of some red wolves into the wild. Id.

In 1986, the FWS issued a final rule outlining a reintroduction plan for red wolves in the 120,000-acre Alligator River National Wildlife Refuge in eastern North Carolina. See 51 Fed.Reg. 41,790. This area was judged the ideal habitat within the red wolf's historic range. Id. at 41,791. Between 1987 and 1992, a total of 42 wolves were released in the Refuge. In 1993, the reintroduction program was expanded to include the release of red wolves in the Pocosin Lakes National Wildlife Refuge in Tennessee. Since reintroduction, some red wolves have wandered from federal refuges onto private property. From available data, as of February 1998 it was estimated that about 41 of the approximately 75 wolves in the wild may now reside on private land.

This case raises a challenge to 50 C.F.R. § 17.84(c), a regulation governing the experimental populations of red wolves reintroduced into North Carolina and Tennessee pursuant to section 10(j). The FWS has extended the takings prohibitions of section 9(a)(1) to the experimental red wolf populations with certain exceptions. See 50 C.F.R. § 17.84(c) (1998). As noted above, the taking provision of section 9(a)(1) prevents landowners from harassing, harming, pursuing, hunting, shooting, wounding, killing, trapping, capturing, or collecting any endangered species. See 16 U.S.C. § 1532(19). However, in order to insure that other agencies and the public would accept the proposed reintroduction, the FWS relaxed the taking standards for wolves found on private land under its authority over experimental populations.

Section 17.84(c) allows a person to take red wolves on private land "[p]rovided that such taking is not intentional or willful, or is in defense of that person's own life or the lives of others." Id. § 17.84(c)(4)(i). Private landowners may also take red wolves on their property "when the wolves are in the act of killing livestock or pets, Provided that freshly wounded or killed livestock or pets are evident." Id. § 17.84(c)(4)(iii).

A landowner may also "harass red wolves found on his or her property ... Provided that all such harassment is by methods that are not lethal or injurious to the red wolf." Id. § 17.84(c)(4)(iv). Finally, landowners may take red wolves after efforts by Service personnel to capture such animals have been abandoned, and such taking has been approved in writing. Id. § 17.84(c)(4)(v). All of these exceptions to the taking prohibition are subject to a 24-hour reporting requirement. Id. § 17.84(c)(4).

C.

. . .

Appellants Charles Gibbs, Richard Mann, Hyde County, and Washington County filed the instant action challenging the federal government's authority to protect red wolves on private land. They seek a declaration that the anti-taking regulation, 50 C.F.R. § 17.84(c), as applied to the red wolves occupying private land in eastern North Carolina, exceeds Congress's power under the interstate Commerce Clause, U.S. Const. art. I, § 8, cl. 3 ("Congress shall have Power ... To regulate Commerce ... among the several States ..."). Appellants also seek an injunction against continued enforcement of the anti-taking regulation on non-federal land. Appellants claim that the red wolves have proven to be a "menace to citizens and animals in the Counties." They further allege that because of the federal regulatory protections surrounding the wolves, North Carolinians cannot effectively defend their property.

On cross-motions for summary judgment, the United States District Court for the Eastern District of North Carolina held that Congress's power to regulate interstate commerce includes the power to regulate conduct that might harm red wolves on private land. See Gibbs v. Babbitt, 31 F.Supp.2d 531 (E.D.N.C.1998). The district court found that the red wolves are "things in interstate commerce" because they have moved across state lines and their movement is followed by "tourists, academics, and scientists." Id. at 535. The court also found that the tourism they generate substantially affects interstate commerce. See id. The private landowners and North Carolina Counties now appeal.

II.

We consider this case under the framework articulated by the Supreme Court in United States v. Lopez, 514 U.S. 549, (1995), and United

States v. Morrison, 120 S.Ct. 1740 (2000), aff'g Brzonkala v. Virginia Polytechnic Institute and State University, 169 F.3d 820 (4th Cir.1999). While Congress's power to pass laws under the Commerce Clause has been interpreted broadly, both *Lopez* and *Morrison* reestablish that the commerce power contains "judicially enforceable outer limits." See *Lopez*, 514 U.S. at 566; *Morrison*, 120 S.Ct. at 1748-49. It is essential to our system of government that the commerce power not extend to effects on inter-state commerce that are so remote that we "would effectually obliterate the distinction between what is national and what is local." National Labor Relations Board v. Jones & Laughlin Steel Corp., 301 U.S. 1, 37, (1937). Indeed, the judiciary has the duty to ensure that federal statutes and regulations are promulgated under one of the enumerated grants of constitutional authority. It is our further duty to independently evaluate whether "a rational basis exist[s] for concluding that a regulated activity sufficiently affect[s] interstate commerce." Lopez, 514 U.S. at 557. . . .

The *Lopez* Court recognized three broad categories of activity that Congress may regulate under its commerce power. 514 U.S. at 558. "First, Congress may regulate the use of the channels of interstate commerce. Second, Congress is empowered to regulate and protect the instrumentalities of interstate commerce, or persons or things in interstate commerce, even though the threat may come only from intrastate activities. Finally, Congress' commerce authority includes the power to regulate those activities having a substantial relation to interstate commerce, i.e., those activities that substantially affect interstate commerce." Id. at 558-59 (citations omitted).

Section 17.84(c) is "not a regulation of the use of the channels of interstate commerce, nor is it an attempt to prohibit the interstate transportation of a commodity through the channels of commerce." Lopez, 514 U.S. at 559. The term "channel of interstate commerce" refers to, inter alia, "navigable rivers, lakes, and canals of the United States; the interstate railroad track system; the interstate highway system; . . . interstate telephone and telegraph lines; air traffic routes; television and radio broadcast frequencies." United States v. Miles, 122 F.3d 235, 245 (5th Cir.1997). This regulation of red wolf takings on private land does not target the movement of wolves or wolf products in the channels of interstate commerce.

This case also does not implicate *Lopez* 's second prong, which protects things in interstate commerce. Although the Service has transported the red wolves interstate for the purposes of study and the reintroduction programs, this is not sufficient to make the red wolf a "thing" in interstate commerce. See, e.g., Lopez, 514 U.S. at 559, (rejecting application of prong two to Gun-Free School Zones Act, despite the fact that the regulated guns likely traveled through interstate commerce); National Assoc. of Home Builders v. Babbitt, 130 F.3d 1041, 1046 (D.C.Cir.1997) ("NAHB ") (rejecting notion that Delhi Sands Flower-Loving Fly was a "thing" in interstate commerce). Therefore, if 50 C.F.R. § 17.84(c) is within the commerce power, it must be sustained under the third prong of *Lopez*.

Under the third *Lopez* test, regulations have been upheld when the regulated activities "arise out of or are connected with a commercial transaction, which viewed in the aggregate, substantially affects interstate commerce." Lopez, 514 U.S. at 561. In *Morrison*, the Supreme Court noted, "In every case where we have sustained federal regulation under *Wickard* 's aggregation principle, the regulated activity was of an apparent commercial character." Morrison, 120 S.Ct. at 1750 n. 4. The Court in *Lopez* likewise placed great emphasis on the "commercial concerns that are central to the Commerce Clause." Lopez, 514 U.S. at 583 (Kennedy, J., concurring); see also Hoffman v. Hunt, 126 F.3d 575, 586-87 (4th Cir.1997) (noting the importance of the distinction between "the regulation of, on the one hand, those activities that are commercial or economic in nature ... and, on the other hand, those activities that are not").

Although the connection to economic or commercial activity plays a central role in whether a regulation will be upheld under the Commerce Clause, economic activity must be understood in broad terms. Indeed, a cramped view of commerce would cripple a foremost federal power and in so doing would eviscerate national authority. The *Lopez* Court's characterization of the regulation of homegrown wheat in Wickard v. Filburn, 317 U.S. 111 (1942), as a case involving economic activity makes clear the breadth of this concept. The Court explained that "[e]ven Wickard, which is perhaps the most far reaching example of Commerce Clause authority over intrastate activity, involved economic activity in a way that the possession of a gun in a school zone does not." Lopez, 514 U.S. at 560; accord Morrison, 120 S.Ct. at 1749-

50. See also Brzonkala, 169 F.3d at 835 (explaining that the Court has a "relatively broad understanding of such [economic] activity"). In fact, our understanding of commerce may not be limited to its "18th-century" forms. See Lopez, 514 U.S. at 574 (Kennedy, J., concurring). While we must enforce meaningful limits on the commerce power, we must also be mindful of the "Court's relatively generous conception of economic activity." Brzonkala, 169 F.3d at 835.

Lopez and *Morrison* rest on the principle that where a federal statute has only a tenuous connection to commerce and infringes on areas of traditional state concern, the courts should not hesitate to exercise their constitutional obligation to hold that the statute exceeds an enumerated federal power. Respect for our federal system of government was integral to those decisions. See Lopez, 514 U.S. at 561 n. 3; Morrison, 120 S.Ct. at 1754-55. Yet *Lopez* also counsels that "[w]here economic activity substantially affects interstate commerce, legislation regulating that activity will be sustained." 514 U.S. at 560. In enforcing limits on the Congress, we must be careful not to overstep the judicial role. To strike down statutes that bear substantially upon commerce is to overstep our own authority even as we fault Congress for exceeding limits on its power. The irony of disregarding limits on ourselves in the course of enforcing limits upon others will assuredly not be lost on those who look to courts to respect restraints imposed by rules of law.

With these basic principles in mind, we consider appellants' challenge to § 17.84(c).

III.

Appellants argue that the federal government cannot limit the taking of red wolves on private land because this activity cannot be squared with any of the three categories that Congress may regulate under its commerce power. Appellants assert that 50 C.F.R. § 17.84(c) is therefore beyond the reach of congressional authority under the Commerce Clause.

We disagree. It was reasonable for Congress and the Fish and Wildlife Service to conclude that § 17.84(c) regulates economic activity. The taking of red wolves implicates a variety of commercial activities and is closely connected to several interstate markets. The regulation in question is also an integral part of the overall federal scheme to protect, preserve, and rehabilitate endangered species, thereby conserving valuable wildlife resources important to the welfare of our country. Invalidating this provision would call into question the historic power of the federal government to preserve scarce resources in one locality for the future benefit of all Americans.

A.

To fall within Congress's commerce power, this regulation must have a "substantial relation to interstate commerce"—it must "substantially affect interstate commerce." Lopez, 514 U.S. at 559. The Supreme Court recently emphasized that "in those cases where we have sustained federal regulation of intrastate activity based upon the activity's substantial effects on interstate commerce, the activity in question has been some sort of economic endeavor." Morrison, 120 S.Ct. at 1750-51. Intrastate activities may be subject to federal regulation if they have a "meaningful connection with [a] particular, identifiable economic enterprise or transaction." Brzonkala, 169 F.3d at 834. We therefore must consider whether the taking of red wolves on private land is "in any sense of the phrase, economic activity." Morrison, 120 S.Ct. at 1751-52.

Unlike the Violence Against Women Act (VAWA) in Morrison and the Gun-Free School Zones Act (GFSZA) in Lopez, § 17.84(c) regulates what is in a meaningful sense economic activity. The Court in Morrison explained that both the VAWA and the GFSZA involved activity that was noneconomic and only tenuously linked to interstate commerce. 120 S.Ct. at 1749-52. Yet the taking of a red wolf on private land is unlike gender-motivated violence or guns near schools. The protection of commercial and economic assets is a primary reason for taking the wolves. Farmers and ranchers take wolves mainly because they are concerned that the animals pose a risk to commercially valuable livestock and crops. Indeed, appellants' arguments focus quite explicitly on these economic concerns—they want freer rein to protect their property and investments in the land. See Appellants' Br. at 10 ("In the face of these threats [from red wolves], North Carolinians cannot effectively defend their property."); id. at 12.

The relationship between red wolf takings and interstate commerce is quite direct—with no red wolves, there will be no red wolf related tourism, no scientific research, and no commercial trade in pelts. We need not "pile inference upon inference," Lopez, 514 U.S. at 567, to reach this conclusion. While a beleaguered species may not presently have the economic impact of a large commercial enterprise, its eradication nonetheless would have a substantial effect on interstate commerce. And through preservation the impact of an endangered species on commerce will only increase.

Because the taking of red wolves can be seen as economic activity in the sense considered by Lopez and Morrison, the individual takings may be aggregated for the purpose of Commerce Clause analysis. See Morrison, 120 S.Ct. at 1750 n. 4. While the taking of one red wolf on private land may not be "substantial," the takings of red wolves in the aggregate have a sufficient impact on interstate commerce to uphold this regulation. This is especially so where, as here, the regulation is but one part of the broader scheme of endangered species legislation.

Further, § 17.84(c) is closely connected to a variety of interstate economic activities. Whether the impact of red wolf takings on any one of these activities qualifies as a substantial effect on interstate commerce is something we need not address. We have no doubt that the effect of the takings on these varied activities in combination qualifies as a substantial one. The first nexus between the challenged regulation and interstate commerce is tourism. The red wolves are part of a $29.2 billion national wildlife-related recreational industry that involves tourism and interstate travel. See Heart of Atlanta Motel, 379 U.S. at 256, (finding it is well-established that "[c]ommerce among the States . . . consists of intercourse and traffic between their citizens" (internal quotation marks omitted)). Many tourists travel to North Carolina from throughout the country for "howling events"—evenings of listening to wolf howls accompanied by educational programs. These howlings are a regular occurrence at the Alligator River National Wildlife Refuge. According to a study conducted by Dr. William E. Rosen of Cornell University, the recovery of the red wolf and increased visitor activities could result in a significant regional economic impact. See William E. Rosen, Red Wolf Recovery in Northeastern North Carolina and the Great Smoky Mountains National Park: Public Attitudes and Economic Impacts (unpublished, Joint Appendix at 633). Rosen estimates that northeastern North Carolina could see an increase of between $39.61 and $183.65 million per year in tourism-related activities, and that the

Great Smoky Mountains National Park could see an increase of between $132.09 and $354.50 million per year. This is hardly a trivial impact on interstate commerce. Appellants understandably seek to criticize the Rosen study, but concede that the howling events attract interstate tourism and that red wolf program volunteers come from all around the country.

While there are no formal congressional findings that the ESA affects interstate commerce, such findings are neither necessary nor sufficient to sustain a statute or regulation. In *Lopez*, the Court said that "Congress normally is not required to make formal findings as to the substantial burdens that an activity has on interstate commerce." 514 U.S. at 562; see also Perez v. United States, 402 U.S. 146, 156, (1971) (particularized findings are not necessary for Congress to legislate). Further, in *Morrison*, the Court emphasized in the face of voluminous congressional findings that "the existence of congressional findings is not sufficient, by itself, to sustain the constitutionality of Commerce Clause legislation." 120 S.Ct. at 1752. In evaluating whether there is a rational basis for the promulgation of a statute or regulation under the commerce power, we often consider congressional committee findings. See Lopez, 514 U.S. at 562. Here, Congress has provided numerous sources of informal findings. Committee reports and legislative debates have emphasized the importance of endangered species to interstate commerce. We independently evaluate the constitutionality of this regulation, but we also take account of congressional judgment and the judgment of the agency designated to implement the statute.

Appellants argue that the tourism rationale relates only to howling events on national park land or wildlife refuges because people do not travel to private land. They reason that without tourism on private land the regulated activity does not substantially affect interstate commerce. Yet this argument misses the mark. Since reintroduction, red wolves have strayed from federal lands onto private lands. Indeed, wolves are known to be "great wanderers." See 60 Fed.Reg. 18,940, 18,943 (1995). In 1998, it was estimated that 41 of the 75 wolves in the wild now live on private land. Because so many members of this threatened species wander on private land, the regulation of takings on private land is essential to the entire program of reintroduction and eventual restoration of the species. Such regulation is necessary to conserve enough red wolves to sustain tourism. Appellants in fact seem unmindful of the history of endangered species regulation. The Endangered Species Acts of 1966 and 1969 initially targeted conservation efforts only on federal lands, but they met with limited success. See Note, Evolution of Wildlife Legislation in the United States: An Analysis of the Legal Efforts to Protect Endangered Species and the Prospects for the Future, 5 Geo. Int'l Envtl. L.Rev. 441, 449-53 (1993). The Endangered Species Act of 1973 was motivated in part by the need to extend takings regulation beyond the limited confines of federal land. See id. at 556. The prohibition of takings on private land was critical to the overall success of the ESA in halting and reversing the near extinction of numerous species. See 16 U.S.C. § 1538(a)(1). The success of many commercial enterprises depends on some regulation of activity on private land, and interstate tourism is no exception.

Tourism, however, is not the only interstate commercial activity affected by the taking of red wolves. The regulation of red wolf takings is also closely connected to a second interstate market—scientific research. Scientific research generates jobs. It also deepens our knowledge of the world in which we live. The red wolf reintroduction program has already generated numerous scientific studies. For example, the red wolf is used as a model for other carnivore reintroductions. See Donald E. Moore III & Roland Smith, The Red Wolf as a Model for Carnivore Reintroductions, 62 Symp. Zool. Soc. Lond. 263 (1990). Scientists have also studied how the red wolf affects small mammal populations and how the wolves interact with the ecosystem as a whole. See, e.g., Bryan T. Kelly, Alligator River National Wildlife Refuge Red Wolf (Canis Rufus) Scat Analysis: Preliminary Analyses of Mammalian Prey Consumed by Year, Season, Pack, Sex, and Age (April 1994) (unpublished, Joint Appendix at 942). By studying the effects of red wolves on the ecosystem, scientists learn about the interdependence of plants and animals, as well as how other threatened species may be reintroduced in the future. Scientific research can also reveal other uses for animals—for instance, approximately 50 percent of all modern medicines are derived from wild plants or animals. See Norman Myers, A Wealth of Wild Species: Storehouse for Human Welfare 4 (1983). Protection of the red wolves on private land thus encourages further research that may have inestimable future value, both for scientific knowledge as well as for commercial development of the red wolf.

The anti-taking regulation is also connected to a third market—the possibility of a renewed trade in fur pelts. Wolves have historically been hunted for their pelts. See Stanley P. Young & Edward A. Goldman, The Wolves of North America I, 165-70 (1964). Congress had the renewal of trade in mind when it enacted the ESA. The Senate Report noted that the protection of an endangered species "may permit the regeneration of that species to a level where controlled exploitation of that species can be resumed. In such a case businessmen may profit from the trading and marketing of that species for an indefinite number of years, where otherwise it would have been completely eliminated from commercial channels." S.Rep. No. 91-526, at 3 (1969), reprinted in 1969 U.S.C.C.A.N. 1413, 1415. The American alligator is a case in point. In 1975, the American alligator was nearing extinction and listed as endangered, but by 1987 conservation efforts restored the species. Now there is a vigorous trade in alligator hides. See Catharine L. Krieps, Sustainable Use of Endangered Species Under CITES: Is it a Sustainable Alternative?, 17 U. Pa. J. Int'l Econ. L. 461, 479-80 (1996) (explaining that many environmentalists are now encouraging the purchase of alligator products to create an incentive for protecting alligators and their habitats). Although alligator hides have more recently been a part of interstate commercial trade and red wolves were sold for their pelts primarily in the nineteenth century, this temporal difference is beside the point. It is not for the judiciary to move from species to species, opining that species A possesses great commercial potential, but species B does not. Assessing the relative scientific value and commercial impact of alligators and red wolves is for Congress and the FWS, informed as they are by biologists, economists, and others whose expertise is best delivered to the political branches, not the courts.

Finally, the taking of red wolves is connected to interstate markets for agricultural products and livestock. For instance, appellant landowners find red wolves a menace because they threaten livestock and other animals of economic and commercial value. By restricting the taking of red wolves, § 17.84(c) is said to impede economic development and commercial activities such as ranching and farming. This effect on commerce, however, still qualifies as a legitimate subject for regulation. It is well-settled under Commerce Clause cases that a regulation can involve the promotion or the restriction of commercial enterprises and development. Indeed, "[t]he motive and purpose of a regulation of interstate commerce are matters for the legislative judgment." United States v. Darby, 312 U.S. 100, 115 (1941). We recognize that

"Congress can regulate interstate commerce for any lawful motive."
United States v. Soderna, 82 F.3d 1370, 1374 (7th Cir.1996). The regulation here targets takings that are economically motivated—farmers take wolves to protect valuable livestock and crops. It is for Congress, not the courts, to balance economic effects—namely whether the negative effects on interstate commerce from red wolf predation are outweighed by the benefits to commerce from a restoration of this species. To say that courts are ill-suited for this act of empirical and political judgment is an understatement. . . .

Section 17.84(c) aims to reverse threatened extinction and conserve the red wolf for both current and future use in interstate commerce. Congress is entitled to make the judgment that conservation is potentially valuable, even if that value cannot be presently ascertained. The Supreme Court has held that the congressional decision to maintain abandoned railroad track is reasonable "even if no future rail use for it is currently foreseeable." Preseault v. ICC, 494 U.S. 1, 19 (1990). The Court reasoned that "[g]iven the long tradition of congressional regulation of railroad abandonments, that is a judgment that Congress is entitled to make." Id. (citations omitted). Similarly, Congress has long been involved in the regulation of scarce and vital natural resources. The full payoff of conservation in the form of tourism, research, and trade may not be foreseeable. Yet it is reasonable for Congress to decide that conservation of species will one day produce a substantial commercial benefit to this country and that failure to preserve a species will result in permanent, though unascertainable, commercial loss. . . .

The protection of the red wolf on both federal and private land substantially affects interstate commerce through tourism, trade, scientific research, and other potential economic activities. To overturn this regulation would start courts down the road to second-guessing all kinds of legislative judgments. There is a "rational basis" as defined by *Lopez* for sustaining this regulation. We therefore hold that the anti-taking provision at issue here involves regulable economic and commercial activity as understood by current Commerce Clause jurisprudence.

B.

This regulation is also sustainable as "an essential part of a larger regulation of economic activity, in which the regulatory scheme could

255

be undercut unless the intrastate activity were regulated." Lopez, 514 U.S. at 561. The Supreme Court in Hodel v. Indiana stated: "A complex regulatory program ... can survive a Commerce Clause challenge without a showing that every single facet of the program is independently and directly related to a valid congressional goal. It is enough that the challenged provisions are an integral part of the regulatory program and that the regulatory scheme when considered as a whole satisfies this test." 452 U.S. 314, 329 n. 17 (1981).

The FWS issued this regulation pursuant to the provisions of the Endangered Species Act, a comprehensive and far-reaching piece of legislation that aims to conserve the health of our national environment. Congress undoubtedly has the constitutional authority to pass legislation for the conservation of endangered species. See Babbitt v. Sweet Home Chapter of Communities for a Great Or., 515 U.S. 687, (1995) (presupposing validity of Endangered Species Act in upholding broad definition of "harm" as including significant habitat modification); see also TVA v. Hill, 437 U.S. at 194, 98 S.Ct. 2279 (emphasizing that Congress has struck a balance in "favor of affording endangered species the highest of priorities" and upholding application of the ESA because "[o]nce the meaning of an enactment is discerned and its constitutionality determined, the judicial process comes to an end").

Appellants repeatedly argue that individual takings of red wolves have only an insubstantial effect on interstate commerce and therefore that the application of the regulation to private landowners is invalid. But we emphasize that the effect on commerce must be viewed not from the taking of one wolf, but from the potential commercial differential between an extinct and a recovered species. A single red wolf taking may be insubstantial by some measures, but that does not invalidate a regulation that is part of the ESA and that seeks conservation not only of any single animal, but also recovery of the species as a whole. The Supreme Court in Lopez was emphatic on this point: "'where a general regulatory statute bears a substantial relation to commerce, the de minimis character of individual instances arising under that statute is of no consequence.'" 514 U.S. at 558 (alteration in original) (quoting Maryland v. Wirtz, 392 U.S. 183, 197 n. 27, (1968)); see also Perez v. United States, 402 U.S. 146, 154, (1971) ("Where the class of activities is regulated and that class is within the reach of federal power, the courts have no power to excise, as trivial, individual instances of the class.").

Once a species has been designated as endangered, there are by definition only a few remaining animals. Therefore, the effects on interstate commerce should not be viewed from the arguably small commercial effect of one local taking, but rather from the effect that single takings multiplied would have on advancing the extinction of a species. Each taking impacts the overall red wolf population, which has an effect on many dimensions of commerce between the states. As the Supreme Court has stated, "[i]f it is interstate commerce that feels the pinch, it does not matter how local the operation which applies the squeeze." Heart of Atlanta Motel, 379 U.S. at 258. Section 17.84(c) must thus be evaluated against the overall congressional goal of restoring red wolves and endangered species generally. It would be perverse indeed if a species nearing extinction were found to be beyond Congress's power to protect while abundant species were subject to full federal regulatory power. Yet under appellants' theory, the more endangered the species, the less authority Congress has to regulate the taking of it. According to this view, endangered species would lie beyond congressional protection because there are too few animals left to make a commercial difference. Such reasoning would eviscerate the comprehensive federal scheme for conserving endangered species and turn congressional judgment on its head. . . .

IV.

. . .

A.

It is imperative to set forth at the outset the historic roles of federal and state authority in this area. The regulated activity at issue here does not involve an "area of traditional state concern," one to which "States lay claim by right of history and expertise." Lopez, 514 U.S. at 580, 583 (Kennedy, J., concurring).

Appellants argue that the regulation infringes on the traditional state control over wildlife. We are cognizant that states play a most important role in regulating wildlife—many comprehensive state hunting and fishing laws attest to it. State control over wildlife, however, is circumscribed by federal regulatory power. In Minnesota v. Mille Lacs

Band of Chippewa Indians, the Supreme Court recently reiterated that "[a]lthough States have important interests in regulating wildlife and natural resources within their borders, this authority is shared with the Federal Government when the Federal Government exercises one of its enumerated constitutional powers." 526 U.S. 172, 204 (1999). In Mille Lacs, the Court upheld Chippewa Indian rights under an 1837 treaty that allowed the Chippewa to hunt, fish, and gather free of territorial, and later state, regulation. Id. These Indian treaty rights were found to be "reconcilable with state sovereignty over natural resources." Id. at 205.

It is true that in the nineteenth century courts followed the legal precept that wildlife was the property of the state. See Geer v. Connecticut, 161 U.S. 519, (1896) (upholding a Connecticut statute that prohibited the interstate transportation of game birds that had been killed within the state). But the principles in Geer were modified early in the twentieth century. See Hughes v. Oklahoma, 441 U.S. 322, 329 (1979) ("The erosion of *Geer* began only 15 years after it was decided."). *Geer* was finally overruled in 1979 by Hughes v. Oklahoma, which held that states do not own the wildlife within their borders and that state laws regulating wildlife are circumscribed by Congress's commerce power. 441 U.S. at 326, 335. In light of *Mille Lacs* and *Hughes*, the activity regulated by § 17.84(c) — the taking of red wolves on private property — is not an area in which the states may assert an exclusive and traditional prerogative in derogation of an enumerated federal power. . . .

Given the history of federal regulation over wildlife and related environmental concerns, it is hard to imagine how this anti-taking regulation trespasses impermissibly upon traditional state functions — either control over wildlife or local land use. *Lopez* and *Morrison* properly caution that States should receive judicial protection from unconstitutional federal encroachments on state matters. Yet endangered wildlife regulation has not been an exclusive or primary state function. In this way the anti-taking regulation is distinctly unlike the GFSZA, which forbade the possession of firearms in a school zone. The Supreme Court explained that the regulation of school zones was within the "general police power" retained by the states. See Lopez, 514 U.S. at 567. The regulation of red wolf taking is also unlike the VAWA, which established a "right to be free from crimes of violence motivated by gender," 42 U.S.C. § 13981(b) (1994). The Supreme Court found that the VAWA impeded on family law and criminal matters of traditional state concern. See Morrison, 120 S.Ct. at 1754-55. The Court noted, "[W]e can think of no better example of the police power, which the Founders denied the National Government and reposed in the States, than the suppression of violent crime and vindication of its victims." Id. at 1754. Unlike the GFSZA and the VAWA, § 17.84(c) does not invade traditional state concerns — it is simply one small part of an ongoing federal effort to preserve the scarcest natural resources for future generations.

In contrast to gender-motivated violence or guns in school yards, the conservation of scarce natural resources is an appropriate and well-recognized area of federal regulation. The federal government has been involved in a variety of conservation efforts since the beginning of this century. In 1900, Congress passed the Lacey Act, which provided penalties for the taking of wildlife in violation of state laws. See Act of May 25, 1900, ch. 553, 31 Stat. 187 (codified as amended 16 U.S.C. § 701 (1994)). The Migratory Bird Treaty Act of 1918 forbade all takings of numerous bird species and explicitly preempted state laws. See 16 U.S.C. §§ 703-12. Furthermore, Congress has regulated wildlife on nonfederal property through numerous statutes, including the Bald Eagle Protection Act of 1940, which prohibits, inter alia, the taking, possession, selling, or exporting of bald eagles or any of their parts. See 16 U.S.C. §§ 668-668d (1994). Similarly, the Marine Mammal Protection Act of 1972 regulates the taking of marine mammals and restricts the importing of marine mammals and their products through an elaborate system of permits. See 16 U.S.C. §§ 1361-1421h (1994 & Supp. III 1997). The Magnuson Fishery Conservation and Management Act of 1976 provides national standards for fishery conservation and management along with an elaborate system of enforcement. See 16 U.S.C. §§ 1801-83 (1994 & Supp. III 1997).

The Supreme Court has repeatedly upheld these statutes and the conservation efforts of Congress with regard to a variety of animal species. In Missouri v. Holland, the Court upheld the Migratory Bird Treaty Act as a necessary and proper means of executing Congress's treaty power. The conservation of endangered wildlife, Justice Holmes stated, was a "matter[ ] of the sharpest exigency for national well being." 252 U.S. 416, 432-33 (1920). In 1977, the Supreme Court held that Congress had the power under the Commerce Clause to grant federal fishing licenses for use in state waters, thereby preempting conflicting state laws. See Douglas v. Seacoast Products, Inc., 431 U.S. 265 (1977). Later in Andrus v. Allard, the Court emphasized that the "assumption that the national commerce power does not reach migratory wildlife is clearly flawed." 444 U.S. 51, 63 n. 19 (1979). . . .

D.

. . . The rationale for this regulation thus stops far short of conferring upon Congress a broad police power. It is instead appellants' arguments for invalidating this regulation that go too far. If the federal government cannot regulate the taking of an endangered or threatened species on private land, its conservation and preservation efforts would be limited to only federal lands. A ruling to this effect would place in peril the entire federal regulatory scheme for wildlife and natural resource conservation.

LUTTIG, Circuit Judge, dissenting:

. . . The killing of even all 41 of the estimated red wolves that live on private property in North Carolina would not constitute an economic activity of the kind held by the Court in *Lopez* and in *Morrison* to be of central concern to the Commerce Clause, if it could be said to constitute an economic activity at all. Morrison, 120 S.Ct. at 1750 ("[A] fair reading of Lopez shows that the noneconomic, criminal nature of the conduct at issue was central to our decision in that case."). It is for this reason that the majority's attempted aggregation is impermissible: "While we need not adopt a categorical rule against aggregating the effects of any noneconomic activity in order to decide these cases, thus far in our Nation's history our cases have upheld Commerce Clause regulation of intrastate activity only where that activity is economic in nature." 120 S.Ct. at 1751 (citations omitted). But even assuming that such is an economic activity, it certainly is not an activity that has a substantial effect on interstate commerce. The number of inferences (not even to mention the amount of speculation) necessary to discern in this activity a substantial effect on interstate commerce is exponentially greater than the number necessary in *Lopez* to show a substantial effect on interstate commerce from the sale of guns near schools or in *Morrison* to show a substantial effect on interstate commerce from domestic assault. The number (and the speculation) is even greater than that necessary in Wickard v. Filburn, 317 U.S. 111 (1942). And, it bears reminding, the regulated activity in *Lopez* and *Wickard* at least was in some sense economic in character.

. . . I would invalidate this particular agency regulation under *Lopez*, *Morrison*, and *Brzonkala*, and instead recognize as the aberration that action of invalidation, rather than the opinions in *Lopez*, *Morrison*, and *Brzonkala*, as does the majority. Compare Morrison, 120 S.Ct. at 1773-74 (Souter, J., dissenting) (similarly to majority, characterizing *Lopez* and *Morrison*, and by implication *Brzonkala*, as aberrational vis-a-vis the sixty years of jurisprudence predating *Lopez* and predicting that *Lopez* and *Morrison* will not be "enduring law"); see also Morrison, 120 S.Ct. at 1777-78 (Breyer, J., dissenting) ("And even were I to accept *Lopez* as an accurate statement of the law, which I do not...."). I would do so without any fear whatsoever that such "would place in peril the entire federal regulatory scheme for wildlife and natural resource conservation," ante at 504, as the majority over-rhetorically predicts would result from the invalidation of this lone regulation. No more so than in *Brzonkala* will "[m]aintaining the integrity of the enumerated powers" by invalidating this single regulation "mean that statutes will topple like falling dominos." *Brzonkala*, 169 F.3d at 897 (Wilkinson, J., concurring).

While it could be lost in a reading of the majority opinion, we do not address here Congress' power over either the channels or instrumentalities of interstate commerce. We do not address activity that is interstate in character. We do not address in this case a statute or a regulation with an express interstate commerce jurisdictional requirement, which would all but ensure constitutional validity. We do not have before us an activity that has obvious economic character and impact, such as is typically the case with non- wildlife natural resources, and even with other wildlife resources. We are not even presented with an activity as to which a plausible case of future economic character and impact can be made.

To the contrary, we are confronted here with an administrative agency regulation of an activity that implicates but a handful of animals, if even that, in one small region of one state. An activity that not only has no current economic character, but one that concededly has had no economic character for well over a century now. An activity that has no foreseeable economic character at all, except upon the baldest (though admittedly most humorous) of speculation that the red wolf pelt trade will once again emerge as a centerpiece of our Nation's economy. And, importantly, an activity that Congress could plainly regulate under its spending power and under its power over federal lands, regardless. . . .

Accordingly, I would faithfully apply in this case the Supreme Court's landmark decisions in *Lopez* and *Morrison*, as I would in any other case. The affirmative reach and the negative limits of the Commerce Clause do not wax and wane depending upon the subject matter of the particular legislation under challenge.

NOTES AND QUESTIONS

1. Why does the majority believes that the regulations challenged in this case regulate "economic activity"? Would the case have come out differently if the regulations had not been considered to regulate economic activity?

2. In justifying federal power to protect the red wolves, the court majority emphasizes that they "are part of a $29.2 billion national wild-life-related recreational industry that involves tourism and interstate travel," that they attract scientific researchers, and that their protection is essential if a plet trade is ever to be revived. Does this imply that Congress's has lesser power to protect a noncharismatic endangered species that does not attract tourists or researchers to cross state lines and that is of less obvious commercial value?

3. In his majority opinion, Chief Judge Wilkinson notes that the federal government has a long history of regulation of wildlife to protect migratory species. Thus, he rejects the argument that the Endangered Species Act impermissibly infringes on what has traditionally been a state function. The federal government does not have nearly as long a history of involvement in regulating pollution than it does in protecting wildlife. Does this mean that Congress has less power to regulate pollution than it has to protect endangered species?

Species Listing Determinations (pp. 934-37)

The U.S. Fish and Wildlife Service (FWS) announced in November 2000 that it was so overwhelmed by the need to make designations of critical habitat under court orders that it would cease listing new species, save for emergency situations, until the end of the 2001 fiscal year. At the time of the FWS announcement, 39 additional species were about to be listed and 236 others were considered candidates for listing. But the FWS was faced with the need to comply with court orders for designating critical habitat that were pending for more than 300 additional species. Michael Grunwald, Endangered List Faces New Peril, Wash. Post, Mar. 12, 2001, p. A1. The agency stated that its budget for listing-related activities was being entirely consumed complying with court orders in existing litigation. Thus, it announced that it would not be able to respond to any more petitions for new listings.

Environmental groups charged that the FWS has created its own problem by intentionally budgeting only $6.3 million of its $1.3 billion budget for listings and designations of critical habitat. They note that the agency has never requested a substantial increase in its budget for listing-related activities. In March 2001, the Bush administration created a furor by asking Congress to impose a moratorium on private lawsuits to force listings and designations of critical habitat. As of April 2001, there were nearly 80 lawsuits pending to force species listing and notices of intent to sue had been served in 95 additional cases. The Species Litigation Act, Wall St. J., April 20, 2001, p. A14. While Congress rejected the proposed moratorium, former Secretary of Interior Bruce Babbitt supported the Bush administration's claim that the listing process had placed impossible demands on federal agencies.

On August 28, 2001, the FWS reached agreement with three environmental organizations to expedite the listing of 29 endangered species most in need of immediate protection in return for deferring by six months the designation of critical habitat for species already listed. By deferring the deadlines for critical habitat designations that were the products of prior lawsuits, the settlement freed up $600,000 that the FWS agreed to redirect to expedite the listing decisions. Center for Biological Diversity, Historic Agreement Reached to Protect 29 Imperiled Species from Coast to Coast, www.biological diversity.org/swcbd/activist/ESA/settlement.html. While this agreement was hailed as a breakthrough, see, e.g., A Victory for Endangered Species, N.Y. Times, Sept. 3, 2001, the basic problem of insufficient resources for species listing and critical habitat designation remains. FWS estimates that it will need at least $120 million simply to process the current backlog it faces.

For the first time a court has reversed a decision to list a species on grounds other than procedural violations. In San Luis & Delta-Mendota Water Auth. v. United States, No. 99-5658 (E.D. Cal. June 23, 2000), a federal district court held that the U.S. Fish and Wildlife Service's decision to list the Sacramento spiltail as threatened was arbitrary and capricious. The court held that the Service had failed to explain why the population size of the species was inadequate in the light of data submitted by California wildlife officials who opposed the listing.

The U.S. Court of Appeals for the D.C. Circuit reversed a lower court that had ordered the Fish and Wildlife Service to conduct on-site counting of goshawks in the Tongass National Forest in Alaska before placing them on the Endangered Species List. Southwest Center for Biological Diversity v. Babbitt, 215 F.3d 58 (D.C. Cir. 2000). The court held that the "best available data" requirement of § 4(b)(1)(A) of the ESA did not require on-site counting prior to making a listing determination.

Even as the U.S. Fish and Wildlife Service (FWS) is struggling to keep up with existing court orders to list species and designate critical habitat, the U.S. Court of Appeals for the Fifth Circuit has made it easier for plaintiffs to force the government to do so. In Sierra Club v. U.S. Fish and Wildlife Service, 245 F.3d 434 (5th Cir. 2001), the court reversed a decision by the FWS not to designate critical habitat for the threatened Gulf sturgeon. The court ruled that a regulation relied upon by the FWS to justify its refusal to designate critical habitat (50 C.F.R. § 402.02) conflicted with the Endangered Species Act because it required federal agencies to consult to avoid jeopardizing endangered species only when agency action could threaten the survival, and not merely the recovery, of a species.

Review of Federal Action: Section 7 and Oregon's "Water War" (pp. 938-52)

On at least three occasions beginning in late June 2001, a group of southern Oregon farmers have defied federal officials by forcing open an irrigation canal that had been shut to protect an endangered bottom-feeding suckerfish and the threatened coho salmon. In April the federal Bureau of Reclamation had ordered federal irrigation water to be cut off to 1,400 farmers and ranchers in the Klamath Basin in order to comply with biological opinions that deemed it necessary to prevent further declines in the water level in Upper Klamath Lake that would jeopardize the species. Douglas Jehl, Officials Loath to Act as Water Meant for Endangered Fish Flows to Dry Western Farms, N.Y. Times, July 9, 2001, p. A8. The area has faced a year of record drought that has left 200,000 acres of farmland parched in the absence of federal irrigation water.

Protection Against Private Action: § 9 (pp. 952-70)

Several cases addressed the question of what the government must prove before getting an injunction against private action likely to "take" an endangered species. In Greenpeace Foundation v. Mineta, 122 F.Supp. 2d 1123 (D. Haw. 2000), a federal court held that there was insufficient evidence that an endangered monk seal eats enough lobster in order to support the conclusion that a lobster fishery harms the seal by reducing its food supply. The court found that a bottomfishing operating in the area did cause a take of the seals, but it declined to issue an injunction shutting it down.

The Ninth Circuit's decision allowing construction of a high school on land used by endangered pygmy owls, discussed on page 967 of the casebook, has now been published at Defenders of Wildlife v. Bernal, 204 F.3d 920 (9th Cir. 2000).

As noted in the casebook on page 967, a federal district court gave the government a year to gather data to support its case seeking an injunction to block the harvesting of 94 acres of private timber located in the home range of a pair of endangered spotted owls. The district court ultimately decided that the government had failed to meet its burden of proof that the timber harvest would harm the endangered owls. The court held that the fact that the male owl of the pair had foraged on part of the 94-acre tract was insufficient to prove a prospective take when the pair had a home range of 3,600 acres and a high rate of reproduction. United States v. West Coast Forest Resources, Ltd. (D. Ore. March 13, 2000).

Private Development of Public Resources
(pp. 975-76)

As discussed on page 976, the Bureau of Land Management adopted new regulations governing grazing on public lands. The decision by the U.S. Court of Appeals for the 10th Circuit upholding these regulations in Public Lands Council v. Babbitt, 145 F.3d 154 (10th Cir. 1998) was upheld by the U.S. Supreme Court in Public Lands Council v. Babbitt, 529 U.S. 728 (2000). In an opinion by Justice Breyer, the Court emphasized that the Taylor Grazing Act creates no private right or title in the public lands covered by a grazing permit.

Prior to leaving office, the Clinton administration took final action to prohibit the construction of new roads for timber harvesting in roadless areas of the National Forest System. 66 Fed. Reg. 3224 (2001). This policy, promulgated on January 5, 2001, was the result of a lengthy rulemaking process in which 1.6 million comments were received from the public. Faced with legal challenges from the timber and paper industries, the regulations were blocked temporarily by a federal judge in Idaho on May 10. After initially declining to defend the regulations in court, the Bush administration announced in July 2001 that it will reconsider them in an effort to scale back the amount of land covered by the policy. Eric Pianin, Administration Revisits Forest Land Rules, Wash. Post, July 7, 2001, p. A2.

The Bush administration also is reconsidering Clinton administration regulations issued in November 2000 to prevent environmental damage from hard rock mining on public lands. 65 Fed. Reg. 69998 (2000). The regulations completed a rulemaking that had been initiated more than a decade before. See Douglas Jehl, Gold Miners Eager for Bush to Roll Back Clinton Rules, N.Y. Times, Aug. 16, 2001, p. A1.

- 9 -
Environmental Enforcement

EPA's Incentives for Self-Policing Policy
(pp. 990-96)

On April 11, 2000, EPA made revisions to its policy on Incentives for Self-Policing, which is excerpted on pp. 990-93 of the casebook. 65 Fed. Reg. 19618 (2000). The agency also adopted a Final Policy on Compliance Incentives for Small Business. 65 Fed. Reg. 19630. The most significant aspect of EPA's policy for encouraging compliance by small businesses is that it provides that EPA will forego all penalties – including recovery of the economic benefit of violations – for small businesses that make a "good faith" effort to comply with regulations either through conducting environmental audits or receiving on-site compliance assistance. Small businesses are defined as companies with 100 or fewer employees on a companywide basis.

The revisions to EPA's Incentives for Self-Policing Policy are relatively minor. One significant change is that EPA has amended its definition of "prompt disclosure" in section D-3 (top of p. 992 in the casebook) to give companies 21 days from the time of discovery to disclose a violation rather than the 10 days allowed under the old policy. The new policy also provides that discovery of the violation need not have been the product of a systematic audit procedure in order for the violator to be eligible for a waiver of criminal penalties. Section 3-C of the old policy required that all conditions in Section D be satisfied. The new policy only requires compliance with subsections 2 through 7 of Section D (omitting subsection 1, which deals with "Systematic Discovery").

The new policy clarifies that repeated noncompliance will not disqualify violations discovered at newly acquired facilities. Finally, the term "compliance management system" replaces the terms "an objective, documented, systematic procedure" in the definition of "Systematic Discovery" in Section D-1, solely to conform the Policy language to terminology more commonly in use by industry. 65 Fed. Reg. 19618, 19621 (2000). The following excerpt should replace the material currently reproduced on pp. 990-93 of the casebook.

EPA, Final Policy Statement on Incentives for Self-Policing of Violations, 65 Fed. Reg. 19,618 (2000)

C. Incentives for Self-Policing

1. No Gravity-Based Penalties

If a regulated entity establishes that it satisfies all of the conditions of Section D of this Policy, EPA will not seek gravity-based penalties for violations of Federal environmental requirements discovered and disclosed by the entity.

2. Reduction of Gravity-Based Penalties by 75%

If a regulated entity establishes that it satisfies all of the conditions of Section D of this Policy except for D(1)—systematic discovery—EPA will reduce by 75% gravity-based penalties for violations of Federal environmental requirements discovered and disclosed by the entity.

3. No Recommendation for Criminal Prosecution

(a) If a regulated entity establishes that it satisfies at least conditions D(2) through D(9) of this Policy, EPA will not recommend to the U.S. Department of Justice or other prosecuting authority that criminal charges be brought against the disclosing entity, as long as EPA determines that the violation is not part of a pattern or practice that demonstrates or involves:

(i) A prevalent management philosophy or practice that conceals or condones environ   mental violations; or

(ii) High-level corporate officials' or managers' conscious involvement in, or willful   blindness to, violations of Federal environmental law;

(b) Whether or not EPA recommends the regulated entity for criminal prosecution under this section, the Agency may recommend for prosecution the criminal acts of individual managers or employees under existing policies guiding the exercise of enforcement discretion.

4. No Routine Request for Environmental Audit Reports

EPA will neither request nor use an environmental audit report to initiate a civil or criminal investigation of an entity. For example, EPA will not request an environmental audit report in routine inspections. If the Agency has independent reason to believe that a violation has occurred, however, EPA may seek any information relevant to identifying violations or determining liability or extent of harm.

D. Conditions

1. Systematic Discovery

The violation was discovered through:

(a) An environmental audit; or

(b) A compliance management system reflecting the regulated entity's due diligence in preventing, detecting, and correcting violations. The regulated entity must provide accurate and complete documentation to the Agency as to how its compliance management system meets the criteria for due diligence outlined in Section B and how the regulated entity discovered the violation through its compliance management system. EPA may require the regulated entity to make publicly available a description of its compliance management system.

2. Voluntary Discovery

The violation was discovered voluntarily and not through a legally mandated monitoring or sampling requirement prescribed by statute, regulation, permit, judicial or administrative order, or consent agreement. For example, the Policy does not apply to:

(a) Emissions violations detected through a continuous emissions monitor (or alternative monitor established in a permit) where any such monitoring is required;

(b) Violations of National Pollutant Discharge Elimination System (NPDES) discharge limits detected through required sampling or monitoring; or

(c) Violations discovered through a compliance audit required to be performed by the terms of a consent order or settlement agreement, unless the audit is a component of agreement terms to implement a comprehensive environmental management system.

3. Prompt Disclosure

The regulated entity fully discloses the specific violation in writing to EPA within 21 days (or within such shorter time as may be required by law) after the entity discovered that the violation has, or may have, occurred. The time at which the entity discovers that a violation has, or may have, occurred begins when any officer, director, employee or agent of the facility has an objectively reasonable basis for believing that a violation has, or may have, occurred.

4. Discovery and Disclosure Independent of Government or Third-Party Plaintiff

(a) The regulated entity discovers and discloses the potential violation to EPA prior to:

(i) The commencement of a Federal, State or local agency inspection or investigation, or the issuance by such agency of an information request to the regulated entity (where EPA determines that the facility did not know that it was under civil investigation, and EPA determines that the entity is otherwise acting in good faith, the Agency may exercise its discretion to reduce or waive civil penalties in accordance with this Policy);

(ii) Notice of a citizen suit;

(iii) The filing of a complaint by a third party;

(iv) The reporting of the violation to EPA (or other government agency) by a "whistleblower" employee, rather than by one authorized to speak on behalf of the regulated entity; or

(v) imminent discovery of the violation by a regulatory agency.

(b) For entities that own or operate multiple facilities, the fact that one facility is already the subject of an investigation, inspection, information request or third-party complaint does not preclude the Agency from exercising its discretion to make the Audit Policy available for violations self-discovered at other facilities owned or operated by the same regulated entity.

5. Correction and Remediation

The regulated entity corrects the violation within 60 calendar days from the date of discovery, certifies in writing that the violation has been corrected, and takes appropriate measures as determined by EPA to remedy any environmental or human harm due to the violation. EPA retains the authority to order an entity to correct a violation within a specific time period shorter than 60 days whenever correction in such shorter period of time is feasible and necessary to protect public health and the environment adequately. If more than 60 days will be needed to correct the violation, the regulated entity must so notify EPA in writing before the 60-day period has passed. Where appropriate, to satisfy conditions D(5) and D(6), EPA may require a regulated entity to enter into a publicly available written agreement, administrative consent order or judicial consent decree as a condition of obtaining relief under the Audit Policy, particularly where compliance or remedial measures are complex or a lengthy schedule for attaining and maintaining compliance or remediating harm is required.

6. Prevent Recurrence

The regulated entity agrees in writing to take steps to prevent a recurrence of the violation. Such steps may include improvements to its environmental auditing or compliance management system.

7. No Repeat Violations

The specific violation (or a closely related violation) has not occurred previously within the past three years at the same facility, and has not occurred within the past five years as part of a pattern at multiple facilities owned or operated by the same entity. For the purposes of this section, a violation is:

(a) Any violation of Federal, State or local environmental law identified in a judicial or administrative order, consent agreement or order, complaint, or notice of violation, conviction or plea agreement; or

(b) Any act or omission for which the regulated entity has previously received penalty mitigation from EPA or a State or local agency.

8. Other Violations Excluded

The violation is not one which (a) resulted in serious actual harm, or may have presented an imminent and substantial endangerment, to human health or the environment, or (b) violates the specific terms of any judicial or administrative order, or consent agreement.

9. Cooperation

The regulated entity cooperates as requested by EPA and provides such information as is necessary and requested by EPA to determine applicability of this Policy.

E. Economic Benefit

EPA retains its full discretion to recover any economic benefit gained as a result of noncompliance to preserve a "level playing field" in which violators do not gain a competitive advantage over regulated entities that do comply. EPA may forgive the entire penalty for violations that meet conditions D(1) through D(9) and, in the Agency's opinion, do not merit any penalty due to the insignificant amount of any economic benefit.

F. Effect on State Law, Regulation or Policy

EPA will work closely with States to encourage their adoption and implementation of policies that reflect the incentives and conditions outlined in this Policy. EPA remains firmly opposed to statutory environmental audit privileges that shield evidence of environmental violations and undermine the public's right to know, as well as to blanket immunities, particularly immunities for violations that reflect criminal conduct, present serious threats or actual harm to health and the environment, allow noncomplying companies to gain an economic advantage over their competitors, or reflect a repeated failure to comply with Federal law. EPA will work with States to address any provisions of State audit privilege or immunity laws that are inconsistent with this Policy and that may prevent a timely and appropriate response to significant environmental violations. The Agency reserves its right to take necessary actions to protect public health or the environment by enforcing against any violations of Federal law.

Enforcement Authorities and Policies: Enforcement Actions and Penalty Policies (pp. 996-1002)

EPA reported in July 2000 that it had instituted a combined total of 3,945 civil, judicial and administrative enforcement actions during fiscal year 1999. These resulted in $166.7 million in civil penalty assessments. A total of 260 companies made disclosures of violations at nearly 1,000 facilities under EPA's Incentives for Self-Policing Policy. EPA conducted 21,000 inspections of facilities. EPA, Office of Enforcement and Compliance Assurance, Annual Report on Enforcement and Compliance Assurance for Fiscal Year 1999 (2000).

The Bush administration has proposed to cut 270 enforcement positions in EPA's Office of Enforcement and Compliance Assurance while providing $25 million in federal grants to states for their enforcement activities. Eric Pianin, Bush Plans to Shift Some EPA Enforcement to States, Wash. Post, July 22, 2001, p. A1. A report issued by the General Accounting Office in July 2001 questioned the plan, finding that it cannot be demonstrated that such cuts can be made at the federal level without impairing the effectiveness of overall enforcement efforts. Another report by EPA's Office of Inspector General found that only a handful of states had aggressive environmental enforcement programs, and it criticized the performance of 44 states in enforcing Clean Water Act standards. Eric Pianin, GAO Issues Warning on EPA Enforcement, Wash. Post, Aug. 23, 2001, p. A23.

Chapter 9. Environmental Enforcement

Professor Clifford Rechtschaffen describes two competing visions of environmental enforcement that dominated controversies over federal-state enforcement relationships during the Clinton Administration. Clifford Rechtschaffen, Competing Visions: EPA and the States Battle for the Future of Environmental Enforcement, 30 Env. L. Rep. 10803 (2000). Under the Clinton administration, EPA's enforcement vision focused on deterrence-based enforcement, while many states had shifted to a conciliatory, cooperation-oriented approach. After surveying the scant empirical literature on what enforcement strategies are most effective, Professor Rechtschaffen argues "that it would be ill-advised to make a wholesale shift away from deterrence-based practices." Id. at 10828.

The Federal-State Enforcement Relationship and *Harmon Industries* (pp. 1003-1010)

The holding by the Eighth Circuit U.S. Court of Appeals in *Harmon Industries* (casebook page 1003) that EPA may not "overfile" under the Resource Conservation and Recovery Act (RCRA) has not settled the controversy over the ability of the federal government to bring an enforcement action independent of a state action. A district court in the Tenth Circuit has refused to follow *Harmon* in a RCRA case. United States v. Power Engineering, 125 F.Supp. 2d 1050 (D. Colo. 2000). The decision was based partially on Tenth Circuit precedent that suggested a contrary result, but it was also based on the district court's direct disagreement with *Harmon's* interpretation of RCRA. The court wrote that:

> As an initial matter, the plain meaning of Section 6926's "in lieu of" language is that an authorized state's regulations supplant those of the Federal Government, as the *Harmon* court conceded. See Harmon, 191 F.3d at 899. It is questionable, however, that "the administration and enforcement of the program are inexorably intertwined" under the RCRA. Id. Indeed, while Section 6926 primarily addresses the administration and enforcement of state regulations by authorized states, Section 6928 concerns the federal enforcement of such regulations. The very structure of the RCRA suggests, therefore, that the administration and enforcement of state regulations are not "inexorably intertwined." The structure of the

sentence containing the "in lieu of" language also suggests that Congress did not intend "in lieu of" to apply to enforcement. Section 6926(b) states that an authorized state "is authorized to carry out [its] program in lieu of the Federal program under this subchapter in such State *and* to issue and enforce permits for the storage, treatment, or disposal of hazardous waste." 42 U.S.C. S 6926(b) (emphasis added). Because the administration of state authorized programs, and the enforcement of state regulations are addressed in separate clauses, the structure of Section 6926(b) indicates Congress' intent that administration and enforcement are not "inexorably intertwined." In addition, the plain language of Section 6926(b) indicates that the "in lieu of" appearing in the first clause does not modify the second clause in which the question of enforcement is explicitly addressed. *Harmon*'s interpretation of the contested sentence in Section 6926(b) renders the second clause superfluous.

United States v. Power Engineering, 125 F.Supp. 2d 1050, 1059 (D. Colo. 2000).

In United States v. Elias, 2000 WL 1099977 (D. Idaho 2000), *Harmon* was used to challenge one of the largest criminal penalties ever imposed for an environmental violation. An Idaho businessman who owns a fertilizer company had been sentenced to 17 years in prison and fined $6.3 million after being successfully prosecuted by the federal government for a criminal violation of RCRA. The businessman, Allan Elias, had been convicted for knowingly endangering an employee by ordering him to clean out a storage tank containing cyanide, without safety equipment. The employee was overcome by cyanide fumes and suffered brain damage. The defendant argued that the federal government had no jurisdiction to prosecute him because Idaho had been delegated authority to operate the RCRA program. The court concluded that although the state program operated "in lieu of" the federal program, it did not foreclose imposition of federal criminal penalties. United States v. Elias, 2000 WL 1099977 (D. Idaho 2000). The court generally agreed with *Harmon*, but noted that when EPA had approved delegation of the RCRA program to Idaho it expressly had reserved authority to impose federal penalties for violations, rather than the penalties specified by state law.

Harmon also has been found to be inapplicable to the Clean Air Act, which does not contain the "in lieu of" language upon which *Harmon* relied, and which also contains language pointing the other way. In United States v. LTV Steel Co., 118 F.Supp. 2d 827 (N.D. Ohio 2000) a steel company argued that its settlement with the city of Cleveland barred EPA from overfiling and imposing penalties on it for violations involving fugitive dust emissions. The court rejected this argument and distinguished *Harmon* by noting that: "Unlike RCRA, the Clean Air Act contains language in its enforcement section which seems to anticipate overfiling. Thus, the Act states that "in determining the amount of any penalty to be assessed under this section . . ., the court [ ] shall take into consideration . . . payment by the violator of penalties previously assessed for the same violation." See 42 U.S.C. § 7413(e)." United States v. LTV Steel Co., 118 F.Supp. 2d 827, 833 (N.D. Ohio 2000). The court also rejected the company's claim that EPA's action was barred by res judicata, noting that EPA and the city of Cleveland were not in privity and were enforcing separate bodies of law.

Criminal Enforcement (pp. 1010-1029)

In July 2000 EPA announced that its criminal enforcement program has resulted in sentences that totaled a record 208 years of prison time. EPA, Office of Enforcement and Compliance Assurance, Annual Report on Enforcement and Compliance Assurance for Fiscal Year 1999 (2000).

Standing in Citizen Enforcement Actions: The Effect of *Laidlaw* (pp. 1071-1081)

Although the Supreme Court's decision in *Laidlaw* is less than two years old, the opinion has been cited in at least 135 subsequent cases. In only a handful of environmental cases have courts distinguished *Laidlaw* and denied standing to a plaintiff in a citizen suit. See, e.g., Atlantic States Legal Foundation v. Babbitt, 2001 U.S. Dist. Lexis 5651 (N.D.N.Y. 2001); Central and South West Services v. EPA, 220 F. 3d 683 (5th Cir. 2000). *Laidlaw* resulted in the Fourth Circuit, sitting en banc, unanimously reversing the panel opinion. Friends of the Earth v.

Chapter 9. Environmental Enforcement

Gaston Copper Recycling Corp., 204 F. 3d 149 (2000) (pp. 1072 & 1081 of the casebook).

Government Preclusion of Citizen Suits (pp. 1081-1083)

The Fifth Circuit has held that a state administrative enforcement action does not bar a citizen suit under the Clean Air Act. Section 304(b)(1)(B) of the Clean Air Act, 42 U.S.C. § 7604(b)(1)(B) bars citizen suits when EPA or a state is "diligently prosecuting a civil action in a court of the United States or a state." In Texans United for a Safe Economy Education Fund v. Crown Central Petroleum Corp., 207 F.3d 789 (5th Cir. 2000), the court reversed a federal trial court that had held that an administrative action by the Texas Natural Resource Conservation Commission barred a citizen suit against an oil refiner. The trial court had concluded that if the agency had the power to award relief that is the "substantial equivalent" of what a court could award, the suit should be precluded. But the Fifth Circuit found that the plain language of the Clean Air Act's citizen suit provision forec1osed such a result.

The Eleventh Amendment and Citizen Suits Against States (pp. 1091-1092)

Tensions in the federal-state enforcement relationship also have been raised in citizen suit litigation in cases in which plaintiffs have sought injunctions against state officials to compel them to enforce federal statutes. Some courts have relied on *Ex parte Young* to permit suits against state officers to proceed. See, e.g., Waste Management Holdings, Inc. v. Gilmore, 252 F.3d 316 (4th Cir. 2001), others have found that states have waived Eleventh Amendment defenses. See, e.g., SDDS, Inc. v. South Dakota, 225 F. 3d 970 (8th Cir. 2000), and Entergy, Arkansas, Inc. v. Nebraska, 210 F. 3d 887 (8th Cir. 2000).

The following case involved a highly publicized challenge to the legality of mountaintop-removal coal mining under federal environmental laws, including the Clean Water Act and the Surface Mining Control and Reclamation Act. West Virginia environmental officials

277

were sued for failure to comply with these laws when they approved mountaintop removal mining operations, which result in the dumping of massive amounts of overburden in valleys, burying streams and drainage areas. After a federal district court found that this practice violated federal law, the state appealed to the U.S. Court of Appeals for the Fourth Circuit where it raised an Eleventh Amendment defense. An excerpt from the Fourth Circuit's decision is reproduced below.

Bragg v. West Virginia Coal Association, 248 F.3d 275 (4th Cir. 2001)

NIEMEYER, Circuit Judge:

. . .

I

Mountaintop-removal coal mining, while not new, only became widespread in West Virginia in the 1990s. Under this method, to reach horizontal seams of coal layered in mountains, the mountaintop rock above the seam is removed and placed in adjacent valleys; the coal is extracted; and the removed rock is then replaced in an effort to achieve the original contour of the mountain. But because rock taken from its natural state and broken up naturally "swells," perhaps by as much as 15 to 25%, the excess rock not returned to the mountain— the "overburden"—remains in the valleys, creating "valley fills." Many valley fills bury intermittent and perennial streams and drainage areas that are near the mountaintop. Over the years, the West Virginia Director of Environmental Protection (the "Director" or "State Director"), as well as the U.S. Army Corps of Engineers, has approved this method of coal mining in West Virginia.

The disruption to the immediate environment created by mountain-top mining is considerable and has provoked sharp differences of opinion between environmentalists and industry players. *See, e.g.,* Penny Loeb, *Shear Madness,* U.S. News & World Rept., Aug. 11, 1997. As Loeb reported these differences of opinion, environmentalists decry the "startling" change in the topography, which leaves the land more subject to floods, results in the pollution of streams and rivers, and has an "incalculable" impact on wildlife. The environmentalists also criticize the mining process itself, which cracks foundations of nearby houses, causes fires, creates dust and noise, and disrupts private wells. The coal companies concede that the process changes the landscape, but note on the positive side that land is reclaimed, that grass, small shrubs, and trees are planted, and that waterfowl ponds are added. Moreover, the companies observe that mining is critical to the West Virginia economy and creates high-paying jobs in the State.

Patricia Bragg . . . alleged that the State Director [of West Virginia's Division of Environment Protection], in granting surface coal mining permits, "engaged in an ongoing pattern and practice of violating his non-discretionary duties under the Surface Mining Control and Reclamation Act [of 1977, 30 U.S.C. § 1201 *et seq.*] and the West Virginia state program approved under that statute." More particularly, she alleged that the Director consistently issued permits to mining operations, without making requisite findings, that (1) authorized valley fills, (2) failed to assure the restoration of original mountain contours, and (3) violated other environmental protection laws. She asserted that the Director violated his federal- and State-law duty to "withhold approval of permit applications that are not complete and accurate and in compliance with all requirements of the state program." She also alleged that the Corps of Engineers breached its duties under federal law. ...

All but two counts of the complaint were settled, and the court resolved Counts 2 and 3 on motions for summary judgment. Both of these counts addressed a West Virginia regulation, enacted to conform with a federal regulation, that established 100 foot "buffer zones" around "perennial" and "intermittent" streams, within which surface mining activities may not disturb the land, unless the State agency "specifically authorizes" such activities after making certain findings. . . . Count 2 alleged that the Director engaged in a pattern and practice of approving mountaintop removal operations without even attempting to make the required findings, and Count 3 alleged that because valley fills inherently have an adverse effect upon stream ecology and cause violations of water quality standards, the findings required by the State regulation could never be made, at least not accurately, for valley fill permits. In entering summary judgment in favor of Bragg, the district court ruled (1) that "the Director has a nondiscretionary duty to make the findings required under the buffer zone rule before authorizing any incursions, including valley fills, within one hundred feet of an intermittent or perennial stream," . . . and (2) that "the Director has a nondiscretionary duty under the buffer zone rule to deny variances for valley fills in intermittent and perennial streams because they necessarily adversely affect stream flow, stream gradient, fish migration, related environmental values, water quality and quantity, and violate state and federal water quality standards." . . . Based on these rulings, the court enjoined the Director "from approving any further surface mining permits under current law that would authorize placement of excess spoil in intermittent and perennial streams for the primary purpose of waste disposal.". . . .

The State Director appealed, challenging not only the district court's substantive rulings on Counts 2 and 3, but also its rulings that the Eleventh Amendment did not bar this suit against him and that the federal court had jurisdiction to consider Bragg's claims. . . .

II

The Surface Mining Control and Reclamation Act of 1977 ("SMCRA") was enacted to strike a balance between the nation's interests in protecting the environment from the adverse effects of surface coal mining and in assuring the coal supply essential to the nation's energy requirements. *See* 30 U.S.C. § 1202(a), (d), (f); *see also Hodel v. Va. Mining & Reclamation Ass'n*, 452 U.S. 264, 268-69. (1981). The Act accomplishes these purposes through a "cooperative federalism," in which responsibility for the regulation of surface coal mining in the United States is shared between the U.S. Secretary of the Interior and State regulatory authorities. *See* H.R.Rep. No. 95-218, at 57 (1977) (hereinafter "Legislative History"), *reprinted in* 1977 U.S.C.C.A.N. 593, 595. Under this scheme, Congress established in SMCRA "minimum national standards" for regulating surface coal mining and encouraged the States, through an offer of exclusive regulatory jurisdiction, to enact their own laws incorporating these minimum standards, as well as any more stringent, but not inconsistent, standards that they might choose. *See* Legislative History, at 167, *reprinted in* 1977 U.S.C.C.A.N. at 698; 30 U.S.C. § 1255(b).

To implement this cooperative federalism, SMCRA directs the U.S. Secretary of the Interior to develop a "federal program" of regulation that embodies the minimum national standards and to consider for approval any "State programs" that are submitted to it for approval. To obtain approval of its program, a State must pass a law that provides for the minimum national standards established as "requirements" in

Chapter 9. Environmental Enforcement

SMCRA and must also demonstrate that it has the capability of enforcing its law. *See* 30 U.S.C. § 1253(a). Once the Secretary is satisfied that a State program meets these requirements and approves the program, the State's laws and regulations implementing the program become operative for the regulation of surface coal mining, and the State officials administer the program, *see id.* § 1252(e), giving the State "exclusive jurisdiction over the regulation of surface coal mining" within its borders, *id.* § 1253(a). If, however, a State fails to submit a program for approval, or a program that it submits is not approved, or approval of a State's program is withdrawn because of ineffective enforcement, then the *federal* program becomes applicable for the State, and the Secretary becomes vested with "exclusive jurisdiction for the regulation and control of surface coal mining and reclamation operations taking place [in the] State." . . .

Thus, SMCRA provides for *either* State regulation of surface coal mining within its borders *or* federal regulation, but not both. The Act expressly provides that one or the other is exclusive, *see* 30 U.S.C. §§ 1253(a), 1254(a), with the exception that an approved State program is always subject to revocation when a State fails to enforce it . . . [A]fter a State enacts statutes and regulations that are approved by the Secretary, these statutes and regulations become operative, and the federal law and regulations, while continuing to provide the "blueprint" against which to evaluate the State's program, "drop out" as operative provisions. . . .

The West Virginia [Coal Mining] Act sets out minimum performance standards that mirror those found in SMCRA, and the State Director has exercised his statutorily granted power to promulgate State regulations that parallel those issued by the Secretary of the Interior pursuant to the federal Act. *See* 38 W. Va.Code St. R. § 2-1 *et seq.* Thus, since the Secretary's approval of the West Virginia program in 1981, the Director has served as the exclusive permitting authority in the State, and West Virginia has maintained "exclusive jurisdiction," with certain exceptions inherent in the federal oversight provisions, over surface mining regulation within its borders.

III

Bragg brought this action against the State Director under the "citizen suit" provision of SMCRA, which provides in relevant part:

[A]ny person having an interest which is or may be adversely affected may commence a civil action on his own behalf to compel compliance with this chapter—

. . .

(2) against the Secretary or the appropriate State regulatory authority to the extent permitted by the eleventh amendment to the Constitution where there is alleged a failure of the Secretary or the appropriate State regulatory authority to perform any act or duty   under this chapter which is not discretionary with the Secretary or with the appropriate State regulatory authority.

The district courts shall have jurisdiction, without regard to the amount in controversy or the citizenship of the parties.

30 U.S.C. § 1270(a)(2).

The State Director asserted below and now contends that, as an official of West Virginia who has been sued in his official capacity, he is immune from suit in federal court under the doctrine of sovereign immunity guaranteed by the Eleventh Amendment. In response to the district court's reliance on *Ex parte Young,* 209 U.S. 123 (1908), to overcome the Eleventh Amendment bar, the Director argues that the *Ex parte Young* exception does not apply because the issues in this case involve enforcement of West Virginia law, not federal law. ... [The] Director concludes that the *Ex parte Young* exception for ongoing *federal* violations does not apply; rather, *Pennhurst State School & Hospital v. Halderman,* 465 U.S. 89 (1984), controls. In *Pennhurst,* the Supreme Court held the *Ex parte Young* doctrine inapplicable to a suit brought against a State official to compel his compliance with State law. *See* 465 U.S. at 106.

Bragg, on the other hand, contends that the *Ex parte Young* exception permits suit against the State Director. She argues first that Congress, by enacting 30 U.S.C. § 1270(a)(2), "authorized citizens to bring *Ex parte Young* suits against State officials who have the responsibility to comply with SMCRA and federally-approved State programs under that Act." Second, she asserts that her suit seeks to enforce federal, not State, law because (1) States with federally approved programs are still bound by federal statutory mandates that govern their activities, and (2) the buffer zone regulation promulgated by West Virginia is federal law. ...

[The Eleventh Amendment] limit on federal judicial power is an essential element of the constitutional design, as immunity "accords the States the respect owed them as members of the federation," ... and protects the States' ability "to govern in accordance with the will of their citizens. "

. . .A State's immunity to suit in federal court is subject to well established and important exceptions, however. *See S.C. State Ports Auth. v. Fed. Maritime Comm'n*, 243 F.3d 165, (4th Cir. 2001) (enumerating six exceptions to Eleventh Amendment immunity). [As the exception at issue here], the Eleventh Amendment does not preclude private individuals from bringing suit against State officials for prospective injunctive or declaratory relief designed to remedy ongoing violations of federal law. . . .

A

Although the *Ex parte Young* exception to the Eleventh Amendment is well established, its precise contours are not. . . . Even though "the State itself will have a continuing interest in the litigation whenever State policies or procedures are at stake," *Coeur d'Alene Tribe,* 521 U.S. at 269; *see also Gr. N. Life Ins. Co. v. Read,* 322 U.S. 47, 51 (1944), a court decree enjoining a State officer from committing future violations of federal law generally will not upset the careful federal balance established by the Constitution and confirmed by the Eleventh Amendment. To preserve this balance, however, "we must ensure that the doctrine of sovereign immunity remains meaningful, while also giving recognition to the need to prevent violations of federal law." *Coeur d'Alene Tribe,* 521 U.S. at 269.

But because this balance is a careful one indeed, the Supreme Court has strictly limited the application of the *Ex parte Young* doctrine to circumstances in which injunctive relief is necessary to "give[ ] life to the Supremacy Clause." . . . And as "it is difficult to think of a greater intrusion on state sovereignty than when a federal court instructs state officials on how to conform their conduct to state law," sovereign immunity also bars a court's grant of any type of relief, whether retrospective or prospective, based upon a State official's violation of State law. *Pennhurst,* 465 U.S. at 106. . . .

[J]ust as the Court did in *Coeur d'Alene Tribe,* we must evaluate the degree to which a State's sovereign interest would be adversely affected by a federal suit seeking injunctive relief against State officials, as well as the extent to which *federal,* rather than State, law must be enforced to vindicate the federal interest.

The respective federal and State interests revealed in this case make the analysis complex because SMCRA was expressly designed to hand over to the States the task of enforcing minimum national standards for surface coal mining, providing only limited federal mechanisms to oversee State enforcement. Thus, because the federal enactment, in furtherance of its design to advance State interests, creates the potential for exclusive State regulatory authority, the federal interest would seem to be better served by encouraging private citizens to enforce their claims relating to the State enforcement efforts in State, rather than federal, court. A more precise evaluation of this interest, however, as it might affect application of *Ex parte Young,* requires us to return to the statutory structure of SMCRA and the methods by which it employs a cooperative federalism.

B

As we have noted, under SMCRA Congress intended to divide responsibility for the regulation of surface coal mining between the federal government and the States. But characterizing the regulatory structure of SMCRA as "cooperative" federalism is not entirely accurate, as the statute does not provide for *shared* regulation of coal mining. Rather, the Act provides for enforcement of either a federal program or a State program, but not both. Thus, in contrast to other "cooperative federalism" statutes, SMCRA exhibits extraordinary deference to the States. *See* Mark Squillace, *Cooperative Federalism Under the Surface Mining Control and Reclamation Act: Is This Any Way to Run a Government?,* 15 Envtl. L. Rep. 10039 (1985) (calling SMCRA's "broad delegation" to States "unparalleled"). . . . The statutory federalism of SMCRA is quite unlike the cooperative regime under the Clean Water Act, 33 U.S.C. § 1251 *et seq.,* which was construed in *Arkansas v. Oklahoma,* 503 U.S. 91 (1992). As the Supreme Court noted there, one of the Clean Water Act's regulations "effectively *incorporate[d]* " State law into the unitary federal enforcement scheme, making State law, in certain circumstances, federal law. *Id.* at 110 (emphasis added). Under SMCRA, in contrast, Congress designed a scheme of mutually exclusive regulation by either the U.S. Secretary of the Interior or the State regulatory authority, depending on whether the State elects to regulate itself or to submit to federal regulation. Because West Virginia is a primacy state, its regulation of surface coal mining on nonfederal lands within its borders is "exclusive." *See* 30 U.S.C. § 1253(a); 30 C.F.R. § 948.10. This federal policy of encouraging "exclusive" State regulation was careful and deliberate. The Act's preliminary findings explain that "because of the diversity in terrain, climate, biologic, chemical, and other physical conditions in areas subject to mining operations, the primary governmental responsibility for developing, authorizing, issuing, and enforcing regulations for surface mining and reclamation operations subject to this chapter should rest with the States." 30 U.S.C. § 1201(f). According to the Act, it is the States, not the federal government, that are to "develop[ ] and implement[ ] a program to achieve the purposes of this chapter." *Id.* § 1202(g). . . .

Even so, SMCRA does manifest an ongoing federal interest in assuring that minimum national standards for surface coal mining are enforced. But when a State fails to enforce these minimum national standards, it does not automatically forfeit the right of exclusive regulation. . . . Until [a] withdrawal [of authority under SMCRA] occurs, because an approved State program must include "a *State law* which provides for the regulation of surface coal mining and reclamation operations in accordance with the requirements of this chapter," 30 U.S.C. § 1253(a)(1) (emphasis added), the minimum national standards are attained by State enforcement of its own law. "[I]t is with an approved state law and with state regulations . . . that mine operators must comply."

In sum, even though the States ultimately remain subject to SMCRA, the Act grants "exclusive jurisdiction" to a primacy State (one with an approved program), thereby conditionally divesting the federal government of *direct* regulatory authority. . . .

Bragg argues, however, that despite the federal government's conditional grant of "exclusive jurisdiction" to West Virginia, the national minimum standards set out in SMCRA retain operative force against West Virginia. For example, her complaint asserted that the State Director had violated nondiscretionary duties found in 30 U.S.C. § 1260, which sets out requirements for permit approval, and in § 1265, which establishes standards for reclaiming mined property and preserving the environment.

To construe SMCRA in the manner urged by Bragg, however, would circumvent the carefully designed balance that Congress established between the federal government and the States because the effect of a citizen suit to enjoin officials in a primacy State to comport with the *federal* provisions establishing the core standards for surface coal mining would end the exclusive State regulation and undermine the federalism established by the Act. Thus, rather than advancing the federal interest in preserving this statutory design, Bragg's interpretation would frustrate it.

While it is true that Congress' desire to implement minimum national standards for surface coal mining drives SMCRA, Congress did not pursue, although it could have, the *direct* regulation of surface coal mining as its preferred course to fulfill this desire. Nor did Congress invite the States to enforce *federal* law directly. By giving States exclusive regulatory control through enforcement of *their own* approved laws, Congress intended that the federal law establishing minimum national standards would "drop out" as operative law and that the State laws would become the sole operative law. *Cf. Nat'l Wildlife Fed'n v. Lujan,* 928 F.2d 453, 464 n. 1 (D.C.Cir.1991) (Wald, J., concurring) (recognizing that the provisions of SMCRA do not "technically apply" in primacy States). Thus, all of the *federal* provisions establishing the minimum national standards are not directly operative in West Virginia so long as it remains a primacy State. . . . The Act's structural provisions creating the facility through which the State can attain and can lose its primacy status remain directly operative. *See, e.g.,* 30 U.S.C. §§ 1253, 1254, 1267, 1271. But these provisions are not at issue in this case. . . .

Because 30 U.S.C. § 1260 establishes minimum standards that have been adopted by West Virginia and approved by the Secretary, *see* W. Va.Code § 22-3-18, any violation of this standard involves State law, not federal law, even though the relevant language in the State law is identical to that in the federal law. Accordingly, any injunction against State officials to enforce this provision would command them to comport with the State's own law, not federal law, because only the State law is operative and directly regulates the issuance of permits. . . .

[The district court's injunction issued] to a State official to comply with the State's law was so abhorrent to the values underlying our federal structure as to fall outside the bounds of the *Ex parte Young* exception. In *Pennhurst,* the Supreme Court stated:

> [I]t is difficult to think of a greater intrusion on state sovereignty than when a federal court instructs state officials on how to conform their conduct to state law. Such a result conflicts directly with the principles of federalism that underlie the Eleventh Amendment. We conclude that *Young* and *Edelman* are inapplicable in a suit against state officials on the basis of state law.

465 U.S. at 106.

To be certain, the state-law claims at issue in *Pennhurst* were of a different character from the claims at issue in this case. In *Pennhurst,* the Supreme Court noted that because the lower court had exercised *pendent* jurisdiction over the state-law claims, *see id.* at 104, 104 S.Ct. 900, an *Ex parte Young* injunction to enforce those claims was not necessary to vindicate the supremacy of federal law, *see id.* at 106. In this case, the federal interest in adjudicating the dispute is undoubtedly stronger, as the rights at issue were created by the State pursuant to a federal invitation to implement a program that met certain minimum standards set by Congress. Moreover, the federal government, through the Secretary's oversight role, retains an important modicum of control over the enforcement of that State law. . . .

Nonetheless, although "the difference between the type of relief barred by the Eleventh Amendment and that permitted under *Ex parte Young* will not in many instances be that between day and night," *Edelman,* 415 U.S. at 667, we conclude that the injunctive relief sought against the State Director in this case "falls on the Eleventh Amendment side of the line" by some distance, *Coeur d'Alene Tribe,* 521 U.S. at 281, and is therefore barred by the Eleventh Amendment. The *Pennhurst* Court made clear that its decision was driven by the indignity to which a State is subject when a federal court orders that State's officers to conform their conduct with their own laws—a concern that is also present in this case. *See* 465 U.S. at 106. In subsequent Eleventh Amendment decisions, the States' dignity interest has played an increasingly critical role. . . . And particularly in the absence of an explicit incorporation of State law into federal law, *cf. Arkansas*, 503 U.S. at 110-11; *Geis v. Bd. of Educ.*, 774 F.2d 575, 581 (3d Cir.1985), States retain a unique interest in the enforcement of their own law against their own officers. This is especially true where, as here, Congress has reserved to the States the "exclusive" right to set the rules by which the regulation of surface mining will be governed. The West Virginia statute and implementing regulations are solely the product of its own sovereignty, enacted pursuant to its democratic processes, and, as was the case in *Pennhurst*, a State's sovereign dignity reserves to its own institutions the task of keeping its officers in line with that law.

Moreover, it is simply not the case that an *Ex parte Young* injunction is necessary to "vindicate the supreme authority of federal law" in this context. *Pennhurst*, 465 U.S. at 106. The SMCRA citizen-suit provision is designed not to vindicate individual rights, but rather to supplement the Secretary's enforcement power under 30 U.S.C. § 1271(b)—a power that is unaffected by the constraints of the Eleventh Amendment. *See Seminole Tribe v. Florida*, 517 U.S. 44, 71 n. 14 (1996) (citing *United States v. Texas*, 143 U.S. 621, 644-45 (1892)). If West Virginia's program no longer comports with the federal blue-print found in SMCRA, the Secretary may instigate an enforcement proceeding and revoke West Virginia's authority to regulate surface mining. Additionally, as part of its approved State program, West Virginia enacted a citizen suit provision that, parroting the language of its federal counterpart, gives affected individuals the right to sue in State court to compel the Director's compliance with the West Virginia Act. *See* W. Va.Code § 22-3-25. Because the West Virginia courts are open to such suits, the federal interest in maintaining the State's compliance with its own program may be fulfilled via suit in that forum, in a manner that does not offend the dignity of the State. *See Coeur d'Alene Tribe*, 521 U.S. at 274 (opinion of Kennedy, J.).

In sum, rather than asking the States to enforce the federal law, Congress through SMCRA invited the States to create their own laws, which would be of "exclusive" force in the regulation of surface mining within their borders. *See Hodel*, 452 U.S. at 289 (noting that under

SMCRA, states "enact and administer their own regulatory programs"). An order from an Article III court instructing an officer of such a State to conform his conduct with a duly enacted State law would create an affront to that State's dignity similar to that created by the orders at issue in *Pennhurst*. And particularly when that State's law specifically provides for its own enforcement in a State forum, the concerns that gave rise to the exception of *Ex parte Young* evaporate.

Accordingly, we conclude that Bragg's claims filed against the State Director in federal court are not authorized by the *Ex parte Young* exception to the Eleventh Amendment.

C

[The court also concluded that West Virginia had not waived its sovereign immunity rights when it agreed to assume responsibility for implementing SMCRA.]

V

For the reasons given, the consent decree of February 17, 2000, is affirmed, but the judgment of the district court enjoining the State Director is vacated, and the case is remanded to the district court with instructions to dismiss Bragg's unsettled claims asserted in Counts 2 and 3 without prejudice to any suit she may wish to pursue in West Virginia State court.

Affirmed in part, vacated in part, and remanded with instructions.

NOTES AND QUESTIONS

1. Is the court correct in believing that federal interests in the sound enforcement of SMCRA can be adequately protected through the mechanism of the federal government's withdrawing enforcement authority from the state?

2. The citizen suit provision of SMCRA is worded differently from the citizen suit provisions in other environmental statutes. Compare it with the Clean Air Act, for example. See 42 U.S.C. § 7604(a). Do those differences suggest that Congress specifically contemplated the kind of citizen suit brought in *Bragg*? Bragg argued that a state's

289

accepting responsibility under SMCRA to implement a program that compiled with the federal statutory minimums amounted to an agreement to have such enforcement actions as these brought against it. Supreme Court precedent makes it clear, though, that Congress' intent to have a state waive its immunity must be "unmistakably clear and unequivocal." The *Bragg* court concluded that the SMCRA language failed this test.

3. How generally applicable is the *Bragg* holding? The court distinguishes the SMCRA version of cooperative federalism from that of the Clean Water Act. Does the holding apply to the Clean Air Act?

Enforcement Against Federal Facilities
(pp. 1092-96)

In California ex rel. Sacramento Metropolitan Air Quality Management District v. United States, 215 F.3d 1005 (9th Cir. 2000), the Ninth Circuit upheld the right of a California state air quality management district to seek penalties in state court from a U.S. Air Force base for Clean Air Act violations. While the federal agency had removed the case to a federal district court, which had held it immune from penalties under the Clean Air Act, the Ninth Circuit ordered the case returned to state court. The court held that the Clean Air Act specifically preserves the rights of state and local governments to seek penalties for violations of state and local air quality regulations in state court.

- 10 -

Protection of the Global Environment

The "Rio+10" Conference and the State of Global Environmental Governance (pp. 1102-09)

Preparations are under way for the next once-a-decade global environmental summit. On September 2-11, 2002, representatives of virtually every nation on earth will gather in Johannesburg, South Africa for the World Summit on Sustainable Development, also known as "Rio+10" because it is the ten-year successor to the Rio Earth Summit held in 1992. The United Nations General Assembly decided in December 2000 that the Commission on Sustainable Development (CSD) would be the entity responsible for organizing the Johannesburg Summit. The CSD was established in December 1992 to ensure effective follow-up of commitments made at the Rio Earth Summit. It functions as a commission of the United Nations Economic and Social Council (ECOSOC), with 53 members.

The Johannesburg summit will evaluate progress that has been made since the Rio Earth Summit in 1992. It will consider what countries have done to date to implement Agenda 21, the obstacles they have encountered, and the lessons that can be learned from this experience. While Agenda 21 itself will not be open for revision, the conference will seek to reach consensus on the state of current environmental conditions and to determine what mid-course corrections need to be made to achieve the goals of Agenda 21. The conference also will consider how advances in technology, science, and communications have changed the world and the implications of future economic and social change on the health of the planet.

The thousands of world leaders and representatives of nongovernmental organizations who meet in Johannesburg will confront an uncertain future for global environmental governance. At previous Earth summits (Stockholm in 1972, Nairobi in 1982, and Rio in 1992)

Chapter 10. Protection of the Global Environment

a remarkable spirit of international cooperation spurred countries to set aside past differences for the sake of the planet's future health. That spirit has been badly shaken by several developments. Progress in implementing the ambitious agenda for global action adopted at the Rio Earth Summit has been disappointing. The United States government has retreated from a position of leadership on global environmental issues. The Bush administration now flatly rejects the Kyoto Protocol to the Framework Convention on Climate Change. While the nations of the world are becoming more economically interdependent, sharp divisions between developing countries and the industrialized world threaten to jeopardize future international cooperation. Never have environmental problems that transcend national boundaries seemed so urgent. Yet the prospects for crafting effective global responses to them never have seemed so uncertain.

Despite decades of international cooperation, many believe that existing institutions of global environmental governance simply are not adequate to meet future challenges. What we call international environmental law now consists of a patchwork of formal and informal agreements, monitored and implemented by a plethora of governmental, quasigovernmental, and nongovernmental organizations. In 1970, there were 52 international agreements pertaining to the environment; in 1999 there were 215 environmental treaties and more than 500 bilateral legal instruments with significant environmental provisions. A total of 21 separate United Nations agencies are involved in some manner in dealing with environmental issues. The policies of other international organizations, such as the World Bank, the International Monetary Fund and the World Trade Organization (WTO), now have profound environmental consequences as well.

Those concerned with developing more effective institutions of global environmental governance are debating several issues. See, e.g., Eileen Claussen, Global Environmental Governance: Issues for the New U.S. Administration, 43 Environment 29 (Jan/Feb 2001). These include the following: How and to what extent should existing institutions of environmental governance be restructured or replaced? How can coordination between them be improved? Should a World Environmental Organization, on a par with the WTO, be created or will more decentralized approaches, built on emerging models of collaborative governance, offer more promise of success? Should new patterns of international governance and political authority be developed and, if so, how can they be reconciled with traditional notions of state sovereignty? Can truly enforceable international environmental obligations be created? International human rights law has evolved to alter older concepts of state sovereignty; how should international environmental law evolve?

Clearly the industrialized world bears the lion's share of the responsibility for problems like global warming and climate change. Yet without the participation of the developing world, any regime for controlling greenhouse gas emissions seems doomed to failure. How can the G-77 and China be mobilized to participate in such a regime? How can governments and individuals be induced to make sacrifices today to prevent problems in the future? Solutions that impose significant costs in the short term on individuals or important industry sectors are politically unpalatable because politics typically does not reward those who place a high value on long-run futures that extend far beyond terms of office. How can poorer nations be given the capacity to comply with international environmental controls that may require significant expenditures? How can notions of national sovereignty be reconciled with the need for collective action to protect the global environment? To what extent should global institutions or treaties be the vehicles for combating environmental problems? While the nations of the world are becoming more interdependent economically, political realignments are devolving more power to smaller units of government. Can effective global governance regimes be designed to ensure broad participation of sovereign nations without undermining national sovereignty?

Global Climate Change: Scientific Developments (pp. 1121-27)

While the full environmental consequences of climate change remain uncertain, confidence in climate forecasts is increasing and the news is not good. The most recent consensus estimate by the Intergovernmental Panel on Climate Change (IGPCC), released in February 2001, warns that the magnitude of global warming will be even greater than previously thought. Intergovernmental Panel on Climate Change, Third Assessment Report (2001). The IGPCC report concluded that average global temperatures will rise by between 2.5 and 10.4 degrees Fahrenheit by 2100, a 60 percent increase over the level forecast just six years ago. The IGPCC found that there is new and stronger evidence that most of the warming observed over the last 50 years is attributable to human activities, which will continue to change the composition of the atmosphere throughout the 21st century.

Following the issuance of the IGPCC report, the Bush administration asked the National Academy of Sciences (NAS) to perform its own assessment of the state of scientific knowledge concerning climate change. On June 6, 2001, the NAS's National Research Council released its report, *Climate Change Science: An Analysis of Some Key Questions*. The report, prepared by a committee of eleven of the nation's leading climate scientists, confirmed the findings of the IGPCC and concluded that global warming could well have "serious adverse societal and ecological impacts by the end of this century." The report agreed that the climatic changes observed during the past several decades are most likely due to human activities, although the committee could not rule out the possibility that the climate's natural variability could be responsible for a significant portion of the trend. The NRC agreed that human-induced warming and sea level rise are expected to continue through the 21st century and beyond, though current predictions of the magnitude and rate of future warming "should be regarded as tentative and subject to future adjustments (either upward or downward)." The following is an excerpt of some of the NRC's key conclusions.

National Research Council, Climate Change Science: An Analysis of Some Key Questions (2001)

Are greenhouse gases causing climate change?

The IPCC's conclusion that most of the observed warming of the last 50 years is likely to have been due to the increase in greenhouse gas concentrations accurately reflects the current thinking of the scientific community on this issue. The stated degree of confidence in the IPCC assessment is higher today than it was ten, or even five years ago, but uncertainty remains because of (1) the level of natural variability inherent in the climate system on time scales of decades to centuries, (2) the questionable ability of models to accurately simulate natural variability on those long time scales, and (3) the degree of confidence that can be placed on reconstructions of global mean tempera-

Chapter 10. Protection of the Global Environment

ture over the past millennium based on proxy evidence. Despite the uncertainties, there is general agreement that the observed warming is real and particularly strong within the past twenty years. Whether it is consistent with the change that would be expected in response to human activities is dependent upon what assumptions one makes about the time history of atmospheric concentrations of the various forcing agents, particularly aerosols.

By how much will temperatures change over the next 100 years and where?

Climate change simulations for the period of 1990 to 2100 based on the IPCC emissions scenarios yield a globally-averaged surface temperature increase by the end of the century of 1.4 to 5.8°C (2.5 to 10.4°F) relative to 1990. The wide range of uncertainty in these estimates reflects both the different assumptions about future concentrations of greenhouse gases and aerosols in the various scenarios considered by the IPCC and the differing climate sensitivities of the various climate models used in the simulations. The range of climate sensitivities implied by these predictions is generally consistent with previously reported values.

The predicted warming is larger over higher latitudes than over low latitudes, especially during winter and spring, and larger over land than over sea. Rainfall rates and the frequency of heavy precipitation events are predicted to increase, particularly over the higher latitudes. Higher evaporation rates would accelerate the drying of soils following rain events, resulting in lower relative humidities and higher daytime temperatures, especially during the warm season. The likelihood that this effect could prove important is greatest in semi-arid regions, such as the U.S. Great Plains. These predictions in the IPCC report are consistent with current understanding of the processes that control local climate. . . .

What will be the consequences of global warming (e.g., extreme weather, health effects) of increases of various magnitude?

In the near term, agriculture and forestry are likely to benefit from carbon dioxide fertilization and an increased water efficiency of some plants at higher atmospheric CO_2 concentrations. The optimal climate for crops may change, requiring significant regional adaptations. Some models project an increased tendency toward drought over semi-arid regions, such as the U.S. Great Plains. Hydrological impacts could be significant over the western United States, where much of the water supply is dependent on the amount of snow pack and the timing of the spring runoff. Increased rainfall rates could impact pollution run-off and flood control. With higher sea level, coastal regions could be subject to increased wind and flood damage even if tropical storms do not change in intensity. A significant warming also could have far reaching implications for ecosystems. The costs and risks involved are difficult to quantify at this point and are, in any case, beyond the scope of this brief report.

Health outcomes in response to climate change are the subject of intense debate. Climate is one of a number of factors influencing the incidence of infectious disease. Cold-related stress would decline in a warmer climate, while heat stress and smog induced respiratory illnesses in major urban areas would increase, if no adaptation occurred. Over much of the United States, adverse health outcomes would likely be mitigated by a strong public health system, relatively high levels of public awareness, and a high standard of living.

Global warming could well have serious adverse societal and ecological impacts by the end of this century, especially if globally-averaged temperature increases approach the upper end of the IPCC projections. Even in the more conservative scenarios, the models project temperatures and sea-levels that continue to increase well beyond the end of this century, suggesting that assessments that examine only the next 100 years may well underestimate the magnitude of the eventual impacts.

Has science determined whether there is a "safe" level of concentration of greenhouse gases?

The question of whether there exists a "safe" level of concentration of greenhouse gases cannot be answered directly because it would require a value judgment of what constitutes an acceptable risk to human welfare and ecosystems in various parts of the world, as well as a more quantitative assessment of the risks and costs associated with the various impacts of global warming. In general, however, risk increases with increases in both the rate and the magnitude of climate change.

Global Climate Change and the Kyoto Protocol (pp. 1127-45)

As noted in the casebook (p. 1128), the nations of the world agreed on a Framework Convention on Climate Change (casebook, pp. 1129-1131) at the Rio Earth Summit in 1992. The framework convention established a process for negotiating limits on emissions of greenhouse gases that resulted in the adoption of the Kyoto Protocol in December 1997 (casebook, pp. 1133-1142). The Kyoto Protocol requires nations in the industrialized world to reduce emissions of greenhouse gases to a level approximately five percent below their 1990 emissions during the period between 2008 and 2012. (The United States is required to reduce its emissions to a level seven percent below 1990 levels; the European Union is required to achieve an eight percent reduction). While reductions of this magnitude would not be enough to reverse many of the adverse effects of climate changes that already have been set in motion, the Kyoto Protocol represents the first global effort to deal with the problem.

As of July 20, 2001, the Kyoto Protocol had been signed by 84 countries and it had been ratified or acceded to by 37 countries. It has not been ratified by the United States or by any other industrialized nation. The nations that have ratified or acceded to the Kyoto Protocol are: Antigua and Barbuda, Azerbaijan, the Bahamas, Barbados, Bolivia, Cyprus, Ecuador, El Salvador, Equatorial Guinea, Fiji, Gambia, Georgia, Guatemala, Guinea, Hondurs, Jamaica, Kiribati, Lesotho, Maldives, Mauritius, Mexico, Micronesia, Mongolia, Nicaragua, Niue, Palau, Panama, Paraguay, Romania, Samoa, Senegal, Trinidad and Tobago, Turkmenistan, Tuvalu, Uruguay, Vanuatu, and Uzbekistan).

Following the 1997 Kyoto conference it had been anticipated that many of the details for implementation of the Kyoto Protocol would be worked out at the November 1998 COP-4 meeting in Buenos Aires. However, the parties ultimately realized that it would take more time to develop consensus on some of the difficult issues that remained. These included: rules and guidelines for emissions trading, joint implementation, and the Clean Development Mechanism (CDM), how to police emissions trades, measurement, reporting and verification issues, the consequences of noncompliance, provisions for technology transfer, and how to treat carbon sinks. These issues proved difficult to resolve and few decisions were reached on them at the COP-5 meeting in Bonn, Germany, held from October 25 to November 24, 1999. At the COP-6 meeting, held from November 13-24, 2000, in The Hague, Netherlands, negotiations ended in an impasse because of sharp disagreements between the United States and the European Union over how to achieve compliance with the emissions limits set by the treaty. The parties subsequently agreed to resume meeting in Bonn in May 2001 in an effort to salvage some agreement.

The U.S. delegation to COP-6 had operated under difficult circumstances because the meeting took place while the outcome of the U.S. presidential election remained in doubt. When the Bush administration ultimately took office in January 2001, there was considerable uncertainty concerning what changes would be made in U.S. policy on climate change. On February 12, 2001, United Nations officials agreed to a request from the United States to postpone the resumption of COP-6 negotiations from May until June or July in order to give the new administration time to conduct "a review of its policy toward the international climate change negotiations." Andrew C. Revkin, Bush Team Under Attack on Emissions Talks, N.Y. Times, Feb.16, 2001, p. A14.

Following her confirmation as EPA Administrator, Christie Whitman signaled that the new administration would act to combat climate change by emphasizing President Bush's campaign pledge to regulate carbon dioxide emissions. On September 29, 2000, during the heat of the presidential campaign, candidate Bush had proposed legislation to require mandatory emissions reductions of carbon dioxide as part of a new strategy to control four pollutants (also including nitrogen oxide, mercury, and sulfur dioxide). Appearing before a Senate committee and later on national television, Administrator Whitman stated that there was no question that global warming was occurring, that the president was very sensitive to the urgency of this issue, and that he had proposed to reduce emissions of carbon dioxide. Whitman repeated these statements at a meeting of European environment ministers in Italy in an effort to reassure them that the United States would act to combat climate change. At the administration's first cabinet meeting, Treasury Secretary Paul O'Neill circulated copies of a speech he had given when CEO of Alcoa calling for a Manhattan Project to mobilize a governmental response to global climate change. These developments shocked conservatives who had expected the new administration to relax environmental regulations. Robert D. Novak, .

Chapter 10. Protection of the Global Environment

. .And Warming, Wash. Post, March 1, 2001, p. A19; Douglas Jehl, Moves on Environment Disappoint Industry, N.Y. Times, March 11, 2001, p. A16. When word leaked that the new president would propose controls on carbon dioxide emissions in his first address to Congress, conservatives flooded the White House with emails protesting the decision. Bush ultimately decided not to mention it during his speech.

On March 13, 2001, Administrator Whitman met with Bush at the White House where the president informed her that he had changed his mind and would no longer support controls on emissions of carbon dioxide. John J. Fialka & Jeanne Cummings, How the President Changed His Mind on Carbon Dioxide, Wall St. J., March 15, 2001, p. A20. In a letter to four Republican Senators opposed to regulating carbon dioxide, President Bush assured them that his administration would not support such proposals. Bush cited uncertainties concerning the science behind global warming and concern that controls on greenhouse gas emissions would harm consumers at a time when the nation faced what he described as "an energy crisis." Douglas Jehl, Bush Ties Policy Shift to an "Energy Crisis," N.Y. Times, March 15, 2001, p. A19.

While Bush had expressed opposition to the Kyoto Protocol during the campaign, his proposal to regulate carbon dioxide emissions led some to believe that his administration would work to persuade the rest of the world to modify the agreement to make it more acceptable to the United States. However, in late March the administration indicated that it considered Kyoto to be "fatally flawed" and "effectively dead." Oh No, Kyoto, The Economist, April 7, 2001, p. 73. European governments were infuriated by the decision and, in particular, by the fact that it was announced without any effort by the U.S. to consult with them. Rage over Global Warming, The Economist, April 7, 2001, p. 18. A meeting of Western Hemisphere environment ministers ended in discord on March 30 when the United States rejected efforts by Latin American nations to persuade the U.S. to back reductions on emissions of greenhouse gases. Douglas Jehl, Hemisphere Conference Ends in Discord on Global Warming, N.Y. Times, March 31, 2001, p. A9.

The U.S. briefly thought it had gained a key ally in its efforts to kill the Kyoto Protocol, when the new Japanese Prime Minister visited President Bush at the White House and expressed sympathy for the U.S. position. This led some to predict that the Kyoto accord would collapse when the COP-6 meeting was resumed in Bonn on July 19, 2001. However, while the COP-6 meeting was in progress, leaders of the other industrialized countries informed President Bush at another summit meeting in Genoa, Italy, that they were prepared to ratify the Kyoto Protocol even without the participation of United States. While the Bush administration promised to propose alternative measures to combat global warming without specifying when, the leaders of the other countries indicated that this would not stop them from pursuing implementation of the Kyoto accord. David E. Sanger & Alessandra Stanley, Allies Tell Bush They'll Act Alone on Climate Accord, N.Y. Times, July 22, 2001, p. A1. After an all-night bargaining session on July 22, 2001, 178 nations meeting at the resumed COP-6 conference reached agreement the following day on provisions to implement the Kyoto accord, with the United States alone in its opposition. Andrew C. Revkin, 178 Nations Reach a Climate Accord; U.S. Only Looks On, N.Y. Times, July 24, 2001, p. A1. As a result of this agreement, it now seems likely that some European countries will ratify the Kyoto Protocol. However, considerable work is still necessary to develop detailed rules and procedures for implementation of the agreement.

Ironically, some of the provisions of the "Core Elements for the Implementation of the Buenos Aires Plan of Action" approved at the resumed COP-6 were the kinds of measures the Clinton administration had proposed, but the European Union had rejected, at the Hague meeting in November 2000. Agreement was reached on how to treat carbon dioxide sinks, which had been a major obstacle to agreement in The Hague. Credit will now be given for carbon dioxide sinks up to 13 million tons of carbon per year. Controversy over the consequences of non-compliance was only resolved at the last minute after the meeting had been extended by one day due to the objections of Japan, Canada and Australia. The question whether to make the rules legally binding was left to the first session of the Conference of the Parties serving as the Meeting of the Parties (COP/MOP) to the Kyoto Protocol after the Kyoto Protocol enters into force.

The agreement establishes a compliance committee consisting of two components. The "facilitative branch" will assist all parties in their implementation of the Protocol while the "enforcement branch" will determine whether developed countries have met their targets and complied with monitoring and reporting requirements. If the enforcement branch finds that a party has failed to comply, it will decide on

Chapter 10. Protection of the Global Environment

the appropriate consequences for the noncompliance. At the insistence of the G-77 and China, the membership of both branches of the compliance committee will be based upon equitable geographical representation.

To encourage compliance, for every ton of emissions by which a party exceeds its target, 1.3 tons will be deducted from that party's assigned amount for the subsequent commitment period. The enforcement branch will be empowered to review detailed plans that every non-complying party will be required to develop to explain how it will meet its reduced target for the subsequent commitment period. Decisions by the enforcement branch can be appealed to the full COP/MOP, which can overturn them only by a three-quarters vote.

Some environmentalists are very critical of the provision adopted on sinks, which will allow countries to claim credit for all kinds of activities designed to promote forest growth. Others view it as a necessary compromise, while worrying that it may create a loophole that will allow a country like Japan to meet half of its emissions reduction commitments simply by changing its forest practices. Another key question now is whether the Kyoto Protocol can work without some form of involvement by the United States, which has only five percent of the world's population, but which produces a quarter of the world's emissions of greenhouse gases.

Surprisingly, a bipartisan group of members of Congress is now urging the Bush administration to resume participation in the Kyoto negotiations. On August 1, 2001, the U.S. Senate Foreign Relations Committee by a 19-0 vote adopted a resolution calling for the United States to participate in international negotiations to reach a binding agreement to reduce emissions of greeenhouse gases to combat climate change. A similar resolution also has passed the House International Relations Committee. Most significantly, the Senate resolution specifies that Senate Resolution 98 (casebook, p. 1133), which passed the Senate 95-0 in 1997, five months before the Kyoto Protocol was negotiated, should not cause the United States to abandon its shared responsibility to help combat global climate change. While noting that developing nations, especially the largest emitters, must be included in any future binding agreement and that such an agreement should not cause serious economic hardship, it calls on the Bush administration to participate in international negotiations to craft a revised Kyoto Protocol or other future binding climate change agreements.

On August 2, 2001, the U.S. Senate Governmental Affairs Committee approved $4.8 billion over 10 years to fund research technologies to combat global warming. "Further delay can only mean that a more difficult problem awaits us in the future," said Sen. Robert Byrd, D-W.Va., co-author with Sen. Ted Stevens, R-Alaska, of the research funding bill. Byrd said a 1997 Senate resolution that he drafted with Sen. Chuck Hagel, R-Neb., and that passed 95-0 five months before the Kyoto treaty, "should not be used as an excuse by the Bush administration to abandon America's shared responsibility to help find a solution to the global climate change dilemma." The Senate Foreign Relations Committee's resolution says any global warming agreement must require mandatory cuts in greenhouse gases, yet it agrees with Bush and the earlier 1997 Senate resolution in saying developing nations should be included and the U.S. economy should not be unduly harmed.

COP-7, the next round of negotiations on the Kyoto Protocol, is scheduled for October in Marrakesh, Morocco. The Bush administration has not said whether they will have any alternative proposal ready by the time of that meeting.

Trade and the Environment: the GATT and the WTO (pp. 1152-1153)

This edition of the casebook inadvertently omits a discussion of what the World Trade Organization (WTO) is and how it came into being, which had appeared in the second edition. The WTO is a product of the Marrakesh Agreement that completed the Uruguay Round of negotiations under the old General Agreement on Tariffs and Trade (GATT) in December 1993. U.S. membership in the WTO was approved by Congress in December 1994, and the WTO came into being on January 1, 1995. The principles established under GATT still remain the centerpiece of the international trading system, which now has been integrated into a new, unified system under the WTO. Unlike GATT's "contracting parties," the WTO has "Members" who are required to attend the organization's ministerial conferences. The WTO's General Council, which reports to the ministerial conference, is responsible for running the day-to-day business of the WTO. Its subsidiary, the General Council on Trade and Goods administers existing trade agreements, the role GATT used to play. The WTO has dispute settlement provisions that are more developed that GATT's by making the formation of dispute settlement panels and the adoption of their decisions automatic, subject to appeal to an Appellate Body of seven members.

The U.S. General Accounting Office issued a report in June 2000 that examined the impact of the WTO's dispute settlement procedures on U.S. laws and regulations. GAO, World Trade Organization: U.S. Experience to Date in Dispute Settlement System (June 2000). The report found that as of April 2000 the United States had initiated 25 cases at the WTO and had been a defendant in 17 cases brought against it by other countries. In 13 of the 25 cases initiated by the United States, the U.S. prevailed in a final WTO dispute settlement ruling; 10 cases were resolved without a rule, and the U.S. did not prevail in the other two. Of the 17 cases brought against the U.S., 10 were resolved without a ruling, the U.S. lost 6 cases and prevailed in only one. A total of 187 complaints had been filed with the WTO during the first five years of its existence, with the U.S. and the European Union being the most active participants in the system. The GAO concluded "that the United States has gained more than it has lost in the WTO dispute settlement system to date. WTO cases have resulted in a substantial number of changes in foreign trade practices, while their effect on U.S. laws and regulations has been minimal." Id. at 4.

Recent protests against WTO have been cited as evidence of strong grassroots support for efforts to develop a fairer system of world trade and economic development that respects environmental and social justice. The director-general of the World Trade Organization has recognized that "in the absence of environmental protection policies, trade will exacerbate existing environmental problems" and that in some circumstances "trade can itself be the cause of environmental problems." When industrialists, government officials, and other members of the world elite gathered in Davos, Switzerland, last January for their annual World Economic Forum, consumer, labor, environmental, and human rights activists gathered in Porto Alegre, Brazil for the first counter forum, called the World Social Forum. This forum highlighted the distributional consequences of policies that fail to consider the social and environmental costs of trade liberalization. Stephen Buckley, Foes Take Moderate Tack on Globalism, Wash. Post, Jan. 27, 2001, p. A15.

Chapter 10. Protection of the Global Environment

The Tuna/Dolphin Controversy, the Panama Agreement and the International Dolphin Conservation Program Act (p. 1153-61)

As noted in the casebook (pp. 1158-1159), the International Dolphin Conservation Act of 1992 (IDCA), Pub. L. 102-523, 106 Stat. 3425, authorized the Secretary of State to enter into international agreements to establish a global moratorium of minimally 5 years to prohibit tuna harvesting with purse-seine nets deployed on or to encircle dolphins or other marine mammals. It also banned the sale, purchase, transport, or shipment in the United States of any tuna that is not "dolphin-safe." Following the enactment of the IDCA, various Central and South American nations that had purse seine fishing vessels located in the Eastern Tropical Pacific Ocean (ETP) along with the United States voluntarily agreed to further dolphin safety by establishing the International Dolphin Conservation Program (IDCP) also known as the "La Jolla Agreement." Nations participating in the IDCP voluntarily agreed to limit dolphin deaths from tuna harvesting in the ETP by maintaining dolphin kill levels at or below established "dolphin mortality limits" assigned to each tuna seine, and to work toward reducing dolphin mortality to levels approaching zero.

In September of 1995, representatives of five major environmental organizations (the Center for Marine Conservation, the Environmental Defense Fund, Greenpeace, the National Wildlife Federation, and the World Wildlife Fund), the Inter-American Tropical Tuna Commission, and 12 ETP nations met in Panama to discuss and negotiate dolphin protection issues. The outcome of these discussions resulted in the Panama Declaration, an international agreement for the protection of dolphins and management of tuna in the Eastern Tropical Pacific Ocean (ETP). It was signed on October 4, 1995, by 12 ETP nations: United States, Mexico, Belize, Columbia, Costa Rica, Ecuador, Honduras, Panama, Vanuatu, Venezuela, France, and Spain. This treaty legally reaffirmed the commitments and objectives of reducing dolphin mortality as established in the IDCP. The treaty also modified the existing U.S. laws on dolphin safety by lifting primary and secondary embargoes on tuna caught in compliance with the IDCP, permitting all tuna in accordance with the IDCP to be introduced into the U.S. tuna market. Finally, "dolphin-safe" was expanded to include ETP tuna caught in purse-seine nets in which no dolphin deaths or serious injuries

304

occurred during their use. Although the Declaration was embraced by many interest groups, many others were strictly opposed to the Panama Declaration, arguing that all it effectively accomplished was the legalization of killing of dolphins.

On August 15, 1997, Congress effectively implemented the Panama Declaration and lifted the ban on tuna imports from nations in compliance with IDCP, by enacting the International Dolphin Conservation Program Act (IDCPA), Pub. L. 105-42, 111 Stat. 1122. This act amended the Marine Mammal Protection Act of 1972 to support the International Dolphin Conservation Program and to implement the 1995 Panama Declaration. It significantly changed the existing MMPA by lifting the ban on tuna imports from all nations complying with the IDCP. It further amended MMPA by requiring U.S. fisherman harvesting tuna to obtain permits issued by the Department of Commerce and requiring a mandatory advisory committee to oversee the IDCP.

Although the IDCPA mirrored the Panama Declaration on most issues, it differed on the issue of dolphin-safe label requirements. The signatory nations of the Panama Declaration sought legislation that would immediately allow tuna caught with purse-seine nets to be labeled dolphin-safe so long as no dolphins were observed to be killed or seriously injured during the set. But there was substantial concern that while there had been great success in decreasing dolphin mortality rate to minimal levels, the repeated use of purse-seine nets may cause significant physiological stress on dolphins that could impede the recovery of depleted dolphin populations. Due to such concern, Congress amended the MMPA to require the Secretary of Commerce to conduct population abundance surveys on depleted dolphin stocks and research into whether the stress imposed on dolphins when encircled or caught in purse nets adversely affected depleted dolphin stocks. The amendments directed the Secretary to make an initial finding on the issue by March 1, 1999, and a final conclusion on the issue by December 31, 2002. Congress provided that, pending the initial or final finding, the existing dolphin-safe label requirements for tuna sold in the United States would stay in force. These requirements permitted use of the dolphin-safe label only on tuna that was not harvested with purse-seine nets intentionally deployed on or to encircle dolphins. This existing standard would stay in effect unless the Secretary's initial or final research concluded there was no adverse impact on the depleted dolphin stock. If the Secretary found no concrete adverse impacts, the dolphin-safe label would default to a new standard, which would permit tuna harvested with purse seine nets to be labeled as dolphin-safe as long as no dolphins were observed to be seriously injured or killed during use of the nets.

On April 29, 1999, the Secretary of Commerce issued an "initial finding" that "there is insufficient evidence that chase and encirclement by the tuna purse seine fishery 'is having a significant adverse impact' on the depleted dolphin stocks in the [Eastern Tropical Pacific Ocean]." 64 Fed.Reg. 24,590 (1999). David Brower, an environmental group, and an animal rights organization brought suit to challenge this finding. They argued that the Secretary had violated the IDPCA by changing dolphin-safe label standards for tuna through an "initial finding" based on insufficient and misconstrued data. In Brower v. Daley, 93 F. Supp. 2d 1071 (N.D.C 2001), the court agreed that the Secretary had acted contrary to the Act by failing to consider the results of congressionally-mandated stress research studies when he made his initial finding to trigger changes in the existing dolphin-safe label standard. The court ordered that the Secretary's finding be set aside until he has an opportunity to consider preliminary results from such studies.

The WTO Upholds France's Asbestos Ban
(pp. 1161-65)

While the *Corrosion Proof Fittings* decision (p. 462) derailed EPA's efforts to ban asbestos in the United States, a growing number of countries throughout the world are enacting asbestos bans. When Spain banned asbestos on July 3, 2001, it became the thirteenth out of fifteen members of the European Union to ban the import and use of the substance. Chile banned asbestos in July 2001 despite a personal plea not to do so by Canadian Prime Minister Jean Chetrien. Argentina followed suit in August 2001. Australia, Saudi Arabia, and Brazilian cities and states accounting for 70 percent of Brazil's market also have banned asbestos use. El Salvador banned asbestos in the mid-1980s.

In September 2000, a WTO panel rejected a challenge by Canada to France's 1996 ban on imports of chrysotile asbestos. World Trade Organization, European Communities – Measures Affecting Asbestos and Asbestos-Containing Products (WT/DS135/R, Sept. 18, 2000). While the panel found that an import ban normally would violate WTO rules promoting free trade, it concluded that a ban on asbestos imports was justified under Article XX(b), the GATT's provision exempting measures necessary to protect life or health.

This decision is highly significant because it represents the first time that a measure restricting trade has been upheld on environmental grounds. Throughout the dispute, Canada argued that France's asbestos ban was not based on adequate scientific research and that it was contrary to international trade rules. The Canadian government claimed that chrysotile asbestos is safer than many alternative products, and that it is perfectly safe to use and install if adequate safety measures are taken. France, supported by the European Union, maintained that asbestos kills approximately 2,000 people in France each year. All five scientific experts consulted by the WTO panel agreed that chrysotile asbestos is carcinogenic and dangerous to human health. Canada appealed the panel's decision to the WTO's Appellate Body, which upheld the decision in March 2001. Canada, the world's second largest producer and the largest exporter of chrysotile asbestos, is particularly concerned that this decision could influence countries in other parts of the world to ban asbestos, particularly in developing countries where the industry has been making a push to expand exports.

NAFTA and the Environment (pp. 1165-68)

As noted in the casebook (p. 1166) the NAFTA environmental side agreement created the North American Commission on Environmental Cooperation (CEC) and gave it authority to investigate complaints by citizens concerning nonenforcement of environmental laws and regulations. As of June 2001, the CEC had completed its assessment of 19 citizen complaints and had found that only two of these warranted preparation of a public factual record. Twelve additional complaints were under review. There is some evidence that NAFTA has increased environmental awareness in Mexico, contributing to a growing environmental movement there. See Pollution Fight Takes Root in Courtrooms of Mexico, San Jose Mercury News, April 30, 2001, p. A11.

Chapter 11 of NAFTA, which is designed to protect foreign investors against arbitrary action by governments, has come under considerable scrutiny as a result of a ruling against Mexico in a case brought by the Metalclad Corporation. Anthony DePalma, NAFTA's Powerful

Little Secret, March 11, 2001, p. C2. Metalclad alleged that Mexico had effectively expropriated a hazardous waste landfill it was building when local officials in Mexico refused to license the project, despite prior assurances to the company by the Mexican government that it would be allowed to operate. Metalclad then invoked Chapter 11's provisions for convening an arbitral tribunal of the International Centre for the Settlement of Investment Disputes. Mexico argued that the permit denial was the result of a change of plans by Metalclad, which had decided to significantly expand its site despite public opposition. The tribunal awarded Metalclad $16.68 million after finding that the locality had exceeded its authority and that a decree by the region's governor declaring the site a protected natural area was tantamount to expropriation without compensation.

In 2000 the Clinton administration agreed to a free trade agreement with Jordan that includes provisions to ensure that labor and environmental standards are enforced. Despite their enthusiasm for trade liberalization, the Business Roundtable refused to endorse the agreement because of its provisions requiring Jordan to enforce its labor laws. Helene Cooper, CEOs Reject Pact Tying Sanctions to Labor Rights, Wall St. J., Feb. 9, 2001, p. A4. When the Bush administration announced the commencement of negotiations with Chile on a free trade agreement, it indicated that it expected the pact to be similar to the U.S.-Jordan agreement. However, both the Bush administration and the Chilean government have expressed opposition to including environmental and labor provisions in such an agreement. Nora Boustany, Latin American Dignitaries Descend on Washington to Air Their Agendas, Wash. Post, Feb. 28,. 2001, p. A29.

International Trade in Hazardous Substances: The *Khian Sea* and the Basel Convention (pp. 1169-73)

Incredibly, the saga of the incinerator ash dumped in Haiti by the *Khian Sea* (casebook, p. 1169) continues sixteen years after the ash was dumped. In November 1988 the *Khian Sea*, renamed the *Pelicano*, arrived in Singapore without its cargo of ash. In a subsequent perjury prosecution against the boat's owners in 1994, the captain testified that the ash had been dumped in the Atlantic and Indian Oceans. Meanwhile, the ash the boat had dumped on the Haitian beach remained there more than a decade after it had been dumped. Greenpeace and other environmental groups organized a "Project Return to Sender" to pressure Philadelphia to take its ash back. In April 2000, the ash was loaded aboard the *Santa Lucia*, which was to take it to Florida where it would be dumped in a landfill in Pompano Beach. However, the Florida Department of Environmental Protection ultimately disapproved of the disposal in January 2001. A Trail of Refuse, N.Y. Times Magazine, Feb. 18, 2001, p. 14.

As noted in the casebook (p. 1173), in March 1994 the second Conference of the Parties (COP-2) to the Basel Convention agreed to ban the export of hazardous wastes intended for final disposal from OECD to non-OECD countries. They also agreed to a ban on the export of wastes intended for recovery and recycling by December 31, 1997. Because this decision was not part of the text of the Basel Convention, at COP-3 in 1995 it was proposed that it be formally added to the Convention as an amendment. This amendment has to be ratified by three-fourths of the parties (62 countries) before it enters into force. As of August 2001, 148 have ratified the Basel Convention, but only 26 countries have ratified the amendment, which therefore has not yet entered into force.

Tort Litigation Against Multinationals: The *Beanal* Case (pp. 1177-81)

International law has evolved to recognize universal human rights to be free from torture and other injustices, as indicated by recent efforts to prosecute former Chilean dictator Agosto Pinochet and those charged with war crimes in the Balkans. International environmental law is evolving more slowly. While the Alien Tort Claims Act has been invoked in the United States in response to human rights abuses, efforts to apply it to environmental damage caused by the actions of multinational corporations in other countries have not been as successful, as indicated by the *Beanal* case (casebook pp. 1177-81).

Following the Fifth Circuit's decision, the very kind of harm feared by plaintiffs in the *Beanal* litigation occurred. The plaintiffs had alleged that overburden dumped by the company's Grasberg mining operation created a risk of landslides that threatened them. On May 4, 2000, a rock-waste containment for the overburden collapsed, causing an adjoining water basin to overflow, killing for workers and spilling waste and water into the Wanagon Valley. Jay Solomon, U.S. Mining Firm, Indonesia at Odds over Latest Spill, Wall St. J. May 8, 2000, p. A30. The Indonesian Ministry of Environmental Affairs stated that it had "warned Freeport a long time ago" about the dangers of its waste containment, but that the company had not acted to correct the problem. Id. On May 24, 2000, Freeport agreed not to continue placing overburden in the Wanagon basin and to temporarily limit production at its Grasberg open pit to an average of no more than 200,000 metric tons of ore per day pending completion of studies concerning how to prevent future spills.

On June 20, 2001, the Exxon Mobil Corporation was sued in federal district court in Washington, D.C. by the International Labor Rights Fund, which represents eleven villagers from Aceh, Indonesia. The lawsuit seeks to hold Exxon Mobil accountable for human rights abuses by Indonesian soldiers guarding the company's oil facilities in Indonesia. It alleges that the company bought military equipment and paid mercenaries who have assisted Indonesian security forces in eforts to crush dissent by torturing and assaulting villagers. Exxon denies responsibility for the behavior of the Indonesian military and says that it condemns the violation of human rights in any form.

Promoting Voluntary Corporate Actions to Protect the Environment (p. 1196-98)

As noted in the casebook, many corporations are committied to achieve improved environmental performance through voluntary programs like the International Organization for Standardization's ISO 14,000 program governing environmental management systems. Several companies also are involved in voluntary product certification programs that allow them to approach consumers with independent certification that they engage in best environmental practices in their global operations. For example, all of Chiquita's banana farms have been certified by the Rainforest Alliance as complying with a Better Banana program, a set of environmental and social best practices that involves significant reductions in pesticide use and water pollution and improved waste management practices. In April 2001 officials of the Canadian timber industry agreed with a coalition of environmental groups to protect from logging 1.5 million acres of coastal rainforest in British Columbia. Jim Carlton, Canada, Timber Firms Agree on Rainforest Pact, Wall St. J., April 4, 2001, p. A2. The agreement follows successful efforts by environmental groups to get large retailers like Home Depot to agree to phase out selling products using wood from old growth forests. A representative of the Natural Resource Defense Council explained that: "The basic goal is for the consumer to ask, 'Where does my wood come from?'" Id. Other environmentalists predicted that the agreement represented "the beginning of the end for old-growth logging." Id.

The Cartagena Protocol on Biosafety (p. 1199)

The Cartegena Protocol on Biosafety to the Convention on Biological Diversity has entered into force and has been signed by virtually every U.S. trading partner. It applies a "precautionary approach" that is being used by opponents of genetically modified organisms (GMOs) to argue that the burden of proof is on the producers of such products to demonstrate the safety of products containing recombinant DNA. Aventis, a French multinational company, has had to recall Starling GMO corn that it had been approved for use solely for animal feed because the product started turning up in human food products. As of July, 2001, 105 countries had signed the protocol and five had either ratified or acceded to it.

The Persistent Organic Pollutants Treaty (pp. 1201-02)

At the Stockholm Convention on POPs on May 22-23, 2001, 91 countries, including the United States, signed the Legally Binding Instrument for Implementing International Action on Certain Persistent Organic Pollutants (the "POPs treaty"). The Convention will enter into force 90 days after 50 countries have ratified it. President Bush announced he will submit the treaty to the Senate for ratification later in 2001. The treaty calls for the immediate elimination of eight POPs: aldrin, chlordane, dieldrin, endrin, heptachlor, hexachlorobenzene, mirex, and toxaphene. The ban will take effect as soon as the treaty enters into force. It is predicted that this will take 3-4 years. The treaty immediately prohibits the production of PCBs and it calls for the phasing out of their remaining uses over time, including their removal from electrical transformers and other equipment by 2025. The treaty also promotes strong actions to minimize releases of by-product POPs, such as dioxins and furans, and actions taken to eliminate these by-products where feasible.

The controversy over proposals to ban DDT was resolved by providing that DDT eventually should be eliminated, but that it could continue to be used for disease vector control by countries that need to use DDT against malaria until affordable alternatives are available to them. The treaty follows the approach supported by the World Health Organization (WHO), and the parties will work in accordance with WHO guidelines. The parties agreed to channel funds and technical assistance to developing countries, with the Global Environmental Facility (GEF) identified as the entity responsible for interim financing.